Théâtre du Gymnase
Boulevart Bonne Nouvelle
Boulevart
Bd St Denis
Rue Meslay
Rue de Bondy
Rue Notre-Dame de
Rue des Jeuneurs
BONNE NOUVELLE
Rue de Cléry
Rue du Caire
Entrepot des Glaces
Rue Chevreau
Rue Grenéta
Rue Mandar
Beaurepaire
ARTS ET METIERS
Rue des Fontaines
Rue Phelipeaux
Rue des Gravilliers
Rue de Montmorency
Rue Michel le Comte
ARCHIVES
BOURG L'ABBÉ
S. SAUVEUR
Rambuteau
Hôtel St Aignan
MARCHÉS
Temple
Rue du Chaume
VIII
S. MERRY
Rue du Plâtre
Rue de la Verrerie
Tour St Jacques
Rivoli
Pl. du Chatelet
PLACE DE L'HOT
MONT DE PIÉTÉ
ILE

THE TURBULENT CITY: PARIS
1783 TO 1871

BOOKS BY ANDRE CASTELOT

The Turbulent City: Paris

King of Rome

Queen of France

THE TURBULENT CITY:
PARIS
1783 to 1871

ANDRE CASTELOT

Translated by Denise Folliot

HARPER & ROW, PUBLISHERS
NEW YORK and EVANSTON

THE TURBULENT CITY: PARIS. Copyright © 1962 by André Storms. Printed in the United States of America. All rights reserved. No part of this book may be used or reproduced in any manner whatsoever without written permission except in the case of brief quotations embodied in critical articles and reviews. For information address Harper & Row, Publishers, Incorporated, 49 East 33rd Street, New York 16, N.Y.

FIRST EDITION

GM

This book is published in France under the title LE GRANDE SIECLE DE PARIS.

Library of Congress catalog card number: 62-14524

TO ALAIN DECAUX

CONTENTS

FLIGHT OVER PARIS

PARIS REVOLTS

1. Latude, or the Thief of Fame	15
2. Maillard, the Consumptive	21
3. Paris Without a King	29
4. Fie! How Horrible!	39
5. "Nothing . . ."	44
6. Pierre Notelet, Parisian Sightseer	50
7. Thérèse-Angélique Aubry, Goddess of Reason	54
8. Bon-Ami	59

PARIS AND THE SABER

1. The Elysée Transformed	67
2. A Melodramatic Coup d'Etat	73
3. The Return	79
4. The Night of Nivôse	87
5. The Step Toward the Throne	96

6. The Pope in Paris 108
7. The Coronation, or the End of Hypocrisy 119
8. Countersign? Conspiracy! 126

PARIS AND THE RETURN OF THE LILIES

1. Paris Occupied 139
2. A Reactionary Chestnut Tree 147
3. Thanks to a Pin 156
4. A *Jolie Laide* 161
5. The Knife 168
6. Dubourg and the Three Glorious Days 175
7. The Noble Faubourg 183
8. Two Women of Paris 189
9. Two Princes 197

PARIS BLEEDS

1. The Infernal Machine 205
2. A Banquet Smelling of Burning 211
3. The Man in the Yellow Coat 220
4. The Orbit of a Comet 228
5. Freedom Goes to the Head 234
6. The Rubicon 240
7. First Steps of the Second Empire 249

PARIS PLAYS AND SUFFERS

1. In Offenbach's Day 257
2. An Acrimonious Parisian 268
3. Virginia 280

4. At "My Aunt's"	287
5. The Last Inhabitant of the Tuileries	293
6. Paris Besieged	300
7. A Mild Spring	311
8. Paris Torn Asunder	318

THE TURBULENT CITY: PARIS
1783 TO 1871

FLIGHT OVER PARIS

On a misty day in November, 1783, thousands of Parisians left the capital, flocked through the little village of Passy and reached the nearby country, that is the gardens of La Muette, where an astonishing spectacle was about to unfold. The skies of Paris had been chosen as the birthplace of a new invention which was to revolutionize the world. A chemist and a physician—Pilâtre de Rozier and François-Laurent, Marquis d'Arlandes—were to fly over the capital for the first time.

The invention was a very recent one. A few months earlier a wallpaper manufacturer of Annonay was musing before his kitchen range, above which his maid had just hung the damp clothes. Suddenly one of his shirts, warmed by the fire, swelled out and began to rise.

Watching it, M. Joseph Montgolfier invented the Montgolfière.

On this November 21 an ascent in the Montgolfière was to be tried from La Muette, and ever since midday thousands of spectators had been invading the park. Full of curiosity they gazed at the balloon, moored on a lawn which would one day be crossed by the Rue d'Andigné. Since they were in the country the elegant women spectators wore country hairstyles, but they went white with jealousy on perceiving a fellow Parisienne displaying a hairstyle *à la montgolfière,* a blue-and-gold balloon—just like that of M. Montgolfier—balanced on an artificial chignon.

The real balloon was made of sky-blue oiled paper enhanced with gold ornaments: the King's monogram, the signs of the zodiac and fleurs-de-lis. It contained twenty cubic meters of air heated by a brazier fed with straw. Round the outside of its orifice was set a circular wicker basket for the intrepid navigators and the provisions of straw. Thus, Pilâtre and his companion would fly over Paris on top of flaming bundles of straw.

The moored balloon's envelope had become unstitched. While it was being hastily repaired the spectators had scattered in the park. It was a long time since there had been any aviary there—the pavilion where Charles IX had his falcons put when they were about to molt—but the public could admire a model dairy and a vast pheasant run which extended beyond the Porte Dauphine, so called in honor of Marie Antoinette on her arrival in France.

Suddenly shouts summoned the spectators. The balloon had been repaired and was about to take off. They came running back, to the great satisfaction of the Marquis d'Arlandes, who had been in despair at seeing so few people around the balloon. He gracefully waved his handkerchief in good-bye and smiled at the pretty women, but the Montgolfière did not seem in a hurry to leave the ground. The hot air had not completely filled the envelope.

"Monsieur le Marquis," cried Pilâtre from the basket, "you are doing nothing and we are not moving."

M. d'Arlandes apologized. He recounted later in the *Journal de Paris* of November 29: "I then poked the brazier. With my fork I seized a bundle of straw which was not catching, no doubt because it was too close-packed. I lifted it and shook it in the middle of the flame. The next moment I felt as though I were being lifted by the armpits, and I said to my dear companion: 'This time we are rising!' "

It was 1:54 in the afternoon.

The balloon gained height and already the aeronauts had a wide view: from the plain of Grenelle to the new Route de la Révolte.* Suddenly the Montgolfière was violently jolted.

"What are you doing?" the Marquis asked his companion anxiously. "Are you dancing?"

---

* The present Boulevards Pershing and Gouvion-Saint-Cyr and the avenues that prolong them as far as Saint-Denis. Louis XV had had this road built thirty years before, after an uprising, so as not to have to cross turbulent Paris on his way from Versailles to Compiègne.

"I'm not moving."

"Ah," cried d'Arlandes. "We've met a new current at last!"

The globe, in fact, was moving toward the southwest. Below the travelers was the little village of Passy—with its terraced houses and mills on the hillside. The shadow of the balloon was thrown onto the rows of a vineyard alongside the Rue Vineuse, whose wine Louis XIII had been so fond of drinking when he came back in the evening from a wolf hunt in the Bois de Boulogne.

A few yards further on, the aerial navigators were over the hill of Chaillot. As they stoked their brazier they saw a rider beneath them descending the hill as fast as his horse would carry him. It was Monseigneur the Duc de Chartres—originator of the balloon demonstration—who was trying to follow the Montgolfière.

On the ridge joining the hill of Chaillot with the rising ground of the Etoile, mirrors of water reflected the sky. They were the reservoirs for the famous fire pump of Chaillot that had just been erected by the brothers Périer.

> Here, by a strange fate, of water
> Fire has become the porter.

This "fire" was composed of several steam engines placed on the bank of the Seine at the corner of the present Rue des Frères-Périer. They worked two lift-and-force pumps. Each of these could raise 97,276 gallons of water a day to the reservoirs placed at a height of 118 feet on open ground that would one day bear the name of Place des Etats-Unis. This machinery, which stopped working only in 1902, carried water to subscribers as far away as the Faubourg Saint-Antoine.

The balloon had just passed the present Place de l'Alma and was about to leave the right bank at the level of the Invalides ferry. All those who had not believed in the miracle, all who had considered the two balloonists' reports to be mere boasting, all the doubters who had not wanted to go to La Muette were at the windows, on the roofs, in the street.

An immense shout went up: "The machine is flying!"

The enthusiasm was indescribable. There were embraces, shouts and applause. Two men had all Paris at their feet, a Paris of 630,000 inhabitants extending from the Faubourg Saint-Honoré to the Faubourg Saint-Antoine and from the Faubourg Saint-Denis to the

Faubourg Saint-Michel. To their left the aerial navigators could see "a field of mud, whose rough, unequal surface upset the most solid coaches, exhausted the horses and annihilated the pedestrians." This was the Champs-Elysées.

When the Duc de Chartres reached the Invalides ferry he could see the blue-and-gold globe above the buildings of the new Military School, all shining white in the pale autumn sun. (In a few months the school was to have a new pupil whose name would seem very strange to his fellow scholars: Napoleone Buonaparte.)

On board the balloon a drama was taking place. The Marquis d'Arlandes had just noticed that the car was dotted with holes. The canvas had caught fire.

"We must go down!" He noted: "At the same time I took my sponge. I easily extinguished the fire that was eating the few holes I could reach, but having noticed that when I leaned on the lower part of the canvas to see if it was holding on to the hoop it came away easily, I repeated to my companion: 'We must go down.'

"He looked down and said to me: 'We are over Paris.'

" 'No matter,' I said.

" 'But look, is there any danger to you? Are you held fast?'

"I examined my side and perceived that there was nothing to fear. With my sponge I hit the principal cords within my reach; they all resisted, only two strings had broken. I then said: 'We can cross Paris.'

"During this operation we had gone very near the roofs. We stoked up the fire and rose with the greatest ease. It seemed to me that we were nearing the towers of Saint-Sulpice."

The northwest wind was now directing the globe toward Notre Dame. Soon its shadow was thrown on the towers of the basilica, whose platforms were black with people. The two balloonists threw in more bundles of straw, and the Montgolfière changed direction. "As we rose, a current of air forced us from this direction and bore us towards the south. On my left I saw a wood that I took to be the Luxembourg."

Beneath the aeronauts there shortly appeared the Bièvre, now a stream, now a lake, a silver ribbon winding among kitchen gardens and cottages, flowing alongside the royal tapestry factory to which the brothers Gobelin—"dealers in scarlet tapestry"—gave their name. The Boulevard Saint-Jacques was crossed at a very low altitude.

"Look out, we are going to hit the windmills!"

They just cleared the windmills of Petit-Gentilly. Arlandes took a bundle of straw and shook it so that it would catch more quickly. The balloon rose and the current carried it to the left. Before them the Bièvre described a great S, winding gently round the Butte-aux-Cailles where the windmills were gaily turning.

Pilâtre de Rozier cried again: "Mind the windmills!"

But the aerostat landed very neatly between the mill of Merveilles and the Moulin-Vieux, about two hundred yards distant. Not without difficulty the first air travelers freed themselves from the envelope which in deflating had covered the two little cars.

It was nineteen minutes past two. The voyage had lasted twenty-five minutes.

The tanners, potters and farmers of Petit-Gentilly came running up the slopes of the Butte-aux-Cailles. In their enthusiasm they threw themselves on Pilâtre de Rozier's overcoat and divided it up. Had it not been for the arrival of the Duc de Chartres, who came galloping up a few moments after the landing, the two balloonists would have been left stark naked.

The Marquis d'Arlandes hastened to find a horse and galloped to La Muette, where the account of the heroic day was to be drawn up. He was greeted "with tears of joy and excitement" (it was fashionable at that time to shed torrents of tears). One grumbler shrugged his shoulders, however, and turned to an old man with long white hair and curious clothes.

"What use can these balloons be?"

The old man—he was more than seventy-seven—had come as a neighbor. He lived, in fact, at Passy, at what is now 62-66 Rue Raynouard. He looked at the grumbler and replied, smiling philosophically: "Monsieur, what use is the child that has just been born?"

The old man was Benjamin Franklin.

The sky over Paris was interesting but its subsoil was no less interesting. Let us now enter one of the Paris sewers, which—indirectly thanks to a pretty woman—underwent a very happy transformation at the end of the eighteenth century. At the end of Louis XV's reign M. Joseph de Laborde, financier by profession, owned the district stretching from the present Rue du Quatre-Septembre to the Rue La Fayette. Unhappily the northern part of his domain was rendered noisome by the passage of the famous sewer, known as the Great Sewer, that came from the Bastille and went to Chaillot. From time to time twenty-two thousand hogsheads of water were poured into this cesspool from a reservoir in the Rue des Filles-du-Calvaire, but once this torrent had passed the sewer became pestilential again. Now, M. de Laborde had a mistress, the famous dancer Guimard. Between pirouettes she seemed to eat only diamonds. Her appetite was so great that she ruined her rich financier, and M. de Laborde had to turn everything into money. He divided up his park—thus giving us the Rues Grétry, Favart and Marivaux—and obtained permission to cut a road across his land situated beyond the boulevard, on condition that "the said sewer be vaulted over by the new road." So the Rue de Provence came into being and a drama, begun five hundred years earlier, approached its climax.

In the twelfth century the roads of Paris, devoid of gutters and paving, appeared for most of the year as stagnant lakes of mud in which only the ducks and pigs paddled about with enthusiasm. "On October 13, 1131, Philippe, eldest son of Louis le Gros, was riding along the Rue Saint-Jean when a pig that was paddling in the filth threw itself under the horse's feet, bringing about the fall of the young prince, who died as a result."

Fifty years later Philippe Auguste, standing by chance at the window of his palace, had to recoil hastily "in great loathing of heart." He had just had a full breath of the "corrupted" stench from the tracks of a cart going up the street and throwing two waves of filth and stinking mud against the walls. The king decided to have his capital paved. But at his death only the four "arms" of Paris, the four principal roads which crossed at the Grand-Châtelet, were paved, with large round stones. However, Philippe Auguste's successors carried on his work and, little by little, all the Paris roads received a surface whose outline was like that of a basin. Into this central gutter ran everything. It was "everything into the road," which overflowed in the smallest shower and stank so much that one was obliged, as a writer in the time of François I tells us, "to carry some flowers or perfume to get rid of the smell."

These streams of water and fetid matter were swallowed up in vast cesspools called "holes." In 1633 the scavengers, or *maistres fifis*, were bold enough to clean out one of these "holes," that of

Ponceau, between the Rue Saint-Denis and the Rue Saint-Martin. Maxime du Camp, who tells us this story, affirms that the first five workmen to enter the sewer immediately fell down dead. The doctors were amazed at this phenomenon and asserted that the poor *maistres fifis* "had been killed by the glance of a basilisk that was doubtless hiding in one of the pits of the sewer." (The basilisk was a kind of serpent with the unpleasant reputation of having a glance capable of killing one at ten paces.) Later on workmen had the courage to repeat the operation in the hole of the Rue Amelot. The work went on for seven months and the *maistres fifis* excavated 6,420 cartloads of matter at least two centuries old. The inhabitants of the district all emigrated, and when they returned they had to have the outer walls of their houses renewed, as they had been eaten away by the mephitic vapors.

All these "holes" discharged their overflow into open drains that ran into the stream of Ménilmontant, whose narrow waters had difficulty in carrying toward the Seine everything entrusted to their sluggish flow. The river, then, was the great sump, and the inhabitants drank its water! In January, 1404, "the river is so full of mud, dung, rubbish, rottenness and filth," declared a royal ordinance, "that it is a great horror and abomination to see." In 1788 things were still no better, which did not prevent Mercier from writing, as seriously as possible, that "the water of the Seine combined all the qualities one could wish: it is murky and disagreeable to look at; but that is what makes it much better than certain waters which, for the most part, hide heterogeneous matter under a pleasing exterior. It is in every point superior to those limpid waters that flow from the Swiss rocks." In short, "it is the most excellent of drinks." Little less than a century later Maxime du Camp was also to assert that the Seine water seemed to him "eminently drinkable." And for centuries Parisians came greedily into the street on hearing the famous cry of: "Wa-ater! Water!"

Admittedly Paris also possessed a great many wells (there were still thirty thousand in 1870, Charles Kunstler tells us), but this water—with which, incidentally, the bread was made—was contaminated by infiltration not only from the drains but also from the cemeteries. When the wind was blowing one could see unhealthy vapors rising from the seventy-three Paris cemeteries, and one can understand the ravages of the plague in Paris.

8 • THE TURBULENT CITY: PARIS

The most important cemetery was the famous Charnel House of the Innocents, in which were buried, during eight hundred years, the dead of twenty-two parishes, not to mention the Hôtel-Dieu, the Châtelet prison and the Morgue, which also carried out their interments there. The bodies were piled twelve or fifteen hundred together in communal graves. In less than thirty years one gravedigger alone had buried ninety thousand, whom he had stacked "like slices of bacon" in the large paupers' grave. From time to time, when this "overflowed," the skeletons were piled on top of the eighty arcades that surrounded the enclosure and sheltered the bodies of those whom their birth or means allowed to have a separate tomb. It was there that in Villon's day was painted the famous fresco of the *Danse macabre*.

The lofts of the cemetery cloister were packed with bones that sometimes fell down onto the stalls of the pedlars or the shops of the public writers, those "repositories of servant girls' tender secrets," which were placed up against the cemetery wall. So—as Sébastien Mercier said—"it is among the worm-eaten remains of thirty generations, it is in the midst of the fetid and cadaverous odor that offends the nostrils, that one sees this girl buying ribbons and that girl dictating love letters."

This beribboned picture did not prevent the wine and milk from going sour in the neighboring cellars, and there was no counting the number of cases of asphyxia and "pale colors." The walls adjoining the cemetery ran with water. "The poor, often dying of contagious diseases, are buried there pell-mell," Voltaire relates. "Dogs come sometimes to gnaw the bones; a dense vapour arises from it; it is pestilential in the heat of summer after the rains; and almost next door to this garbage heap are the Opéra, the Palais Royal, the royal Louvre. The filth of the privies is taken a league away, and for twelve hundred years the rotting bodies from which this filth was produced have been stacked in the same town. In vain does the example of so many European towns put Paris to the blush; it will never reform."

Louis XVI decided to prove the contrary, and on November 9, 1785, the Council of State ordered the Cemetery of the Innocents to be abolished and the bones to be taken, by night, to the catacombs. "Imagine," wrote Mercier, "the flaming torches, that enormous grave, those different layers of corpses suddenly disturbed, those crumbling bones, those scattered fires fed by the coffin planks, the moving shadows of those funeral crosses, that dreadful enclosure suddenly illuminated in the silence of the night. The inhabitants of the square waking up, leaving their beds. Some stand at the windows, half-naked; others descend; the whole neighborhood comes running."

In 1786 and 1787 the operation had to be renewed. Too many bodies still remained in the cemetery, and eight times during the nineteenth century the former site of the cemetery was excavated. On the last occasion, in 1860, 813 cartloads of bones were taken out.

On the site today, at the very spot where a tall stone lantern used to burn day and night, the pretty nymphs of Jean Goujon and Pajou laugh and play in the clear water that seems to flow from their urns.

But further down, under the thick layer of cement that was put over the graves, there are still bones. They sleep there, as elsewhere in Paris, on the sites of former cemeteries.

There were so many tombs that could not be found.

Under the recreation ground of a school in the Boulevard Saint-Marcel still lies the body of Mirabeau, who was expelled from the Panthéon when the opening of the iron chest in the Tuileries proved that the celebrated tribune was an expert at playing a double game. (Evidence of his complicity with the court while championing the Revolution.) Beneath the Eiffel Tower rest hundreds of bodies. They are the victims of the Massacre of Saint Bartholomew who were buried in the Ile des Cygnes, which in the sixteenth century extended as far as the present Avenue Bosquet. Under the market in the Rue de l'Ave-Maria still sleep Rabelais, the Man in the Iron Mask, Maurigron, Quélus and Saint-Mégrin, Henri III's three minions and Jean Nicot who brought to France "the nicotine herb," Nicot's herb, otherwise tobacco. Poor Jean Nicot, who has left his name only to the poison extracted from his discovery!

On leaving the Villiers Métro station one enters the former site of the Errancis cemetery. There, whenever the ground is opened, bones appear and are taken to the catacombs, but there are still many left. Perhaps, beneath the pavements of the Boulevard de Courcelles, between the Rue du Rocher and the Parc Monceau, there still remain the bodies of Robespierre, Saint-Just, Couthon, Charlotte Corday, Philippe-Egalité and Madame Elisabeth.

In 1864, when a drain was being dug in the Rue de la Paix, which runs above the former cemetery of the Capucine Convent, the remains of the Duchesse de Guise were discovered. It was known that the body of the Marquise de Pompadour (née Antoinette Poisson) had been interred near at hand in the vault of the La Trémoille family (which, incidentally, caused the Princess de Talmont to remark that "the honored bones of the La Trémoille family must be very surprised at finding fishbones [*arêtes des Poisson*] near them"). The wooden paving of the Rue de la Paix was dug up in the hopes of finding the pretty Marquise's body, but the work had to stop, for they came across the tomb of Cardinal Dubois, Louis XV's First Minister, whose vault had been turned into a cesspool. There was some thought of calling in the successors to the *maistres fifis,* but it was finally decided to abandon the search, and Mme. de Pompadour still sleeps her last sleep under the pavement of the Rue de la Paix.

Above all this corruption ran a medieval network of 1,065 streets, 104 culs-de-sac, 27 passages, 56 squares, 34 quays and 15 boulevards. The town swarmed with carriages, sedan chairs and pedestrians and was alive with the bellowings of coachmen and the cries of hundreds of small tradesmen shouting in sharp and piercing tones:
"Tinder for muskets! May God be thanked!"
"Oysters in the shell!"
"Fine cherries, one sou the pound!"
"Chimneys cleaned from top to bottom!"
"Fine bouquets! Roses and buds for lasses and lads!"
"All these discordant cries," wrote Mercier, "form a whole of which one can have no idea without having heard it. The idiom of these traveling criers has to be studied in order to distinguish its meaning. . . . As the endings have nearly all the same tone, it is only usage that teaches the learned servant girls not to mistake them, and they form an unintelligible cacophony for everyone else."

In the street no one walked, they ran, scarcely taking time to ogle the girls in the dress shops who worked behind the counters "in a line, one after the other." The Parisian hastened to the walks where it was fashionable to show oneself. "The most beautiful garden," wrote Mercier, "is deserted at a certain hour, on a certain day, because on that day it is customary to foregather elsewhere. No reason can be seen for this exclusive preference, but this tacit convention is rigorously observed." The Palais Royal, the Champs-Elysées and the Tuileries were rarely abandoned. "The double rank of pretty women who line the great alley in the Tuileries, close to each other on a long line of chairs and gazing with as much freedom as they are gazed at, is like a living flowerbed of many colors." They did not speak *français,* but *françoué.* Until the day of his death Louis-Philippe said *moé* for *moi* and *roué* for *roi.* Moreover the Parisian had much difficulty in palatalizing the double l, and never managed to pronounce *Versailles, paille* or *bouillon* correctly. This did not prevent his possessing the art of conversation to an extent that has never been equaled. "Each stroke was like the stroke of an oar, light yet deep. One never stayed long on a subject, but there was a prevailing atmosphere that made all the ideas return to the matter in question. Arguments on each side were discussed with singular rapidity. It brought a refinement of pleasure to be found only in a highly organized society which has set up subtle rules that are always observed."

These qualities could also be found, to a lesser degree, of course, but somewhat surprisingly, in the worker or artisan. On the eve of the Revolution there was confident talk in shops and workrooms of metaphysics and the new ideas. The people had begun to read. Works of philosophy and politics had reached the street. A traveler was dumbfounded at seeing "coachmen on their boxes, soldiers at their posts and police commissioners in their stations" all reading. From this came a disorder that increased and finally carried all before it. Restif de La Bretonne explained it: "The workers in the capital have become unmanageable because they have read in our books a truth that is too strong for them." They also became "unmanageable" because they heard hotheads like Councilor d'Eprémesnil proclaim "that the kingdom must be *debourbonized."* For most Parisians it was not *debourbonizing* that was needed, but *de-Austrianizing* Versailles. The hate they bore Marie Antoinette leaves one gasping. Where were the 200,000 lovers throwing their hats in the air whom the old Duc de Brissac, Governor of Paris, showed the little Dauphine from the balcony of the Tuileries? How far away it all was! Now the public preferred to applaud philosophers or Members of Parliament like Councilor Fréteau, who exclaimed when the affair of the Queen's necklace came to light:

"Great and fortunate affair! A cardinal a thief, the Queen implicated in a forgery! What mud on the crozier and the scepter! What a triumph for the ideas of liberty!"

These "ideas of liberty," by the way, were to lead Councilor Fréteau, on June 14, 1794, to lose his head in the Place du Trône-Renversé.

All these bourgeois of Paris, by giving vent to their "ideas of liberty" were to set going the terrible machine whose mechanism they could not check and that would finish by crushing them. What urged them on? Pride. Mme. Roland could never forget that when, as a child, a lady of quality had asked her to tea, she had been received in the servants' hall.

"What was it made the Revolution?" Napoleon was to ask. "It was vanity. Liberty was only the pretext."

Let us leave for the moment these vain gentlemen of the robe and consider their wives or mistresses, the Parisienne of 1785, whether she were rich bourgeoise, a lady of the lesser nobility or a kept woman. See her in the morning, "in the youth of the day" according to the pretty expression of the time, half-dressed, wearing a low-cut bodice and reclining on her couch, as, with beating heart, she awaits her hairdresser. He, of course, is Léonard, the great Léonard. The moment he enters he becomes lost in meditation, while his client holds her breath. Suddenly he has it: he rushes to the kitchen, returns with a cauliflower, a bundle of leeks, three carrots and a turnip, and fashions a headdress *à la jardinière* for the excited and overjoyed lady. Very often, when Léonard was working on his structures, he would see a whole whirlwind of visitors around his client. The Parisienne of the eighteenth century knew no shame, and with her indecency became a grace. Friends and admirers surrounded her and, dressed in her "bed cloak," she smiled at their follies. Lively maidservants fluttered about the room, and a sprightly abbé could be heard humming a popular tune as he fanned himself in his armchair. Or else his opinion was asked on a new "peach flower" material the merchant had just brought.

"What does the abbé say?"

And the abbé pronounced an authoritative opinion.

The day was beginning. The fashionable Parisienne amused herself, danced, talked scandal, broke with her lover and took another and, in the evening, went to drink ratafia at the Pont de Neuilly and eat macaroons. Ratafia didn't taste very good and macaroons were fattening, but this was the thing to do at two o'clock in the morning. As she went to bed her maid tidied her hair for the night in the style called *battant-l'oeil*. (In this style the side hair was dressed well forward over the face, particularly at the temples, so that the least breath of air made the eyes blink [*battre*].) Freudeberg's engraving, described by the Goncourt brothers, shows her chemise slipping from her bare breast, and her frilled underskirt swelling round the high heels of her mules. "The woman calls for her candles and behind her, in a frame lit by the fading glow, a cupid laughs like the god of her dreams and the angel of her night."

These pretty heads surrounded by frills, these frail Parisian weathercocks who, one day, would wake in astonishment to find themselves mounting Sanson's steep ladder, possessed a delicate feeling for the proprieties, a "worldly sense," a delicacy of manners and hearts that today seems quite forgotten. Mme. Dillon had the Prince de Guéménée for her lover. This fact was known to everyone—even her husband. Yet, "on arriving at Hautefontaine," said someone, "one was sure Mme. Dillon was the Prince's mistress, and when one had stayed there for six weeks one doubted it."

Certainly Parisiennes rarely loved their husbands. But could they be blamed? In those days one did not make one's own marriage; it was made for one, and this paradoxical situation has provided us with many delightful sayings. I do not know where I read the remark of the young Parisienne greatly loved by her husband, who begged her to call him *tu*.

"*Eh bien! va-t'en!*" she replied.

There is also the story of the little Comtesse de Forcalquier who, having been slapped by her husband, hoped to obtain a separation. Not succeeding—there was as yet no divorce—she entered her husband's study and declared, joining gesture to word: "Here is your slap, monsieur. I can do nothing with it!"

It is only fair to say that the husbands had just as much wit. Witness that sublime cuckold who, surprising his wife in the most compromising situation with an adolescent whose only costume was a powdered wig, exclaimed: "What impudence, madame! Supposing it had been anyone else but myself!"

Love affairs were all that mattered and were yielded to without remorse.

On her deathbed Mme. de Groslier said to her confessor: "Father, I was young, I was pretty, I was told so and I believed it; judge of the rest."

And she died.

These last words remind one of a saying reported by Pierre Bessand-Massenet. In Mme. de La Briche's salon could be seen a pretty, ill young woman, suffering from serious disease of the lungs and knowing she had not long to live. One day she seemed more pensive than usual.

"What are you dreaming of, madame?" someone asked her.

"I regret myself," she murmured.

She was regretting everything that went to make her: that good breeding, that grace, that politeness of the heart, that free yet elegant gallantry, above all that perpetual search for distraction which prevented her becoming aware of the stench rising from the rotten heart of the age, a miasma which was a harbinger of catastrophe.

PARIS REVOLTS

1
Latude, or the Thief of Fame

On the day following July 14, 1789, the Parisians crowded round the Bastille, which the "patriot" Palloy—he was never to be called anything else—at the head of five hundred workmen, each paid forty-five sous a day, had begun to demolish. He was tearing down the old fortress not by order of the King, to whom it belonged, but on his own authority.

The women, wearing Bastille bonnets (a muslin tower with two rows of black lace crenellations), looked admiringly at the heroes of the day, the conquerors of the fortress, who strutted about wearing coats on which was embroidered a mural crown. On the evening of the 14th of July there were 633 heroes. At the end of July the number had risen to 863. What surprised Lenotre was that the figure stopped there. (Taking part in the assault on the impregnable fortress seems to have provided a long lease of life, since the budget of 1874 still made mention of pensioners under the title of "conqueror of the Bastille.")

Through all the dust stirred up by the demolishing picks, beneath the stones hurtling from the tall façade, their fall applauded by the crowd, a gray-haired man was showing people round the celebrated fortress. He seemed quite at home. In fact he had spent two long periods of imprisonment there during his thirty-five years of captivity.

This man was Latude. His real name was Danry, but having learned that a gentleman from his part of the country, Vissec de La Tude, had died without issue, he had declared himself his son. Moreover, he had altered his "father's" name and claimed to be called Masers, Vicomte de La Tude. (On his liberation this title enabled him to obtain a handsome pension from Louis XVI.)

Thirty-five years of captivity! What had he done to merit such a punishment? It had all begun forty years earlier, on April 26, 1749, with an attempted fraud. On that day Danry bought six glass bubbles, called "Prince Rupert's drops." These toys, shaped like pears, exploded noisily when the points were broken. Danry placed them in a box, tying the points to the lid in such a way that when the box was opened there would be an explosion, and then sprinkled the whole with a fine powder of alum and vitriol. The packet, carefully wrapped, was sent to "Mme. la Marquise de Pompadour, at Court." The following day Danry went to Versailles, managed to see the royal favorite's chief valet and alleged that he had heard two individuals uttering threats against the Marquise in the Tuileries gardens. He had followed them, he said, and had seen them put a large packet in the post. Danry said that was all he knew about it, "but, being devoted to Mme. de Pompadour's interests, he had hurried to reveal what he had seen."

The packet arrived on the following day. Quesnay, the King's doctor, was charged with opening it, surrounding himself with all the usual precautions. He declared that the "machine" was hardly dangerous, but that it was perhaps a question of an attempted assassination by "amateurs." The vitriol, certainly, might cause some damage. Danry was suspected and he was asked to write an account of the affair. The unhappy man was lost: an expert compared his writing with that of the address, and the future Latude was sent to the Bastille. Instead of telling the truth, the prisoner stuck to his lie—then he confessed. This might not have merited thirty-five years in prison, but with his exaltation, his rages, his lies, his obstinacy, his epistolary excesses (when he had no ink he wrote with his blood), Danry ended by being thought mad. In those days madmen were not treated, they were shut up. And then Latude decided to escape. He escaped three times, was recaptured and kept in prison not for his "crime," but for absconding.

His second escape, carried out with the help of a rope ladder that can still be seen in the Carnavalet Museum, was almost miraculous.

On his conducted tours of the Bastille Latude related his adventure several times a day in the same words he was later to use in his memoirs: "In our room my friend d'Aligre and myself had a chimney whose flue came out at the top of the tower, but like all the chimneys in the Bastille it was full of gratings and bars that in some places hardly left room for the smoke to pass. Had we gained the summit of the tower we would have had below us an abyss of nearly two hundred feet, a moat filled with water and dominated by a high wall, which had also to be crossed. We were alone, without tools, without materials, spied on every instant of the day and night and watched by a crowd of sentries who surrounded the Bastille."

In six months, with the help of two iron feet from the table in their cell, the two men succeeded in loosening the chimney gratings.

"These iron bars were fastened by a very hard cement that we could soften only by squirting water with our mouths into the holes we had made."

It was the governor who, without intending to, provided the materials for constructing the rope ladder. Latude demanded shirts. He already had seven, but did not consider them good enough. The administration made him three dozen, at twenty livres the shirt—four thousand present-day francs. The shirts were unraveled and rolled into balls of thread and then plaited, and on Wednesday, February 25, 1756, the two prisoners climbed to the top of the tower and lowered themselves into the moat.

"Finally, after nine hours of toil and fear, waist-deep in water, having wrenched out stones from the surrounding wall, we managed to make, in a wall four and a half feet thick, a hole large enough to get through. We were saved!"

Rearrested at Amsterdam, Latude was returned to the Bastille and put into a dungeon. If one is to believe the prisoner's memoirs, and Alexandre Dumas in his *History of Louis XVI*, "the food was worse than would be given to a pig or a dog. He had no blanket and was dressed in rotting rags."

"Oh, Madame de Pompadour!" exclaimed Dumas."What a terrible account you must have had to render to God!"

It would have been to Latude's interest, instead of acting as a guide in July, 1789, to have copied M. de Beaumarchais's example and to have gathered up and burned the prison archives, which were being thrown into the fortress moats. Posterity would then not have been able to read the documents showing that the truth was quite different. "Danry is in a very bad temper," noted the Bastille commandant. "He sends for us at eight o'clock in the evening to tell us to send his turnkey to the market to buy fish"—it was an abstinence day—"saying that he cannot eat eggs, artichokes or spinach. Danry is just as exacting on meat days. He swore like a trooper and said to me: 'Commander, when I'm given fowl, it should at least be well larded.'"

Here is another report: "The individual Danry demands more blankets. So far he has refused to accept the trousers M. de Rochebrune had made for him, which are very good, lined with excellent leather, and with silk garters, all very well made." During the whole of this period "dressing gowns lined with rabbit fur, waistcoats lined with silk plush, gloves and fur bonnets" were provided for the prisoner simply on his asking. Of course, truffled chicken and silk garters, however well made they are, do not equal freedom. But the legend of the Bastille was beginning.

In the prison courtyard Parisians, white with retrospective fear, were shown "an iron corset invented to hold a man in every joint and fix him in perpetual immobility." This was a medieval horseman's armor which came from the store of ancient arms kept in the Bastille.

"Here, exposed to the light of day, is a no less destructive machine, but no one has been able to guess at its name or actual use!" It was a clandestine printing press seized from a certain François Lenormand in 1786.

It was affirmed that the Bastille had been the scene of secret executions, as witness the bones found in the bastion. The discovery of "the remains of the martyrs of liberty" enabled Mirabeau to exclaim: "The Ministers lacked foresight; they forgot to eat the bones!"

Actually, the bones were those of Protestant prisoners buried there because they had no right to the consecrated ground of St. Paul's cemetery.

For a few coppers Parisians were able to take home "crusts" of a few hairs' thickness formed on the vaults of the dungeons "by the prisoners' breath."

The Bastille became the fashionable promenade. All Paris went to the Faubourg Saint-Antoine to contemplate "its victory over despotism." Mme. de Genlis and her pupils, the children of the Duc d'Orléans, Beaumarchais and many advanced intellects might be seen there. All Paris wanted to see "the breach" by which, under fire from the garrison, the assailants rushed in to free the prisoners. All Paris wanted to touch the cannons which, from the battlements, had fired on the people. Paris forgot that the governor gave orders to fire only when the assailants had entered the enclosure. Paris forgot that not one of the fifteen cannon on top of the towers had opened fire. A single gun charged with grapeshot fired one or two rounds in the courtyard. Paris forgot that there could have been no "breach" for the simple reason that, being attacked with cries of "Long live the King!" the Bastille had opened its gates. "The Bastille was not taken by force," wrote Elie, one of the most famous "conquerors," who cannot be accused of partiality. "It yielded before being attacked, on the promise I gave, on the word of a French officer, that no harm would be done to anyone if it yielded."

One knows how this promise was kept.

"Resistance was nonexistent," related Pasquier, who went there as a spectator with pretty Louise Contat of the Comédie-Française. "Only a few rifle shots were fired. . . . What I saw perfectly was the action of the soldiers lining the platforms of the towers, who raised the butts of their rifles in the air and expressed, by all the usual means in such circumstances, their desire to surrender."

Paris forgot that the Bastille had been attacked only to find arms for defense against both "brigands" and the royal army, in case the latter should attack the town to restore order. For ten years Paris had been hungry; for ten years want had been an endemic condition that facilitated the creation of "spontaneous anarchism," but in attacking the royal castle Paris had had no thought of freeing the victims of despotism. They were thought of only when night came. The cell doors had to be forced, for the conquerors were engaged in carrying the keys in triumph from wineshop to wineshop. Seven prisoners were found: two madmen, who were quickly sent to Charenton, four forgers, and the Comte de Solages, imprisoned for incest and guilty, according to his uncle, "of atrocious crimes." It was not a very brilliant haul. The number was padded out by adding a Comte de Lorges, "old man, hero and martyr"—who had never existed. This did not prevent Michelet from describing his beard falling to his waist.

The demolition itself was magnified. If letters addressed to the authorities by Palloy are to be believed, "bourgeois, artists, workmen" hastened to take part in it. It is enough to read the papers left by the "Patriot" to be convinced that the true Parisians made no attempt to lend a hand in knocking down the abominable fortress. During the demolition—Palloy reckoned it up—there were four insurrections and eight assassinations. The unfortunate Patriot was himself wounded twice.

I realize that the truth is very disappointing. It is much better to believe in the fifteen cannons belching grapeshot and in the magnificent outburst of all the people of Paris rushing to attack the horrible jail and save the innocent victims of arbitrary power. Let us go on believing the legend. It is such a fine one! Like the Parisians of 1789 who wept with joy as they watched the Bastille disappear a little more each day under the demolishers' picks, one can go and admire No. 21 Boulevard Bonne-Nouvelle, or the house built on the corner of the Rue de Bourgogne and the Place du Palais-Bourbon. These houses were constructed of stones watered by the tears of the "victims of tyranny," in other words of stones from the Bastille. To get an idea of the thickness of its terrible walls one has only to visit the Square Henri-Gailli, opposite the Pont Sully. Here one can see the foundations of the Freedom Tower, so called because prisoners living there were free to walk in the enclosure. These remains were found at the top of the Rue Saint-Antoine, in 1899 when the tunnel for the Métro was being dug, and brought to their present position stone by stone.

We might mention, too, that the present roadway of the Pont de la Concorde (the pavements are modern) was constructed in 1790 from stones taken from Charles V's old fortress, the Bastille.

2
Maillard, the Consumptive

On that July 14 a man named Stanislas-Marie Maillard was seen brandishing a flag and being the first to enter the Bastille. He was seen again on June 20, and August 10, 1792, when he was to play his part in the attack on the Tuileries. On September 2, 1792, the day of the massacres, he was to preside over the improvised tribunal in the Abbaye prison.

When the affair was over he went back home, asking nothing more than to be able to take care of his lungs, for the fierce Maillard, the man whom some historians have depicted with a knife between his teeth, yelling, shouting, leading *sans-culottes* and *tricoteuses* in the assault, was actually a quiet, pale young bookkeeper to a bailiff, a young man who spat blood and, undermined by consumption, was to die before the end of the Revolution.

Moreover, Maillard seems to have taken a hand in revolutionary events only in order to avoid the worst. He was to prove this on September 2 when by himself he saved two or three hundred royalists. It was perhaps partly owing to him that the imprisoned royalty had to leave Versailles on October 5, 1789, but it was certainly thanks to his initiative and coolness that the archives of the Hôtel de Ville were saved and the storm diverted from Paris.

On Sunday, October 4, 1789, the eve of the drama, he had shuddered with all Paris as he read in the *Courrier de Versailles* the distorted account of the previous Thursday's "orgy." In the presence of the King and Queen—that "jade," the Parisians called her—a banquet had been given by the garrison. The tricolor cockade, so the *Courrier* affirmed, had been trampled underfoot. The guests had refused to drink the health of the nation. A banquet! When Paris lacked bread! "Senseless people," wrote the pamphleteer, "open your eyes at last, rouse yourself from your lethargy!"

On this bright autumn Sunday the Parisians walked to the Palais Royal or on the boulevards, talking of nothing but "the insult to the nation."

The night of October 4-5 fell on Paris. Here and there the tocsin was rung, as though to prevent the town from sleeping. At six o'clock in the morning, in the Saint-Eustache district, a little girl was seen to snatch up a drum and begin to beat it, shouting the while. Gradually women collected, and the procession that formed set off for the Hôtel de Ville.

This was "the first squad," as an eyewitness tells us. They were "young, robed in white, hair dressed and powdered, with an engaging air that presaged no evil intent." As they marched gaily along they forced the women they met to follow them.

"Come along! We are going to Versailles!"

At the Porte Saint-Antoine they carried off with them a young girl of seventeen, Louise Chabry, called Louison, a sculptor's apprentice, who with her parents was watching the ever-increasing groups pass by. And a little flower girl of twenty, Françoise Rolin, living in the Rue de la Poterie near the Halles, was seized as she left home "to go to market."

During the first part of the morning groups from all parts of the town were going in the direction of the Place de Grève. To the young girls with "hair dressed and powdered" were now joined an increasing number of unbrushed and disheveled viragoes and also men, mainly from the Saint-Antoine and Saint-Marceaux faubourgs. Together with the most excited of the women the men rushed at one of the doors of the Hôtel de Ville, freed the prisoners and gave them money to buy clothes. Then the women broke open the armory, seized eight hundred rifles and the municipal cash box—one may fight for liberty and yet not despise a little profit. Real harpies, carrying torches, wanted to burn the town archives.

It was at this point that Maillard appeared.

"I rushed toward them," he said later, giving his evidence to the commission of inquiry. "I took away their torches, which incidentally nearly cost me my life."

The women had only one cry: "To Versailles! To Versailles!" "In order to forestall the evil these women might commit"—these are his own words—Maillard decided to put himself at their head.

"Detachments left for the different districts to recruit other women, who were told to meet them in the Place Louis XV."

Maillard remained with the chief body of the troop, which, preceded by a drummer, marched toward the Place Louis XV (now the Place de la Concorde). Again, as they went, the fishwives forced the women they met to march with them. Among these were two shop girls from the Rue Saint-Honoré, a second-hand clothes dealer from the Rue Saint-André-des-Arcs, a lace worker from the Rue Meslée, a charwoman from the Rue Froidmanteau, a nurse from the Rue Bailleul, a dyer from the Rue de la Calande, who was harnessed to one of the four cannons taken from the Hôtel de Ville. They even carried off a marquise, whom the women forced out of her carriage by the Louvre gate. (Maillard intervened and managed to get *her* let off.)

A horse guard rode by the column.

"Are you going to Versailles?" cried one of the fishwives. "Tell the Queen we shall soon be there to cut her throat."

In the Place Louis XV and the Champs-Elysées six to seven thousand women were gathered. Some were armed wtih broomsticks, according to Maillard's account, others with pitchforks, swords, skewers and old pistols. Here and there a few muskets were to be seen, but they were carried by men disguised as women. Beards spread over lawn shawls, and boots emerged from striped skirts. This is not a royalist legend: there exist 392 depositions for these October days that are very precise on the point. The reason for the masquerade is given by a contemporary: "They were less likely to decide to repel women by armed force."

Not without difficulty Maillard succeeded in giving his "army" some appearance of order. By now six or seven drummers and two cannons headed the procession.

As the marchers entered Chaillot, along the river, shutters were heard closing. The inhabitants were barricading themselves at the approach of the mob. The women, who were hungry and thirsty, knocked at the doors and even wanted to break them down. Not succeeding, they avenged themselves by tearing down sign boards. Maillard grew angry.

"I told them they would do themselves no credit by acting like this and that I would retire from their leadership if they behaved so, and that their actions might be looked on with disapproval, whereas, if they went on peacefully and honestly, all the citizens of the capital would be grateful to them. They finally yielded to my reproaches and advice."

Everything continued in a more or less orderly fashion until Sèvres, when the vanguard dispatched by Maillard into the town found no "refreshment for the ladies" except eight four-pound loaves, which were cut up "in little portions." The "ladies" thereupon scattered into the town, "took benches and other pieces of wood," as Maillard related, "and set about breaking down the doors and destroying the signs of all the shopkeepers."

But thanks to a few jugs of wine somehow procured the "army" continued on the march. Rain had begun to fall. Soon, muddy and soaked, the women shouted to passers-by: "See what a state we are in, but the jade will pay us dearly!"

Some of them sharpened enormous kitchen knives on the milestones.

"How glad I should be if I could open her belly with this knife and tear out her heart by thrusting my arm in up to the elbow!"

Maillard was appalled at having to make his entry into Versailles with such a crew. He was also disturbed by the presence of the cannons at the head of the procession.

"I made them form a circle and told them that the two cannons they had should not be dragged at the head. Although they had no ammunition, they might be suspected of evil intentions and they ought rather to display gaiety than cause a riot in Versailles. . . . They consented to do as I wished. As a result the cannons were placed in the rear and I proposed that they should sing 'Long live Henri IV!' as they entered Versailles and shout, 'Long live the King!' They did not cease repeating this among the people of that town, who were waiting for them and cried, 'Long live our women of Paris!'"

On arriving in front of the Hôtel des Menus-Plaisirs, where the Assembly was in session, the army halted, and Maillard and a delegation of women received permission to enter the session chamber.

"The people lack bread," declared the women's leader to the Assembly. "They are in despair, their arms are raised and they will certainly be led into some excesses. We ask permission to search the houses suspected of hoarding flour. It is for the Assembly to avert the shedding of blood, but the Assembly contains enemies of the people, who are the cause of the famine. Wicked men are giving money and bonds to the millers to make sure that they do not grind."

From every corner of the hall cries broke out: "The names, the names! Name them, name them!"

After a few seconds' hesitation Maillard said absurdly: "The Archbishop of Paris has given two hundred livres to a miller to stop grinding."

While the deputies raised a shout of indignation a few "advanced" representatives approved, and yelled: "It is the Archbishop of Paris!"

The disorder grew, as gradually the women, who had managed to slip into the hall through a side door, began calling to the representatives, straddling the benches, taking off their stockings and even their skirts to dry them, and crying out in cadence: "Bread! Bread! Bread!"

Some of them kissed the deputies, even the Bishop of Langres, while the Vicomte de Mirabeau "caressed the prettiest bosoms." It was finally decided, in the midst of indescribable disorder, to send the president of the Assembly, Monnier, to the castle to explain to the King the sad state of the capital, where one was obliged to queue for a whole day to buy a piece of terribly costly bread. A delegation composed of a few deputies and about ten women set off with the President. "We were on foot, in the mud, under a heavy rain," he later related. "A considerable crowd of Versailles inhabitants lined the avenue leading to the château. The women of Paris formed various groups, mixed with a certain number of men, mostly dressed in rags, their eyes wild, their gestures menacing, and uttering horrible yells. They were armed with a few muskets, old pikes, axes, iron-tipped sticks or long poles with sword or knife blades on the end." (These were the rearguard of Maillard's army.) "Small detachments of the bodyguards were on patrol and galloped by quickly, in the midst of cries and boos." Not far from the gate, in front of the rows of troops defending the approaches to the royal courtyard, two young women threw themselves at Monnier's feet. They were the sculptor's apprentice and the flower girl, Louison Chabry and Françoise Rolin. They wanted "to go to the King."

"You have only to follow me," Monnier replied.

Not without difficulty the little band passed the horsemen, entered the gates and were shown into the royal antechamber. The president, Louison and four other women were shown into the presence of the King, who was in the Council Room. The little sculptor's apprentice was appointed spokeswoman for her companions. She advanced toward Louis XVI, who was waiting for her surrounded by a few of his gentlemen, and fell fainting with emotion, having only the strength to murmur: "Bread! Bread!"

When she came to she saw the King bending over her and helping her to drink a little wine in a large gold goblet. Then he made her smell spirits.

"My poor women," sighed the King. "I have no bread in my pocket, but you can go to the pantries, where you will find provisions, not as much as there used to be, but in any case you will take what is there."

From the courtyard could be heard insults to the Queen.

"We want her head to take to Paris on the end of a pike!"

The King turned to Louison and asked sadly: "Have you come to harm the Queen?"

The poor child denied it in a trembling voice.

"The Queen agrees to come to Paris with me," went on the King. Louison fell on her knees, asking to kiss the royal hand.

"You deserve better than that," Louis declared, raising the girl and kissing her.

The delegation withdrew enchanted and appeared in the courtyard crying: "Long live the King! Tomorrow we shall have bread!"

Louison and Françoise—who had been received only by the minister Saint-Priest—were booed. It was felt without doubt they had been bought. They had received money. They had brought no written promise. No paper from the King. The two girls were punched and kicked. Two women put garters round their necks and dragged them to a lantern. Luckily, other women and two guards intervened. The two unfortunate women were sent back to the château. Louis XVI agreed to show himself on the balcony with Louison and declare to the crowd that the little working girl had not received a single copper. The King then wrote in his own hand the order to send corn from Senlis and Lagny to Paris, and he handed a deputy a letter for the town of Paris. When Louison and Françoise reappeared in the courtyard they were acclaimed. People danced round them, crying, "Long live the King!" and it was a happy procession that returned to the Assembly, where the royal note was read. "I am deeply touched by the insufficiency of supplies for Paris. I shall continue to second the zeal and efforts of the municipality by all the means and all the resources in my power, and I have given the most positive orders for the free circulation of corn on all the roads and for the transport of that intended for my good city of Paris."

A copy of the letter was handed to Maillard, who immediately left for Paris in company with Louison, Françoise and two hundred women. With the King's permission the whole delegation was piled into court carriages provided by the Messageries du Roi.

Toward midnight, at the end of the Avenue de Versailles, the carriages crossed the Paris National Guard, "as wet as ducks, floundering and stumbling in the mud." The regular army of Parisians marched very slowly in ranks of six, drums beating, flags flapping in the wind and rain, but behind them was a mob: fifteen thousand "volunteers," brandishing blunderbusses, halberds and even whips. At the head of this invasion marched Lafayette, whom the Parisians had forced to take the lead. After resisting for a long time he mounted his famous white horse—in reality a broken-down old nag—and took the road to Versailles.

At two o'clock in the morning Maillard, convinced that the affair was over, arrived at the Hôtel de Ville in company with 150 women who had refused to leave him. When the King's letter was handed over, the Mayor invited everyone to supper and gave them meat, rice and "as much as they wanted to drink." Poor Louison had not ceased being threatened by her companions, who reproached her for letting herself be kissed by the King. "In the heat of the wine" they once more wanted to hang the girl and the municipality sent her home with an armed escort to protect her.

It was nearly six in the morning when Maillard, accompanied by about ten female admirers, went to bed in a furnished room in the Rue Grenelle-Saint-Honoré. He was dead beat and wanted only to rest. But two hours later ten or twelve women dragged him from his bed. He must put himself at their head to go and present a laurel wreath to M. de Lafayette, who would soon be returning to Paris. Maillard got up and started off bravely, but at the entrance to Paris the little group was met by a messenger. He brought grave news. At dawn the château had been invaded by the Parisians, and the royal family, prisoners of the capital, would sleep that night in the Tuileries. Nevertheless, Maillard went on, on foot. At Viroflay he met the procession. The heads of the two bodyguards killed that morning as they were defending the entrance to the Queen's apartment were carried first. A barber of Sèvres had been forced to powder and arrange them. "After this vanguard came an immense, hideous and grotesque crowd

... a tragic masquerade of soldiers, bandits, drunken women holding on with difficulty astride the cannons."

Instead of the Hundred Swiss, with starched ruffs and striped doublets who habitually preceded His Majesty when he entered his good city of Paris, instead of the bodyguards and mayoral guards prancing on their black horses, the carriage was surrounded by a nameless mob of disheveled viragoes, yelling and drunken, covered with tricolor rosettes from their heads to the bottom of their skirts. Instead of the silver trumpets—four in front and four behind—sounding high and clear, there were cries of: "To the lantern! Down with the clergy!" At the back, between two rows of National Guards, marched the disarmed bodyguards and soldiers of the Flanders Regiment.

At the Chaillot barrier—it was then pitch dark—Mayor Bailly, correct and cold, presented the King with the keys of the city on a gold platter and declared without the least irony—of which he would have been quite incapable: "What a wonderful day, sire, on which the Parisians hold Your Majesty and his family in their city."

A battalion of mendicant friars, Franciscans, Recollets, Capuchins and Picpusians hastily armed, gave the salute. Louis XVI turned his head and "furtively wiped away a tear."

But the "wonderful day" was not yet finished. Before going to the Tuileries Lafayette took "his prisoners" to the Hôtel de Ville, where the crowd acclaimed the royal family. Here were not the drunken escort but the real people of Paris, delighted at being able to shout: "Long live the King! Long live the Queen! Long live the Dauphin! Long live us all!"

Maillard, the consumptive Maillard, could do no more. Since the previous day he had walked nearly forty-five miles. He returned quickly to his room while the crowd in the square wept with joy. Without doubt as he went to bed Maillard, like all the other Parisians that evening, must have thought that the Revolution was ended.

It had barely begun.

3
Paris Without a King

On Tuesday, June 21, 1791, at seven o'clock in the morning—a heavy, stormy morning—Lemoine, the King's valet, rose from his camp bed, which was set up every evening right in his master's bedroom in the Tuileries, and approached the royal bed.

"Sire, it is seven o'clock."

No answer. Astonished by this silence he opened the curtains: the bed was empty. Stupidly he looked at the cord still tied by one end to his arm, the other having been placed on the previous evening within reach of the royal hand. Pierre Hubert, a servant occupied in tidying Lemoine's bed, approached. Perhaps the King had spent the night with the Queen? Although this seemed a little surprising, the two men decided to wait. Half an hour later Lemoine, who was beginning to show anxiety, told Hubert "to inquire in the Queen's apartments whether the King was not there." The boy came back a few moments later bringing the reply given him by one of the Queen's lady's maids: "It is not yet day."

The sun was already high, but this meant that Marie Antoinette's shutters and curtains had not yet been opened.

But Hubert brought back another piece of information. He had it from Lenoble, *a garçon de toilette,* whom he had met as he came back.

"There is no one in M. le Dauphin's room."

The lamplighter had observed this at seven o'clock. He had informed J. A. Duperrier, an officer of the Queen's wardrobe, but the latter had shrugged his shoulders, thinking it was a joke.

In distress Lemoine crossed the royal bedroom and through a small dressing room entered the little prince's bedroom: it was empty. Fearfully, the valet then descended the little internal staircase that enabled the King to visit the Queen or to go to his forge or archives on the ground floor. These two rooms also were empty. At the foot of the stairs was a door giving onto the Queen's alcove. Lemoine did not dare knock and went back by the central corridor to the entrance to the Queen's apartment. There he found a whole group of servants waiting in front of the door which was "closed from within with bolts and bars." The waiting women to Madame Royale and the Dauphin were also there, announcing the disappearance of the royal children and of Mesdames Brunier and de Neuville.

Someone knocked, timidly at first, then more loudly. There was no reply. A servant was then bold enough to go round by the way Lemoine had taken. He pushed open the door of Marie Antoinette's apartment, which led onto the corridor, and entered the alcove. The bed was empty. He crossed the room and opened the door to the crowd, which spread out into the bedroom.

The incredible news was soon known and spread from the kitchens in the basement to the attics on the fourth floor of the Pavillon de Marsan. It reached the town; from the streets rose "a murmur like the roaring of a wave urged on by the tempest" recounted an eyewitness. The cry went from window to window and from door to door: "The King has gone! The King has gone!"

A quarter of an hour later a great crowd was moving toward the Tuileries. Seeing the Carrousel fill with people, a captain of the riflemen of the National Guard, a certain Dubois of the Roule division, who was looking through a window, seemed very astonished. Alone of all the inhabitants of the château, and perhaps even of Paris, he still knew nothing. He asked questions; he was answered and at first shrugged his shoulders. At half past ten on the previous evening he had accompanied the Queen to her apartment. One of his men had then put his mattress across the single door, and was it possible that she was not in her room that morning? Saber in hand, he entered the room and to his stupefaction discovered a false wardrobe transformed into a door and communicating with the great gallery. He then had to admit the facts.

After gazing at the long, gray façade, the people finally entered the château. The National Guard did not stop them. A cherry seller installed herself on the Queen's bed, crying: "Come on! Cherries, fine cherries at six sous the livre!"

One question was in everybody's mouth: how had the King and the Queen managed to leave this bastion?

A wag fastened a notice to the château wall: "Citizens are warned that a fat man has escaped from the Tuileries. Those who find him are asked to bring him back to his lodging. They will be given a moderate reward."

Another notice on the gate said: "Lodgings to let."

A great clamor arose from the Louvre gates. It preceded General Lafayette, Bailly, the mayor of Paris and Beauharnais, president of the Assembly, who were crossing the Pont Royal. Lafayette pushed his way through the crowd, which did not spare its insults. Only a few days earlier the general had declared: "I will answer for the King with my head!"

This would enable Danton to shout logically, a little later: "We must have the King or your head!"

The three masters of Paris, abused, jostled and booed, managed to take refuge in the guardroom of the château, where the officers who had been on duty since the night before cut a sorry figure. Gouvion, the major general, was appalled and Captain Dubois was still amazed. Beauharnais and Bailly were limp. The former decided to go to the Assembly and officially inform the deputies of the "terrible news."

Lafayette turned to Bailly. "Do you think the arrest of the King and his family is necessary to the public safety?"

Bailly agreed, but who would dare give the order to send couriers in all directions and to "run down" Louis XVI?

"Very well! I shall take the responsibility on myself," declared Lafayette with a superior smile, and he dictated to Romeuf, his aide-de-camp:

"The enemies of the Revolution having carried off the King" (this was the spontaneous phrasing), "the bearer is charged with warning all good citizens. They are enjoined, in the name of their country in danger, to snatch him from their hands and bring him back to the bosom of the National Assembly. This is about to meet, but meanwhile I take upon myself all responsibility for the present order."

And after signing, he added in his own writing: "This order extends to the whole royal family."

This act was a real "coup d'état." One must think back to an age when royalty still had immense prestige in France in order to realize the seriousness of such an initiative.

The paper went from hand to hand and was hastily copied. About fifteen officers or improvised couriers seized the copies and hurried to the stables in order to ride out in all directions. Few of them passed the barriers. The people stopped them, "thinking they were in the King's suite."

In spite of his coup d'état Lafayette was not very hopeful.

"They have too much start on us for us to be able to reach them," he sighed, turning to Romeuf and handing him one of the copies. "But we must do something."

Paris, in fact, was becoming tumultuous. The sky was heavy and the threatening storm did nothing to help calm people's minds.

Bailly had shut himself up in the Hôtel de Ville and listened to the dull murmur that rose toward him. He dictated the first "communiqué" to his clerk, Dejoly.

"The King was carried away last night, around two o'clock, without anyone's knowing what road he has taken. As soon as the municipality was informed of this departure it took prompt measures to discover his route. . . . All good citizens are called on to show courage and, above all, good order. In consequence the Council decrees that the fronts of all houses shall be illuminated on this coming night and those following."

Other measures were taken. All the bells of Paris rang the tocsin, the drums beat the general alarm, the barriers were closed, the batteries on the Pont-Neuf fired salvoes. In the Assembly, at the opening of the session, a deputy proposed "that the largest artillery in Paris should fire alarm signals every ten minutes."

"Couriers are better than cannon," he was answered.

At this point Beauharnais, who was presiding, rose to speak.

"It has just been announced to me that one of M. de Lafayette's aides-de-camp, sent in pursuit of the King, has been stopped by the people. He asks to appear."

It was Romeuf, who on going to find a horse had not even been able to cross the Place de la Concorde; the laborers working on the bridge had prevented him.

He was applauded for his courage and given a decree of the Assembly, laying down that "should the said couriers meet any individuals of the royal family, public functionaries, National Guards or troops of the line they shall be expected to take all necessary measures to halt the said carrying off" (of the King).

Romeuf left the session hall and, strong in his title of envoy of the Assembly, was proceeding to the Soissons road when he was brought the deposition of the postilion, who on the previous night had driven two women to the relay station at Claye, on the Metz road. These were the two waiting women to the Children of France who had also disappeared. At about four o'clock in the morning the postilion had seen the arrival of a large berlin coming from Paris. He had admittedly not been able to see the people inside, but he added that his journey had been ordered "on behalf of M. Fersen."

All Paris knew the name of Fersen, friend of the Queen. Without doubt they were on the track of the fugitives. Without further delay Romeuf went to the Saint-Martin barrier, where he learned that one of his comrades carrying Lafayette's order had succeeded in passing the barrier. He had gone through there around midday, that is an hour previously. For all that, Romeuf set off at a gallop toward Bondy.

They were both on the right road, the one taken ten hours before by the royal family, who had decided that night to flee from the Revolution.

Two long days went by.

The Assembly was in permanent session. The only event of importance after Romeuf's departure had been the reading of a letter left by the King, which had been greeted first with anxiety and then with relief and contempt. It contained only complaints and grievances which showed the gulf separating the monarchy from the representatives of the nation. The King had left slamming the door—that was all. What did he intend to do? What were his plans? One could almost gain the impression that the sovereign was resigned to abandoning his kingdom to anyone who wanted to take it.

Since then, with stoicism and turning their minds to other things or dozing, the deputies had been occupied in drawing up the new penal code or solving customs problems. Even the importation of merchandise from Madagascar and the best way of allowing the entry of smoked salmon into France did not shake them out of their torpor.

There was no news of the fugitives. Reports merely piled up on the Assembly table. A wave of suspicions and denunciations, starting from Paris, began to spread over the whole of France. Trunks, boxes and parcels carried by public transport were searched and even a case containing a layette was confiscated. Throughout Tuesday the "noble legislators" had received "the expression of their purest patriotism" from the outlying communes of Paris. To these sentiments the deputies replied that "the patriotism of the citizens of Paris was equal to the serious circumstances."

The Parisians were constantly coming for news, but the deputies knew no more than they did. Everyone slaked his thirst for information by reading the papers and pamphlets sold by the hawkers which announced the departure of the King "through the tunnels in the Tuileries," or "by boat, disguised as a National Guard," while "his wife was dressed in peasant's costume." It was declared that Louis XVI had stabbed and thrown into the Seine the "two sentries who had tried to oppose his flight" and that the bodies had been found "in the nets at Saint-Cloud." It was alleged that the royal family had been arrested at Senlis, while others swore that it was at Meaux or Château-Thierry.

At ten o'clock on Wednesday evening the deputies obtained a suspension of the session. They hurried to the cafés and restaurants near the Manège. A few representatives who had not even the energy to leave their seats slumbered where they were. Suddenly a clamor arose. Cries could be heard: "The King is arrested! The King is taken!"

The session was immediately resumed and two men, white with dust and exhausted, were almost carried into the hall. One was the surgeon Mangin, who had left Varennes that same Wednesday, at two o'clock in the morning after Louis XVI had been recognized by Judge Destez of Varennes. He had stopped only to change horses at each station and to collect the reports from the town halls of Clermont and Sainte-Menehould. At eight o'clock in the morning he had arrived at Châlons and had continued on his way in company with the celebrated Palloy, who, having finished demolishing the Bastille, was still "exploiting the Revolution," to use Lenotre's very apt phrase. The Patriot had arrived at Châlons with Bodan, one of Lafayette's messengers who had set off after the first pursuers, but Bodan had gone on alone to meet the royal berlin.

Now that the game was played out Palloy considered that nothing would be better for his fame than for him to go with the surgeon. Later he was even to try to make people believe that he had been as far as Varennes.

The two men galloped together as far as Bondy, where Mangin

succeeded in giving his companion the slip. But Palloy was tenacious and managed to rejoin the man from Varennes in front of the Assembly hall. It was ten o'clock at night. Mangin had been galloping since two o'clock in the morning and had therefore done the journey from Varennes to Paris in about twenty hours.

Mangin laid a bundle of papers on the table. In a tense silence one of the secretaries rose and read: "Gentlemen, in our present state of alarm we authorize M. Mangin, surgeon of Varennes, to leave immediately in order to inform the National Assembly that His Majesty is here and to beg it to indicate the course we should follow. Signed: the municipal officers of Varennes."

A murmur arose from the bays . . . Varennes? Where was that? But there was no time for questions, as the secretary was already reading the dispatches from the municipalities of Sainte-Menehould and Clermont-en-Argonne. They smelled of powder: "Towns garrisoned . . . The country is in danger! . . . More troops are about to arrive! . . . Help us quickly! . . . come without loss of time!"

These lines set off an immense tumult; proposals came from all sides.

"Seize Bouillé!"

"Dismiss him!"

"No horses should be given to the posting stations!"

"See that no one leaves Paris tonight."

The deputy Toulongeon established calm and made the Assembly's responsibilities clear to it by declaring gravely: "We have arrived at perhaps the most painful and most solemn moment ever enshrined by history in the annals of a nation."

There was applause. And the deputies immediately decided to take "the most urgent and active measures . . . to protect the person of the King. In fulfillment of these dispositions MM. de Latour-Maubourg, Pétion and Barnave will proceed to Varennes, and to any other places where they find it necessary to go, with the title and character of 'Commissioner of the National Assembly.' They will be accompanied by M. Dumas, Adjutant-General of the Army, charged with carrying out their orders."

At two o'clock in the morning, the excitement having died down, the commissioners, political opponents, met in Comte de Latour-Maubourg's peaceful house in the Rue Saint-Dominique and discussed matters "with much constraint," in company with Lafayette, the Minister Duport and Tracy, the deputy for Moulins. "There was much talk as to the course which would be taken with regard to the King," Pétion wrote. Everyone said that "that fat pig was a great nuisance." "Will he be interned?" said one. "Will he reign?" said another. "Will he be given advice?"

Lafayette, relieved, and with one weight less on his shoulders, "grinned" and joked. Shortly before four o'clock the three deputies went to fetch Dumas in the Rue Thévenot and then proceeded to the Saint-Martin barrier. When they got there, and in spite of the presence of two ushers from the Assembly on the box of the coach, the National Guard wanted to stop the travelers from going on their way. There was some argument, and not without difficulty the soldiers finally let the deputies pass.

It was broad daylight, on Thursday, June 23, when the coach rolled into the paved streets of Bondy.

For forty-eight hours a "quiet but terrible excitement spread throughout the capital," as a contemporary newspaper observed. In the stuffy atmosphere of that sweltering week, under a sky heavy with a storm that never broke, passions rose to white heat. Journalists and pamphleteers full of hate, paid scribblers and authors wrote thousands of words for the people to feed on. The whole affair was now known: how the fugitives had been able to leave the Tuileries, how they had been recognized at Sainte-Menehould and arrested at Varennes, thanks to Drouet; how the troops, stationed by Bouillé in the villages of the Marne and the Argonne, had made peace with the population.

At the Palais Royal there swarmed groups of people who cried out: "Frenchmen, dethrone your King; nominate judges from among your deputies to condemn him, if need be, to death. Deliver up your Queen to the furies; let her be torn in pieces!"

In the Faubourg Saint-Germain a fishwife could be heard saying "she proposed to eat the Queen's heart on a spit." How had such a gulf been formed between the sovereigns and the French?

Twenty years separated them. On the King's part, twenty years of good will and love for his subjects, but twenty years, too, of ignorance, blunders, mistakes, hesitations and, above all, of insensibility and weakness.

On the Queen's part, twenty years of charm, goodness and generosity, but twenty years, too, of blind friendships, overtenacious rancor, excessive expenditure, twenty years of pride, coquetry, frivolity and, above all, twenty years of mockery and impertinence.

It was in the forest of Bondy that the first clash took place between Paris and those who were again to become its prisoners. "A crowd of madmen"—the expression is from Mathieu Dumas—issued from the wood and threw themselves on the National Guards surrounding the royal berlin. "In vain were they driven back; they slipped under the horses and between the wheels" in their attack on the carriage. "A thick cloud of dust made it impossible to see further than one hundred paces . . . but the cries could be heard from afar off." "There was talk of nothing but flaying the guards," said Moustier, "cutting them to pieces and tying them to the carriage wheels."

In all the noise the Queen was the most often attacked. Harridans screamed: "The bitch, the slut, the whore!"

And when Marie Antoinette, to calm the crowd besieging the berlin, lifted up the little Dauphin, who was crying, a voice lashed out: "It's no good her showing us her son; we know very well it's not fat Louis's."

The King heard the insult, turned pale, but said nothing. Tears rolled down from the Queen's eyes and the Dauphin uttered "cries of terror."

When the berlin moved forward again it was laden with men and *tricoteuses*. They were everywhere, on the seats, on the shaft, on the mudguards and even on the box. "It was a hideous and sinister spectacle." A little further on there was another incident. The mounted National Guards, who had been accompanying the carriage since Meaux, and the foot grenadiers commanded by Captain Lefebvre, the future Duke of Danzig, began to fight, each claiming that the "post of honor" near the berlin was due to them. "The fray grew lively and bayonets flashed around the carriage."

Dumas had lost his voice and could not make himself heard. Barnave then leaned right out of the window, shouting above the tumult: "Remember, colonel, you must answer with your head for the safety of the royal family!"

Spurred on by the young deputy's voice, Dumas managed to free the carriage and the future Marshal Lefebvre's grenadiers won their point.

Near Pantin the procession became more orderly. Behind the King's berlin, that funeral car of the monarchy surmounted by a band of "madmen," came a long farm cart covered with palms in which were Drouet, Guillaume and the little band of Varennais who had stopped the King in the vaulted passage of Saint-Gengoult.

At the barrier Lafayette was waiting. The carriages stopped. Louis XVI asked for a glass of wine, "which he drank right off." Then, to the sound of drums, the procession skirted Paris by the "new boulevards." Since leaving Varennes the unhappy prisoners had been accompanied by an immense and ceaseless tumult, a concert of howls. Now, apart from the sound of the drums beating a funereal rhythm, there was silence.

It was a crushing, insulting silence, a hundred times worse, perhaps, than the insults in the forest of Bondy. The National Guard lined the road, with reversed muskets as for a funeral. Behind the soldiers were the people, "calm, but somber," their hats firmly on their heads. Many of the men were "armed with pikes, sabers and knives." The berlin, still laden with its groups of "patriots" reached the Etoile barrier and went down the Champs-Elysées. "There was an immense crowd of people," wrote Pétion, "and it seemed as though the whole of Paris and its surroundings were gathered in the Champs-Elysées. No more imposing spectacle has ever been presented to men's eyes. The roofs of the houses were covered with men, women and children."

Marie Antoinette appeared to be suffering cruelly; the Dauphin "stood at one of the windows looking at the people"; as for Louis XVI, who seemed to have a mantle of lead on his shoulders, he looked at the multitude with a dazed eye, "the look of a drunken man," reported a witness. The three bodyguards who had left with Louis XVI were chained together on the seat; one of them was weeping.

"Before the carriage went eight cannons and as many behind, with the fuse lit. . . . The only radiant face was that of M. de Lafayette, who was riding a superb battle horse. A large white plume in his hat marked him out from a distance. He commanded the whole crowd with the dignity of a hero; he really appeared like a demigod."

And the bitter, thick, whirling dust still entered through the lowered windows, covering the women's dresses and the King's brown plush clothes with a layer of white, mingling with the sweat and painting black lines on the faces of those poor people, who were a thousand miles from understanding the reasons for all this hate.

The crowd had left only a narrow channel across the Place de la Concorde and the carriages followed it. Once they had entered the garden, the swing bridge, in front of which, eighteen months later, the scaffold would be permanently erected, was closed.

4

Fie! How Horrible!

In the courtyard of the La Force prison, on the morning of September 3, 1792, two trembling women were sitting next to each other on a stone bench. Around them the crowded courtyard, generally full of noise, was plunged into stupor. The silent prisoners in the yard—"rogues of aristocrats"—were terrified. From time to time two half-drunk *sans-culottes,* their clothes stained with blood, went up to one of the unfortunates and dragged him to the office, where an improvised tribunal was being held.

On the previous evening the "September massacres" had begun in all the Paris prisons. The news of the imminent capture of Verdun by the army of the Prince of Brunswick—the man who had threatened the capital with military force "if the least outrage is committed against Their Majesties the King and Queen"—had caused a wave of panic. At the tribune of the Assembly Danton had shouted: "One section of the people will hasten to the frontiers, another will dig trenches and the third, with pikes, will defend the interior of our towns. Paris will second these great efforts. . . . We need daring, still more daring, and France will be saved!"

The "daring" consisted first of all in going to massacre those prisoners who had been held since August 10, the date of the fall of royalty.

At about ten in the morning two men staggered toward one of the women, pulled her to her feet and took her to the office of the tribunal, where bloodstained arms were propped against the walls. Through the half-opened door leading into the Rue du Roi-de-Sicile, bright in the sunshine, the presence of the murderers awaiting their prey could be divined.

The president of the tribunal was the pale, the elegant, the refined Hébert. At the Fraternal Society of the Two Sexes he had met a former nun and married her. It was idyllic. When speaking of her husband, she would sigh: "His hands are as pure as his soul!" These were the hands which, every day, wrote ignominies and filth, for Hébert was the famous Père Duchesne. That day he was presiding over the slaughter at La Force.

"Who are you?" he asked the woman, pale with terror, who was pushed in front of him.

She murmured: "Marie-Louise de Savoie-Carignan, Princesse de Lamballe."

"Your occupation?"

"Superintendent of the Queen's household." And she fainted.

The Princesse de Lamballe was, indeed, so emotional that she fell in a faint when she saw "a lobster in a picture," but this time the unhappy woman had some reason for losing her senses. Married very young to the son of the Duc de Penthièvre, she had been widowed at nineteen. Her husband, after leading a disordered existence, had died in terrible suffering from the after-effects of a love affair. Having made of the princess her "inseparable" friend—in the fashion of the time—Marie Antoinette had tired of her and her too frequent swoons.

Mme. de Lamballe, in semi-disgrace, had gone to live with her neurasthenic father-in-law. But when the Revolution came and when she learned that the Queen was in danger, the princess had hastened to rejoin her. So that on the morning of June 20 Marie Antoinette and Mme. de Lamballe had been together when the Parisians had invaded the château in the hope of making the King reverse his veto of the Assembly's decree condemning the priests who refused to take the oath. The maddened mob broke in locked doors, overturned the beds in the Queen's apartment, and surrounded the King as he stood on a table in an antechamber on the "garden side" of the Tuileries, as the actors of the King's theatre called it. Marie Antoinette, her children and the Princesse de Lamballe had taken refuge behind the great table in the Council Room, on the "courtyard side" of the Carrousel. There the rioters had found them. Since then not a night had passed without the Princesse de Lamballe's reliving the scene. With sweaty faces and bare arms the men marched past, brandishing pikes and hatchets above the table, waving a handful of sticks carrying a notice: "To the lantern with Marie Antoinette!" and even displaying a piece of meat on a plate which they called "aristocrat's heart." Shattered doors lay on the ground. Everywhere one walked on broken glass. The masquerade did not end until eight in the evening, when Louis XVI was finally able to rejoin his family. The Princesse de Lamballe looked at him horrified when he appeared. He had forgotten to take off the red bonnet the rioters had put on his head.

Henceforth the château was no more than a wreck battered by the tempest. Like shipwrecked people, Louis XVI, Marie Antoinette and their cousin lived there in anguish, listening to the sinister rumors that reached them. During the six weeks that separated the two attacks the unfortunate people sometimes wished for final, sudden engulfment. Anything seemed preferable to that slow agony.

During the night of August 9-10 the tocsin began to ring. The Princesse de Lamballe and Marie Antoinette, who had not gone to bed, watched the sun rise on the last day of the monarchy. The sky was as red as blood. At about four o'clock the tocsin ceased, but the heavy silence that followed the peals of bells seemed to them even fuller of anguish. All Paris was marching on the Tuileries.

In the gardens and the courtyards the troops who were to defend the château fell in. Louis XVI went downstairs. From a window the Princesse de Lamballe saw her gloomy cousin waddle past the men who were going to die for him. A great cry of "Long live the nation!" drowned the acclamations of the Swiss Guards and royalist sections of the National Guard. Some gunners left their cannon and came to insult the King. "Down with the veto! Down with the fat pig!"

It seemed useless to resist. And so, shortly afterward, the royal family had followed Roederer's advice and taken refuge in the Manège, where the Assembly was sitting. In this way Louis XVI, Marie Antoinette, Madame Elisabeth and the Princesse de Lamballe advanced toward their death. The little Dauphin, who amused himself in kicking the leaves in the garden, was to know the most atrocious of destinies. Only Marie-Thérèse, "weeping softly" on her aunt's arm, was one day to return to the Tuileries.

There followed three days of nightmare. The royal family had been shut up in a little office behind the President's chair. From this cupboard, which was unbearably hot, the princess could hear the defending cannons and muskets of the Swiss Guards rage not far away. Then the cannon fire died down and only a few isolated shots could be heard. Finally there was silence: the Tuileries had succumbed. Then, like a wreck thrown up on the shore after the tempest, the victorious rioters carried their trophies to the Manège. The prisoners saw brought into the hall their jewels, their silver, the letters from their desks, boxes of correspondence, even trunks found in their apartments and clothes.

In the evening the prisoners were shut up in little cells in the Feuillants convent. At the end of the corridor, behind a grille, a mad crowd shouted threats of death. "When one of the ladies appeared at a door of the apartment," wrote an eyewitness, "she was obliged by the terrifying cries to return at once. Every time I looked at the grille I thought I was in a menagerie watching the fury of the wild beasts when someone approaches the bars." The princess thought only of the Queen. "I fear she is lost," she sighed.

On August 13, packed into one coach, the unhappy people set out for their prison, the keep of the Temple. The tower was not ready and they had to camp in the lodgings of the archivist to the order. Mme. de Lamballe slept in a little, windowless room between the Queen's bedroom and that of the Dauphin. During the night of August 19-20 she and Mme. de Tourzel had been taken off to the La Force prison. Marie Antoinette had thrown herself into her departing friend's arms and then, embracing her children's governess, she had said quietly: "If we are not so fortunate as to meet again, look well after Mme. de Lamballe. On all essential occasions be the spokeswoman and as far as possible avoid her having to answer embarrassing questions."

Now, on the morning of September 3, the Princesse de Lamballe was alone before Hébert.

"Did you have any knowledge of the plots of August 10?"

Naturally she denied it.

"Swear liberty, equality, hatred of the King, the Queen and royalty."

The Duc de Penthièvre had paid some of the men there to save his daughter-in-law. One of them whispered in the princess's ear: "Swear, or you are dead."

The princess pressed her hands together. On one of her fingers sparkled a ring set with a blue stone and containing some white hair plaited in a love knot, with the motto: "They are whitened by misfortune." It was the Queen's hair. She let her hands fall and straightened herself proudly in the dress she had not taken off since August 10.

"I shall easily swear to the two first; I cannot swear the last; it is not in my heart."

Hébert rose and smiled graciously.

"Set Madame at large."

And the princess was dragged to the entry to the prison, where No. 2 Rue du Roi-de-Sicile now stands. Two heaps of corpses lay there.

"Fie! How horrible!" exclaimed the poor woman.

Then a murderer named Nicolas pushed the condemned woman to the corner of the Rue des Ballets. A barber called Charlat knocked off her bonnet with the end of his pike, wounding her forehead, and a second later she fell, pierced with stabs. The killers were only now to "set her at large." Near the conduit of the Rue Saint-Antoine they sawed off her head with a knife and tore out her heart and genitals. One man placed the head with its long, fair hair on the end of a pike, another ran the heart through with his saber and a third made himself a pair of mustaches from the victim's pubic hair. Four men—a cabinetmaker from the Rue du Faubourg-Saint-Antoine, a chessboard maker from the Rue Popincourt, a gunner from the Montreuil section and a young drummer from the Halles—harnessed themselves to the body and the joyous band set off for the Temple to show the victim's head to the Queen.

The headless body, which was one large wound, bumped over the cobbles. When they reached what is now 113 Boulevard Beaumarchais, they washed the head in a bucket of water.

The commissioners on guard in the Temple had not been able to prevent the killers from yelling at the bottom of the little tower where the royal family was still living that the Queen should come to the window.

Marie Antoinette was still ignorant of what was going on. She had been playing backgammon with the King. A confused noise was coming from the garden. It was doubtless "Patriot" Palloy's workmen who were building a wall around the tower. Suddenly a piercing cry came from the little dining room. Cléry, the King's valet, appeared in the room, haggard, his eyes full of horror. He looked at the Queen and was silent. He could not say that he had just seen, framed in a window, on the end of a pike, the severed head of the Princesse de Lamballe with its fair hair floating in the wind.

A yell rose from the courtyard: "As she doesn't show herself we must go up and make her kiss the head of her whore!"

Marie Antoinette had not understood the words. "They are spreading the rumor that you and your family are no longer in the tower," one of the commissioners explained kindly, as he closed the curtains. "They want you to appear at the window, but we shall not allow it."

The cries grew. Other municipal officers appeared in the room; they were ghastly pale. Marie Antoinette, seized with anguish, asked what was being kept from her. There was a tall fellow there, whose sword knocked against the furniture. Marie Antoinette looked at him and the man explained calmly: "They want to hide from you the head of the Lamballe, which has been brought here to show you how the people takes its revenge on tyrants. I advise you to appear."

But Marie Antoinette did not hear the end of the speech. "Frozen with horror," without a cry, she had fainted.

5

"Nothing . . ."

There exists in the National Archives a very curious series of small, ruled notebooks bound in gray cloth. But in what kind of ivory tower did the good diarist live? Next to the date of July 14, 1789, one can read the simple little word: "Nothing." On June 20, the date of the Oath of the Tennis Court, he simply notes that he has been hunting. For the whole of the month of July, 1791, when, after the Varennes odyssey, the royal family had been practically prisoners in the Tuileries, he has recalled only having been to mass.

And during the beginning of the year 1792, while the dull rumblings of the Revolution were heard, this "nothing," the extraordinary *nothing,* returns like a litany and is displayed on all the ruled pages. Having retired to his home in the course of the summer of that same bloody year, while the capital was in a tumult, while Paris was preparing to assault the Tuileries, while feverish days followed feverish days, the diarist recopied in his calm, fine handwriting a long labor that had taken him several days. His spectacles on his nose, he wrote: "From 1775 to 1791 I went out 2,636 times." And he put down his pen, satisfied.

On the morning of August 10, a few moments before the people attacked the Tuileries, he happened to be in the garden of the château. He did not look at the royal troops, drawn up in battle formation. He sighed: "How early the leaves are falling this year!"

Five months later the Convention declared this man "guilty of conspiracy against public liberty and of attempts against the safety of the state." For the author of the gray notebooks was King Louis XVI.

And this man was to know how to die like a king.

It was the night of January 20-21, 1793, a cold, rainy night. The streets were flooded with melting snow. An oppressive anxiety reigned over Paris. At about three o'clock in the morning, following a denunciation to the Committee of Public Safety, the gendarmes were to order back to their houses the five-hundred-odd conspirators of Baron de Batz, who intended to kidnap the King on his way from the Temple to the scaffold. The drums were beating. Those who belonged to the armed sections were hurrying to their meeting points to be at their fixed posts before daylight. But there were many Parisians who had no obligation to take part in this terrible day and who remained at home, with windows and doors closed. At dawn on this misty, pale Monday the Convention, the Commune, the Executive Council and the Jacobins would begin their session. The attitude of Dumouriez, who had left the army and was at the gates of Paris, the assassination on the previous evening at the Palais Royal of the regicide deputy, Lepeletier de Saint-Fargeau, and the discovery of Baron de Batz's conspiracy had caused precautions to be doubled.

It was five o'clock. All the troops in the capital were under arms. The footsteps of the soldiers rang out in the cold night. The horses' hoofs hammered on the greasy, wet roads. In all Paris no one thought of sleep.

Except in the Temple the King was sleeping.

The King slept. Indeed, he was sleeping profoundly. He had fallen asleep half an hour after midnight after a long interview with his confessor, Abbé Edgeworth de Firmont; after, too, the heartbreaking scene of farewell with his family. At half past eight in the evening all five of them had gathered together. For a quarter of an hour no one was able to utter a word. There were neither tears nor sobs, but cries so piercing as to be heard outside the tower. Then calm was restored. Louis had made his son swear, holding the child's little hands in his own, "never to think of avenging his death." And a few minutes later the child, sobbing, had begged the commissioners to let him "go to see the gentlemen of the Convention that he might pray them on his knees not to put his papa to death."

The King slept. Cléry, his valet, entered the icy bedroom to light the fire. At the noise the condemned man awoke.

"Has five o'clock struck?"

"By several church towers, sire, but not yet by your clock."

"I have slept well. I needed it."

The King rose quickly and dressed with the aid of his valet. He put on gray trousers, white silk stockings, a white waistcoat and a brown coat. Several municipal officers had come in and were present at this last *lever*. Complete silence reigned in the feebly-lit bedroom. Louis emptied his pockets and put various objects on the chimney piece, then he retired into his oratory with his confessor. Meanwhile Cléry placed a mahogany chest in the middle of the room, covered it with a large white cloth and arranged it as an altar.

A few moments later Abbé Edgeworth began mass, served by the valet. The King was on his knees. The municipal officers, with their hats on, watched the scene. The flame of the two candles in their silver sticks sparkled on the white flowers of the yellow glazed wallpaper. The green damask of the bed and chairs was lost in the shadows. The King took communion. On the chimney piece the gilded clock on its gray marble pedestal pointed to six o'clock.

Mass was now over and the terrible waiting began. The minutes went slowly by. A misty day began and a sad light fell from the window obstructed by heavy bars and by the shade placed outside. The movements of the town could be heard in the distance. Detachments of cavalry entered the grounds and the voices of officers and the sound of cannons ceaselessly moved about could be heard.

"They are coming," said the King calmly.

He had asked for scissors, so that Cléry could cut his hair, but they had been refused. "The executioner is good enough for him."

Louis was cold and went to the fire. Suddenly the noise grew louder, doors opened, heavy bolts rose and fell with a clash. It was nearly nine o'clock.

The door opened and General Santerre came in, wearing his hat. At that time the famous brewer of the Faubourg Saint-Antoine was the most adulated man in Paris. He owed part of his popularity to his good heart—his brewery had become a kind of soup kitchen—but also to the excellence of his beer, which flowed like water for the patriots. A commander of the Paris National Guard, he was followed by commissioners, a deputation from the Department and gendarmes, whom he drew up in two ranks.

"Have you come for me?" asked the King in a steady voice.

"Yes."

Louis took up his will and held it out to one of the municipal officers, a man called Roux, who was a conforming priest.

"That has nothing to do with me," Roux said. "I am not here to do your errands but to take you to the scaffold."

"Quite true," sighed Louis XVI gently.

"I was behind the King, near the chimney piece," Cléry was later to write. "He turned to me and I handed him his overcoat. 'I do not need it,' he said. 'Just give me my hat.' I gave it to him. His hand met mine, which he pressed for the last time. 'Gentlemen,' he said, addressing the municipal officers, 'I should wish for Cléry to remain with my son, who is used to his attentions. I hope the Commune will accede to this request.' "

Then, as no one replied, he looked at Santerre. "Let us go!"

"I remained alone in the bedroom," Cléry went on. "I was pierced with grief and almost without feeling. The drums and trumpets announced that His Majesty had left the tower."

Surrounded by gendarmes, the King crossed the garden bristling with pikes and twice turned round toward the old tower where, on the third floor, the Queen, Madame Elisabeth, Madame Royale and the Dauphin were peeping out and listening with anguish.

Louis took a seat in the coach of the Minister of Justice. At his side was the Abbé Edgeworth. On the outside seat, where only silhouettes could be discerned through the mist, sat two gendarmes.

Riding the finest horse from his brewery—a gigantic animal that, on fair days, was "disguised" as an elephant—Santerre preceded the condemned man's coach. Before and behind was a considerable body of foot and mounted soldiers, cannons and, above all, drums, a multitude of drums that beat ceaselessly. Along the route—the Rue du Temple and the boulevards—and on both sides of the road were four rows of troops; the streets were almost deserted. There was no one at the windows; the sun was hidden behind a thick fog.

"More than once during the journey," the general-brewer was to relate, "I had the carriage stopped to ask if the condemned man wanted to ask for anything. In front of the Ministry of the Marine, after giving the word to halt, I approached the door for the last time, asking if 'one' had anything to write, or to say, and if 'one' wanted to speak. 'One' answered no."

At the corner of the Boulevard Bonne-Nouvelle and the Rue de la Lune—by Charles V's former rampart—Baron de Batz was posted. He was still under the impression that his friends were ready to leap forward at his signal. The rolling of the drums came nearer, became immense, deafening. As the carriage was passing, de Batz waved his hat above his head and cried above the dull rumbling: "To us, my friends! All those who wish to save the King!"

Only three or four voices replied, that was all. Around them were only armed men. A patrol surged down on them. Two young men were killed and de Batz was only just able to escape. The King, who was reading the prayers for the dying in his confessor's breviary, did not appear to have noticed the incident.

At twenty past ten the procession entered the Place de la Révolution, now the Place de la Concorde, where twenty thousand men were massed. On the terrace of the Tuileries some onlookers, barely two rows, were looking through lorgnettes. The drums continued to beat. The carriage stopped at the foot of the scaffold erected between the Champs-Elysées and the pedestal of the statue of Louis XV, which had just been pulled down. The King, feeling that the coach had stopped moving, raised his eyes, closed the breviary, keeping his finger in to mark the page, and said to the abbé: "We are there, unless I am mistaken."

The abbé bowed in silence. Louis reopened the book and calmly read the last verses of the unfinished psalm. The executioner opened the door. When the King had descended three assistants surrounded him and wanted to take his coat off him, but he pushed them away violently. He took off his waistcoat himself, opened his shirt collar and then knelt at the feet of the abbé, asking for his last blessing. As he rose Sanson's servants approached.

"What do you want?"

"To bind your hands."

"Bind my hands? No, I shall never consent!"

But the abbé murmured: "Suffer this outrage as a final resemblance to the God who will be your recompense."

Louis held out his hands. "Do what you please!"

His wrists were quickly bound behind his back with a handkerchief; Sanson lopped off his hair with a pair of scissors. The King painfully mounted the steep steps to the scaffold. Suddenly he advanced with briskness to the edge of the platform. He made a sign to the drummers immediately in front of him. Impressed, they stopped beating.

"Frenchmen," cried the King in a voice that could be heard on the other side of the square, "I die innocent. I pardon the authors of my death, I pray God that the blood which is about to be spilt will never fall on the head of France! And you, unhappy people . . ."

"I immediately brandished my saber," Santerre related. "The drums began to roll and not another word could be heard. The King stamped his foot and cried to them to be silent; my aides-de-camp urged the executioner to do his work. Finally, Sanson and his servants dragged Louis down and bound him. He continued to speak with animation, but nothing was heard, on account of the drums, except the terrible cry stifled by the fall of the knife."

This was all boasting. Neither Santerre, nor the future General Beaufranchet, who was perhaps a natural son of Louis XV and was also present, was the author of the famous roll of drums. It would appear to have been General Berruyer, who was in command of the troops drawn up in the Place de la Révolution, who gave the order. Besides, a few minutes after the execution Berruyer arrived on the first floor of what is now the Ministry of the Marine, from which the commissioners of the Commune had watched.

"Did you see that Capet wanted to speak to the people? Do you know that fool Santerre lost his head and let him go on, and if I had not immediately ordered a roll of drums to cover the tyrant's voice I do not know what would have happened."

But right through the Revolution Santerre continued to repeat his boast. Only when the trouble was over he no longer lay claim to the famous order. The time had come to moderate his republican ardor.

"That poor Louis XVI was an excellent man," he would sigh, "a man I loved greatly. I still regret him. Right up to the end I thought that when he arrived at the foot of the scaffold his pardon would be asked. I had even soothed the King with my hope of this, I was so horrified by the idea of his death, when, suddenly, I was ordered to have the drums beaten. I had to obey!"

It was too late, and nobody believed him. For everyone, he had become "the infamous Santerre." Half ruined, his brewery closed, he was no more than an outlaw in "his" Paris. Neither the Consulate nor the Empire called on his services. And yet he ceaselessly harassed the authorities to obtain his reinstatement in the army. Had he not fought in the Vendée? But his very name settled his affair. "No reply," was written in the margin of his letters. Even the republicans forgot that, in a way, it was from his premises that freedom had taken her first flight. Was it not to his brewery that the keys of the Bastille had been taken the day after July 14, 1789? Was it not at his house that certain great revolutionary days had been organized? Nobody wanted to remember.

When he died, on February 6, 1809, the man who had received the adulation of a whole people had not a single friend to follow his coffin. The memory of January 21, 1793, accompanied him to the tomb.

6

Pierre Notelet, Parisian Sightseer

Nothing is more exciting for a historian than to find, in some attic in the provinces, a packet of yellowed letters that will enable him to bring to history some details from "little history." Jules Mazé—one of the most distinguished men I have ever known—told me shortly before his death of his joy on discovering by chance one day in his own home in the Ardennes the complete correspondence of Pierre Notelet. This Pierre Notelet, a merchant, was the brother-in-law of Claude Barbier, master tailor to the sons of Louis XVI and great-grandfather of Jules Mazé. It was to the Barbier family, who had remained in the Ardennes, that Notelet wrote letters during the Terror recounting the events he had witnessed and taken part in.

On the morning of Sunday, September 2, Pierre Notelet left his house. "It seemed to me," he wrote, "that I was about to witness a drama that would be mentioned in history." He went first to the Place de l'Abbaye and was astonished at seeing so many peaceful shopkeepers placidly watching the massacre of the prisoners.

"There was no danger; the killing was very quiet," a young girl was to say that same evening when she was scolded for coming home late.

A rumor ran through the crowd that "there was a massacre at the Carmelites," and Notelet went to the prison in the Rue de Vaugirard, where nearly two hundred priests were held, then went to a convent in the Rue d'Assas. There was a gendarme on duty there and the merchant recognized one of his former employees.

"May I enter? Just for a glance?"

"A glance is dangerous! But I know you are not suspect; come, I shall lend you a saber and you can join the others."

Notelet started. "Oh," replied the gendarme, laughing, "you will not be forced to operate. I shall get you a job as overseer somewhere and you can see the business as though you were in your own armchair."

In transcribing Notelet's letters Jules Mazé has given us the scene that followed. The president—the commissioner for the section—sat down at the table, opened a register and sighed: "Let us begin." Two priests left the sacristy, where the prisoners had been assembled, not without difficulty. They came to the table, carrying their breviaries. They were very pale, but seemed resolute. The commissioner made them state their name and profession and then asked them to take the oath of the civil constitution of the clergy.

"That is impossible for us."

The judge sighed and ordered them, with a gesture, to go into the garden. That simple gesture was a death sentence. One could hear cries of pain, the rattling of weapons, howls and then the inevitable cry of "Long live the nation!" The same scene was repeated. Notelet, overcome by the cries, "regretted having entered this hell and cursed his curiosity. At one moment he was able to glance into the garden." He perceived a pile of corpses in front of the short flight of steps and near the corpses the murderers who, "taking advantage of a pause, were calmly smoking their pipes."

Notelet managed to leave without drawing anyone's attention. "Night had come, the garden was lit by feeble lanterns." The street was peaceful. "Shopkeepers were enjoying the air in front of their doors, servant girls were going to market, nurses taking children for walks and boys playing on the pavement."

Today nothing has changed at 70 Rue de Vaugirard. The décor is the same. There is the corridor, at the foot of the stairs, where Notelet stood; there is the short flight of steps where 176 priests were massacred; there is the garden in which the murderers pursued their victims; there is the well—between 4 Rue d'Assas and 102 Rue de Rennes—into which the bodies were thrown.

For some time after his visit to Rue de Vaugirard Pierre Notelet went out less frequently. But it is true that he had only to lean out of his window at 404 Rue Saint-Honoré—which still stands—to witness an astonishing spectacle: the reflections of the crowd watching the tumbrils pass. "All these people seemed to be waiting for a carnival procession," he wrote to his brother-in-law, recounting the passing of Charlotte Corday. "Suddenly a storm broke. Large drops of rain fell in the dust. The crowd became agitated; one could hear the 'Carmagnole' being sung. Suddenly there were cries of 'There she is! There she is!' She was superb in a long red shift that clung to her body in the rain. One might have thought she was a statue, her face was so calm. Behind the tumbril young girls were holding hands and dancing. For at least eight days I was in love with Charlotte Corday."

"There was a large crowd for the Queen," he wrote three months later, "and many people who were pretending to laugh wanted to weep. In the street I heard a mother say to her daughter: 'Above all, don't cry when you see her; you will get us guillotined.' The tumbril looked like a dung cart; it bumped over the cobbles and you could hear it crack as though it would break. Poor Marie Antoinette was as though insensible but had kept her air of grandeur. When the cart passed under my windows a woman cried: 'Death to the Austrian!' Marie Antoinette heard; she looked at the woman and I saw an expression of contempt, immediately effaced, come into her eyes. I said to myself that the Queen must know that Fury." Notelet hurried downstairs and questioned the wife of a neighboring grocer, and learned that the harridan was a former waiting woman from the château.

The Girondins, too, passed under the window. The last cart contained a corpse, that of Valazé, who had stabbed himself before the tribunal. "Maman," said a child, "come and see. They are bringing a dead man. Will they cut off his head?"

Notelet became more and more attracted to the spectacle and one day he decided to disguise himself as a *sans-culotte* and follow the cart taking Hébert, the celebrated Père Duchesne, to the Place de la Révolution. "Hébert appeared on the platform supported by two men; his face was convulsed, his jaw hung down and his eyes opened and closed ceaselessly. Terrifying acclamations arose, there was applause and the heads of the crowd moved about like the waves of a stormy sea. There was silence for a moment. Hébert was on the plank, with his head in the *lunette* and the knife did not fall. There was a murmur of astonishment; the executioners were laughing and seemed to be very amused. The people then realized that they were purposely prolonging Hébert's agony. I felt oppressed and it seemed to me as though the knife were suspended over my own head. At last it fell."

As he was returning to the Rue Saint-Honoré, Pierre Notelet saw a little dog licking the blood that had flowed from the scaffold. "His mistress noticed this and threatened him with her finger, saying smilingly: 'Stop it, naughty!' "

The ground about the scaffold was so impregnated with blood that one could follow the path of those who had crossed the square. Can one pass that spot without evoking the beseeching voice of Mme. Du Barry: "Just another moment, Mr. Executioner," or without remembering that convent of Carmelites guillotined there? Before mounting the steep ladder the nuns came one by one to bow before their superior, asking her permission to die.

Nearly all those women of the eighteenth century, who seemed so frivolous, carried their *savoir-vivre* to the point of *savoir-mourir*. Such was the Duchesse de Gramont, Choiseul's sister, who to the end treated the executioner's servants as she had formerly treated her coachmen. In contrast to this insolence, though it does not lack style, was the death of young Thérèse de Stainville, Princess of Monaco. An hour before the execution she declared she was pregnant and, according to law, Fouquier-Tinville sent "the Monaco woman" to the hospital for an examination. The next morning the public prosecutor received a "very urgent" letter. He opened it. It was from the princess, who informed him that she was not pregnant. "I did not soil my mouth with this lie from fear of death nor in order to avoid it, but in order to have one day longer so as to cut my hair myself and not to give it away as cut by the executioner. This is the only legacy I can leave my children and it must be pure." "Very urgent," she had written, and the same day Thérèse de Stainville mounted the scaffold. At the same time as her head fell in the Place du "Trône Renversé" Robespierre was arrested. It was perhaps with this last victim of the Terror in mind, as M. Bessand-Massenet recalls, that M. Bertin, professor in the Arts School of Paris, exclaimed fifty years ago in a speech that is too much forgotten: "We are in the course of lavishing homage and even statues on the heroes of the Revolution, but I am very much afraid that we have mistaken our heroes and have not sought them on the right side."

7

Thérèse-Angélique Aubry, Goddess of Reason

At the end of the Restoration a woman of about sixty, poorly dressed, was prowling round the Opéra. After gazing for a long time at the posters, she continued with faltering step on her way to her small lodgings in 43 Rue du Faubourg-Montmartre.

This poor woman was called Thérèse-Angélique Aubry and had been a dancer at the Opéra. Forty years before she had been "such a living model of that antique perfection that has been handed down to us by our artistic monuments," a contemporary tells us, that "she played goddesses." How many times had she personified Venus and Diana! In how many ballets and operas had she finally descended from the flies in a rigging to punish the wicked and permit the lovers to love!

Now she was nothing, but she liked to remember the great hour of her life. A specialist in divinities, she it was who, under the Terror, had been chosen to incarnate the "Goddess of Reason" in Notre Dame. The account of the ceremony was recorded by Hébert in his newspaper:

"On the site of the altar, or rather of that mountebanks' stage, the throne of Liberty had been erected. No dead statue was placed there, but a living image of that divinity, a masterpiece of nature, as my colleague Chaumette has said. A charming woman, beautiful as the goddess she represented, was seated on a mount, a red bonnet on her head and holding a pike. She was surrounded by all the pretty devils from the Opéra who in their turn had excommunicated the shavelings by singing patriotic hymns better than the angels.

"Come down, O Liberty, daughter of nature. . . ."

She remembered. Preceded by drums and seated on a beribboned chair carried by four strong men from the Halles, she had crossed Paris to the Convention, where the president, amid the applause of the representatives of the nation, had given her "the sweetest accolade as a sign of the respect and constant love that republicans will always have for liberty."

All the deputies had insisted on accompanying the divinity back to her temple, the former Notre Dame. The rain had been pouring down for several days and the streets of Paris were like a swamp. The dancers and deputies had been forced, with some loss of dignity, to jump from puddle to puddle and to paddle in the mud, but in the evening of her life Thérèse-Angélique remembered only the kiss from the president and the patriotic hymns that had greeted her appearance in the temple of philosophy.

She remembered with emotion the Paris of her twenties—Paris under the Terror. She remembered Chateaubriand's concierge who, when eagerly questioned by the writer after the Revolution, replied: "Ah! Monsieur le Vicomte, those were the days! Every day there went past the windows little duchesses whose necks were white as snow and they were cut. Now it's all over. The people's pleasures have been taken from them!"

What a "pleasure," too, was the spectacle of the street. The streets of Paris were then the setting for the feasts of "Virtue," for the feasts of "Young People" or of "Old People"—all the people over seventy embraced each other, if a print is to be believed—and above all for the famous "patriotic and fraternal banquets."

"On these spartan tables," wrote the *Journal de Paris,* "there is no need for cloths or napkins or anything bordering on luxury. In this state of simplicity, worthy of the golden age, how many hearts are disposed to fraternity, to sweet equality and even to friendship! Fond mothers and fathers, surrounded by their children, enjoy with delight the first fruits of the Revolution."

One should beware of journalists, for the reality was quite different. We know this thanks to Edme Monnet, a member of the Convention. "It is very curious," he wrote, "to go through the streets and public squares of Paris during the so-called fraternal repasts. I have witnessed a series of scenes all more or less disgusting, more or less grotesque. In one place there is drunkenness in all its most revolting aspects; farther on, amid every symptom of gaiety, conversation of cannibals; elsewhere talk of massacre and arson."

But she who had been the Goddess of Liberty wanted to remember only the houses covered with patriotic inscriptions, shops with republican signboards—one bookseller having even called his shop "A Notre Dame de la Guillotine"—and, above all, that joyous crowd that always wanted to return home as late as possible. What a spectacle it was. Jules Bertaut has written: "The Revolution was the street, the triumph of the street, the dictatorship of the street. Everyone out of doors, a whole people feverishly coming and going, a whole city swarming, overflowing with curiosity for the unbelievable new things presented to its eyes." *

Together with the rest of Paris Thérèse-Angélique had been present at the feast of the Supreme Being, celebrated on June 8, 1794, in front of the Tuileries. She had seen Robespierre, in his famous coat of blue nankeen, set fire to the effigy of Atheism dressed in 114 ells of cloth that citizen Ruggieri had covered with sulphur and powder. In burning, Atheism was supposed to give way to a statue of Wisdom, which had been built inside the effigy, but in the midst of the flames the second statue seemed in a bad way. "It was the most dreary Wis-

* *Les Parisiens sous la Révolution* (Amiot-Dumont).

dom one had ever seen," an eyewitness recounts. Her neck appeared to have been severed by an axe, she was looking sadly at her feet, and she was blackened by smoke.

After the burning the participants had set off for the Champs-de-Mars, where, with the help of a great many carts, a symbolic mountain had been erected. There to the strains of the hymn "Father of the Universe" old men crowned with vine leaves were supposed to bless adolescents, children were supposed to throw flowers to the sky, and virgins were supposed to swear "to marry only citizens who had served the fatherland"; but this fine program had been somewhat shortened. It was appallingly hot and everyone was dying of thirst. Robespierre was horrified to see some of his colleagues settle comfortably on "his mountain" and unpack their provisions.

In the Paris of 1793 and 1794 life had been completely changed by the issuing of paper money. As Mercier says, it "created as many tradesmen as there were men. . . . Imagination roamed among regions of fancied riches." In this epoch the marriage ceremony took place in the Temple *décadaire* (The Revolutionary calender abolished the week and divided each month into three *décades* of ten days each.) before the statue of Hymen. Thirty or forty couples would sit there side by side, and utter the sacramental "yes" with one voice. Then the newlyweds would pass in turn before the registrar to the sound of an orchestra playing "appropriate music." When a Negro married a white woman—this happened in the Temple of Peace in the Xth *arrondissement*—he was greeted with an air from *Azéma:*

> Ivory and ebony
> Make attractive jewels.

If an old woman married a young man the imperturbable orchestra played the refrain from *Le Prisonnier:*

> Young husband, elderly wife
> Will have an unhappy married life.

If the guests wanted "to be in the swim" they had to wear informal dress *à la Patriote,* or gowns *à la Constitution.* Some people thought that these sartorial changes were insufficient and—like the citizen designer Wicar, David's pupil—hoped that the ladies would soon abandon "the ridiculously puffed-out kerchiefs that concealed their most agreeable charms" and go about naked to the waist. For his part the sculptor Espercieux wanted to see the men adopt helmet and chlamys "as in Athens."

While waiting for the chance to transform the Parisians into Spartans, the innovators joyfully busied themselves with the costumes of the National Guard. "Each section," Jules Bertaut tells us, "wanted to have its own uniforms, its own colors and its own special adornments; here the grenade and fur bonnet; there horsehair plumes falling from the head. What French heart would not beat at the thought of playing soldiers!" Indeed, there had been an unheard-of craze for the Parisian guard. This troop of bourgeois periodically disguised as soldiers, in which every class mingled, gave rise to picturesque stories.

"Keep in step; you're marching like a priest," cried an officer to one of his men.

"It's your fault, captain, I'm wearing the shoes you made me and they're horribly uncomfortable," replied the soldier to his shoemaker-officer.

On May 24, 1794, the government commissioned the great David to create a national costume. The painter designed a "dress for the French citizen at home," consisting of a tunic, breeches and a round bonnet topped with a plume. For winter this costume was embellished by a blue cape floating from the shoulders. Only David's friends had the courage to go about dressed like this. But the unfortunate pupils of the Ecole de Mars had to wear a costume "half Roman and half Scotch," bare legs and a Polish tunic adorned with swallows' nests as epaulettes. A heavy antique sword worn in a tiger-skin belt completed the picture.

Added to that the poor pupils of the Ecole de Mars, these future leaders of the republican army, were served herb soups "in the Spartan style," after which the Ecole de Mars perished, undermined by dysentery, bronchitis and rheumatism. A street in Neuilly perpetuates its sad memory.

In 1794 the future of Paris promised to be even *more* wonderful, if one were to believe the *Institutions* of Saint-Just. Here is an example:

"If a man leaves a friend, he is bound to explain his reasons in the temples. If he refuses, he is banished.

"He who does not believe in friendship, or who has no friends, is banished.

"Procreation is obligatory, for spouses who have no child during the first seven years of their union, or who do not adopt one, are separated by law and must leave each other.

"Assassins will be dressed in black for the whole of their lives and will be put to death if they abandon this dress. Men who have always lived lives without reproach will wear a white scarf at the age of sixty."

The fall of Citizen Saint-Just, in company with his friend Robespierre, was the only thing that prevented these rules from being put into practice. In France ridicule no longer killed.

8
Bon-Ami

At 398 Rue Honoré a family of artisans lived happily and peacefully. The Terror was at its height; every day tumbrils passed under the windows, rumbling heavily over the cobbled street and shaking the ornaments on the furniture, but this did not prevent the household from leading a pleasant existence, particularly as the family had the happiness of possessing a charming lodger, who cheerfully took the workingman's daughters to botanize at Issy, to picnic at Meudon or wander in the deserted roadways of the Champs-Elysées. In the evening he read them poetry. They adored him. The elder girl, Eléonore, was secretly in love with him and pretty Babet, the younger, called him *Bon-Ami*. A visitor has described the lodger as "well combed and powdered, wearing a very clean dressing gown and lounging in a large armchair in front of a table laden with beautiful fruit, fresh butter, pure milk and aromatic coffee. The whole family, father, mother and children, sought to divine his every wish at a glance so as immediately to forestall it."

One day Bon-Ami noticed that the gentle Babet was always overshadowed by "an unnatural sadness." He pressed her with questions and the girl confessed that she was in love with the lodger's best friend, who was called Philippe. He, too, was languishing, and steps were quickly taken for the two turtledoves to marry. In the autumn of 1793 the whole house was concerned only with this idyll.

And yet Bon-Ami had other cares at that time: his name was Maximilien Robespierre.

What a contrast with the quiet life of 398 Rue Honoré, the needlework of the Duplay girls, the sound of the carpenter's plane in the yard—what a contrast with the Paris of 1794, plunged more deeply into blood each day through the will of the Duplays' lodger, dear, adorable Bon-Ami!

As a matter of fact the Parisians had already begun to sicken at the smell of blood; the "national chopper" had lost its popularity. When the carts passed, shutters were closed and it was even difficult to know where to erect the scaffold that had long since left the former Place Louis XV. Sanson's assistants, who were sent to set up the framework of the guillotine, had to flee from the Place de la Bastille as a result of protests from the surrounding inhabitants, and the sinister machine finally found its way to the present Place de la Nation.

Robespierre may perhaps have wanted to stop the slaughter but, tired and listless, he let things go on, imagining that "the war he was maintaining with the scaffold was the war of virtue against crime." All Robespierre is in that word "virtue." "Virtue," he said himself, "without which the Terror is deadly." A year earlier this bloody violence had been salutary; the country was in danger. But in the summer of 1794, when the "enemies from inside were muzzled," the system was all the more useless since the armies of the young Republic were everywhere successful. "The victories are like Furies in pursuit of Robespierre," Barère, the Convention member, was to say. Yet the guillotine continued to mow people down every day, even making gaps in the ranks of the Convention. So as to feel safer the deputies huddled together on their benches, while some of the rows remained empty. All trembled, and from this fear was born the courage of despair. Robespierre felt the revolt coming. He guessed at the agreement that was being prepared between parties he had carefully divided.

On July 26, 1794, he mounted the tribune of the Convention. After protesting against the calumnies that showed him as a tyrant, he spoke of a new "purge" that had become necessary. But he named nobody. Having uttered his final phrase in which he called on the people "who are feared, who are flattered and who are despised," he left the tribune.

The heat was appalling. The word "purge" brought out the sweat on the foreheads of the deputies. "The names . . . give the names!" cried several voices.

Indifferent, Robespierre returned to his seat and did not deign to reply. This silence was to be his fall. There was panic among the enemies of the Incorruptible. They outdid each other in platitudes and voted for the speech to be printed. But all felt that they were marked. The Marais and the Montagne—the center and the extreme left (there had been no right for a long time)—united in face of the danger. While Robespierre went to be applauded at the Jacobin Club, and during the whole of that night the deputies plotted and prepared the hard day that followed. It was the night of supreme fear. The Revolution was about to complete its work of self-destruction.

On the morning of July 27, curled and powdered and wearing a sky-blue silk suit, the Incorruptible appeared on the threshold of the Duplays' house. Eléonore, with a touching look, arranged the folds of her idol's cravat, while the carpenter pressed his hand and murmured: "Be prudent, Maximilien." The dictator went off to the Convention and turned round for the last time, making a farewell gesture for the whole family standing in the doorway. He was never to see them again.

It was noon. Heavy storm clouds began to cover the sky of Paris. Inside the Convention hall it was as hot as an oven. Saint-Just, who had been chosen by Robespierre to denounce the traitors, "the enemies of virtue" to use his own words, began to speak and could not get beyond the second sentence. No parliamentary assembly has ever witnessed such complete disorder. Everything had been carefully arranged. Tallien, who had received a terrified letter from his mistress, Thérèse Cabarrus, imprisoned in the Conciergerie and about to appear before the dreaded Revolutionary Tribunal, had two heads at stake: his own and that of the future Notre-Dame de Thermidor. He leaped to the tribune to replace Saint-Just. Robespierre left his seat in his turn and tried to speak. The uproar grew louder.

On the evening before, at the Jacobin Club, Maximilien had committed the error of denouncing Billaud and Collot d'Herbois. Knowing that they were lost if the Incorruptible came unscathed out of the business, they both took command of operations. Collot, who happily for the conspirators was presiding over the session, rang his bell continuously, firmly decided to allow speech only to the attacking side and to refuse it to those who were already figuring as the accused.

Three men were now clinging to the tribune: Maximilien, Billaud, who was yelling himself hoarse, and Tallien, who had taken out a dagger with which he was threatening Robespierre. But Billaud's vocal cords were beginning to thicken and Collot's arm to weary. Other partisans immediately replaced them. Thuriot, a former friend of Danton, took the bell from the President's failing hand and rang it with force, while Tallien and Barère, replacing the now speechless Billaud, delivered speech after speech. Robespierre, who had returned to his seat, tried in vain to get in a word. Yells, even from the center, answered him. There were cries of "Down with the tyrant!" Robespierre's breath was taken away. His pale complexion had turned yellow. The words stuck in his throat. It was then that Garnier, from Aube, hurled in his face the famous phrase: "The blood of Danton is choking you!"

Suddenly came the cry they had been awaiting for three hours: "I demand a decree of accusation against Robespierre." It was a certain Louchet who had found the ultimate courage. He was hardly known up to that time and was never to be heard of again.

A terrible silence followed the shouting and weighed on the Assembly. The Convention, horrified at its own audacity, said nothing. For a few moments only the sounds of breathing could be heard. Finally the deputies plucked up courage. Applause, at first scattered, broke out. The proposal was accepted and voted by a show of hands. The case was heard. It was nearly four o'clock.

Gendarmes entered the hall and arrested Robespierre, Saint-Just and Couthon. Robespierre's brother and Lebas joined them voluntarily, and the prisoners were taken away. The paralytic Couthon was not even given time to sit in his little invalid carriage worked with two wheels. Ushers carried him out in their arms.

It might be thought that, having sent their master to the guillotine, the gentlemen of the Convention would have palavered at length, congratulated each other on their courage and on still having their heads on their shoulders, and then have hurried to the café for refreshment. They had shouted so much and it was so hot. But not at all. Deputies in those days were conscientious and hardly had the tumult and the shouting died down than they gave order for "drying and burning the seaweed that grows in the Glénans islands in the Quimperlé district."

The affair, however, was far from being over. The Paris Commune, often more powerful than the Convention, had been informed hour by hour of what was going on within the Assembly. By a spontaneous impulse it had the tocsin rung and the sections assembled. The square in front of the Hôtel de Ville bristled with pikes. Insurrection was in the air and was only waiting for a sign which Robespierre alone could give.

In the meantime, while the Convention was busy with the Breton seaweed and the alarm was being sounded by order of the Commune, each prisoner, accompanied by a few gendarmes, left the Convention and crossed Paris to the prison assigned to him. At the Luxembourg, the head jailer, horrified at hearing the name of Robespierre, shut his gate violently and refused to accept the prisoner. In front of every prison to which Lebas, Couthon and the younger Robespierre were taken the same scene was repeated. The Commune had presumably given precise orders only a few moments earlier. Faced with this unexpected reaction from a jailer, Robespierre was the first to be annoyed. He did not believe in the efficacy of a rising to give him back power. With his respect for the law, he greatly preferred to appear before the Revolutionary Tribunal. What a fine trial it would be!

But something had to be done. They could not remain indefinitely before locked gates, particularly as a crowd was gathering and turning hostile. The gendarmes were glad to obey their prisoner, who, returning to his cab, told them to take him to the municipal police, in other words to open the gates of freedom for him. He was at home in the offices of the Committee of Public Safety. But once there, in the Quai des Orfèvres, he remained for two hours, undecided about what course to pursue. He did not like "those people" of the Commune. He thought them "immoral."

"In saving yourself, you save freedom," an emissary of the municipality told him.

And yet, at nine o'clock in the evening, almost in spite of himself, he made his way to the Hôtel de Ville, where the other prisoners whom the Commune had cleverly been able to free had already gone. On his arrival he began to hesitate again. Saint-Just urged him to act, but he could not bring himself to do so. Should he summon Paris to arms against the Convention and thus go outside the law? This Rubicon was too difficult for him to cross.

Roederer has written: "Which of us ever saw Robespierre in action? He was a paralytic when it was a question of acting."

During this time the Convention had abandoned its seaweed and was occupied with the census of cattle that daily arrived in Paris. Being informed of events the members of the Assembly grew terrified. It appeared that the troops of the Commune were nearing the Tuileries. Hanriot—"Robespierre's donkey," as the Parisians had nicknamed him—marched on the Convention, then, no one knows why, hesitated and retreated. The deputies quickly regained courage, declared the "Robespierrists" to be "outlaws"—which meant death without trial— and charged Barras to put down the growing revolt.

Night had fallen. Barras, who was beginning to understand the machinery of these famous revolutionary days, made the first move. He made his way to the Place de l'Hôtel de Ville with two columns of gendarmes and soldiers. One went by the quays, the other by the Rue Saint-Honoré.

Meanwhile, in front of the Hôtel de Ville, where the Parisian troops were massed, waiting had become tiresome. Robespierre's decision still did not come. It was soon two o'clock in the morning, and when the defenders of the Commune heard the Convention's decree read at the crossroads they began to feel a strong desire to go to bed. The ranks became progressively thinner.

Barras, who had knowledge of the password, met little resistance as he entered the square. He went into the Hôtel de Ville and appeared in the room where the masters of the day before were gathered. Shots rang out. Lebas killed himself, Couthon lost his balance and rolled from the chair in which he had been put. The younger Robespierre jumped out the window and broke his thigh. Maximilien was seriously wounded by a bullet in the jaw. Had he wished to kill himself, or had a gendarme shot him? One will never know. He fell, staining with his blood a sheet of paper on which he had just written the first two letters of his name. This document can still be seen in the

Carnavalet Museum. It is the call to insurrection. Robespierre *had* decided—but too late.

An hour later Robespierre, his cotton stockings down to his ankles and his sky-blue suit all spotted with blood, was lying on the table in the courtroom of the Committee of Public Safety. He had been transported to the place where he had reigned for over a year. A box containing a few bits of ration bread had been placed under his head for a pillow. In his hand he held a little bag of white leather on which could be read: "*Au Grand Monarque,* Lecourt, furnisher to the King." He used it to wipe away the clotted blood from his mouth. With a movement of pity someone handed him some sheets of paper with which he tried to staunch his wound. At about four o'clock in the morning a surgeon came to dress it. The body of Lebas; Couthon, still in the arms of two gendarmes; Saint-Just, as haughty as ever; and the younger Robespierre, who was dying, were taken to the Tuileries.

It was now broad daylight. The people filed past Maximilien Robespierre, still stretched out, as though at a show. "So that's a tyrant. He's not much!" "He's a pretty kind of king!"

During the morning, as the deputies left the Convention reeling with fatigue after a session of twenty-four hours, the prisoners were taken to the Conciergerie. At each crossroads the procession halted. Insults rained down on Robespierre, who was borne in a chair by four men.

At three o'clock in the afternoon the accused were brought from prison to the Revolutionary Tribunal. The public prosecutor, Fouquier-Tinville, was to plead against his former leaders. There were about twenty of them, huddled on benches. There was no interrogation, no defense, for the outlaws. Before sentence of death was passed there was simply an identification by two people present. And so two employees who were there by chance affirmed that they recognized the first accused to be Maximilien Robespierre, the man who, the day before, had been revered as a god.

It was five o'clock. Sanson's horses were pawing the ground in the courtyard of the Palais de Justice. For this occasion the guillotine was set up again in the Place de la Révolution, so that the carts could stop for a few moments in the Rue Honoré in front of the house where Danton, on the point of perishing, had predicted Robespierre's end.

There was another stop a little further on, in front of the Duplays' house. The shutters were closed, and all were either in flight or arrested. Filth was thrown at the condemned men. Women danced round the carts, and a child, dipping a broom into a bucket of blood on a neighboring butcher's stall, daubed the front of the house with it. Robespierre closed his eyes.

The cart full of dying men—most of them were seriously wounded—arrived at last at the foot of the guillotine. The journey had lasted more than an hour. The populace howled. Those whose limbs were broken had to be hoisted onto the platform. Couthon, who was the first, was thrown onto the scaffold. It was impossible to stretch the paralytic out on the swing plank. His limbs refused and he had to be laid out on his side. It took a full quarter of an hour to get his head into the *lunette*. Robespierre was guillotined last but one. One of the executioner's servants tore off the bandage supporting his jaw. The terrible wound appeared; blood gushed out. The pain made Maximilien utter an atrocious cry that could be heard at the other end of the square. All was over.

At the same time, without further delay, those at the Committee of Public Safety who had supported, followed and praised him turned their coats and hastily sent a circular letter to the armies, announcing that "oppression and the modern Catilinas" had disappeared. "All hearts are opened to tender effusions. And in Paris joy," they added, "has taken the place of consternation."

The joy, however, was not entirely general. Certain small Paris workmen, a few bourgeois called into business regretted the government that had just fallen. It was with them in mind that Maximilien's epitaph was written:

> Passer-by, whoe'er you are, no tears for me must shed.
> If I still lived, you would be dead.

More than half a century later, a young man—Victorien Sardou—was eagerly questioning Babet concerning the man who for her had never ceased to be Bon-Ami.

"You would certainly have loved him," she sighed. "He was so good, so affectionate!"

PARIS AND THE SABER

1

The Elysée Transformed

At the beginning of the Directory the Elysée Palace knew the saddest hours in its history. Its proprietor, Bathilde d'Orléans, former Duchesse de Bourbon, called Citizeness Vérité, being completely ruined by the Revolution, had let it for eighteen thousand francs a year to a pair of newly-rich bourgeois: Citizen and Citizeness Hovyn, who had come from Courtrai together with their daughter, who was saddled with the unusual first name of Liévine. Bathilde had kept only a few rooms for herself; the three tenants, with no servant, occupied the immense château by themselves, and were terribly bored. One detail was the despair of that excellent housewife, Mme. Hovyn: to go from the kitchen to the dining room she had to open and close twenty doors.

The poor things could not sleep for boredom. Perhaps they then evoked with a touch of envy the shades of the *berceuses* of M. de Beaujon, their predecessor at the Elysée. Beaujon, the king of finance, had been nearly blind and half paralyzed, and his sole, sad nourishment was an occasional spoonful of spinach. Every evening, leaving his guests to feast at leisure, he had his wheeled armchair pushed up to his bed. Once he was in bed, his *berceuses* were introduced in a cool rustle of satin sliding over the floor. There were five or six of them, with ravishing figures, pretty enough to tempt a saint, and, grouped round the head of the bed, they began to chatter. These young people should on no account be thought of as loose women hired for the occasion; they came from the best society, lived in the Elysée and possessed lackeys, carriages and horses. As he listened to their futile conversations made up of nothing—that eighteenth-century *nothing,* that inimitable *nothing,* that *nothing* whose flavor has been lost forever—M. de Beaujon sank gently into slumber and forgot the sufferings of his poor body.

Lacking *berceuses,* and in order to feel less lonely, the Hovyns decided to transform the Elysée into a public dance hall. The Parisians, happy at finding themselves still alive after all the torment, were consumed with a strong appetite for quadrilles and Paris possessed nearly two thousand dance halls. They had sprung up everywhere and, as the Vicomte d'Almeras relates, in places where one was most surprised to find them: in the Jesuit novitiate, in the Carmelite convent in the Marais, in the Filles Sainte-Marie, in the seminary of Saint Sulpice, in the garden of the Carmelites, where the orchestra sat up against the wall of the sacristy whose steps had been covered in blood from the priests assassinated in September, 1792. Even above the gate of the former cemetery of Saint Sulpice a pink transparency announced: "Zephyrs' Dance Hall."

Dancing gave the opportunity for criticizing the government, and *"Bals des Victimes"* were given in the Hôtel Thélusson, Rue de Provence, or in an old house in the Faubourg Saint-Germain. The fashion was to have one's hair cut short at the nape of the neck, as though one were going to the scaffold. Greetings were exchanged *à la victime,* imitating the movement of a head being inserted in the *lunette.*

In spite of these "good" examples, and although she had barely escaped the scaffold, the Duchesse de Bourbon had not the heart to dance, and was horrified at seeing her palace opened to the public. But her dismay was of short duration. A few weeks after the opening of the "Elysée Hall" a decrepit coach, flanked by gendarmes, came on the order of the Directory to conduct Citizeness Vérité politely to the Spanish frontier.

The landlady being thus out of the way, the Hovyns transformed the palace into a really vast palais de danse. And what did they dance there? The *Walse,* which came from Germany in 1797.

> Waltz! of every dance the best,
> Favouring love so much,
> When, amorously to me pressed,
> I dared that curve to touch,
> Sweet curve of snowy breast.

The "sweet curve" was not very difficult to find. It was, so to speak, to hand, for at that time women were seeking Grecian simplicity and wore their dresses so low as to "send their charms galloping," to use an expression of the time. It will be remembered that David's pupil Wicar, a member of the "Patriotic Society of Arts," had urged, during the Terror, the abandonment of kerchiefs covering the "most agreeable charms"; fashion was soon completely to satisfy him with the appearance, when the torment was over, of dresses *à l'Omphale,* or *au lever de l'Aurore,* creations so attractively transparent that one dressmaker sold an "apron kerchief," which the *Journal des Dames* recommended in these terms: "If one considers the fine transparency of the dress that often serves also as a chemise, one will acknowledge in this accessory the same usefulness as in the aprons of savages."

A poet of that time could certainly not be taxed with exaggeration when he wrote, concerning this grecomania:

> Compliments were what she sought
> In her thin and gauzy dress,
> But a cold was all she caught.

After the ball at the Elysée the Parisiennes, who, as Mercier reports, had no longer to worry about their "figure and their corsets, could eat their fill. They devoured stuffed turkey and anchovy tarts; they ate for the rentier, the soldier, the clerk, for every employee of the Republic, and as they devoured they spoke all the ill they could of that same Republic. Nothing was more horrible than the present regime; if they danced it was to annoy it, for they had heard that the two councils—the Elders and the Five Hundred—did not care for dances. They added that dancing was the only thing that would not perish in France. And yet these women who cursed the appalling regime were daughters, sisters and wives of tradesmen to the Republic. They never ceased eating; they no longer drank wine, because of the weakness of their nerves, but they swallowed *Kirschwasser,* maraschino and all the West Indian liqueurs."

Ices were also eaten at the Elysée. Garchy, the fashionable ice-cream vendor, had set up a counter in one of the drawing rooms. There were served "divine ices yellow with apricots or rounded with succulent peaches" and accompanied by almond biscuits. Garchy rarely appeared himself. He had his own establishment, the famous Frascati, at the corner of the boulevard and the present Rue de Richelieu, then Rue de la Loi. A royalist, he had been wounded on October 5, 1795, fighting against the troops of "General Vendémiaire." The old Jacobins took their revenge one evening by invading his eight salons decorated "in the antique style" and seriously wounding several customers. The Etruscan chairs were hurled against the orange-wood paneling. Mme. Garchy, who had recently had a child, fainted. The establishment also included ballrooms, gaming rooms and, above all, a little garden twenty-six yards by thirteen in which Parisians could eat the famous ices under arbors of wisteria and Virginia creeper.

Frascati and the Elysée had a formidable rival: the Hôtel Richelieu dance hall. "In this enchanted place," wrote a habitué, "a hundred perfumed goddesses, crowned with roses, drift about in Athenian dresses and try in turn to catch the eyes of our *Incroyables* with their rumpled hair and Turkish slippers. There the women are nymphs, sultanas, savages. Their breasts are bare, their arms are bare. The men are, by contrast, too carelessly dressed. They sometimes remind me of those lackeys who, under the old regime, would dance in the drawing room once a year, at midnight on Shrove Tuesday, twenty minutes before putting their masters to bed." There were crowds there and, according to the same witness, no ball in Paris was to be compared with that of the Hôtel Richelieu. All others would have to yield to it, "like rose hips to roses."

The Hovyns, however, had no intention of giving way to their competition and organized traveling shows and other attractions in the Elysée park. A sheep was sent up in a balloon and then left it "thanks to a well-arranged mechanism," landing by parachute and bleating loudly, as one may imagine. Another evening the Hovyns had the idea of inviting a new diplomat of whom all Paris was talking. He was a Turk—a real Turk—accredited to the Republic by the Sublime Porte.

As Lenotre has said, "Since the Revolution was waging war against the whole of Europe, representatives of foreign powers were a marked rarity." And this was a Turk "with soft gazelle's eyes," wearing a goffered bonnet surmounted by a turban. When he gave audience he presented two lozenges to women accompanied by their husbands. Women who came alone received a dozen. To young ladies chaperoned by their mothers he offered drops of attar of roses, saying: "Come without your mother."

When it was known that he had accepted the Hovyns' invitation there was wild excitement. There was a great crush at the Elysée, although the price of tickets had been put up from three to five francs. All the belles of the Directory were there. The mistress of Barras, Mlle. Lange, whose beauty, it appears, was "virginal," was presented to him. "She is beautiful," His Excellency declared.

When he saw Mme. Tallien, half-naked, as fashion required, he stopped, dazzled by the opulent forms of the woman reputed to be the most beautiful in Paris. The diplomat was seen to pull himself together, assemble all his knowledge of the French language, gaze amorously at Mme. Tallien and come out with this compliment: "Public beauty!"

This was quite true. "This woman," said a contemporary, "flaunts the most insolent luxury in the midst of public poverty. . . . She sets the tone for the impurest elements in Paris of both sexes." She had just left Tallien, who, as she admitted frankly, had been merely "a lifebelt" for her, and had fallen into the arms of Barras, "King of Paris and of vice." This enabled her to be all-powerful in the government offices and to allow herself the luxury of giving a length of uniform cloth to a general who had only one suit, and that one quite threadbare. She had announced the happy outcome of her negotiations by crying to him across a drawing room full of guests: "Well, my friend, now you have your breeches!"

The general had bowed, but was never to forget. His name was Napoleon Bonaparte. Thanks to Barras he had been able to save the dying Convention by cannonading, on the steps of Saint-Roch, the royalists setting out to attack the regime. He had become the lover and then the husband of Mme. Tallien's best friend, Josephine de Beauharnais, who had also been Barras's mistress. The two women had similar tastes—even in dress, as can be seen from this letter sent by

Mme. Tallien the day before a party: "The feast would be very dull without you. I beg you to come with that peach-flower underskirt you like so much and which I do not dislike and whose fellow I propose to display myself."

In spite of the presence of Mme. Tallien and occasional appearances by Mme. Bonaparte, the Elysée's receipts began to fall off. The Turk could not be invited every evening, and so the Hovyns announced another balloon ascent. But this time a "member of the fair sex" would take to the air in the company of the famous aeronaut Jacques Garnerin, who made his exhibitions more exciting by leaving his balloon at 1,950 feet and landing by parachute. But, incredibly enough, the Directory was much more prudish than has been claimed, and the government forbade the exhibition on the pretext that to watch "two persons of different sex rising publicly into the air was indecent and immoral."

The Elysée Dance Hall finally disappeared and M. Hovyn died, perhaps of grief. Under the Consulate Liévine went into association with Velloni *fils,* and they announced the opening of the "hamlet of Chantilly, formerly the Elysée-Bourbon, having two entrances from the Champs-Elysées and from the Faubourg Saint-Honoré on the corner of the Rue Marigny." There were to be *"haltes anglaises,* consisting of every kind of cold meat, as well as fork lunches and other lunches served in the cottages of the hamlet." Liévine and Velloni also recommended their "new sparkling citron water," their "Dutch beer house where there would be served white beer of the finest quality, with various pastries, the whole very choice and most cleanly and respectably run. Nothing has been neglected to make this the most pleasant and elegant resort." The Parisians came in crowds but the establishment's vogue was very short, and Liévine, who by the terms of the partnership received only ten sous for a gentleman and six for a lady, decided to find another source of income. She would surround the Elysée with shops and divide up the palace into about thirty middle-class apartments.

One courtyard flat on the first floor, consisting of three low-ceilinged rooms, was let to a family from the Beauce, Mme. Boussand tells us. They had a little boy "with blue eyes, fair hair and a frail smile." He would come back from school crying: his schoolmates beat him because he looked like a girl. His name was Alfred de Vigny.

2
A Melodramatic Coup d'Etat

On the morning of November 10, 1799—19 Brumaire, Year VIII— a traveling carriage containing two men was crossing the Place de la Concorde and passed by the spot where, six years and ten months before, King Louis XVI's scaffold had been erected.

"My friend," said one of the occupants of the carriage, "tomorrow we shall either sleep in the Luxembourg or end here."

At that time the Luxembourg was the seat of the government; the man who had just spoken was called Bourrienne and was General Bonaparte's secretary. Together with his friend the aide-de-camp La Valette, he was going to Saint-Cloud, where the future emperor had planned that day to overthrow the Directory and take the place of the five "kings": Barras, Roger Ducos, Sieyès, Gohier and Moulin.

When in the previous month Paris had learned of Bonaparte's disembarkment at Fréjus, the town had seemed intoxicated. People embraced each other, jumped for joy, and applauded. "This return is drunk to even in the cabarets," a contemporary newspaper wrote. "It is sung in the streets." France was about to rediscover its soul and Paris its life. Until that evening of 21 Vendémiaire, when the news ran through the town, everything had seemed dead. Paris had the "spleen," as the expression then went. Even vice was beginning to leave it indifferent. The unheard-of corruption of Barras's government no longer caused scandal. Immorality was complete. Comte Fleury tells the story of the Parisian who first married the niece of a rich aunt and then divorced her in order to marry the aunt herself, who was eighty-two. When the old woman died he remarried the niece. There was also mentioned the case of the man, widowed of two sisters, who wanted to marry their mother. It all seemed quite natural. There was no belief in anything. The working-class population of the suburbs turned away from politics. Resignedly the people of Paris had let successive royalist or Jacobin conspiracies fight for a dying France. Nothing could be worse than the present regime.

The streets of Paris reflected both the poverty of the inhabitants and the luxury of the tradesmen, tax collectors and their mistresses who lived on the body of the dying Republic. A passer-by, going from the Odéon to the Louvre, met only eight cabs and one private carriage. At the barriers one met decrepit coaches drawn by old nags harnessed with rope. In contrast, outside Tivoli was a real tangle of phaetons, *wiskeys, dulcinés* and *bobgheis,* all shining with gold and precious stones.

When they saw Bonaparte again, even in his curious half-civilian, half-oriental costume of tubular hat, green overcoat and Turkish scimitar, everyone heaved a sigh of relief. All the rottenness would now be swept away. A coup d'état seemed inevitable. Could he take power legally, ask for a revision of the Constitution? The procedure under law would require nine years. And so, on the general's return, many superior officers, offering their sword to their future master, came regularly to "Citizen Bonaparte's" house in the Rue de la Victoire asking for an interview. On the evening of 17 Brumaire they all received an invitation for six o'clock on the following morning. This meeting before dawn surprised them, but they went boldly in the dead of night to the Rue de la Victoire. Seeing the streams of people, they understood: it was "for today."

General Debelle appeared in civilian clothes.

"What, aren't you in uniform?" said a surprised friend.

"I didn't know . . . but wait, it will not take long."

And, turning to a gunner, the orderly of one of the officers, he said: "Lend me your uniform, my man." And in the street the two men changed clothes.

In the darkness could be heard the thundering voice of General Lefebvre: "Let's throw all those b—— lawyers in the river!"

This had not been necessary; the lawyers had done just what was wanted. The Elders—most of whom, having been previously won over, only asked to be convinced—were made to believe that an anarchist plot had been discovered. One of the deputies devoted to Bonaparte—a certain Cornet, who was to serve all the regimes—had read at the tribune one of those speeches of which politicians in those days had the secret. It quite seriously spoke of the "skeleton of the Republic" fallen into "the hands of the vultures which fought over its fleshless limbs."

The "hands of the vultures" apparently symbolized the Parisians of the suburbs, who had become very passive but whose reactions were still feared. Formerly they never hesitated to invade the debating chamber on the slightest pretext in order to impose their will. So the Elders hastened to vote that the legislative body should be transferred on the following day to Saint-Cloud, far from the "hands of the vultures," and that General Bonaparte should be nominated commander of the Paris garrison.

On his way to take the oath of fidelity before the Elders, the general, at the head of a dazzling procession, went along the boulevards in the direction of the Tuileries. The crowd acclaimed him. The banker Ouvrard, who lived on the corner of the Rue Chaussée d'Antin, saw the sight, heard the cries, decided, like Morny much later, that when a clean sweep is being made it is better to be at the right end of the broom handle, and hastened to let Bonaparte know that his coffers were open to him.

Two of the five kings, Sieyès and Roger Ducos, were of the plot, but the other three still knew nothing. Gohier and Moulin, disturbed by the sound of marching in the town, sought out Barras, who refused to receive them: he was shaving and was about to have a bath. He had no suspicions of anything. When he got out of his bath Bonaparte offered him, through Talleyrand, a nice little sum of money—Ouvrard's money—that decided him to leave immediately for his estate at Grosbois. The arbiter of the situation, he thus shamelessly abandoned his two colleagues and "escaped ignominiously from history."

There therefore remained only two kings out of five; the Directory was practically extinguished. Yet the great unknown element was the second chamber: the Five Hundred, among whom were still many Jacobins, relics of the terrible Convention. How would these react?

On this cold, misty November day Saint-Cloud presented an unexpected sight. The refreshment houses were crammed with deputies and with Parisians who had come along as though it were a theatre. "The dinners of some of the members of parliament stuck in their throats. If Bonaparte succeeded, what would become of them? One of them, however, cheered by some Suresnes wine, was soon strutting around. "You see, my head is still on my shoulders." "It's not your best feature," a colleague retorted.

Troops who were bivouacked in the avenue leading to the château considered the situation from their own point of view.

"It's time to chuck all these orators out; with all their chatter they've left us for six months without pay or shoes. We don't need so many governors."

Unfortunately for the conspirators the Five Hundred's battalion of guards was also on duty at Saint-Cloud and saw no reason to overthrow its masters.

"Keep calm and count on us," the grenadiers shouted to the deputies as they went to the château.

The sightseers interrupted their lunch to watch Bonaparte's carriage go by, followed by that of Bourrienne. When they arrived in the courtyard the carriages drew up and the general got out briskly.

The two chambers—the Grand Salon for the Elders and the Orangerie for the Five Hundred—were not in readiness. Deputies of both assemblies mixed together began an awkward meeting in the open air. They gossiped and asked questions, looking anxiously at the profusion of uniforms. The Five Hundred spoke loud and firm: "Ah! he wants to be a Caesar, a Cromwell! We must see about that!"

The Elders weakened. Those who were in the plot did not dare to speak so openly. A wind of opposition began to rise. At one o'clock the Orangerie was ready. The Five Hundred had put on their togas and ample red cloaks designed by David. They took their places and immediately there was a storm, with shouts of: "No dictatorship! We are free here! Bayonets do not frighten us!"

The president—Lucien Bonaparte, the general's brother—tried in vain to restore some semblance of calm. Very fortunately these gentlemen, who took themselves for Romans, had a predilection for effective scenes. One of them proposed taking the oath to the Constitution. Perhaps new blood would thereby be infused into the dying Directory. Lucien agreed. In order to gain time he was ready to swear fidelity to the regime he would shortly overthrow. Each deputy therefore mounted the tribune, stretched out his arm with a fine sweep of his toga, pronounced the oath and returned to his place.

All the rites were scrupulously respected. The conspirators thus had two good hours before them.

On the first floor, in the Grand Cabinet, Bonaparte paced nervously up and down while Sieyès shivered over a small wood fire. Every ten minutes La Valette brought the latest news. It was not very encouraging. The general felt the danger; if he did not intervene personally all would be lost. He decided to begin with the Elders. It was they, he hoped, who would carry the Five Hundred with them.

Followed by his general staff, he entered the Grand Salon. Finding the eyes of all the legislators turned on him, Bonaparte lost his assurance. His speech was a lamentable one. He repeated himself and stammered: "If I am a traitor, be you all Brutuses. . . . I declare that when this is over I shall be nothing more in the Republic than the arm upholding what you will have established."

The Elders were quite willing to be Brutuses, but demanded names. How could Bonaparte give them, since the supposed terrorist plot did not exist? He became flustered, realized he was ridiculous and got violent. He uttered threats, turning to the grenadiers on guard: "And you, brave grenadiers, whom I see around this place, if any orator, in the pay of foreigners, dares pronounce against your general the word 'outlaw,' may the thunder of war crush him instantly."

By invoking military power the apprentice dictator finally succeeded in making the Assembly hostile. Murmurs were heard. Not knowing what to say, Bonaparte remembered a phrase that had been very effective with the Arabs of the Divan at Cairo and hurled it at the astonished deputies: "Remember that I march accompanied by the God of Fortune and the God of War."

The Assembly muttered. "General," whispered Bourrienne, dragging Bonaparte to the door, "you must leave. You don't know what you are saying."

With the Five Hundred it was much worse. And yet engravings have popularized and magnified the scene. There one can see Bonaparte, watched by two grenadiers, opening his arms in a noble gesture to the deputies surrounding him. One of the Five Hundred lifts a dagger and a soldier interposes himself. Lucien defends himself nobly. The reality did not have this legendary grandeur. In fact, as Vandal has written, "it was a hand-to-hand fight." The moment Bonaparte entered the fray broke out with unheard-of violence. Deputies, spectators and soldiers fought like ragamuffins; one of the deputies caught his foot in his toga and went sprawling. Bonaparte was half fainting and did not know what was going on. He recovered consciousness only outside the hall from which he had been dragged by an officer who had taken him unceremoniously by the shoulders.

He went back to the Grand Cabinet. He was still so disturbed that he declared to the ex-abbé Sieyès: "General, they want to make me an outlaw!" The terrible measure of exclusion was, indeed, voted a few minutes later. When the news was brought to Bonaparte, he unsheathed his sword, brandished it, opened the window and yelled: "To arms!" A second later the hero of Italy appeared in the courtyard, crying: "My horse!"

On seeing the arrival of the kicking, snorting, rearing animal Bonaparte started. He did not possess a saddle horse and in his stable in the Rue de la Victoire there was only a cabriolet. One could not take France in a cabriolet, and so Admiral Bruix had promised to lend him a mount for the day of the coup d'état. Two men had difficulty in holding the beast. Not without trouble Bonaparte mounted and tried to sit his horse nobly. In his feverish anxiety he scratched the pimples covering his cheeks. He was bleeding, which enabled him to assert that the Five Hundred had tried to assassinate him. The soldiers seemed ready to "cross the Rubicon," but the grenadiers of the legislative body hesitated. It was past five, daylight was fading, the November fog filled the park and he had to make an end before night. Lucien had just sent his brother an anguished appeal: "In less than ten minutes I shall have to interrupt the session or I cannot answer for anything." Bonaparte finally gave precise orders. A few moments later the president of the Five Hundred arrived on the parade ground surrounded by soldiers who had removed him from his chair. "The appearance of legality" had thus come to join the actors in the coup d'état.

Lucien mounted a horse, addressed himself particularly to the grenadiers, entrusted them with the task of expelling the "representatives with stilettos" who were besieging the tribune and swore that he would kill his own brother if the latter attacked liberty. The guard acclaimed the orator. Bonaparte could then give the order to march.

The drums beat the charge. It was the knell of the regime. The soldiers invaded the Orangerie with fixed bayonets. There was immediately a general stampede. The robed Five Hundred in their ridiculous Roman disguise jumped through the windows and disappeared in the park. A few recalcitrants hung on to their chairs; the soldiers picked them up bodily and put them outside. Those who resisted too strongly felt the steel of the bayonets stroking their spines.

Outside there was a rout, a wild flight into the night. In order to run faster, the deputies abandoned their robes in ditches and on lawns, purple stains trailing in the fog.

Ten years earlier Mirabeau had cried to young Dreux-Brézé, who paled under his plumes: "We will leave here only if forced by bayonets!"

His prediction was now fulfilled. The Revolution was dead.

The next day—*décadi,* day of rest—Paris woke up under the Consulate. They had seen so much during the last ten years that at first the Parisians gave few outward signs of their joy. "One would think one had returned to the first days of liberty," wrote an eyewitness, "but the experience of the last ten years can be felt, and suspicion mingles with contentment." In the evening this suspicion gradually disappeared when the municipal processions, preceded by drums and trumpets, came to the crossroads to announce the creation of consuls and the disappearance of the directors. There were shouts of "Down with the Jacobins! Long live Bonaparte! Long live peace!"

Bonaparte, it was affirmed, was peace. There was not a pamphlet, not a poster, not an article, not a manifesto that on the day following Brumaire did not affirm the universal desire of the population: peace.

And yet, alas, they would have to wait fifteen years before they found peace again.

3

The Return

In the spring of 1800 a man, a little over thirty, went down the Champs-Elysées with beating heart. He possessed a passport in the name of "Lassagne, native of Neuchâtel in Switzerland," but his real name was Vicomte François-René de Chateaubriand. He had left

France eight years before and was now re-entering Paris on tiptoe with false papers. He had disembarked at Calais, a few days earlier, from the Dover packet boat and had been struck by the miserable air of the inhabitants. On the road his stupefaction grew. From Calais to Paris he saw hardly any men, "but blackened and sunburned women, their feet bare, their heads uncovered or tied up in a handkerchief. As they plowed the fields one might have taken them for slaves. . . . Everywhere there were mud and dust, dung or rubbish." After a brief stay with Mme. de Lindsay at Ternes, "Citizen Lassagne" walked along the Champs-Elysées. Suddenly he stopped, amazed; he could hear the sounds of violin, clarinet and tambourine. The garden was full of *bastringues* (public dance halls) where the Parisians were dancing. The "dance mania" of the Directory was not over and on some days Paris resembled a vast palais de danse. Chateaubriand went on. The Place Louis XV was bare. "It had the ruined, melancholy air of an old amphitheatre." The exile could not tear his eyes from "the spot in the sky" where the guillotine had risen. "I seemed to see my brother and sister-in-law, in their shifts, bound by the side of the bloodstained machine."

Still under his false name, Chateaubriand had rented an entresol apartment in the Rue de Lille, not far from the Rue des Saints-Pères. He worked part of the night, while two turtledoves he had bought cooed above his table. They cooed so much that they prevented the writer from sleeping. When evening came he shut them up in his little traveling trunk, but they sounded even louder. Chateaubriand then decided to go out "to make excursions in various directions." He was not the only one thus wandering round Paris. On every side, wrote the Prince de Léon, another who had returned, one heard nothing but: "Do you remember? It was there . . . it was here."

For the "ordered world" was beginning to be reborn. The "re-entrants" looked at each other timidly, "like people who have escaped a shipwreck and meet each other on a desert island." They recounted how they had lived. It had not always been easy for the transplanted Parisians. No doubt, at the beginning, the beautiful émigrées had danced "breathlessly while their châteaux burned." But tragedy in Watteau dress had lasted only a short time and they had to adapt themselves. The Marquise de Vuillaume had kept a café, Mme. de Virieu a dressmaking establishment, the Duchesse de Guiche had become a nurse, the Marquise de Jumilhac a sewing maid, Mme. de Lamartinière a garment mender and Mme. de Rocheplate a costermonger. "In Soho," wrote Pierre Bessand-Massenet, "was opened a restaurant where one could eat 'real French cooking' at fabulously low prices; one was received by a La Rochefoucauld, who, at busy moments, did not hesitate to bring the client's dishes himself, a napkin under his arm." Mme. de Flahaut and her friends made hats. "We worked around a large table," wrote Vicomte Walsch. "The girls were recruited among our sisters, our cousins and the young people we loved; for in exile one loves perhaps better than in one's homeland those beloved beings who play the part of consoling angels." And at the end of each week the vicomte went off to try to sell the goods; if he came back unsuccessful, one of the "consoling angels" would sigh: "It's going badly; we shan't be able to dance tomorrow."

The Marquise de La Tour du Pin became a farmer in America somewhere between the Great Lakes and the Green Mountains, and the marquise's butter was soon famous all around. "I made it up carefully into little pats, stamping them with our monogram, and placed them attractively in a very clean basket on a fine napkin. My cream was always fresh. This brought me quite a good sum of money every day."

Chance, or Providence, sometimes threw these Parisiennes from their boudoirs right into the Vendée war. Such was the delicate Mme. de Lescure who, as she herself admitted, had no passion for heroism. When, on August 10, she found herself surrounded in Paris by the unrestrained mob that was rushing to plunder the Tuileries, she had lost her head and begun to cry with them: "Break everything! Long live the *sans-culottes!*"

But this woman, even while she laughed at her own cowardice, had known how to rally her Chouans to the fight. During the whole of the terrible retreat of the "royal army" she never left her husband, who was mortally wounded and carried on a litter. She had remained for days on horseback, hunted by the republicans, had spent her nights crouching in a furrow and in a ruined cottage had given birth to twin daughters, while her own mother lay in a swoon beside her.

All those who returned spoke of their fears, their terror even, as they approached the first French post. In what way would the republicans greet these *ci-devant?* Mme. de Boigne, who was to return to France a little later, would relate how with beating heart she had entered the customs office. She had remained standing in front of the clerk, who slowly took down her particulars. The chief officer approached. "Write, 'as beautiful as an angel,' " he ordered. "That will be shorter and will not tire madame so much." This officer must have been a Parisian, and suddenly Mme. de Boigne felt at home again.

Once they had returned to Paris, a contemporary tells us, the émigrés were "conquered by the spirit of sociability and equality." They risked going into society and went to see the reigning queen, the ravishing Mme. Récamier, who had dethroned Mme. Tallien. Her first remark was always: "Would you like to see my bedroom?" She was, indeed, not a little proud of her modern furniture. "All the furniture is elegant," a woman visitor related. "The bed is white and gold, with fringes; the steps leading up to it are of precious wood; the room is hung with taffeta draperies, but what struck me most was a kind of white marble tripod standing at the foot of one of the steps on which was placed a golden lamp, with the figure of a genie holding an urn from which he poured oil into the lamp."

How many men would have liked to know that white-and-gold bed! But she contented herself with gracefully rejecting her suitors and blushing to be so beautiful.

As M. de Chateaubriand's turtledoves continued to coo, the writer abandoned his *Génie du Christianisme* and went off to wander about Paris, where one rubbed shoulders with "the assassins of one's kin." Yet the *septembriseurs* had changed their district and, Chateaubriand relates, "had become hawkers of cooked pears at street corners, but they were often obliged to take to their heels, because the people, who recognized them, overturned their stalls and wanted to brain them." For all that, Phrygian bonnets, egalitarian triangles and fasces were still painted on the walls and restaurants, and a placard at the entrance of one establishment continued to announce: "Here we take pride in the title of citizen." So the reactionaries were in the habit of shouting loudly: "Citizeness Angot, open some oysters for me!"

From three o'clock to seven the restaurants were full, mealtimes varying according to class and profession. Between ten and eleven in the morning it was fashionable to have "a fork luncheon." At midday a Parisian of 1800 would have felt himself dishonored if he had swallowed anything. He had had a large breakfast in the morning, but did not sit down to table again until six o'clock; only the common people ate at three o'clock or at five. In the following year the famous Véry's restaurant was opened at the Tuileries, its décor being inspired by the excavations at Herculaneum. The menu gave a choice of nine kinds of soup, seven kinds of pâté, twenty-five sorts of hors d'oeuvres, boiled beef seasoned with twenty different sauces, thirty-one entrées of fowl and twenty-eight of veal or lamb. Finally fifteen roasts, twenty-eight fish and forty-four side dishes—vegetables or eggs—tempted the appetite. "I defy the most intrepid trencherman to have any appetite left when he has finished dining at this restaurant," declared a traveler. "But if there is a little room still in his stomach he can soon fill it by making his choice from thirty-one desserts."

At around two or three in the morning it was fashionable to take tea. This was a meal composed of meat, game, punch, in fact of everything—except tea. Those who were not hungry went to eat ices at Mazurier's, a lemonade seller at the entrance to the Champs-Elysées.

Chateaubriand, too, frequented the Champs-Elysées. He had chosen a little café, "because of the nightingales hung in cages around the room." This made a change from turtledoves. Or else he would go and sit in the Café du Caveau at the Palais-Royal, where a viola player sang ballads in honor of the First Consul to the customers drinking liqueurs or punch:

> Through his virtues and his charms
> He deserves to be our father.

The ballad singer sometimes made way for a savage who, crouching in a cardboard grotto, went through an astonishing performance, beating a big drum, uttering cannibalistic yells at the sight of so much fresh meat. This savage was in reality a Parisian, who had been Robespierre's coachman, or so it was affirmed. Wandering about the Palais Royal provided an endless spectacle. From early morning a young woman with protruding eyes would chant: "This is the beautiful Madeleine . . . the beautiful Madeleine who sells hot cakes. Feast yourselves; they are the people's joy." The "beautiful Madeleine" was to pass to posterity since she gave her name to the cakes, which have come down to our day and which, under the Consulate, were really "the people's joy."

One could also wander along the boulevards. The Boulevard du Temple, with its showmen, its tumblers, its prostitutes, was a colorful spectacle in itself. Panoramas, rope dancers' booths, little theatres were all black with people. Every class could be met there. "The scarcity of workmen," wrote the *Débats,* "has brought a hitherto unknown affluence to the lower classes which permits the artisan to satisfy his old leanings to debauchery and the kind of instinct that leads him to pleasures of which he formerly had no idea." And everywhere there was dancing. The same issue of the *Journal des Débats* tells us that in many of the taverns converted into dance halls "the discordant sound of a violin summons the artisan, the soldier, the grisette, the water carrier." Pleasure was within reach of all purses, excepting those of poets, and Chateaubriand, who had wandered one evening among the rope dancers of the Quai des Théatins, now the Quai Voltaire, had been forced to flee, for lack of money, pursued by the laughter of the spectators and the cries of the waiters: "Refreshments, messieurs, refreshments!"

What could one do in Paris, in 1800, if one had no money? We are told by the *Journal des Débats:* "Cross the Tuileries at seven in the evening, the crowds are there; the beauty of the weather, the richness of the most majestic garden in Europe are calculated to engage us in a stroll. . . . Go to the Champs-Elysées; the same crowd, the same elegance and more variety. The brilliant equipages going to the Bois, or returning, fill the eye agreeably and conduce to conversation, on account of the thousands of anecdotes about their owners. Night comes, you turn your head and you see the Elysées-Bourbon, whose illumination is halfway between the last rays of day and the pale light of the moon. You draw near: an orchestra is heard and catches your imagination for an instant. Do you wish to enter? It costs only fifteen sous or seventy-five centimes. Such a cheap pleasure cannot be a real pleasure, and you continue on your way. To your left, in the distance, other lights shine through the trees; it is the 'Italian Garden.' It is too far; you will go another day. Let us return, but what stops you? It is the crowd under every tree in the Champs-Elysées. What is it? Here a piano, there a harp, next to it a guitar, further on a whole concert. Do you stop at the square which was called after Louis XV and which has lost its name without having yet found another that pleases everyone? More lights, and a sign: CORAZZA, ICE CREAMS. You must go to bed; you are tired; take the boulevards. What a lot of people! Go on, go on, you will soon find more. . . . See what richness, what light, what freshness, how many pretty women all different, and young men all alike . . . luxury, nature, day, night, women, prostitutes, vice, decency, all are mingled." The article is entitled: "This Is Paris!"

A week before May 8, shortly after eight o'clock in the evening, in the shops of the Rue de l'Arbre-Sec or the Rue Saint-Honoré—they stayed open in summer until night—you might have met a fashionable young man, one of those young men "all alike," wearing a very short coat adorned with yellow buttons. His shirt came very high and as he pulled up the ends of his cravat he would ask in affected tones: "Your shop seems to me to do a good business, a great many people must come here. Tell me, what do they say about that humbug of a Bonaparte?"

Sometimes the shopkeepers would show the young man the door—how could anyone dare to speak so cavalierly of the hero of Italy? The young man went off, laughing; he seemed delighted, for it was Bonaparte himself. At two o'clock in the morning of May 4, having been to the performance at the Opéra, he had left to rejoin the army and cross the Saint-Bernard pass. Fifteen days later, when the news of Marengo reached Paris, everyone went mad. The population rushed into the streets; all the shops closed.

"At midday," a police report tells us, "at the first cannon shot most of the workers left their workshops, assembled in the streets and squares and listened eagerly to the news. They gathered in large groups round the notice boards that the Prefect of Police, on the orders of the government, had put up in the city and, in particular, in the suburbs. Cries of 'Long live the Republic! Long live Bonaparte!' were followed by broad remarks and gay sallies. In the suburbs one was struck by the frankness with which everyone spoke of the number of men we had lost or who had been taken prisoner. 'It is not like the old days,' someone said in the Rue Victor. 'Now at least we know everything.' The cabarets were full until eleven in the evening, and not a glass of wine but was drunk to the Republic, the First Consul and the armies."

When it became known, on the morning of July 3, that Bonaparte had come back during the night, there was a fresh explosion of enthusiasm. Increasingly large groups of workmen invaded the garden of the château. The Consul had to show himself on the balcony. He was greeted by a great acclamation. In the evening the shops in the center of the town displayed suitable symbols and illuminated decorations. There was only one false note, in the Passage Feydeau: a "silhouette painter" felt the need to display the portrait of Louis XVI. In the "Faubourg Antoine," the former crucible of revolution, the enthusiasm was indescribable. It was as bright as day, bonfires burned even on the roofs and, toward the east, the sky was such a vivid red that it seemed as though an immense fire had broken out among the cabinetmakers of the neighborhood.

All Paris went to the Carrousel on the occasion of the customary parade that took place every *quintidi*. This was two days after the return of the conqueror. At noon precisely, Bonaparte appeared in the porch of the château behind a mameluke with a bow in his hand. He received an enormous ovation. Wearing his simple gray suit, he mounted a white horse caparisoned in orange velvet. Behind him was a glittering crowd of plumed and gilded aides-de-camp. "None of his portraits is like him," wrote Charles Nodier, who saw him on this day of glory. "It is impossible to catch the character of his face, but his physiognomy is overwhelming. . . . His face is very long, his complexion like gray stone, his eyes very deep set, very large, fixed and sparkling like crystal."

According to the accepted custom since Ventôse, Bonaparte took up his place facing the château, on the spot where the little triumphal arch now stands. While the military band played its slow, solemn marches, the troops filed past, a symphony of blue coats, yellow leather, red epaulettes, white-gaitered legs, vermilion plumes, tall skin caps. Napoleon bent his eyes "sparkling like crystal" on these men with whom he would conquer Europe.

France's convalescence was nearly over. There remained only the drama of the royalist extremists, unrepentant Chouans who refused to let themselves be "pacified," and they were proceeded against with implacable severity. The inhabitants of the Faubourg Saint-Germain— tucked away in their houses in the Rues Grenelle, de l'Université or Saint-Dominique—would also continue to stand up against Bonaparte, but being naturally more peaceful than the Chouans they would be satisfied with irony and sulks. The Emperor was to have his revenge, however, when he saw drawn up in an antechamber the new chamberlains "engaged" on the occasion of his marriage to Marie-Louise. There was a Ségur, a Noailles, a Gontaut, a Chabot, a Béarn, a Turenne, a Contades. The palace marshal then asked Napoleon to be good enough to indicate those who were to begin their service.

"It's all the same to me."

"But, sire . . ."

"Very well," decided the former gentleman cadet, Napoleon Buonaparte, considering the batch as though it were a question of choosing spare horses, "very well, take the fair one and the one with curly hair!"

4
The Night of Nivôse

The affair of the infernal machine—which exploded at the beginning of Christmas night, 1800—began, so to speak, almost exactly one year before. On Thursday, December 26, 1799, passers-by crossing the Place Vendôme wrapped up against the terribly cold weather could have seen a man of twenty-five—bright-eyed, sharp-faced, with powdered hair—walking up and down. This man, whose name was Hyde de Neuville, was head of the royalist agency in Paris and, like many others in those troubled times, had chosen the profession of conspirator. At that moment he was conspiring against the First Consul, but as Georges Cadoudal was to say to him one day: "Hyde de Neuville, do you know what we ought to advise the King if he comes back to the throne? We ought to tell him that he would do well to have us both shot, for we shall never be anything but conspirators; we've formed the habit!"

Yet, on this day following the Christmas of 1799, Hyde was not thinking of suppressing Bonaparte. He was waiting for Talleyrand, who was to take him to the Consul so that he might ask if Bonaparte would agree to receive General d'Andigné, commander of the royalist troops of Anjou. Perhaps, if the two men managed to convince him, Bonaparte would accept the commander-in-chief's sword that "King" Louis XVIII wanted to give him.

In the carriage Hyde gave only half an ear to Talleyrand, ready to betray his master, who asked his companion to convey to the Comte d'Artois that he was "entirely devoted" to him. Hyde remembered only one of the minister's sentences: "If Bonaparte lasts a year, he will go far."

The little drawing room into which the conspirator was ushered was icy. The heating reflected the poverty of the new government: Bonaparte had found only sixty thousand francs in the coffers. Suddenly a small, thin man, his hair plastered over his temples, his walk hesitating, crossed the room, leaned against the chimney piece and raised his head. It was the First Consul.

"He looked at me with such an expression," Hyde related, "and with such penetration that I quite lost countenance." An appointment was made for the next day. Bonaparte agreed to receive the envoy of the "King of France." They talked first of peace in the west, which according to Bonaparte "could be made in five minutes." The two Chouans were not of this opinion.

"But what do you want in order to stop the civil war?" asked the Consul.

"Two things," Hyde replied. "Louis XVIII to reign legitimately over France and Bonaparte to cover her with his fame."

Their voices quickly rose.

"If you do not make peace I shall march against you with 100,000 men!"

"We shall try to prove that we are worthy to fight with you."

"I shall burn your towns."

"We shall live in cottages."

"I shall set fire to your cottages."

"We shall take to the woods."

The conversation was going badly, to say the least of it. Bonaparte tried charm.

"The Bourbons are out of luck, and you have done everything for them that you should. You are brave, take up the cause of glory, fight under my flag!"

The two royalists declined the offer; they preferred the white flag. The interview was a complete failure; d'Andigné could do nothing but return to the west, while Hyde and his Parisian friends quite naturally resumed their plan of murdering the First Consul. This is not surprising. Vandal wrote: "Having seen so many fall and die around them, they had come to hold their lives and those of others cheaply. Constantly in danger of being killed, they did not hesitate at the idea of suppressing their adversary by the most expeditious means." It seemed all the more necessary to strike him down since on February 19, 1800, Bonaparte was going to take up residence in the Tuileries. The procession to the palace was composed merely of the Consul's coach, a present from the Emperor of Austria, and some debilitated cabs—public vehicles whose numbers had been covered up with strips of paper. It showed the poverty of the regime; but by taking possession of the King's palace, by daring to install himself in Louis XVI's apartments, Bonaparte became even more markedly the Usurper, the man to overthrow—a man all the more dangerous in that the mass of the country was for him.

The conspirators considered all possible means: a pistol shot to be fired at Bonaparte's back during a review in the Carrousel, a barrel of powder to be placed in a cellar at the Tuileries. Hate was embedded deeply in the royalists' hearts. One could hear a woman from the best society wish, perfectly naturally, that "her eyes were stilettoes to stab the tyrant of kings when she saw him at the theatre." The Chouans soon decided on a plan to kill the Consul, inspired by the attacks on coaches at which these gentlemen excelled. When he went to Malmaison Bonaparte was escorted by only fifty mounted grenadiers. Now, Neuilly, Puteaux, Nanterre and Rueil were only small villages separated by wasteland that bore an evil reputation and was dotted with quarries in which a whole troop could hide before attacking the escort. Georges Cadoudal—*chouannerie* personified—came to Paris and formed the excellent idea of "walking along the road to Malmaison," but after this "essential step," as he called it, what was to be done? He found it necessary to leave for London in order to come to agreement with the English princes and government.

In his absence, others of the Parisian royalists continued to put forward scheme after scheme, and each one tended to work on his own, as, for example, the Chevalier de Limoëlan, a former officer in the King's navy. He was thirty-two years old, slim, distinguished, white-skinned, thin-faced and near-sighted and—when he was not disguised in order to escape Fouché's hirelings—had fair hair and chestnut eyebrows. He seemed to wish to settle down and there exists a letter from him addressed to the "citizen Minister of Police" in which he declared that he aspired only to the greatest tranquillity. Moreover, he desired to remain in Paris because he feared he would not have this tranquillity in Brittany. Now, he had a curious fashion of living "tranquilly." His landlord, a pastry cook in the Rue Neuve-Saint-Roch, observed with astonishment that almost every day de Limoëlan left his room with a different appearance. One day he would be wearing an "oaten" wig, on the next day his hair would be the deepest black, the day after his face would be framed in thick whiskers, real mutton-chops. When he went out with fair hair this meant that he was going to Versailles to see his fiancée, Anne-Marie. The rest of the time, in spite of his declarations to the "citizen minister," he was conspiring, in company with his friend Saint-Régent, like himself a former sailor. Limoëlan had also taken on his former messenger Carbon, a great specialist in attacking coaches since his master had no further need of servants.

All three sought means to be rid of the "tyrant." The means had been supplied by their implacable enemies, the extreme republicans, who at that time were called the "exclusives," their horrible past having "excluded" them from every position. They haunted the cabarets at the barriers, brooded over their rancor and plotted around wine-stained tables. Some of these "anarchists," whose leader was the Jacobin Chevalier, had formed a scheme to kill the First Consul by setting off in front of his carriage an infernal machine which imitated the one an Italian engineer had used in 1585 at the siege of Antwerp. The machine consisted of a barrel hooped with iron and filled with gunpowder, inflammable material and shot. It was fired by means of a gun, whose cannon had been sawed off, and the trigger was worked from a distance by a string. Unhappily for the exclusives, the police got wind of the affair and on November 7, 1800, all the conspirators were arrested. But Limoëlan and Saint-Régent decided to adopt the exclusives' scheme for the benfit of the royalist cause.

On orders from his former master, Carbon went on December 17 to a certain Lambel, a grain merchant of the Rue Meslée, introducing himself as a traveling merchant on his way to Laval to sell brown sugar and bring back cloth. He said he was looking for a carriage and horse and had heard that Lambel had an outfit to sell. Without haggling Carbon bought a poor cart with shafts and an old, tired black mare, which would certainly not have reached Laval. On December 20 Carbon came to fetch his purchases and, after getting the horse shod by the blacksmith Legros, left it, together with the cart, in a stable at 19 Rue Paradis, by the walls of Saint-Lazare, which belonged to one Thomas, a "coach hirer." On December 22 Carbon took a large barrel on a handcart to the cooper Baroux of the Rue de l'Echiquier and asked him to put on four iron hoops. When the work was done he took the cask to the Rue Paradis. Meanwhile Saint-Régent, who lived, among other addresses, in the Rue d'Aguesseau at the house of a Mme. Jourdan, was making experiments on the marble chimney piece in his room. The daughter of the house, young Marie-Antoinette, saw him place pieces of tinder, phosphorous matches, cane, a compass and a watch on it.

"I am going to set fire to the tinder," he explained. "It must burn in two seconds."

The operation seemed not to be perfected, for the tinder took twenty-five seconds to burn. The conspirators had, indeed, abandoned the firing method chosen by the Jacobins. The procedure seemed too rapid and there would certainly be no time to retire before the explosion. The old system of a fuse seemed preferable, although a certain difficulty was presented by the problem of regulating the time for burning to the speed of the horses and the distance to be covered.

Where would they work? It was announced in the newspapers that on the evening of December 24 the First Consul was to go to the Opéra, at that time on the site of the present Place Louvois, to hear Haydn's oratorio *The Creation*. The "incomparable" Garat would be singing, and on this occasion the choir of the Théâtre Feydeau would be joined to that of the national theatre. The best scheme would doubtless be to take advantage of this evening outing to place the machine at some point in the route.

On December 22 Saint-Régent went by cab to the Place du Carrousel just in front of the Hôtel de Longueville, which faced the Tuileries and in 1800 housed the Consul's stables. The square was at that time narrow, dark and cramped. The entry to the château was between two pavilions used by the bodyguard. On one of them could be read: "August 10, 1792. Royalty is abolished in France, it will never be re-established." As the coachman was later to recount, Saint-Régent looked at the long, gray façade and the dome crowning the central pavilion, drew out his watch and then, turning his back on the "palace of the government," seemed to reflect. He was then at the corner of the square and of the Rue Saint-Nicaise, at the spot where later would stand the statue of Gambetta—until its removal in 1954. This road, once running round the inside of Charles V's rampart, was parallel to the château; for a few dozen yards it crossed the Carrousel and formed one side of the square. On reflection Saint-Régent considered it an excellent spot. The cart with its barrel would be placed in the Rue Saint-Nicaise, toward the Rue Saint-Honoré and about twenty yards from the square. One of them would keep watch on that spot, in front of the Hôtel de Longueville at the end of the Carrousel, and would consequently see the carriage come out of the Tuileries and be able to give the signal to the man who was to fire the machine.

On December 24, around half past five in the evening, when many Parisians were preparing the *réveillon*—midnight mass had not been reintroduced, but the ceremonies were permitted in private churches —Carbon and Limoëlan arrived in the Rue de Paradis. They had put on carters' blue blouses. They harnessed the black mare, put straw and all the horse's litter under the barrel and then went to the Porte Saint-Denis. Two men were waiting for them there, two conspirators whose names the police were never to know. They took the cask and carried it a short way off to the house of Citizeness Vallon, ironer and sister of Carbon. Soon they returned with Saint-Régent, who was also wearing a blue blouse. The barrel was now filled with powder and was so heavy that the five men had difficulty in placing it on the cart. Leaving their two mysterious accomplices, Limoëlan, Saint-Régent and Carbon then proceeded to the Carrousel by the Rue Neuve-Egalité, now the Rue d'Aboukir, thus following the traces of Charles V's old walls. Limoëlan held the horse's bridle, while his two companions gathered as much grit and pebbles as they could find and put these projectiles under the cover of the cart. Carbon left them at the Place des Victoires and a few moments later Limoëlan and Saint-Régent arrived at the Carrousel.

It was seven o'clock. The night was misty and cold. The escort was ordered for eight and they therefore had an hour to wait. The two men walked up and down the ill-lit street. At half past seven they separated. Limoëlan took up his post before the Hôtel de Longueville, where the Rue Saint-Nicaise entered the Place du Carrousel. Saint-Régent had fixed the fuse which, according to his calculations, should burn for seven or eight seconds. A few moments before eight o'clock he lit his pipe, turned the cart so that it blocked half the road, then spied a girl of fourteen—little Pensol, daughter of a baker of the Rue du Bac—gave her twelve sous and asked her to hold the horse while he secured the cover of the cart.

Eight o'clock sounded in the neighboring church of Saint-Roch. The horsemen came out of the courtyard, preceding the Consul's carriage. Saint-Régent heard the hoofs striking the damp road and brought his pipe close to the tinder, waiting for the signal to be given by Limoëlan, but the latter did not move. If Lenotre is to be believed, Limoëlan was dreaming. "In the anxiety of what was about to happen," he writes, "his thoughts had taken an unexpected turn. They were in the peaceful house of Versailles, near the woman who was thinking of him, who had perhaps guessed his anguish, who was certainly praying for him." This "dream" is not to be found in the "Trial of Saint-Régent, Carbon and Others," that nevertheless provides us with all the details we want. Limoëlan does not seem the kind of man to start dreaming at such a time. Did Lenotre, to whom history owes so much, let his imagination wander here? One fact is certain: the machine exploded too late; the Consul's carriage had almost reached the Rue Saint-Honoré when the barrel burst, mowing down the rear of the escort, killing about ten people, wounding twenty-eight and damaging forty-six houses. Did Saint-Régent not see Limoëlan's signal? Did the tinder take too long to burn, as it had on Mme. Jourdan's chimney piece? Or did Limoëlan hesitate, on seeing the little girl Saint-Régent had stationed at the horse's head? No one knows.

The terrible explosion had splintered the windows of the First Consul's carriage. For all that Bonaparte ordered his coachman to take him to the Opéra. The public had heard the explosion, but thought it was a salvo announcing some victory. When, shortly after Bonaparte's arrival, the spectators learned of the outrage they turned toward the consular box and great applause rose toward the man who had saved

France from anarchy. The future Emperor bowed and then hastened back to the Tuileries.

The salon on the ground floor, leading onto the terrace, was already crowded with officials who had come on hearing the news. There was but one opinion among them: all the Chevalier's accomplices had not been arrested and the Jacobins had done the deed. The details which were beginning to go the rounds supported this hypothesis: a cask stuffed with shot, placed on a cart and exploding as the head of the government passed, was not this the plan conceived by the exclusives? Incidentally, the conspirators had not yet gone for trial, assuredly their accomplices wanted to save them by destroying the master of France. Bonaparte himself gave no thought to the Chouans either.

"This is the work of the Jacobins!" he cried as he entered the salon. "It is they who wished to assassinate me. Neither priests nor nobles are mixed up in it. I know what to believe and I am not to be imposed on. It is the *septembriseurs,* wretches covered with mud who are in open revolt, permanently conspiring against all governments. If they cannot be chained up they must be crushed; France must be purged of this disgusting scum! There must be no pity for such wretches!"

Bourrienne, who relates the scene, adds: "One must have seen Bonaparte's animated countenance, his gestures, always rare but expressive, and heard the sound of his voice to be able to form an idea of the anger with which he uttered these words." Fouché, the chief of police, accused the Chouans, one of the few to do so. Bonaparte looked at him with contempt: undoubtedly the regicide, the assassin of Lyons, wanted to save his former friends. Fouché fell silent. "The cleverest actor," wrote Bourrienne, "could not reproduce his calm attitude during Bonaparte's bursts of anger, his reticence, his patience in letting himself be accused."

"Fouché has reasons for being silent," the First Consul was to say to his secretary. "It is understandable that he should deal gently with a band of men steeped in blood and crimes. Was he not one of their leaders?"

Fouché let this pass—which did not prevent his taking the opportunity carefully to prepare a list of 130 names of *septembriseurs* belonging to "that class of men who, for ten years, have been guilty of every crime." (The future Duke of Otranto forgot the firing squads of Lyons.) He signed the list, adding without irony: "All these men have not been taken with a dagger in their hand, but all are universally known to be capable of sharpening and taking one." And eleven days after the outrage, Bonaparte passed a decree deporting about one hundred extremists to the Seychelles.

Meanwhile, at the same time as he got rid of his compromising friends, Fouché continued his inquiry. He had had some fragments of the black mare picked up in the Rue Saint-Nicaise and had summoned all the horse dealers in Paris. On 6 Nivôse, two days after Christmas, the grain merchant, Lambel, recognized the black horse he had sold Carbon. On the following day the coach hirer Thomas came to say that the equipage had been kept in his stable, and the blacksmith Legros said that he had shod the horse. All gave Carbon's description. It did not take long to identify him. The Chouans in Paris each had his index card. The eldest of the former servant's nieces underwent a long interrogation and ended by confessing that her uncle was hiding with the nuns of the Rue Notre-Dame-des-Champs. On 28 Nivôse—January 18—Carbon was arrested. He denied everything at first, then gave the authorities the names of Saint-Régent and Limoëlan. The head of the conspiracy could not be found, but Saint-Régent, who was wandering about Paris without daring to ask anyone for shelter, was finally arrested on January 25, 1801, by a policeman who met him by chance in the Rue du Four.

In the criminal court Carbon tried to save his own head by proving that he had left his accomplices in the Place des Victoires more than an hour before the outrage. For all that, he was condemned to death with Saint-Régent, who begged his judges to send him to the scaffold as soon as possible. They were executed on April 19 to the prolonged applause of the crowd.

Hidden in the abandoned cellars of the church of Saint Laurent, Limoëlan could hear from his retreat the ballad that was being sung in all the streets and squares of Paris:

> An infernal machine,
> Of quite a new design,
> Caused a dreadful scene
> As it sprang its mine.
> Everywhere around
> Men and houses hit the ground.

> The Consul in his car
> Was just then driving by
> To the Opéra. . . .

The Chevalier managed to escape to Brittany. There he received a letter from his fiancée breaking the engagement. She had made a vow to take the veil if the man she loved managed to save his life. She entered a convent, while Limoëlan settled in the United States. He never ceased thinking of her who, behind the bars of a Carmelite convent, continued to pray for him. "The angel who was the instrument of my conversion," he confessed, "showed me the road I must follow." He received the tonsure, was ordained priest under the name of Abbé de Clorivière, and became almoner to the Convent of the Visitation at Georgetown. Since September 28, 1826, he has reposed in the crypt of the chapel he had built and which still stands—that chapel, adorned by him with the portraits of Louis XVIII and Charles X, in which, every December 24, he would prostrate himself during the whole of Christmas Eve, asking God to pardon him.

5
The Step Toward the Throne

On the evening of February 12, 1804, a jailer going his rounds in the sinister tower of the Temple, which had become a political prison, heard a faint rattle from a cell. He opened the door; a body, hung by a cravat, was swinging from the window bars. The prisoner was still breathing. He was revived, not without difficulty, and advantage was taken of his comatose condition to question him. He had been arrested that same morning in the Rue Saint-Sauveur and was called Bouvard de Lozier. He was one of those fanatical royalists, more or less in the pay of England, one of those impenitent Chouans who had schemed to assassinate Bonaparte. He was implicated in the conspiracy of Cadoudal, the terrible Georges, who at that moment was hidden somewhere in Paris and keeping all the police of the capital overworked. The town seemed to be in a state of siege, the streets scoured by patrols, the walls covered with posters giving the description of Georges and his accomplices and announcing "that those who conceal brigands will be put on the same footing as the brigands themselves." Copies of a pamphlet printed in London and declaring that "killing is not assassination" were secretly passed from hand to hand. In short, as Fouché put it, "the air was full of daggers."

"I live in perpetual suspicion," Bonaparte confessed to his brother Joseph. "Every day new plots against my life spring up. The Bourbons make me their sole target!"

The prisoner Bouvard de Lozier, still gasping, however managed to speak at some length, "A man who has just quitted the gates of the tomb and is still overhung by the shadows of death demands vengeance against those who, by their perfidy, have hurled him into the abyss in which he now finds himself."

This preamble is a little surprising. As Lenotre has already remarked, it is not "the style of a hanged man." It is not impossible that Bouvard de Lozier may have been slightly strangled by the police, in order to loosen his tongue. The night before, Louis Picot, Cadoudal's valet, had been well and truly tortured at the Prefecture. However that may be, Bouvard announced that before taking action the conspirators were awaiting the arrival of a prince of the Bourbon family.

Immediately the Channel coast and the frontiers were put under observation. The Councilor of State Réal, who was then head of the police, asked Citizen Shée, the Prefect of the Bas-Rhin, if the Duc d'Enghien—according to him the leader of the émigrés who had taken refuge in the kingdom of Baden—was still at Ettenheim. "The information you gather," enjoined Réal, "must be prompt and sure. If the duke is no longer in that town you will inform me immediately."

The prefect instructed a gendarme, who went to Ettenheim and questioned an innkeeper, but the latter pronounced the name of the Marquis de Thumery, who was with the duke, in the German fashion: in his mouth *t* became *d,* the final syllable became *rey* and the gendarme understood him to say that General Dumouriez was at Ettenheim.

When the report reached the Tuileries on March 8 Bonaparte flew into a terrifying rage. So Dumouriez, that traitor to the Republic, that deserter who had gone over to the enemy, had joined the Duc d'Enghien! Like a caged bear the First Consul paced up and down his office.

"Am I a dog to be crushed in the street, while my murderers are sacred? My person is attacked. . . . I shall give back war for war. . . . I shall know how to punish the plots. The guilty man's head will give me justice."

On the next day, March 9, after a mad pursuit through the Ecoles district, Cadoudal was arrested with his friend Léridan at the corner of the Rue des Fossés-Monsieur-le-Prince. He was interrogated.

"What did you come to do in Paris?"

"I came to attack the First Consul."

"Did you have many people around you?"

"No, because I was not to attack the First Consul until there was a prince in Paris and he is not yet here."

"The plan, then, was conceived and was to be carried out in agreement with a former French prince?"

"Yes, citizen judge."

According to Léridan, the "prince" had already come to Paris on several occasions to give Cadoudal instructions. Greeted with great respect, he was a man of about thirty-five, with slender figure, fair hair and elegant dress. He was indeed a prince, but the Prince de Polignac.

Bonaparte's anger knew no bounds. "The Bourbons think they can shed my blood like that of the vilest animals. My blood is as good as theirs. I shall repay them the terror they wish to inspire in me. . . . I shall show them the kind of man they are dealing with!"

On March 10 the First Consul held a Council in the Tuileries, with his two puppet colleagues Cambacérès and Lebrun, Réal, Murat, the great judge Régnier, Fouché and Talleyrand. These two last would do everything they could—and it would not be difficult—to push Bonaparte into digging an impassable gulf between the France of yesterday and the imperial France of the morrow. In this way the future Emperor, who had not been involved in the Revolution, would become the accomplice of the Convention. It was well calculated and Bonaparte immediately gave them proof of this by saying to the regicide Cambacérès, who was of the opinion that before violating a frontier one might perhaps get some complementary information: "You are very sparing now of the blood of the Bourbons!"

That same day, at ten o'clock in the evening, Méneval found Bonaparte leaning over a vast mahogany table lit by torches, looking at a large map of the Rhine district which was spread out on the table. The First Consul was calculating distances and drawing up timetables. Suddenly he straightened up and dictated a note to Berthier: "Citizen minister, you will please give the order to General Ordener to go post haste in the night to Strasbourg. The aim of his mission is to advance on Ettenheim, surround the town and carry off the Duc d'Enghien, Dumouriez, an English colonel...."

For an hour, in the sleeping palace, Bonaparte dictated, carefully preparing all the details of the ambush.

It was at Malmaison that Bonaparte learned of the success of the operation. The arrest had taken place without incident. A note from Major Charlot, leader of the expedition, brought him proof that the gendarme sent to Ettenheim had confused Thumery and Dumouriez, but the major ended his letter by repeating a confidence made by the prisoner as they sped in a post chaise from Rhinau to Strasbourg.

"I consider Bonaparte to be a great man, but, being a prince of the House of Bourbon, I have vowed him an implacable hatred as also to the French on whom I shall make war at every opportunity."

Irritated by these words Bonaparte refused to dwell on the gendarme's mistake. He made no change in his orders. Forty-eight hours later, as the Duc d'Enghien, after a short halt at Strasbourg, was already approaching Paris, a second courier brought to Malmaison the papers seized at Ettenheim. Documents proved that the duke was at the head of a real antirepublican network having ramifications as far as Alsace. The copy of a letter showed that the prince had pondered on the eventuality of Bonaparte's death. "It is very important for me to remain near the frontiers," he wrote to his grandfather. "For, as things are at the moment, the death of a man can bring about a total change." Enghien was doubtless thinking of the death of the dictator on the battlefield, but Bonaparte saw in it only an allusion to the success of Cadoudal's schemes. The draft of a long letter, addressed by the prince to Sir Charles Stuart, impeached the last of the Condés. The Duc d'Enghien, he wrote, begged "that His Britannic Majesty would of his goodness consider him for employment in any way and in any rank against his implacable enemies ... by deigning to entrust him with the command of a few auxiliary troops among whom he could place some former officers faithful to his nation and the deserters who might join them. The number would be great at this moment, in all the troubles of the Republic. The Duc d'Enghien, during a stay of two years on the French frontiers, has been brought to a positive conviction of this."

So, as Mme. Melchior-Bonnet writes objectively in her biography of the Duc d'Enghien: "Faced with these overwhelming documents, what could be the weight, in Bonaparte's mind, of the fact that this scion of the Condés disapproved every attempt at assassination and had no intention but to make war? In the eyes of the heirs of the Revolution, the Duc d'Enghien, paid with English gold, was betraying the new France. With or without Dumouriez, his guilt seemed certain. He was waiting for the suitable time to cross the frontier and bore the appearance of an émigré seized—out of France, it is true—with weapons in his hand, a crime which revolutionary laws punished with death."

The decision was taken. And in spite of Josephine's supplications, Joseph's representations and, perhaps, Murat's disgust, Bonaparte followed Talleyrand's advice. Coldly, he carried out what he was later to call "a sacrifice necessary to his safety and to his greatness." After a meeting with both consuls he dictated the minutes: "Sitting of 29 Ventôse, Year XII. The government decrees that the former Duc d'Enghien, charged with having borne arms against the Republic, with having been and still being in the pay of England, with taking part in plots hatched by this latter power against the internal and external security of the Republic, shall be brought before a military commission composed of seven members nominated by the governor-general of Paris and to meet at Vincennes." On transmitting the order to the governor-general of Paris, the future King Murat, Bonaparte emphasized that "all must be finished in the night." Enghien, in fact, was expected to arrive during the evening.

The postilions had driven the berlin so rapidly that the prisoner and his escort of gendarmes arrived at one o'clock on that Tuesday, March 20, at the barrier of La Villette. The journey had taken less than sixty hours; meals had been served to the prisoner in the carriage itself and the prince had been able to stretch his legs only by a short walk in the bare countryside with his faithful Mohilof, the dog that had come with him from Ettenheim. After driving round the outside of Paris the equipage, still surrounded by its detachment of gendarmes, entered the capital by the Rue de Sèvres and stopped in the Rue du Bac, in the courtyard of the Ministry for Foreign Relations. The lieutenant of gendarmes, who had accompanied the prince from Strasbourg, asked for his orders. These took some time in coming and it was not until shortly before five that they set off again. The berlin left Paris. Enghien did not hide his surprise. Soon he perceived through the falling darkness the high towers and a medieval pile dominated by the mass of a square keep. The drawbridge was lowered. The prince was at Vincennes, which had served as prison to his ancestor, the Great Condé. Nothing was ready for the reception of the man who was already "the condemned." The governor, Major Harel, a former Jacobin, invited the prince to go up to his own apartment on the first floor of the Tour du Bois. A wood fire crackled in the chimney. The prince sat down, Mohilof at his feet. The major did not know his prisoner's identity; it was only a few minutes before that he had been informed of the arrival "of an individual whose name must not be known," but when Mme. Harel caught a glimpse of the Duc d'Enghien she burst into tears. She had recognized him, although she had not seen him for fifteen years. By an astonishing coincidence the young woman was the prince's foster-sister. The prisoner himself had noticed nothing.

An hour later the room was ready. Surrounded by gendarmes, the duke, with Mohilof at his heels, followed Harel, who crossed the courtyard, bearing a lantern, in the direction of the King's pavilion. A fine rain had begun to fall. The prince mounted the great stone staircase—that staircase which Louis XIV and Mlle. de La Vallière, as young lovers, had mounted so often. The room was vast: a bed, a table and two chairs were insufficient furnishings. Although panes were missing from the window and the room was dusty, it was not a cell. Enghien seemed less uneasy. While he shared with Mohilof a meager repast brought in by a neighboring innkeeper he made plans for the future. If they would allow him, he would like to shoot hares in the forest. He would give his word not to escape.

When he had finished eating, Enghien threw himself on the bed, exhausted by his long journey. He sank immediately into deep sleep and did not hear the muffled sound of the troops being drawn up in battle formation under his windows.

One by one, in the falling rain, the officers picked by Murat from a list drawn up by Bonaparte arrived at Vincennes and gathered in the salon of the Tour du Bois, which was already transformed into a courtroom. What was expected of them? They knew merely that they had come to try "an émigré prince captured bearing arms on our frontiers." Suddenly a man entered, dripping with rain. It was Murat's aide-de-camp. He brought the dossier, a dossier of five pages. The questions were all prepared. That was all they were given to help them decide on a man's life.

At that same hour Talleyrand was arriving to sup with the Princesse de Luynes. The news of the capture of the Duc d'Enghien was the general topic of conversation. Someone approached the minister, asking him what would be the prisoner's fate.

"He will be shot," Talleyrand replied calmly.

At Vincennes the grave was already prepared. That afternoon Harel had given orders for a hole to be dug in the angle of the Tour de la Reine "for burying garbage." It would only have to be slightly enlarged.

Toward midnight the grating of a lock made the prince wake suddenly. Officers and gendarmes crowded into the bedroom.

"Why so soon? Day has not yet broken."

"You are to be tried."

"For what?"

"For having tried to assassinate the First Consul."

Enghien tried to understand. He was heard to murmur: "Let me see, let me see. . . ." He rose and dressed.

"It seems to me that a few hours later would have suited both you and myself. I was sleeping so well."

They crossed the dripping courtyard. The prince noticed detachments of grenadiers, cuirassiers and gendarmes waiting with arms at the order.

In a little room next to the "courtroom" a captain questioned the prisoner. Enghien recounted his life, admitted having received a pension from England—had not his property been confiscated by the Republic?—and declared that he had never had any contact with Cadoudal and Dumouriez. He had taken part in no plot; he fought openly. As for Pichegru, who had been arrested on February 28 and was imprisoned in the Temple, the duke declared he did not know him.

"I congratulate myself on not having known him when I think of the vile methods he wished to use—if this is true."

The brief interrogation was over. He was handed a pen.

"Before signing the present report," wrote Enghien, "I earnestly request a private audience with the First Consul. My name, my rank, my habit of thought and the horror of my situation give me hope that he will not refuse my request."

The judges deliberated. Should there not be a suspension of the trial in order to transmit the prisoner's legitimate request to the First Consul? Councilor Réal should have been there that evening but he was sleeping, and Bonaparte's order telling him to go at once to Vincennes had been placed on his bedside table. When he opened it, in the middle of the night, all was already over. There is no doubt that Réal would have transmitted the prince's request to his master. One may well think that after this meeting between the soldier of Rivoli and the soldier of Berstheim no blood would have been shed. But in the Councilor's absence Savary was in command. The judges were there "to judge without intermission." Let them obey!

The door of the salon was opened. A few officers came up from the courtyard. Savary, standing behind the chair of the president, General Hulin, warmed himself at the fire. The prince entered the room, surrounded by gendarmes. One may imagine with what curiosity, with what interest, those officers—of whom six out of seven were soldiers of the Republic—looked at the Bourbon with long, chestnut hair, with clear eyes and aquiline nose, the last of the Condés, whom they were to try without documents, without even being able to let him have a lawyer. It was not a trial but an assassination.

"Have you taken up arms against France?"

"Look at me, I am a Bourbon; it is you who have taken up arms against me. I have defended the rights of my family. A Condé can return to France only bearing arms. My birth and my opinions make me a perpetual enemy of your government."

According to Savary's memoirs Hulin then made allusion to Cadoudal's plot.

"You will never make us believe that you were indifferent to events whose results would be so important to you."

"Monsieur, I understand you very well," Enghien is said to have replied after a silence. "My intention was not to remain indifferent.

I had asked England if I might serve in her armies and I was given the reply that I could not serve in them but that I should remain on the Rhine, where I would shortly have a role to play, and I was waiting. Monsieur, I have no more to say to you."

If these were really the words spoken by the prince, this half confession could appease the conscience of the judges and enable them to believe in a certain amount of complicity with Georges Cadoudal.

"Take away the accused and clear the room."

The deliberations were short. Hulin dictated to the clerk: "The council deliberating in secret, the president has counted the votes, beginning with the most junior officer. The president being the last to give his opinion, the unanimity of votes declares the accused guilty and in virtue of . . ." The general stopped. In virtue of what law were they to condemn this cousin of Louis XVI, who in fighting the regicide Republic had tried to avenge his dead and recapture what had been taken from him? Hulin hesitated, and then went on. The judgment could be completed later on. "And in virtue of article —— of the law of —— which states —— has consequently condemned him to death, and orders that the present judgment should be immediately carried out at the suit of the judge advocate."

According to certain historians, Bonaparte enjoined Murat that "the sentence, if, as I cannot doubt, it carries the death penalty, should be immediately carried out and the condemned man buried in a corner of the fortress." It is not impossible that this document, of which only copies exist, may be authentic, yet, in that case, would Hulin have dared to take up his pen once more to request the First Consul to grant the prisoner the audience he begged?

"What are you doing now?" Savary said, seeing the president begin his letter.

"I am writing to the First Consul."

The executioner cut short any argument. "Your affair is over. The rest is my business!"

Enghien was no longer sleepy. He chatted with the officer of gendarmes, Lieutenant Noirot, who had served under the old regime. A few forgotten names, names that were already of another age, sounded in the bare room: Chantilly, the Comte de Crussol, the colonel of the

Navarre Cavalry. Suddenly the key grated in the lock. It was Harel, who entered the room carrying a lantern and followed by a gendarme.

"Monsieur, please follow me."

Resignedly he rose, took his coat, whistled to Mohilof and followed the major, accompanied by Lieutenant Noirot and the gendarme. It was still raining and the lantern made the puddles in the courtyard glisten. The little group did not go to the right, but to the left, quitted the courtyard of the château by the carriage gate and crossed the parade ground between the keep and the Sainte-Chapelle. The troops were still there; in the darkness could be heard the clink of weapons and the sound of horses' hoofs pawing the ground impatiently. A little farther on Hulin turned right. The last of the Condés was now walking on the grass that Saint Louis had trodden with his bare feet when, on a fine morning in 1239, he took the road to Paris bearing the heavy stretcher covered with cloth of gold on which lay Christ's crown of thorns. That night, across the same courtyard, his distant descendant walked to his death.

They had arrived at the foot of the high Tour du Diable. Harel raised his lamp. A postern gate stood out from the shadows. The key squeaked in the rusty lock and they entered a vast circular room whose shadows were not dispersed by the yellow lantern light. The major went to the head of a staircase leading down into the gloom. Enghien stood still. His anguished voice echoed under the tall stone vault. "Where are you taking me? If I am to be buried alive in a dungeon I would rather die."

There was a silence. Each man could hear his heart beating.

"Monsieur," said Harel finally in stifled tones, "please follow me and summon all your courage."

Did the prince understand? The idea that the First Consul had decided on his death after the mere appearance of a trial was far from his thoughts.

The staircase seemed endless; finally the icy air struck their faces. The condemned man was standing on a flight of steps over the moat. A few slippery steps more and he touched the grass soaked by the rain which was now falling in torrents. The shadows of the four men and the dog were thrown by the lantern in the officer's hand onto the two high walls of the enceinte and the counterscarp which seemed to be crushing the miserable procession with their great mass. The path, winding through the bottom of the moat, twice passed the foot of the foundations to the governor's and superintendent's towers which swelled the rampart. The prisoner and his jailers went round the enormous corner tower which jutted out, the Tour de la Reine. Suddenly Enghien divined, rather than saw, massed in the darkness behind a curtain of rain, detachments of all the troops that had entered the château. Here and there the wavering lights of lanterns pierced the obscurity and glistened for a moment on the dripping weapons. In front, drawn up in two ranks, a squad of sixteen gendarmes waited with their arms at the ready. Enghien finally understood.

He saw a warrant officer come toward him. The man carried a lantern, halted two paces away, and not without difficulty unfolded a piece of paper. It was the sentence. His voice rose and echoed between the high walls. Between each sentence the rain pattering on the helmets could be heard. The text seemed to be framed by two dates.

"Replied that his name was Louis-Antoine-Henri de Bourbon, Duc d'Enghien, born at Chantilly on August 2, 1772.

. . . .

"Done, concluded and judged without intermission, at Vincennes, on the day, month and hour hereafter mentioned: 30 Ventôse, Year XII of the Republic, at two o'clock in the morning."

From August 2, 1772, to 30 Ventôse, Year XII. He was not yet thirty-two.

"Is there anyone who will render me a last service?"

Noirot stepped forward, then, having listened to the prince, who spoke in his ear, he turned toward the squad.

"Gendarmes, has one of you a pair of scissors?"

"I have."

The object passed from hand to hand. Enghien cut off a lock of his hair, took off the gold ring from his finger and slipped them into a letter he had written before going to bed to Princess Charlotte de Rohan.

"Will you see that this is given to the Princesse de Rohan-Rochefort?"

In a strong voice he asked for a priest. The answer was given from the drawbridge spanning the moat.

"No pious mummery!" It was Savary's voice.

Enghien, chasing away Mohilof, who was still sticking close to him, walked toward a stunted apple tree growing at the foot of the wall. He knelt down, meditated for a moment, then rose. He was heard to murmur: "I must die then, and by the hand of Frenchmen."

Savary's sharp voice once more cut through the shadows. "Adjutant, give the order to fire!"

The warrant officer took off his hat. It was the signal. The volley fired, rumbled and echoed for a long time. A thick smoke made the night even darker. The gendarmes came forward and turned the body over. Its face, hit by several balls, was unrecognizable. One of the men searched the dead man, took his watch and a few papers, and then the corpse was thrown into the garbage pit, face downward in the water filling the bottom of the hole. A stone fell onto the neck and the trench was hastily filled up with shovels of earth.

A few moments later there was nothing at the bottom of the moat except Mohilof running round the mound of mud and howling at death.

Ten days before he died, Napoleon reopened his will and added these lines:

"I had the Duc d'Enghien arrested and sentenced because it was necessary for the safety, interest and honor of the French people when, on his own admission, the Comte d'Artois was maintaining sixty assassins in Paris. In similar circumstances I should still do the same."

After this confession it would be childish to reproach Savary with his ferocious haste and Réal with his deep sleep. The night of Vincennes was indeed Bonaparte's work. It was he, and he alone, who, in full knowledge of what he was doing, made of the Duc d'Enghien "dust before his time."

An abyss of blood was now dug between the Bourbons and Napoleon. In the eyes of the regicides the First Consul had shed the same blood as themselves. He had become one of them. They could offer him a crown without fearing that he would be a General Monck. They did not delay. Less than eight days later they begged him to make "his work as immortal as his glory."

The body of the unhappy man rotting in the garbage pit served as a step toward the new throne.

6

The Pope in Paris

It was a Sunday, Sunday, May 20, 1804, or more exactly, *Décadi,* 30 Floréal, Year XII, day of the shepherd's crook, for the revolutionary calendar was still in force. Floréal was drawing to a close and Prairial would begin in a few hours, but the weather was cheerless and the roads of Paris were covered with thick mud.

Massed on the pavements—a novelty due to the Consulate—the cheerful Parisians were watching a strange spectacle. Preceded by a mounted band, an orchestra in a tiered wagon, and dragoons of the gendarmerie flanked by a cohort of plumed and gilded generals, followed by a corps of trumpets and kettledrums, fifteen to twenty civilians on horseback and wearing silk stockings and short breeches were trying, without much success, to appear good horsemen. These gentlemen—since the previous day one no longer said "citizen"— the mayors of Paris, the presidents and chancelors of the Legislative Body and the Senate, were on their way to the principal squares of the capital to read the decree proclaiming Napoleon Bonaparte Emperor of the French "for the glory and happiness of the Republic." When the reading was over, the masquerade—the expression comes from Fontanes, president of the Legislative Body—set off again to a brisk march that made their horses rear. The president's horse, as he later related, nearly "threw him twenty times into the mud."

The Parisians contemplated this carnival procession—again in Fontanes's words—with applause, of course, but without any wild enthusiasm. The majority were doubtless pleased to see that "the factions were abolished" and that "the revolutionary furies" were now no more than an unpleasant memory. The onlookers had shown a certain pleasure at the effacing of the inscription *"Dix aoust"* written, perhaps, in blood, which for nearly twelve years had been seen on the Tuileries walls, but for all that the people were a little taken aback by this sudden return to forms that it had imagined were definitely banished. That very morning the *Moniteur* had stated that one should give "to the French princes and princesses the title of 'Imperial Highness' " and that "the sisters of the Emperor would bear the same title."

As a matter of fact the second part of this notice was the last act of real comedy that had been played out at Saint-Cloud during the preceding two days. Napoleon had not hidden his satisfaction at hearing himself called "sire," even by his valet, whose ear had had the honor to be pinched. The time was past when he had said to Roederer that the Tuileries were "as melancholy as greatness." Now greatness delighted him for it would enable him, for the good of France, to speak to the sovereigns of Europe as an equal. Unfortunately something had dimmed his joy. On the evening of May 18, the day the Senate had come to proclaim him Emperor, a storm had burst. Before they went in to dinner Duroc, the governor of the palace, had informed the guests of the style in which the new dignitaries should henceforth be addressed. The two former Consuls, together with the sixteen marshals, would be called Monseigneur, ministers would be Excellency, the Emperor's brothers, Joseph and Louis Bonaparte (Napoleon was on bad terms with Jerome and Lucien) would become Imperial Highnesses, and their wives—Julie and Hortense—Princesses. So on several occasions during dinner the new Emperor openly referred to "Princess Louis" and "Princess Joseph." When these titles were announced two ladies paled visibly: Napoleon's sisters Mmes. Murat and Bacciocchi. They were, in fact, nothing, while the Emperor's sisters-in-law and "that Beauharnais woman" were everything. Elisa confined herself to treating the ladies present with haughtiness, but Caroline, who had less self-control according to a witness, "drank glass after glass of water to try to steady herself and appear to be occupied, but she was overcome by tears." Napoleon wanted to treat the matter jestingly and began to tease the two women. The haughtiness and glasses of water redoubled. The next day, after a family dinner, Caroline and Elisa burst out in complaints, tears and reproaches. Mme. Murat dared to exclaim: "Why must I and my sisters be condemned to obscurity and contempt while foreign women are loaded with honor and dignities?"

The "foreign women"—the Empress, her daughter Hortense and Julie Clary—said nothing, but the Emperor grew angry. "To listen to you anyone would think I had stolen your inheritance from the late King our father!"

The tone of the argument grew heated and Caroline went so far as to faint. Seeing this body stretched out on the carpet of his wife's drawing room, Napoleon gave way, and on the morning of May 20 the two new princesses could read the official announcement of their victory in the *Moniteur*.

In Rome Madame Letizia read this issue of the *Moniteur* and hoped to be promoted to the rank of Empress Dowager. Without waiting for that, her friends began to call her Majesty. Napoleon shrugged his shoulders. It was better to treat it as a joke. But after the women came the men. Admittedly, MM. Murat, Bacciocchi and Borghese were not allowed, at least for some time, into the imperial drawing room with their wives; yet it was Joseph who began to sulk. He was covered with gold, looked on himself as heir to the Empire . . . but was not. Napoleon, in fact, had reserved to himself the right to adopt a successor if he had no children. Joseph's reaction was absurd! Collateral heredity could be justified only if Charles Bonaparte—*"Monsieur Père"*—had been Emperor. It was from this absurdity, as Frédéric Masson has shown, that all the follies of Madame Letizia and her children were to derive.

Meanwhile other false notes were heard. "Bonaparte, you are ruining yourself," Rouget de Lisle dared to write to the Emperor. "And what is worse, you are ruining France with you!" "The first captain of the world, and he wants to be called Majesty!" Paul-Louis Courier wrote contemptuously. "He is a Bonaparte and makes himself a king!"

"He was only an ordinary man after all," sighed Beethoven. And with an angry stroke he crossed out the subtitle of his Third Symphony: *"Buonaparte"* and wrote: *"Sinfonia eroica composta per festeggiare il sovvenire di un grand uomo."* For Ludwig van Beethoven the genius of the Revolution was dead.

Some Parisians were not deceived either, but it was laughingly that they declared that the Republic was dying of "a caesarean operation."

> Great parents of the Republic state
> Who of your politics love to prate,
> I feel most deeply for your pain.
> Come, follow in the funeral train
> Of your poor daughter, lately dead
> When of an Emperor brought to bed.

In the new Caesar's opinion this "great cortege" would be the coronation, not only a solemn coronation but a religious consecration that would enable him to escape the ceremony of the raising on the shield in the Champ de Mars with which Napoleon was threatened by the old revolutionaries, who were in love with antiquity and remembered the great feasts of the Year II.

"Times have changed," the Emperor had explained frankly. "The people were then their own masters and everything had to be done before them. Let us be careful not to give them the idea that things are still the same!"

A ceremony at Notre Dame, for example, a religious coronation, would make Napoleon I the anointed of the Lord, an Emperor "by the grace of God." Although he did without it himself, he considered that a "society without religion was like a ship without a compass," and he stated: "Everything that tends to render sacred the one who governs is a great good." The coronation would thus relegate to second place the democratic right bestowed by the coming plebiscite. The divine right that would take its place would make the new Emperor the equal of the European sovereigns. The result could bring nothing but good to France—at least, so Napoleon thought—and, if the Pope agreed to come to Paris, the new dynasty would be definitely strengthened.

"We must judge the advantage we shall gain from this," said Napoleon, "by the displeasure it will cause our enemies."

But would the Pope be willing to leave Rome? Would religion, in the words of young Beyle, come to consecrate tyranny?

Six years before, General Bonaparte (as he wrote to the Directory) considered the Holy See as an "old machine" which "would go out of order" at the first opportunity. This opportunity had not been long in coming, and at four o'clock on the morning of February 20, 1798, the predecessor of the present Pope, Pius VI, stripped of his pontifical ring, had been hustled into a carriage. Surrounded by gendarmes, he had been dragged across Italy to die at Valence. Since this, to say the least, unfortunate event, France and the Holy See had, of course, signed the Concordat. Yet the Curia was not a little scandalized when, through Cardinal Fesch, the new Emperor's uncle, it learned of Napoleon's pretensions. So, "General Vendémiaire" was daring to summon Pius VII to Paris, as though he were a mere chaplain! Even Charlemagne had made the journey, and Clément VII would only crown Charles V at Boulogne. Some of the Roman cardinals considered that the gesture asked of the Holy Father would simultaneously sanction all the laws and acts of France for the past ten years against which the Vatican had had to protest. There was also the political question. By going to Paris would not Pius VII become the enemy of the European sovereigns, in particular those of the house of Bourbon? There was still the problem of the former French bishops who emigrated at the beginning of the Revolution and who, once the Usurper's invitation was known, had written to the Pope tracing a terrible picture of heretical France and reminding His Holiness of the words formerly addressed to Eugene III: "See, O Father of us all, to what point your religion has been surprised!"

Pius VII's "religion" had been "surprised" infinitely more than the unfortunate exiles imagined, since His Holiness maintained epistolary relations with Josephine and had received from her a magnificent rochet costing 711 francs 11 centimes. Now, the former mistress of Barras—and of so many others—having contracted only a civil marriage with General Bonaparte, could only be the Emperor's concubine. Pius VII was unaware of this. He was even unaware of the Empress's Christian name, continuing to call her Victoire in his letters: *Carrissimae in Christo Filiae nostrae Victoriae, Gallorum Imperatrici.*

Meanwhile negotiations were begun between the Vatican and the Tuileries. In Rome Fesch, that nonentity in purple, and in Paris Talleyrand, a former bishop, now married, conducted the talks in the Emperor's name. At the beginning Cardinal Borgia, instructed by the Secretary of State, Cardinal Consalvi, to see what could be obtained on the temporal side, spoke of the cession to the Holy See of Avignon, the Romagna, Bologna, the district of Ferrara, the duchies of Parma and Piacenza. He was given to understand that this was not the time for jokes, and soon everything was confined to the canonical side. In return for his coming to Paris Pius VII demanded the abolition of divorce and the forbidding of Sunday labor. From Paris he was given the vaguest possible assurances and it was affirmed that "for the rest" the Pope and the Emperor could settle matters in personal conversation. Besides, Talleyrand took it on himself to state the case in somewhat undiplomatic language. How could the Holy See take so much persuading? "Were not the temples reopened, the altars re-erected, worship re-established, the chapters endowed, the seminaries founded, twenty millions destined for paying the priests in charge, the possessions of the Church's estates assured?" Pius VII gave way.

When the papal "abdication" was known in Europe there was a considerable amount of critical comment. In Paris the plan was far from meeting with unanimous approbation. The philosophers were indignant, the Protestants considered the ceremony incompatible with the famous freedom of worship, the Republicans were exasperated and the Royalists showed their anger or despair by flooding the country with leaflets, pamphlets and caricatures. Joseph de Maistre described the action the Sovereign Pontiff was preparing as "apostasy," and spoke slightingly of Pius VII as a "worthless buffoon." History was to falsify this insult.

A cold rain was falling on Sunday, November 25, when the papal cortege, composed of sixty cardinals, prelates, abbés and employees of all kinds, on its way from Nemours entered the Forest of Fontainebleau by the long hill of Bourron.

Pius VII was tired. Bandits had robbed him near Piacenza and at Lyons Cardinal Borgia had died from the effects of a sudden illness. His Holiness had left Rome twenty-three days before, and though he considered that the pace was too rapid and incompatible with the dignity that should accompany the journeys of a successor to Saint Peter, the date of the ceremony had been postponed several times and for his part Napoleon considered this journey too slow. "The Pope would be much less tired if he shortened the length of his trip," he declared, and he pressed for speed in the last stages so that, after Lyons, the cortege seemed to be rushing on. In order to make his entry into Fontainebleau with all his entourage the Pope had had to postpone his arrival and at Nemours the abstinence supper prepared for the Friday had been eaten, as breakfast, on Sunday morning at half past nine. Fortunately it was cold; cod, sole and trout had "kept."

On this Sunday, November 25, in Advent—naturally His Holiness refused to admit that it was *quartidi*, 4 Frimaire, day of medlars—the Pope was reaching the end of a journey from which he expected so much "for religion in France." He knew, for everything had been carefully arranged, that it was in the middle of the forest that he would meet the Emperor. Napoleon had said: "As I am going to my palace at Fontainebleau, which is on the route, I shall thus be able to enjoy His Holiness's company a day earlier."

At the top of the hill, by Saint Hérem's cross, the cortege halted. The door of the papal coach was opened and Pius VII perceived not far away, mounted on a horse, a hunter in a green coat. It was the Emperor, who, in order to avoid the appearance of going to meet the Holy Father, was pretending to be in the middle of a wolf hunt. Napoleon, motionless on his mount, did not seem in the least anxious to "enjoy His Holiness's company" one minute earlier. Pius VII hesitated. Between them was muddy ground. He looked at his white slippers embroidered with gold, then made up his mind to walk through the mud to meet Napoleon. Once the Holy Father had taken the first step Napoleon hastened to dismount, to go to meet his guest and to embrace him. There was no question of genuflecting. Besides, the ground was not suitable. Almost at the same instant the imperial carriage advanced in such a way that both of the men had to take a step backward. This maneuver, which had been carefully foreseen, enabled Napoleon to enter the carriage quite naturally by the right-hand door, while the Pope entered on the left. At this point witnesses disagree. Did the Emperor carelessly take the place of honor, or did he enter the carriage first—by Italian politeness—in order to leave the right to his guest? No one knows. However, during the journey from Saint Hérem's cross to the château the carriage was preceded by mamelukes. The Pope must surely have been somewhat surprised by this pagan escort, a rather unexpected one for the head of the Church. His surprise grew when, on arrival at the palace, he was asked to visit the Empress "to pay his compliments." He accepted, but found it unsuitable to attend the musical entertainment to be given on the next day, 5 Frimaire, day of the pig, in the apartments of *carissimae Victoriae,* and retired, visibly worried. Would he be treated as a temporal sovereign until he reached Notre Dame? With this devil of a Corsican everything was possible!

The Emperor seemed even more worried. He admitted that for six days, because of family quarrels, he had not slept. Napoleon had decided that his "old woman," as he called Josephine, would receive the holy oils as well as himself. This was sentimental, not to say capricious, for since the fourteenth century only Marie de Médicis had been anointed.

"I never loved her blindly," Napoleon explained to Roederer (which, incidentally, was not true). "If I am making her an Empress, it is from justice. I am above all a just man. If I had been thrown into prison instead of mounting the throne, she would have shared in my misfortunes. It is just that she should have a part in my greatness."

This "greatness" was also keeping Joseph from his sleep. "The crowning of the Empress," he said, "is contrary to my interests; it tends to give the children of Louis and Hortense superior claims to mine; it prejudices the rights of my children in that it makes Louis's children the grandchildren of an Empress while mine will be the sons of a bourgeoise."

Napoleon had heard this and exploded with rage. "If he talks about his rights and interests to me, he wounds me in my most sensitive spot. It is as though he said to a passionate lover that he had f—— his mistress. My mistress is power! Josephine shall be crowned! She shall be crowned even if it costs me 200,000 men."

Let us hope—in order to please the historians who support the thesis of a pacifist Napoleon—that anger sometimes induced Napoleon to say things he did not mean. Faced with this threatened hecatomb, Joseph gave way and came to Fontainebleau to make his apology. Napoleon showed his satisfaction. "I am called on to change the face of the world. At least, I believe so. Remain therefore within a system of hereditary monarchy which promises you so many advantages."

But for all that the Emperor could not sleep. He admitted himself that he had "to wage a pitched battle" in order to force his sisters and sisters-in-law to carry the Empress's train in Notre Dame. These ladies became so worked up—they too suffered from insomnia—that it was agreed that they should not carry the mantle but "support" it. In exchange they were each offered a chamberlain to carry the train of their own dresses. This threatened to cause a certain amount of shoving in Josephine's wake. Fortunately Joseph, Louis, Cambacérès and Lebrun, entrusted with carrying Napoleon's mantle, were not so exigent.

These two mantles of purple velvet sown with golden bees, these sixty-five yards of cloth, were destined, incidentally, to have a checkered history. In 1814, when Louis XVIII returned, the canons to whom the mantles had been entrusted wanted to display royalist sentiments and asked permission of the Minister of the King's Household to cut up the "so-called imperial mantles" to make liturgical ornaments, that is, cushions for the stalls in which the chapter sat. The idea must have seemed a kind of revenge, and the coronation mantles of "M. and Mme. Buonaparte" were cut up. In fact on February 7, 1815, the parts really "spoiled by the N's and the bees" were sold for three hundred francs, according to the *Registre capitulaire inédit*.* The same register records the dismay of the canons, six weeks later, on the return of the Emperor, who sent for the mantles through Montesquiou. The venerable priests thought they would have to go and hide. Fortunately Napoleon had other cares. One hundred days later the Emperor returned to exile and until 1848, when the future Napoleon III finally intervened, the canons were at leisure to sit down on the mantles, one of which, borne by two kings and two consuls, had enveloped the shoulders of the master of Europe while the other had been "supported" by three queens.

On Wednesday, November 28, at two o'clock in the afternoon—7 Frimaire, day of the cauliflower—the "two halves of the world" drove in a coach toward Paris. It was misty and cold: 30° F. Night had fallen when the procession reached the Barrière d'Italie. At ten to seven the carriage stopped in front of the Pavillon de Flore, where the Pope was living. Napoleon had done things well and the Holy Father's bedroom was an exact reproduction of the one he occupied in Rome in the Monte-Cavallo palace.

One may well think that as he went to sleep that evening in the Tuileries, which had been the scene of so much violence during the past ten years, Pius VII must have felt his heart beat a little faster. From his windows he could see the lake where David—the same David who was now preparing his brushes to immortalize the coronation—had placed the statue of Atheism ten years before for the feast of the Supreme Being. Through the leafless trees of the garden Pius VII could distinguish the site of the guillotine on which so many priests had been executed. On his right he could see the spot where Robespierre—again according to David's plans—had, in the name of

* I must thank M. Joly, curator of the museum of Notre Dame, who allowed me to consult his valuable registers.

the Republic, proclaimed the existence of the Supreme Being, while the crowd sang an air condemning "the superstitions of religion."

The following morning Pius VII was wakened by a strange noise. He listened and recognized a rhythmical chanting: "We want the Holy Father! We want the Holy Father!" Hastily donning "a kind of white dressing jacket," the Pope opened his window and appeared on the balcony. An immense crowd was there, the crowd of June 20, of August 10, of the September days, of 20 Prairial . . . and this crowd immediately fell silent, then knelt. Here and there sobs were heard. With a wide gesture the Pope gave his blessing. This scene was repeated twenty times each day.

The prelates in his suite, who had shown some anxiety on entering that terrible Paris, began to recover their assurance. Those whom the writers of official reports continued, for the sake of brevity, to call the "individuals" of the papal suite, had been lodged all over the place. Some of them had even been put in "furnished rooms" in the Hôtel des Indes and the Hôtel de Genève. The splendors of the imperial kitchens and cellars entirely allayed their fears. The Pope drank only water, but for all that those in charge of serving him ordered five bottles of Chambertin for each of his meals. On 8 Frimaire alone, the eminences, monsignori and other employees swallowed 320 pounds of meat and two dozen chickens. Signor M., a chamberlain reported, was even seen to leave the table with a stuffed fowl under his arm. He ate it later standing at his bedside table.

Pius VII did not notice these details; he had other worries. He had been asked to leave Rome to crown and anoint an Emperor and an Empress and as December 2 drew nearer his role became progressively slenderer. Napoleon seemed to have forgotten that "everything that tended to render sacred the one who governed was a great good." For him the Pope was only a magnificent supernumerary. He would seem to have been made to come merely because he could wear a beautiful white tiara which would look well in the procession, as well as the mameluke Roustan's turban.

First of all the Emperor asked the Pope not to take part in the actual coronation itself. Napoleon thought himself strong enough to place the crown on his own head and that of the Empress. During this time His Holiness could mutter a little prayer at his leisure. This passive role was such a handicap to David that in his famous picture one can see the Pope blessing the two principal personages, one of whom, incidentally, has his back rudely turned. Before the departure it had been decided that the Roman Pontifical would be used, not the ceremony reserved for the king of the Romans crowned Emperor at Rome, but the service *Pro Rege coronando*. It would be enough to substitute *Imperator* for *Rex*. At Napoleon's instigation, a committee formed for the purpose submitted to the Pope, who was obliged to agree to it, a hash of rites from Rome, Rheims, Germany and elsewhere. The Emperor's first care had been to suppress or transform, in the text to be spoken by the Pope, certain verbs he considered displeasing, such as *eligimus* (whom we have elected) and, for the handing over of the sword, *concessum*, which became *oblatum* (which I offer you). As for the anointing, Napoleon did not see himself, like the kings of France, lying on his face before the officiant, having been anointed through the holes in his gown on the chest, the middle of the back and "the folds of the arms." He thought it quite enough to be anointed on the head and hands, which required neither a humble posture nor special clothes.

Pius VII assembled his strength to fight against the Emperor's claim to a *Te Deum* after the constitutional oath. This would be asking the Church to sanction the freedom of worship that Napoleon would mention in his text. The Emperor proposed that during this time His Holiness might withdraw from the ceremony and "do what he considers proper." This time Pius VII would not yield; during the oath he would leave the basilica. On the evening of the coronation the Emperor asked that he might be spared taking communion and, consequently, confessing. Pius VII sighed deeply. "No doubt a time will come when his conscience will advise it. Until then let us not burden his or ours."

The consecration would of itself have required a state of grace and, consequently, confession, but for Napoleon it was merely a ceremony comparable to the crowning or the constitutional oath. Josephine, however, felt she was going to receive what was almost a sacrament and that very evening, throwing herself at the feet of the horrified Pope, she informed him that she was not married to Napoleon. Pius VII nearly fainted. So they had dared bring him from Rome to bless a concubine, to give the triple anointing with the chrism reserved for bishops to a couple living in mortal sin! This time he refused to overlook matters; he would rather leave at once, or at least before the following morning, if the sacrilege were not repaired. Napoleon, in his turn, was forced to yield. He had been tricked by Josephine. It was not so much "the concubine's" religious feelings that had made her throw herself at the Pope's feet as the fear of being one day repudiated, as the family was recommending. In the evening of December 1 Fesch married his nephew and niece. Napoleon raged. What stupidity! Once more his wife had taken him in. Josephine was radiant. The blessing she had received would strengthen her marriage, or so she thought.

That evening a theatre in Paris was advertising a free performance of *Stupidity Has Its Uses*, a play in one act.

7

The Coronation, or the End of Hypocrisy

During the freezing night of December 1-2 no one in Paris slept. The streets, in which a real blizzard was blowing, were as animated as in daylight. Carriages cost sixty to seventy-two francs to hire. One could not get a modest cabriolet for less than thirty francs. From round about, members of deputations and communal delegates, who for economy's sake had lodged in the suburbs, were constantly arriving. At two o'clock in the morning the hairdressers began to work on their clients. The first to be served—the less important in the hierarchy —did not dare move from their chairs as they sat waiting for the moment to put on their court robes, which were more décolletés than one would have thought possible. "A decent woman," as the *Gazette de France* remarked that same morning, "could show her bosom, her arms and her shoulders, but the modesty of the day absolutely required a well-dressed woman to hide her neck, to the extent of muffling up her chin." The men who were to take part in this ballet parade—former soldiers of the Year II richly provided for, former revolutionaries, now sobered down, nobles obliged to marry for money—began to put on the disguises specially contrived for them by Isabey and David, which made them look as though they had escaped from a court ball of the Valois or had come from a fancy-dress evening with the theme of *Les Riches Heures du Duc de Berry*.

At six o'clock in the morning the doors of Notre Dame were opened and delegations and guests began to assemble in their appointed places. The cannons began to thunder. When the sun rose everything was enveloped in mist. A few snowflakes were whirling. Along the route to be taken by the double procession—those of the Pope and of the Emperor—the crowd was already massed behind three ranks of soldiers. For 15 sous one could get a place on the rung of a ladder. Windows cost 400 francs, balconies 600—150,000 present-day francs. All the houses were decorated, the poorest with white sheets dotted with pine branches. The city had undergone "an exceptional cleaning," as the newspapers remarked. The 11 Frimaire was the day of wax, which was doubly symbolic. The roads had been sanded from the Tuileries to Notre Dame, by the Rue Saint-Honoré, and from Notre Dame to the Tuileries, by the Rue Saint-Denis and the boulevards, which latter route would be traveled at night by the light of 500 torches.

It was eight o'clock when Thiard, who had come to take the oath as the new chamberlain, arrived at the Tuileries—even on the morning of his coronation Napoleon went on with his work. Thiard was stupefied by Napoleon's dress. He had already put on his white satin breeches embroidered with gold ears of corn, his white silk stockings and his Henri IV style ruff, but by way of a dressing gown he was wearing the coat of his uniform as colonel of the *chasseurs de la garde*. The Empress appeared, sparkling with diamonds and with 163 dozen emeralds. Napoleon then put on his purple velvet coat, his little red cloak in the Henri III style adorned with 10,000 francs worth of laurel leaves and bees embroidered in gold. When he had put on his black felt hat with white plumes and buckled on his sword, whose jasper hilt carried the Regent diamond, Napoleon turned to his wife and ordered: "Let someone look for Raguineau. He must come at once. I want to speak to him."

Raguineau was Josephine's notary. On the eve of his civil marriage Bonaparte had accompanied his "fiancée" to the lawyer and had tactfully remained in the clerks' office. "The door to Raguineau's office was ajar," Bourrienne related, "and Bonaparte distinctly heard him doing his best to dissuade Mme. de Beauharnais from the marriage she was about to contract. 'You are making a great mistake,' he said to her. 'You will repent it; you are being foolish. You are going to marry a man who has nothing but his cape and sword!' "

The notary, amazed at being called to the Tuileries on the morning of the coronation, entered the room. Napoleon was there, in full costume, resplendent. "Well, M. Raguineau, have I nothing but my cape and sword?"

At half past eight, when the Pope's procession was being drawn up, there was trouble in front of the Pavillon de Flore. The cross bearer, Monsignor Speroni, declared that he could not take a seat in a coach; the pontifical ceremonial required a mule. There were none in the imperial stables; he was offered a horse, or, it was suggested, he could go on foot. This was no good. The outriders were obliged to make a search, and finally discovered a donkey belonging to a fruiterer of the Rue de Doyenné, who agreed to hire out her animal for sixty-seven francs. The donkey was caparisoned in velvet, Speroni was assured it was a badly-grown mule, and the procession was able to set off, preceded by dragoons. But the appearance of the cross bearer, wearing a curious three-cornered hat and perched on the fruiterer's donkey, aroused hilarity. Jeers burst forth: "Here's the Pope's mule; it's the one you kiss!"

Speroni seemed delighted and waved his cross in all directions. The laughter had hardly died down when, following the heralds at arms, the Pope's carriage appeared, lined with white velvet, surmounted by the pontifical tiara and drawn by eight gray horses. Pius VII would have preferred to be carried, as in Rome, on the *sedia gestatoria* borne by twelve valets in his livery of red damask and surrounded by the oriental *flabelli* of ostrich and peacock feathers, but it was explained that this method of progress would unfortunately remind the Parisians of the procession of the Goddess of Reason who, eleven years before, had been perched on a flowered chair and carried by the *sans-culottes* from Notre Dame to the Tuileries. Followed by all the deputies, the woman who had "dethroned the former Holy Virgin" had taken exactly the same route as the Holy Father on that morning of December 2. Pius VII did not insist.

On arriving at the archbishopric, the Pope put on his wide, heavy cope of cloth of gold, entered the basilica by a long canvas corridor and took his seat on the throne placed for him in the choir. The waiting began.

All the guests were there, soon frozen, installed in rows facing not the altar but each other. At the bottom of the church, hiding the central door and obstructing the nave, was an enormous erection of papier mâché on which were written in gold letters the words "Honor, Fatherland" and "Napoleon, Emperor of the French." This was the imperial throne. At the top, on a dais reached by twenty-four rather steep steps, were perched the Emperor's chair and, a little below, the smaller one of the Empress. It was around the foot of this monument that the diplomatic corps and the ministers were installed, while halfway between the throne and the altar were the members of the Senate and Legislative Body, the magistrates and high officers of the crown. Near the altar, in the front row, were ten archbishops and forty bishops, who had had to robe themselves in the police headquarters. In the side aisles and transepts the delegations were massed, and the guests were in the galleries. The waiting continued.

With chattering teeth the congregation conversed or looked at the strange appearance of Notre Dame, whose pillars and walls were hidden, like the façade, under a cardboard casing that gave the basilica an air of being an antique temple or a Jesuit church. "So much work has been done," an eyewitness sighed, "that God Himself would lose His bearings." Another long hour went by.

At eleven o'clock a murmur came from the parvis. A military fanfare sounded. They were the trumpets and kettledrums of the carabineers preceding the cuirassiers, the cavalry, the mamelukes and the long train of carriages. The pale winter sun had dispersed the mist and gilded "a whole world on wheels": the Emperor's coach, drawn by eight dun-colored horses with white plumes. Groups of green-and-gold pages were clustered on the carriage crowned with olive and laurel branches, eagles, palms, coats of arms, crowns, allegorical figures and bees. All this glittered with gold. Inside could be seen Napoleon and Josephine, a symphony in red and gold; opposite them two people in "Spanish" dress, two silvered and feathered silhouettes: these were the Emperor's two brothers. The Parisians, who had been shouting "Begin!" for the past hour, were somewhat surprised at this masquerade. The Pope and the guests in Notre Dame had yet another hour to wait.

At the archbishopric the Emperor and Empress put on their "state robes," the two famous purple velvet mantles, partly hiding Napoleon's long "antique" robe of white satin embroidered in gold and Josephine's dress of silver brocade. The Empress was no longer very young. It is said that just before leaving the Tuileries Isabey helped her to make up and now she lingered to give the final touches. At last the procession made its way to the basilica by the long corridor. Napoleon's three sisters and two sisters-in-law "supported" Josephine's mantle, while Joseph, Louis and the two ex-consuls "carried" the Emperor's. Then came a crowd of people in blue velvet and white satin, a-flutter with plumes. These were the marshals appointed to carry the regalia. General Bonaparte's former companions had distributed among themselves the silver-gilt scepter, the hand of justice adorned with pearls and the orb of silver gilt. All this, like the crown of gold laurel leaves the Emperor had on his head, had been made by the jeweler Biennais in his shop at the sign of the "Violet Monkey." The bill came to seven thousand francs. Kellermann, Lefebvre and Pérignon were carrying the regalia of Charlemagne that Napoleon had insisted should be brought since they used to figure in the kings' coronations. Their authenticity was doubtful. The crown had disappeared during the Revolution and a new one had had to be made. The sword and scepter had, perhaps, been saved, but apparently dated from the reign of Charles V.

The moment the Emperor appeared in the nave all those present rose and cried, "Long live the Emperor!" The two orchestras struck up a warlike march. They were to play practically without interruption during the whole of the long ceremony and the musicians had had 12,137 pages of music copied for them. Sticking up among the orchestras could be seen those instruments intended to accompany the voices of the cantors and to which the name "serpents" was given on account of their curious shape.

It was noon. The ceremony began in the choir, where the prie-dieu for the Emperor and Empress were placed. The congregation could see hardly anything of the anointing and crowning. Napoleon had no intention of letting the former Jacobins see him on his knees before the Pope, or with his face and hands smeared with oil. First came the religious oath: the Emperor "swore before God and His angels to promote and preserve the law, justice and peace of the Church," though this did not prevent him, eight years later, from arresting the Pope and keeping him a prisoner until the fall of the regime. Then followed the prayers, the interminable litanies of the revised and expurgated text, and then the unctions. The mass began. The vestments were white, as the Pope was saying the mass of Our Lady in time of Advent. After the Alleluia came the traditional ceremony of the regalia and, finally, the crowning. Napoleon advanced to the altar, took off his laurel leaf crown from the Violet Monkey, took up Charlemagne's crown—that emblem "which he had won by his sword alone" —placed it on his head, took it off, put on his laurels again, and then prepared to crown the Empress. He could not conceal his joy, the Duchesse d'Abrantès reported, "as he watched the Empress advance toward him, and when she knelt down, when the tears she could no longer repress rolled down onto her clasped hands, at that moment Napoleon, or rather Bonaparte, was for her her true providence and there then arose between those two beings one of those fleeting moments, unique in one's life, which fill the emptiness of many years. . . . When he was on the point of finally crowning her who was his lucky star, as it was presumed, he was *coquettish* for her, if I can use such a word. He arranged that little crown surmounting the diamond diadem, put it on, took it off, replaced it yet again."

In reality—although the Duchesse d'Abrantès was unaware of this —Napoleon was looking for the catch in the diadem into which the crown fitted, that groove which can be seen in the drawing David made that morning. For David was present, and ceaselessly made his admirable sketches, fixed the persons, mentally arranged the "groups," with Madame Letizia dominating the composition—whereas Napoleon's mother was still sulking in Italy and did not come to the ceremony. (On returning to his studio David would resume his sketches and undress his figures. Nothing is more surprising than those drawings in which one sees the Holy Father naked in an armchair, wearing simply his tiara.)

The Emperor and Empress, with the Pope, now approached the great throne where the enthronement and the kiss given by His Holiness to the new sovereign were to take place. Was it at that moment that Napoleon turned round to Joseph and murmured: "Joseph, if our father could see us now"?

At the foot of the steep stairs the princes and princesses, the latter with delight, let fall the mantles. Josephine and Napoleon, pulled backward by the weight of sixty-five yards of cloth, wavered and nearly fell over.

"*Vivat Imperator in aeternum,*" intoned the Pope in a weak voice. The choirs burst forth and, after the *Te Deum*, the Pope continued mass. At the offertory the ballet of two hundred people began again. Napoleon and Josephine bravely descended the steep steps. The Pope was presented with the enamel basin; the water was poured from a ewer. Both basin and ewer had been used at Louis XVI's coronation; the lilies had simply been replaced by Victories, but the L's were still there.

Admittedly, the Emperor, having remounted his scaffolding, yawned excessively; admittedly, as they walked to the archbishopric, he drew Fesch's attention by poking him in the back with his scepter; admittedly the congregation was not very composed and ate rolls and cold meat sold by tradesmen who had managed to get into the basilica; but the ballet envisaged by the ceremonial had gone off without a hitch. Thanks to numerous rehearsals in the Tuileries with models, the former Jacobins and former warrant officers had played their part as well as the Talleyands, Ségurs or Rohans, who had been "taken on" by the new court. Moreover, unique event, of the 5,151,576 francs allowed for expenses they had managed to save 1,319,064 francs.

While the mass was ending Napoleon glanced several times at Josephine, who was such a pretty Empress and so young-looking that on their return to the Tuileries that evening he made her keep her crown on during their supper alone together.

Mass was over. The Pope returned to the archbishopric and was not present at the civil ceremony, which finished at about three o'clock. With one hand on the Gospels Napoleon cried in a loud voice, which could be heard from one end of the church to the other, that oath he would not be able to keep. "I swear to maintain the integrity of the territory of the Republic and to respect and cause to be respected the laws of the Concordat and freedom of worship; to respect and cause to be respected equality of rights, political and civil freedom and the irrevocability of the sales of national property, to levy no duty and establish no tax except by virtue of the law, to maintain the institution of the Legion of Honor, to govern with the interest, happiness and glory of the French people as my sole aim."

The herald at arms announced: "The most glorious and most august Napoleon, Emperor of the French, is consecrated and enthroned!"

The ceremony was over.

The evening before, when Napoleon had received the official—and faked—figures of the plebiscite, the president of Neufchâteau congratulated him on "having brought the vessel of the Republic into port." The Emperor had brought it in merely to put it in dry dock. There was no more talk of republic. The word persisted for three years on the coins, but after Tilsit it disappeared. On this coronation day the nation had once more become the people—"my people," the Emperor was to say—and the citizens "faithful subjects." The old order had come back. At least this was being honest. The coronation firmly marked the end of a piece of hypocrisy.

8

Countersign? Conspiracy!

It was half past three in the morning, and it was raining. One could see no farther than ten paces. The sentry sheltering in his box in front of the barracks in the Rue Popincourt, in the La Roquette district, listened to the rain pattering down and waited, as men on duty always do, to be relieved so that he could return to the guardroom and the straw-heaped bench. In any case, mounting guard, even in the pouring rain and in the cheerless Rue Popincourt, was a hundred times better than being bored, like many of his comrades, at Moscow, where the snow had already made its appearance. It was, indeed, 1812, the night of October 22-23, 1812. Napoleon, the Emperor of the West, was at home from Hamburg to Naples and from Brest to Moscow. But what was he doing among those savages? It was known in Paris, through letters from Russia, that without having fought a great battle the Emperor had already lost a quarter of his soldiers. On the previous evening of October 22, as Louis Madelin relates, Mme. d'Audenarde, the wife of the Emperor's equerry, had written to tell her husband how long "eight months of impatience and grief" seemed to her.

Eight months! The army had left only *five* months before. But the time seemed endless to everyone. The hours of anxiety and waiting went by terribly slowly. The couriers took more than a fortnight to bring any news, and without knowing exactly why people were expecting a misfortune. Yet Paris was still unaware that four days previously the Grand Army had left the Russian capital and begun a retreat that was soon to be transformed into an appalling disaster.

It was certainly better to be in the Rue Popincourt!

Suddenly, through the curtain of rain, the sentry perceived three shadows approaching.

"Halt!"

The shadows stood still.

"Who goes there?"

"Conspiracy!"

It was, in fact, the countersign for the night of October 22-23, all the more appropriate in that the three soaking men who had just halted in front of 51 Rue Popincourt had formed the scheme of overthrowing the French Empire that night by themselves. One was a corporal of the Paris guard; his name was Jean-Auguste Rateau and he had obtained leave for that night and for the occasion was wearing the uniform of an aide-de-camp. The second, André Boutreux, a bachelor of law who had come from Rennes to Paris "to make his fortune in poetry," thought that all roads led to the muses and was playing the part in this affair of a police commissioner. The third, the leader of the operation, was fifty-eight years old, had a round face, chestnut hair and a yellow complexion and was wearing the uniform of a divisional general. In reality he was only a brigadier general and had been put on the retired list. We should add that he had also just escaped from prison, where the imperial government had placed him. His name was Claude-François Malet.

Alain Decaux, his most recent biographer, has shown that General Malet was by no means a republican hero as we have been led to believe. He was an embittered man, all the more so as he was responsible for his own disgrace. Add to that his almost incredible bad luck, and one will understand the motives that led him on. He had succeeded in making himself odious and antipathetic to all the governments that had employed him. Under the Directory he sank to the lowest form of demagogy by flattering his soldiers; under the Consulate, having been made commander of the Charente department, he had endless disputes with the civil authorities and in between bombarded his chiefs with lists of denunciations in which he included the ministers in power; under the Empire, having been posted to the Vendée, he proclaimed his loyalty and at the same time went to the Isle of Oléron to visit the exclusives arrested after the Nivôse outrage, comforted them and opened his purse to them. After a brief suspension he was sent to Italy, where he became "surveyor of the pontifical states." In Rome he took money from the owners of gambling houses and confiscated a prize vessel for himself. In short, "a thief," as Napoleon said when he had the dishonest general retired.

Malet considered himself persecuted. He chafed until the day in 1807 when he met a band of republican conspirators who were looking for a general to put at their head. That day Malet had a revelation. He had at last found his vocation; henceforth he would conspire.

His first conspiracy, during one of the Emperor's absences, consisted in having twelve thousand posters put up in Paris announcing that the Senate had just voted Napoleon's overthrow. The idea was to profit by the astonishment, to seize power and establish a dictatorship. Denounced by one of his accomplices, Malet found himself one morning in a cell in the prison of La Force. This did not at all prevent the conspirator from continuing with his schemes. He could scheme now more easily as he had near him his fellow prisoners, who were all recruits ready for anything and having little to lose. This time the general fixed the fall of the "tyrant" for June 29, 1809. On that day—the Emperor being at Schoenbrunn—the government would be present in a body at the *Te Deum* to be sung in Notre Dame for the capture of Vienna. Malet conceived the idea, once he had escaped and while his accomplices shut the doors of the basilica, of presenting himself in full uniform during the ceremony and announcing to the assembly the death of Napoleon. According to the ever-hopeful Malet the surprise would be so great that the ministers and grand dignitaries would hasten to give their adherence to the new government.

A prisoner placed in the prison of La Force as a spy denounced Malet to the police. This time the minister thought the general was a madman, and after transferring him to the prison of Sainte-Pélagie sent him to the hospital that Dr. Dubuisson, following the example of the famous Belhomme, had just set up at 303 Faubourg Saint-

Antoine for political prisoners. Malet began conspiring again in company with a fellow prisoner, Abbé Lafon, a convinced royalist. Malet was by preference a republican, but being a conspirator above all else considered that as the "Corsican" had to be suppressed he could even associate with the devil to do it. On this occasion he remembered that he had begun his military career as a musketeer under Louis XV and agreed to include in *his* government royalist personalities who were, incidentally, no more informed of their nomination than the exclusives. It is said that the two men played at chess for the names of the future ministers. This time the death of Napoleon, killed by a bullet at Moscow, was to be announced to the troops of the Paris garrison. With the help of forged orders and alleged senatus consultums creating a new government, the troops would be led to the police prefecture, the Hôtel de Ville, the military headquarters and the ministries.

Where the accomplices were concerned Malet had a stroke of genius. They must create accomplices *in spite of themselves,* that is choose enemies of the Empire, make them believe in Napoleon's death and in the creation of a new government. Where were these accomplices to be found? In prison, of course. Malet first thought of General Lahorie—Victor Fanneau de La Horie—detained in La Force, wrongfully, of course, for complicity in Moreau's conspiracy. With him would be associated another prisoner in La Force, General Guidal, accused, with more reason, of having wanted to sell Toulon to the English for thirty thousand francs. Since the doors of La Force were to be opened, Lafon insisted that they should free a poor devil of a royalist agent, the Corsican Boccheciampe, who might be of some use.

As Malet could not appear before the troops alone, he needed two companions: an aide-de-camp and a police commissioner. They came to volunteer. One of the general's companions in captivity was sometimes visited by a young relative, a corporal of the Paris guard, Jean-Auguste Rateau. One day Malet took him by the arm, led him into the garden and asked him "if he was ambitious to get on."

"Ah! general!" replied the corporal. "I ask nothing better!"

"Well," announced Malet, "I am thinking of you. You are young, just the age for noble ambitions. I think the opportunity will soon arise for me to be of use to you. I shall shortly be charged with the execution of certain orders from the Senate. Would you like to be my aide-de-camp?" The corporal nearly fainted with joy.

Matters were just as simple with the poet Boutreux. He had come to see Lafon and to ask the abbé to get him "a good position." Malet took him aside one day and confided: "The Prince Royal of Sweden is going to disembark in the north and cut the Emperor's retreat. The moment it is learned that His Majesty has succumbed everything will be ready for the establishment of a new government. Incidentally I am entrusted with an important part in the future regime." And the general offered him "an excellent position as police commissioner."

This is why, at half past three in the morning of Thursday, October 23, 1812, Malet, who had cleverly escaped over the wall, presented himself with his two companions before the sentry of the Popincourt barracks. Lafon, who had escaped at the same time, was trembling in every limb and preferred to rejoin his accomplice when everything should be over, that is at nine o'clock at staff headquarters in the Place Vendôme.

The sentry, seeing the gold braid on Malet's uniform, called the sergeant of the guard. The latter came running and jumped to attention.

"Where is your commanding officer?" Malet asked brusquely.

The commander of the Xth Cohort, which was stationed at Rue Popincourt, Major Soulier, lived a short way off. For him there was only one god—the Emperor. His anguish can be imagined when Malet roused him, declaring: "Major, the Emperor died on October 7 last under the walls of Moscow. The imperial government is overthrown."

The unhappy man began to sob, while Malet read him the forged documents: senatorial acts, nomination to the rank of general, order to occupy with his cohort the Hôtel de Ville and to prepare, in cooperation with the Prefect of the Seine, rooms suitable for the new government to meet in.

"Imagine my position while this was being read," Major Soulier later told the war council. "I soaked four shirts with my sweat."

He was sweating so much, in fact, that he did not dare get out of bed and, at Malet's request, sent for his adjutant, Captain Piquerel.

"Ah, captain! What sad news I have to tell you! My poor friend, the Emperor is dead!"

"Is it possible?" murmured the officer, stupefied and overwhelmed.

"Go to the section, arm the cohort and place yourself fully at the general's disposition."

The little group returned to the barracks. They did not dare sound reveille for fear of alarming the district. Under the still falling rain the corporals in charge woke the men, who came down in small groups, buttoning up their tunics. When the cohort was assembled —it was already past five o'clock—Boutreux, wearing his tricolor scarf, began in a trembling voice to read the senatus consultum announcing the death of the Emperor and the creation of the new government. Second Lieutenant Gomont, who was standing behind his men, misheard what the poet-commissioner was muttering. "I imagined," he declared later, "that it was to nominate a Regent, seeing that His Majesty the King of Rome was still too young."

It was a surprising thing that this officer was the only one that morning to think of the King of Rome. Neither the prefects nor the ministers would think of saying that with the Emperor dead Napoleon II ascended the imperial throne.

At six o'clock in the morning Malet, accompanied by Rateau and Boutreux and followed by Captain Piquerel at the head of nearly all the cohort's companies, was on his way to the prison of La Force, whose crumbling façade opened on to the Rue des Boulets at the corner of the Rue du Roi-de-Sicile. Malet handed the jailer Bault— Marie Antoinette's former warder at the Conciergerie—the order to free General Lahorie and Guidal, together with the Corsican Boccheciampe. Bault hesitated. He was not in the habit of obeying orders dated from "staff headquarters in the Place Vendôme." He came under the Ministry of Police.

"Have these prisoners brought out at once, or you will answer for it!" cried Malet.

"Permit me to have a word with the Prefect of Police."

This time Boutreux intervened. "The minister is suspended, there is no prefect. The Emperor is dead."

Bault still hesitated. Malet turned to the cohort. "Soldiers, do your duty! You have arms; they are outside the law. Make them act without delay!"

This time the jailer yielded and a few moments later the two generals, bewildered and understanding nothing of this sudden freedom, appeared in the office and found themselves in Malet's presence. He threw himself into the arms of Lahorie, whom he had not seen for eighteen years, and was introduced to Guidal, whom he did not know. Malet told them what was going on and, when their first surprise was over, announced that they had orders to arrest the Minister Savary, the Prefect Pasquier, Desmarets the head of Security, the Prince High Chancellor Cambacérès and the Minister of War, Clarke. Guidal and Lahorie did not seem in the least frightened. Napoleon's death had taken them out of prison and it was quite natural that the new government should employ them without delay—were they not enemies of the regime? Besides, they had seen so much since 1792.

"I thought it was another 18 Brumaire," Lahorie was to say, "and I followed Malet just as I followed Bonaparte."

Suddenly a completely bewildered person entered the office: it was the Corsican Boccheciampe. His release interrupted the work in which he was engaged: "The alphabetical list of synonyms employed by the Italian poets to express the names of the gods, goddesses, the sky and the earth." He was consoled by Malet, who immediately nominated him Prefect of the Seine.

While the leader of the conspiracy went to the headquarters, Lahorie and Boutreux, followed by about sixty men, arrived at the police prefecture, which was then in the Rue de Jérusalem, a sordid alley in the Ile de la Cité. In spite of the early hour, the prefect, Baron Pasquier, was at work. Suddenly he saw in the doorway of his office Lahorie, in civilian clothes and wearing his hat, still accompanied by Boutreux with his scarf. The general did not beat about the bush. "The Emperor is dead. You are no longer prefect. I arrest you."

Pale and with trembling hands, the baron had difficulty in pulling himself together. He tried to read the documents his visitor handed him, but, on his own avowal, "an unfortunate giddiness confused his judgment."

"This is your successor," continued Lahorie, pushing Boutreux toward the prefect.

Pasquier rose quickly and "gracefully" yielded his chair to the poet, a mere police commissioner at four o'clock in the morning and head of the Paris police at seven. Somewhat confused, Boutreux sat down, while Lahorie, on a sheet of the prefecture's headed paper, wrote an order to confine the prefect in the prison of La Force. A second lieutenant of the cohort was summoned and the prisoner given into his charge. Before leaving his office, Pasquier bowed deeply to his successor and to the general and then asked that he might be taken to a neighboring apothecary "to swallow some medicine that might do him good." On arrival at the prison he was taken aback to meet the famous police officer Desmarets, head of Security, whom an officer of the cohort had arrested with equal ease.

"What is going on?" the police officer asked in Latin.

"I do not know," murmured Pasquier. "But it is certainly something very strange."

Lahorie, leaving Boutreux alone with his new greatness, went to the central Ministry of Police, where Guidal, Captain Piquerel and the bulk of the troops from the Popincourt barracks were waiting for him. The office of Savary, Duc de Rovigo, was shut. They knocked, and His Excellency opened the door himself, in his nightshirt.

"You are arrested," declared Lahorie. "Think yourself lucky to have fallen into my hands. No harm will come to you."

Seeing the minister's astonishment, he added, as he sat down and drew up a committal order: "The Emperor was killed under the walls of Moscow on October 8."

"You are telling me stories. I had a letter from him today and I can let you read it."

This was untrue, but Savary was beginning to regain his wits.

"Do you recognize me?" he cried, turning to the soldiers who filled the room.

But the men had difficulty in "recognizing" this man in a nightshirt as His Excellency.

"Do you know the man you are obeying in carrying out this deed? He is a state prisoner, a conspirator!"

Meanwhile Lahorie, who had gone out, returned with General Guidal, who rushed toward Savary with bloodshot eyes. He tripped over a fallen chair, gave a shout of pain and, rubbing his leg, advanced on the minister.

"Do you know me?"

"No, I do not."

"I am the General Guidal you had arrested at Marseilles."

"Ah!" replied Savary. "I know about that. Have you come here to dishonor yourself by a cowardly assassination?"

"No," answered Guidal. "I shall not kill you, but you must come with me."

The Duc de Rovigo yielded. He dressed under the jeering eyes of the soldiers and a quarter of an hour later Guidal handed him over to Bault, who was more and more astonished. He had been given the prefect, the Minister of Police and the head of Security to guard and the three orders were signed by Guidal, his former prisoner.

At the same hour Major Soulier, having changed his shirt for the last time, placed himself at the head of the last remaining company from the Rue Popincourt and, following Malet's orders, occupied the Hôtel de Ville without the least difficulty. He had informed the prefect, Comte Frochot, of his mission and the latter had yielded with such good grace that it had not even been necessary to send him to prison.

"There is room in the great hall for your new government," he declared. "As for your general staff, they can occupy the basement of the Hôtel de Ville. They will do very well there."

And so the conspiracy continued on its way, helped by men who were not in the secret and so played their part all the more naturally. The machine was well set in motion. At the barracks of the Minimes and of La Courtille dispatch riders arrived with documents signed by Malet and ordering the regiments to take up arms and occupy, in the name of the new government, the Palais Royal, the Quai Voltaire, the Senate, the Treasury and the principal Paris barriers, while the bulk of the troops were to gather in the Place Vendôme, where Malet himself would be. All obeyed, even Colonel Rabre, commander of the Paris guard. In brief, at a quarter to ten on the morning of Friday, October 23, Malet was master of three-quarters of Paris. Once they were sure of the Minister of War and of Cambacérès they would merely have to fetch the Empress from Saint-Cloud.

And what of Boccheciampe? At this point Alain Decaux must be heard: "It will be remembered that Malet had, very graciously, nominated Boccheciampe Prefect of the Seine. The Corsican therefore went to the Hôtel de Ville to find Major Soulier, take possession of the building and replace Frochot. When he arrived in front of the ancient and majestic building he stopped, contemplated the monument with respect—and that was all. He was dressed in a miserable, threadbare suit, he was unbelievably lacking in grace, he had a terrible accent. He said to himself that no one would ever be willing to acknowledge

him as the new prefect. When he had for a long time contemplated the Hôtel de Ville he went away, humbly, sadly."
This was the limit of his activity as Prefect of the Seine.

Surprisingly enough, the only man who played his part badly that day was General Malet. Having left his unwitting accomplices he arrived in the Place Vendôme with his corporal-orderly. Behind them the reassuring tread of the 1st company of the Xth Cohort rang out on the wet pavement. It had finally stopped raining, but heavy rain clouds were chasing over Paris.

The military governor of Paris was General Hulin. He was a very determined man and had proved it on the taking of the Bastille and again in 1804, as we have seen, by presiding over the council of war charged with executing the Duc d'Enghien. He was in bed with his wife when General Malet arrived to announce the Emperor's death.

"The Senate, assembled last night, abolished the Imperial Government and I have been appointed to replace you. I have indeed a more painful duty to fulfill, which is to place you under temporary arrest and to seal your papers."

Hulin frowned and looked at this unknown general suspiciously. As though in answer to his thoughts, a small voice came from under the bedclothes. It was Mme. Hulin taking part in the conversation. "But, my dear, if this gentleman is to replace you he must have orders to communicate to you."

"Quite right," exclaimed Hulin. "Quite right. Monsieur, I demand to see your orders."

"Willingly, general," replied Malet. "Let us go into your office."

On arriving in the office—that office Malet hoped shortly to occupy —the conspirator took a pistol from his pocket and shot Hulin, saying, as though in a melodrama: "My orders? Here they are!"

Hulin fell, seriously wounded in the jaw. He was to recover, but the bullet could never be extracted and henceforth the Parisians were always to call him "General *Bouffe-la-Balle.*" While Mme. Hulin uttered shrieks that could be heard from one end of the Place Vendôme to the other, Malet proceeded to the office of the head of the general staff, Colonel Doucet. There he found Major Laborde, the adjutant. The two men—they were police officers wearing military uniform—had just been carefully scrutinizing the orders handed to them by a lieutenant of the Xth Cohort. Seeing the name of General

Malet, Laborde started. He knew of the man. The whole thing could only be a conspiracy. So when the general entered the office announcing that he was taking over the command of the 1st Military Division, Doucet refused to let himself be overborne and replied calmly: "I obey only the orders of the legitimate government—orders signed by the superior authorities and with signatures well known to me. If yours were such, you would find me ready to obey them."

Instead of ordering Rateau to fetch some soldiers of the cohort, Malet preferred to argue. "My orders are signed by me; they should be enough for you. I am responsible for them. If you do not obey you do not know what risk you are running. Harm will come to you."

Doucet remained imperturbable.

"Obey, I tell you!"

"Never!"

Malet took out his pistol, but Laborde had rushed at him and Doucet threw him to the ground.

"Dragoons, to us!" Laborde shouted on the staircase. "They are trying to murder your chief of staff."

While the corporal escaped the cavalry rushed into the office and bound the general. At that moment a man pushed open the door and gazed bewildered at the scene.

"What do you want?"

"Some information about one of my relatives who . . ."

He was given to understand that this was "not the moment." The man bowed and vanished. It was Abbé Lafon. He was to reappear only at the return of the Bourbons.

A minute later Laborde strode onto the balcony over the square. Detachments of all the troops of the garrison were there, assembled on Malet's orders. With a blow the staff officer pushed Malet into the front. "Soldiers!"cried Doucet. "Your Emperor is not dead. You are the dupes of an absurd tale. The man we have just arrested is only an impostor. . . ."

A great cry of "Long live the Emperor!" interrupted him. "In Malet's staring eyes," writes his latest biographer, "appeared a terrible despair, that of a man helplessly watching his dreams crumble."

With Malet bound, Lahorie and Guidal arrested, Boutreux and Lafon in flight and Rateau returned to his barracks, the conspiracy still went on its way, although it had lost its leaders. The troops set in motion by Malet continued to act and a series of misunderstandings followed that brought the affair very near farce. Laborde ran to the police prefecture to undeceive the men of the Xth Cohort, got himself arrested by the officer in charge as an "outlaw" and was brought back to the headquarters of the Place Vendôme, where he made "a very noticeable entrance." There was difficulty in finding Savary, who was "lost" in one of the Paris prisons. But the most picturesque incident was undoubtedly the return of Baron Pasquier to his prefecture. The soldiers on guard thought he had escaped and wanted to rearrest him. The prefect managed to slip from their hand and took refuge in a pharmacy, borrowed a wig and dress from the chemist's wife and thus disguised, it is said, escaped his pursuers.

Paris roared with laughter. Savary, arrested in his nightshirt and "going to prison in place of the man who had come to take his office, his carriage and, practically, his bed," was the object of all the jests.

The epilogue was less amusing. Malet appeared before the Council of War together with twenty-three involuntary accomplices, guilty of credulity. Not without grace he took all responsibility for the affair on himself. His co-accused were all innocent.

"Then who are your accomplices?" asked the president of the tribunal.

"France as a whole, and yourself, Monsieur le Président, if I had succeeded."

This half madman lacked neither character nor wit. He was condemned to death, as were Lahorie, Guidal, Boccheciampe, Rateau—Boutreux was still in flight—and nine officers and warrant officers guilty of having forgotten the King of Rome, guilty of not having thought of shouting: "The Emperor is dead! Long live the Emperor!" As the Prefect Frochot, who was merely retired, said: "That wretched King of Rome, one never thinks of him!"

This forgetfulness irritated Napoleon more than anything else. In the carriage bringing him back at full speed from Russia he was amazed at having to acknowledge the facts. "Among all those soldiers and functionaries to whom my death was announced not one thought of my son!"

The day after his return to the Tuileries he cried to his ministers:

"Your oaths, your principles, your doctrines! You make me tremble for the future.".

The future was becoming dark, indeed. That fugitive from a mental home had shaken the enormous imperial machine by his theatrical conspiracy. The royalists considered Malet to be "the man who had opened the door to hope." He had only set it ajar, but it opened wide when the famous XXIXth bulletin appeared, frankly admitting the Russian disaster. "The government is not unshakable," Mme. de Coigny was able to write hopefully. "Its army is beaten and its police can be kidnaped. So its civil and military power can be routed."

It was the famous "beginning of the end."

Less than a week after the affair, on Thursday, October 29, at three o'clock in the afternoon, the twelve condemned men—Rateau and one of the officers had been pardoned *in extremis*—were placed up against the Farmers-General Wall at the Grenelle barrier. Not one of them would have his eyes bandaged.

Boutreux, when he was finally found, was to be executed at the same place on the following January 30.

"Remember October 29," Malet shouted to the crowd. "I fall, but I am not the last of the Romans!"

After the third fusillade there were only bodies lying on the worn grass. The corpses were loaded onto carts, which set off for the Clamart cemetery.

It began to rain, as it had on the previous Friday. And the rain enlarged the wide pool of blood lying at the exact spot of what is now the entrance to the Dupleix Métro station.

PARIS AND THE RETURN OF THE LILIES

1

Paris Occupied

The Empire was crumbling.

On the morning of March 28, 1814, the Prussian vanguard was approaching Paris. Enemy cavalry had been seen at Claye and Napoleon was still on the other side of the Marne. What would the regent, Empress Marie-Louise, do? By throwing herself into the arms of her father, the Emperor Francis II, by welcoming the Tsar and the King of Prussia at the Tuileries, she might perhaps avoid the worst. Perhaps the reign of Napoleon II would be considered as the only possible solution. At ten o'clock in the evening the Council met in the château and the discussion was long. Everyone except King Joseph thought that to leave Paris would be a grave error. By going they would leave the field open to the Bourbons. A vote was taken and was almost unanimous: the Empress and the government must stay. It was then that Joseph read out a letter already several days old from Napoleon: "You should not under any circumstances permit the Empress and the King of Rome to fall into the hands of the enemy. If they advance on Paris in such force that all resistance becomes impossible, send the regent, my son, the grand dignitaries and the Treasure in the direction of the Loire."

The master had spoken. All yielded, but all knew that by abandoning Paris the Empress was losing her crown.

It was three o'clock in the morning. In the courtyard of the Carrousel Talleyrand entered his carriage and from his thin lips let fall the remark: "So here is the end of all this. Well, this is losing a winning game!"

During the night Marmont sent a note from the advance posts: "The enemy is gaining ground. We may be surrounded this evening."

It was every man for himself. The exodus began at nine o'clock in the morning under a rainy sky. Dully, the Parisians watched in silence as the long procession went up the Champs-Elysées. A squadron of grenadiers and *chasseurs* preceded the green berlins with the imperial arms in which were huddled the Empress, the King of Rome, Madame Letizia, the Queen of Westphalia, Cambacérès, the ladies of honor and the ministers. The King of Rome's pages were seated in great "gondolas" harnessed to eight horses. Then, surrounded by lancers of the guard, came the heavy coronation coaches, whose gilt shone through the morning mist. Inside could be seen harness and spare saddles thrown onto the satin cushions. Finally, bringing up the rear and rolling noisily over the paving, went the wagons containing the crown jewels, the coronation costumes, the imperial sword, the silver, the enamel service and the treasure: thirty-two little barrels of gold.

Of the whole gigantic empire there remained only this caricature of the epoch, this caravan trailing gilded bric-a-brac after it.

At about six in the evening the Prefect of Police, Baron Pasquier, saw his cousin Mme. de Rémusat, lady-in-waiting to Marie-Louise, enter his office. She was accompanied by M. de Talleyrand, who seemed oddly embarrassed.

"You know, cousin, that M. de Talleyrand has been ordered to leave to join the Empress. Is this not most unfortunate? No one will then be left to negotiate with the foreigners, no one whose name bears sufficient weight. You must be more greatly aware of this drawback than anyone else, you who will have the burden of a great responsibility. You can see that M. de Talleyrand is in a dilemma, for how can he not obey, and yet what a misfortune if he really had to go!"

Although bewildered by this strange approach, the prefect appeared to agree, but what could he do? The prince said nothing, but Mme. de Rémusat spoke for him. Could not the baron station a few men at the barrier with the task of arousing the crowd "and being so strong in their protests and cries that they would force the prince to retrace his steps"? Pasquier was of the opinion that it did not beseem a prefect of police to act as an *agent provocateur* and stir up a riot.

"But you have a much simpler way of gaining your ends, and one without danger. M. de Rémusat has a command in the National Guard and is surely in charge of one of the barriers. Let M. de Talleyrand present himself at this barrier in order to leave and let M. de Rémusat do with his National Guards what you are asking me to do through the people."

And so it was done. When, that same evening, M. de Talleyrand presented himself in his traveling berlin at the Bonshommes barrier, he found M. de Rémusat, who refused to let him pass and told the prince to return home. M. de Talleyrand affected extreme annoyance and went to complain to the bodyguard at the Roule barrier at the end of the Faubourg Saint-Honoré. The officer in command explained that the order could obviously not concern the Prince of Benevento and, with a zeal not foreseen by the program, offered His Excellency an escort to Versailles.

But the prince exclaimed that he wished for no favors—it was for him, the Emperor's minister, to give an example of obedience. And he ordered his coachman to return to the Rue Saint-Florentin.

The former Bishop of Autun was now able to betray his master in all tranquillity and to safeguard his own interests. It so happened that, on that day, the latter were the same as those of France. This was pure coincidence. On the following morning, from the top floor of his house, he could see the white smoke of the cannons outlined in the east against the gray, leaden sky. On the other side the hills of Chaillot and Saint-Cloud were almost ink-blue.

While M. de Talleyrand was waiting for his hour to strike, the enemy—Prussians, Austrians, Russians, Swedes and English—were preparing, for the first time since the Hundred Years' War, to take Paris. One hundred and ten thousand men were disposed between Vincennes and Saint-Denis. Facing them, forty-two thousand soldiers, the remnants of Marmont's and Mortier's corps, National Guards, pupils of the Military Academy and even the storekeepers from the depots occupied the plain of Romainville, or assembled on the slopes of Buttes-Chaumont, Montmartre, Ménilmontant and Belleville. Moncey, on the extreme left, defended Clichy; Ornano's cavalry, on the extreme right, protected the Seine.

All Paris was in the streets. Groups of onlookers commented on events. Where was Napoleon? Nobody quite knew. On the 28th he had still been at Saint-Dizier. Doubtless he was pressing forward; doubtless he would suddenly appear at the rear of the enemy. Who was governing? Certainly not M. de Talleyrand, who was being very careful not to show himself. Only King Joseph remained in Paris, but the Emperor's brother was shortly to leave for the Loire, having authorized the marshals to yield the city the moment all resistance appeared useless.

Paris did not take the situation tragically. On the boulevards and café terraces the elegants ordered lemonade and creams, while the bourgeois and *grisettes* moved off toward the barriers. They gazed defiantly at the suburbanites who were camping in front of the shops and in the doorways along the external boulevards, eating enormous loaves of black bread that they had cooked "almost under the cannon." They had with them their cattle, for which the customs officers, never looking beyond the rules, had obliged them to pay an entry fee. The faubourgs were black with people. The cannon were quite near. People queued at one house in Belleville which bore the notice: "Here the battle can be seen for two sous." While the brandy sellers cried: "Take a sip! Have a nip!" little groups of soldiers went by surrounding their prisoners. They were questioned, and everyone could form his own idea of the approaching combat.

Mortier had entrenched himself in old redoubts erected in front of the village of La Villette, but the Russians attacked his flank and the Prussians his front. Soon the French had to fall back and battle was joined in the Grande-Rue of La Villette. The Prussian guard managed to force a bridge over the canal and suddenly debouched on the other side of the road near the point where the village joined Paris. Taken from the rear, Mortier managed to break through and approach the surrounding wall.

Blücher was now occupying Montmartre and calmly bombarding

Paris. Already, from the barriers, could be seen the Cossacks' long lances and enormous whips.

In front of the Clichy barrier Moncey had erected barricades with the help of the pupils from the Military Academy. From his H.Q.—Père Lathuile's wineshop at No. 7 of the present Avenue de Clichy—the marshal directed a heroic resistance. From the Roule to the Poissonière barriers he managed to contain the flood of Cossacks. But at the end of the afternoon resistance became impossible. Marmont signed the surrender in a shop in La Chapelle run by the wine merchant Thouront, at the sign of the "Little Garden," the second house on the left as one leaves the Saint-Denis barrier.

All through the night the city rang with the steps of men and horses. According to the agreement the imperial army was evacuating Paris. That same night Napoleon arrived at the post station of Frometeau, near Juvisy, only to learn that in a few hours the allies would make their entry into the capital. There was nothing for him to do but retrace his steps. At six o'clock in the morning he arrived at Fontainebleau, where for fifteen days he was to live through a spiritual agony a hundred times worse, perhaps, than the physical agony of Saint Helena.

At dawn the Parisians were again moving toward the outer boulevards. "Near the Martyrs barrier," relates an eyewitness in an account that has been forgotten, "there was a corps of Russian musicians, who were playing. A few French of both sexes were calmly listening. Near them were horses killed in the battle. We went to Montmartre. The streets were full of Russian and German soldiers. Several were sleeping, others dressing. Some waxed their mustaches or shaved their companions. Most of them had a white band round their left arm." The enemy armies were composed of such a mixture of uniforms that many mistakes had arisen. At Rothière Cossacks had been seen to fire at the English. And so the high command had ordered the wearing of a white armband for all combatants. But the Parisians—who had a slight tendency to relate everything to themselves—imagined that this distinctive sign was worn by the allies in honor of Louis XVIII, brother of Louis XVI, who nineteen years before had proclaimed himself "King of France and of Navarre," on the official announcement of the death in the Temple of the little Dauphin. This misunderstanding was cleverly exploited by the royalists of the Faubourg Saint-Germain whose hearts had been beating with hope ever since the "beginning of the end" announced by M. de Talleyrand. A little group of young men bearing names great in France hastened to wear cockades, armbands and sashes of immaculate white and to mount their horses. As the first act in the handkerchief revolution they were seen at nine o'clock in the morning parading round the Place de la Concorde while the crowd awaited the entry of the allied troops. One of them—the too famous Maubreuil—had fastened the cross of his Legion of Honor to his horse's tail. A M. de Vauvineux had tied his handkerchief to a broom handle and, at the top of the Rue de Rivoli, was waving his improvised flag and crying: "Long live the King!" The squad of hotheads went up the boulevards to cries of "Let us avenge the Duc d'Enghien's death!" "Rally to the Bourbons!"

The Parisians massed on the pavements replied mockingly: "The Bourbons? Never heard of them!"

Were there any left? Had they not all died on the scaffold?

In vain the little group of hotheads strode excitedly along the boulevards from the Rue Choiseul to the Madeleine. The Parisians watched them, astonished. Only a few ladies of the aristocracy responded.

At noon the head of the Russian army appeared and passed under the gate at Saint-Denis. "What a moment!" a contemporary wrote. "One could have heard a fly passing. From a hatter on the Boulevard Bonne-Nouvelle I had obtained a small place at the window of his wife's bedroom, and through my eye glasses I watched, not without deep emotion, the faces of the curious crowding in the side lane opposite me, above the roadway which singularly patriotic hands had strewn with leaves. The feet of the Ukrainian horses as they trampled this greenery were the only sound in the silence. In the little streets running off the boulevards were perched on benches, and even on the boxes of their carriages, many rich women who, forgetful of their husbands, brothers or sons, dead by Russian bayonets, occasionally interrupted the gloomy watchfulness of the public by sending cries of joy, bouquets and even kisses to the enemy column."

Near the Madeleine, when the Tsar appeared with the King of Prussia at his side, women from the Faubourg Saint-Germain, casting aside modesty in order to see Alexander better, mounted behind the

Russian officers' horses. Others kissed the horse's mane and the Emperor's boots, while he smiled, touched and quite bewildered by this welcome.

On arriving at the *rond-point* the sovereigns halted. The troops passed by them, uttering shouts of joy. By the end of the day the Cossacks had built their straw huts on the Champs-Elysées and were wandering through the town. "The Rue Saint-Honoré presented a most extraordinary appearance," wrote an eyewitness, an Englishman who happened to be in Paris. "At one and the same time one could see Germans, Russians and Asiatics from the Great Wall of China, to the shores of the Caspian and of the Black Sea. There were Cossacks with their sheepskins, their long lances, their thick red beards, and the little whip called a knout hanging round their necks; Kalmouks and other Tartar tribes, remarkable for their flat noses, their little eyes and their deep red complexion; Bashkirs and Tunguses from Siberia, armed with bows and arrows, Circassian chiefs, born at the foot of the Caucasus, dressed entirely in shining coats of steel mail and wearing on their heads tall, pointed caps, exactly like those worn in England in the twelfth and thirteenth centuries. . . . Many of the Russian officers were barely out of their childhood. They wore a tight sash above the hips, their padded chests jutted out, their tangled hair came down to their shoulders. . . . The Russian carriages moving among this crowd were harnessed with ropes and driven by coachmen with long beards and dressed in dark robes, their heads covered with small-brimmed flat hats. Such was the equipage of General Sacken, governor general of Paris."

A few regiments were camped at Ranelagh and sought to demolish dance and entertainment halls or anything that could be burnt to warm themselves. They even entered a scenery store and began to cut up a canvas depicting trees.

"What!" said the proprietor. "You have a wood nearby [the Bois de Boulogne] and you want to burn my forest!"

The Russians considered this a very just observation, and began to cut down the Bois de Boulogne.

Meanwhile Alexander was installed with the Prince de Talleyrand, whose hour had now come. It was he who would set aside the regency of Marie-Louise and obtain from the allies the return of the Bourbons. He even organized a little manifestation at the Opéra, where, that same evening, Alexander went to see a performance of *La Vestale*. The ladies threw white cockades and acclaimed the Tsar and during the interval one of the actors, Lays, advanced to the footlights and sang:

> Of Alexander I sing!
> Long live this mighty king!
> Without dictating laws
> Or making any claim,
> This highly noble prince
> Has won a triple fame:
> An upright and heroic man,
> He brought the Bourbons back again.

This was not very brilliant, and lacked modesty! On the staircases and in the foyers the royalists embraced each other. The Restoration was accomplished.

On the following day the senators declared the Emperor deposed, nominated M. de Talleyrand president of the provisional government and declared that "the French people freely call to the throne Louis-Stanislas-Xavier, brother of the last King," that King whom certain of the senators had, incidentally, sent to the guillotine.

"The French people" thus directly implicated were actually ignorant even of the existence of this Louis-Stanislas-Xavier who was imposed on them by senators Napoleon had nominated. Besides, they called on him in vain, for the King, who was living in England, was kept to his bed by a serious attack of gout. It was his brother, Monsieur, the Comte d'Artois, who was the first of the family to take possession of the Tuileries. On April 8 the prince made his entry into Paris.

Napoleon's marshals, a little embarrassed at being there, and the members of the provisional government headed by Talleyrand, waited at the Bondy barrier. After a speech by the Prince of Benevento they set out for Notre Dame. In the Faubourg and the Rue Saint-Denis the welcome was tepid—the workers regretted the Emperor—but in the center of the town there was a wild reception. From every window there floated bed linen, nobly called white flags, the ground was strewn with white flowers, the women wore lilies in their dresses and hats. There were shouts, embraces, tears.

"It is quite incomprehensible," exclaimed Ney. "Here is a man arrived out of the blue, whom yesterday they did not know, and they are already full of enthusiasm for him!"

The Parisians were principally full of enthusiasm for peace. For them any man—even one as insignificant as the brother of Louis-Stanislas-Xavier—was much more attractive to them than a warrior with his sword perpetually drawn and cavalcading from Madrid to Moscow.

The Comte d'Artois, with tears in his eyes, was completely overcome by his incomprehensible triumph. He kept on repeating: "I am so happy, Monsieur de Talleyrand. Come along, come along! I am so happy." This was lacking in eloquence. So for the benefit of the *Moniteur* the words were altered and Monsieur was made to say: "Nothing is changed in France. There is merely one Frenchman more."

2

A Reactionary Chestnut Tree

On May 3, 1814, Louis XVIII, in his turn, made his "joyous entry" into Paris. The King, Madame Royale, now the Duchesse d'Angoulême, the Duc de Bourbon and his father the old Prince de Condé, who was not quite sure what it was all about, had taken their seats in a barouche drawn by eight white horses from the imperial stables and driven by grooms wearing the Emperor's livery. The carriage was preceded, or followed—witnesses do not agree on this point—by the imperial guard. Some of the veterans had pulled their fur caps right over their eyes. They preferred not to see the spectacle. "Their jaws tightened with impotent rage." It was not the entry of Louis XVIII, but the funeral of Napoleon, who on that same day arrived in an English ship at the island of Elba, in sight of his "cabbage patch" of Portoferraio.

On entering the Tuileries Louis XVIII murmured:

> Il aurait volontiers écrit sur son chapeau:
> C'est moi qui suis Guillot, berger de ce troupeau.

All the palace walls, the furniture, the ironwork and the lamps were, in fact, covered with imperial crowns and the cursed letter N. Eagles hovered on the ceilings, bees buzzed in the drapery, the carpets were sown with violets. Even the bath taps were covered with veritable swarms. During the past month the shop signs in Paris had been transformed, lilies taking the place of violets, but at the Tuileries the royalist ladies had confined themselves to sticking strips of paper over the portraits of the imperial family. Madame Royale directed operations and began eagerly to chase the bees from the carpets. It was decided to sew fleurs-de-lis on top of them. On the ceilings the eagles were transformed into swans and the N's into two L's back to back. Yet the Comte d'Artois thought not enough progress was being made, among other places in the throne room, and was constantly coming to complain to his brother. Louis XVIII, who was less disturbed by the imperial flora and fauna, replied: "If you insist, I shall put his bust on my chimney piece."

"The system I have adopted," he wrote later, "and which my ministers perseveringly follow is founded on the maxim that one must not be King of two peoples, and all the efforts of my government are aimed at causing these two peoples, who only too obviously exist, to form in the end one only." His aim was to assemble all the French "under the flag of pardon and oblivion." It was a hard task. The fanatics purged all those who, even from afar, had approached "the man whom shame forbids one to mention." But Louis XVIII did his best to find excuses with which he prompted the guilty. Old M. de Barentin was trying one day to exculpate himself.

"I did not, strictly speaking, take an oath to Bonaparte."

"I quite understand you," replied the King, smiling indulgently. "At your age one only does things by halves. You did not take an oath, you took an oathlet."

"With wit one gets out of everything," he was fond of saying, and he proved it. One day, amid the public acclamations of "Long live the King!" a workingman shouted: "Long live the fat pig!" The unfortunate man was immediately arrested and taken before the public prosecutor, who decided to prosecute him for "seditious remarks." The minister of justice, hoping for congratulations, went smirking to the King to make his report. Louis XVIII pounced on him: "What! This prosecutor thought that 'Long live the fat pig!'

was addressed to the King of France? And you have not dismissed him? Really, you are not very good at your job."

Louis XVIII did not succeed in disarming the opposition. Everywhere he was lampooned and sung about. The army set the example. The officers slapped his statue and the men when playing cards announced "pig of clubs" or "pig of diamonds."

"The crowd," wrote Henry Houssaye, "gathers round the windows of the print sellers in which are displayed portraits of Napoleon, Marie-Louise and Napoleon II. People go to see the cosmorama of the island of Elba in the Boulevard du Temple. Launay's foundry in the Place de la Fidélité, where the statue from the Vendôme column was taken, has become a place of pilgrimage. In the Rue Tiquetonne a former sergeant-major of the hussars shows Arcole, Austerlitz and Tilsit in his magic lantern. At the Comédie-Française the pit thrice applauds this sentence from *Edouard en Ecosse:* 'Only a dishonest man could speak in such a way of a hero.' At the Palais Royal someone writes, 'Long live the Emperor!' with a diamond on a shop window and passers-by amuse themselves by scratching under the inscription: 'Approved, approved, approved.'. . . On July 19, in the Faubourg Saint-Martin, and on August 18, in the Rue des Vieilles-Haudriettes, workers sing revolutionary refrains and Bonapartist couplets. On September 17 Louis XVIII is greeted in the Boulevard du Montparnasse with a few acclamations, to which the crowd replies by shouting, 'Long live the Emperor!' "

The funeral of the actress Mlle. Rancourt nearly degenerated into a real riot. The vicar of Saint-Roch, Abbé Marduel, had refused to send a priest to the bedside of the former tragedienne, and then had opposed the holding of any religious service. Now, Mlle. Rancourt, after leading a somewhat dissolute life, had become very pious, taking the collection at Saint-Roch, providing the blessed bread, opening her purse for Abbé Marduel's poor and receiving the vicar to dinner. It was only when she died that the abbé remembered that she was excommunicated and he refused to give any blessing. So when the funeral procession left the Rue du Helder, where Mlle. Rancourt had lived, demonstrators seized the horses' heads and made them go to Saint-Roch. As the church was closed, the doors were forced, candles lit and the coffin solemnly carried to the choir. A crowd gathered, and soon five or six thousand people invaded the

Rue Saint-Honoré and the neighboring streets. An eyewitness noted the remarks that were exchanged. "They thought her a good Christian as regards money, but a bad one as regards principles."

"Although the good Rancourt was charitable to a fault, because she died an actress the church is to be closed to her. . . ."

"And by the very vicar who exploited her money for alms to the church!"

"They refused to receive her body! This is a return to the conclusions of the old regime."

The crowd grew stormy. There were shouts of: "To the Tuileries! To the Tuileries!"

The King gave order to require "the clergy of Saint-Roch to provide the honors of divine service." Naturally the extremists declared it was a scandal and were supported by the poor Duchesse d'Angoulême.

To bring about the return of what no longer existed was for Madame Royale, Marie Antoinette's daughter, almost a sacred duty, and that in every sphere. "All the old traditions seem to have taken refuge under the duchess's skirts." Admittedly everything reminded her of the drama. The very landscape she saw every time she went to a window in her apartments reminded her of the bloody tragedy in which her parents had perished. To her left she saw the "waterside" terrace where she used to play with her brother. To her right, toward the Pavillon de Marsan, was the road taken by the royal family on the morning of August 10, the first stage toward the Temple. In front of her, through the soft green foliage, she could almost see the square where her father and her mother, on a morning in January and a morning in October . . . What a nightmare! Often, too, she would look at a large chestnut tree at the end of the great tree-lined roadway, whose branches were taller than those of any other tree in the old garden. This was "the tree of the Swiss." At its foot were buried the bodies of the last defenders of royalty, the unhappy Swiss Guards whom the Parisians had massacred in the garden on the evening of the attack on the Tuileries. Often, when Madame Royale was still in exile, she had been told the beautiful story of the Paris chestnut tree, which every spring, during the Revolution and then during the usurpation of M. de Bonaparte, was covered with flowers long before the other trees of its species in the great roadway. God thus decked the tomb of the martyrs who had been refused burial in Christian ground. Doubtless the tree owed its early flowering only to the blood with which it had been watered on August 10, 1792, but in spite of this fertilizer, which it was preferred not to mention, the chestnut tree had become a place of pilgrimage for the royalists.

In the year following the return of the lilies the tree did not wait for the official date of spring to bud. On the first Sunday in March, 1815, strollers remarked that in the middle of the still denuded garden the chestnut tree was covered with buds that were already beginning to open. Without doubt the tree would be in flower by the first days of April, the first anniversary of the King's return. The tree of the Swiss, a royalist tree, would not otherwise celebrate the fall of the Usurper.

It was March 5—Sunday, March 5. On that day, at about half past one in the afternoon, Baron de Vitrolles gave the King a telegram that had just been handed to him by "M. Chappe, Director of the Telegraph." Louis XVIII read it and then threw the paper on the table.

"Do you know what this is?"

"No, sire, I do not."

"Well," returned Louis XVIII in a voice that remained unchanged. "Bonaparte has just disembarked on the Provence coast. This telegram must be taken to the Minister for War and he will see what he has to do."

The Minister for War was at that time Marshal Soult, Duke of Dalmatia by the grace of Napoleon. The man who had "led the battle" at Austerlitz was now to have to fight the man to whom he owed everything. Vitrolles hurried into his carriage and drove to the Rue Saint-Dominique as quickly as the Sunday crowds would let him. Suddenly he saw Soult, who was sauntering along the parapet of the Pont-Royal. The marshal was on foot, followed by one of his servants carrying his ministerial portfolio. Vitrolles stopped his carriage. Soult approached, and there, as the baron was later to relate, "amid all the people passing round us, from my seat in the carriage, I held the telegram open before the eyes of the marshal, who was standing near the door."

Soult showed no anxiety, and the government merely inserted a decree in the *Moniteur* declaring "Napoleon Bonaparte a traitor and rebel for having entered the Var department with armed force" and enjoining "all governors commanding armed forces, National Guards, civil authorities and even simple citizens to hunt him down."

Only the Baron de Vitrolles saw the danger. He staked everything on Monsieur, Louis XVIII's brother. He was persuaded that the future Charles X could "by his good grace and knightly eloquence" sway the regiments. He went to the Pavillon de Marsan, where he learned that the Comte d'Artois was at vespers.

"At vespers," Vitrolles said to himself as he waited in the hall. "At vespers! How can anyone be at vespers in such circumstances? James II lost his kingdom for a mass. Will these people lose theirs for vespers?"

There was only one explanation: Louis XVIII distrusted his brother and had thought fit to hide the news from him. A quarter of an hour later, indeed, when he had Vitrolles shown into his office, Monsieur appeared to know nothing.

"Well," he asked cheerfully, "do you bring me news of our travelers?"

The "travelers" were the Duc and Duchesse d'Angoulême, who were on an official voyage to Bordeaux. Obviously the King's brother had not read the telegram, so the Secretary of State, contrary to etiquette, was bold enough to ask him a question.

"Has Monsieur not seen the King since mass?"

"Yes, I have seen him."

Then, as though speaking of an event of no importance, he added carelessly: "By the way, this news of the disembarkation, what do you think of it?"

Vitrolles tried to conceal his stupefaction and explained the gravity of the situation to the Comte d'Artois.

"The troops will be loyal only if the princes lead them. It is you, monseigneur, who can best assure the loyalty of the army and reawaken zeal and love for the royal cause among the population."

Louis XVIII's brother paced silently up and down his office. Vitrolles followed him. "I could observe that he listened to me," he wrote later, "only from the speed of his steps, which quickened as my words became more urgent, so that finally, without noticing it, we were almost running."

The silence and the hurried walk continuing, Vitrolles recommenced his exhortations. Finally the future Charles X remarked impatiently, without stopping: "Well, I think you are right and that we must grease our boots."

"No, monseigneur," insisted the panting minister. "You must leave without waiting to grease your boots."

The behavior of all the people sent to "hunt down" one man is well known. There was not a regiment that set out to fight the "traitor and rebel" that, on seeing him, did not begin to shout, "Long live the Emperor!" And one morning a wag hung a notice on the railings of the Vendôme column: "Napoleon to Louis XVIII: My good brother, it is useless to send me any more soldiers. I have enough."

On Sunday, March 12, the Parisians learned of Napoleon's entry into Lyons and of the flight of the Comte d'Artois and the Duc d'Orléans, who had set out to meet him. At the Tuileries the strollers noticed that the buds of the royalist chestnut tree had opened in less than a week. The tree of the Swiss was covered with bright green leaves.

Not far off the most extravagant schemes were being mooted. Marmont had come to find the King. His abandonment of 1814 haunted him, and he wished to fight the Emperor by every possible means. According to him there was only one solution: to transform the château into a redoubt.

"The palace must be so prepared that a battery of heavy guns would be needed to demolish it."

Louis XVIII and his throne would be placed at the heart of this fortress and they would shut themselves up with provisions for two months and with three thousand men of the King's household, stage soldiers, perhaps, but who would be "excellent for this purpose," the marshal declared. As for the other members of the royal family, the Duc de Raguse dispatched them offhandedly, in all directions.

"And supposing the King were struck on the head by a projectile from one of the heavy guns?" Marmont envisaged the prospect cheerfully:

"The Comte d'Artois, your nephews and your cousins are without. When Your Majesty is dead your rights and titles pass to another."

Louis XVIII preferred to keep his rights for himself. Perhaps he would listen to the scheme arranged by Blacas. According to his favorite, the King, on the approach of the "tiger," should enter an open barouche, together with his first gentleman-in-waiting. The carriage would be followed by the peers and deputies on horseback—as well as they could, for some of them had not ridden since the reign of Louis XVI. This procession would advance to meet the Emperor and ask him what he had come for. Embarrassed for a reply, M. de Bonaparte would retire. Vitrolles, without moving a muscle, proposed that the procession should be preceded by the Archbishop of Paris bearing the Blessed Sacrament, "like St. Martin going to meet the King of the Visigoths."

On the morning of March 19, Palm Sunday, a courier announced that Napoleon had entered Auxerre and had immediately continued his march on Paris. That very evening he might arrive at Fontainebleau. In the garden the Sunday strollers saw the tree of the Swiss covered with flower buds just about to open. Perhaps the royalist tree, by flowering much earlier than usual, wanted to console the King. For his departure was decided. At half past eleven in the evening the carriages drew up in the courtyard under the rain. The royal berlin was stationed in front of the vestibule of the Pavillon de Flore. Bodyguards and National Guards came out of the guardroom and mingled with the courtiers and officers on duty. The door opened. An usher bearing two torches appeared, and then the King, supported by Blacas. Nothing was heard but groans and sobs. Not without difficulty the old King made his way through a crowd of kneeling faithful to his carriage and sat at the back of the berlin. He made a final gesture of farewell. Surrounded by bodyguards, the carriage moved off toward the Saint-Martin barrier. The royal household left the château and for a few hours silence fell on the deserted palace. The departure had been so hurried that Louis XVIII's slippers had been left behind.

"It is my slippers that I most regret," the King was to confide to Macdonald before he went to Ghent. "One day, my dear marshal, you will know what it is to lose slippers that have taken the shape of your feet."

The following morning, the famous 20th of March, 1815, the Parisians came to look at the long, gray façade of the château. The white flag had been taken away. "The crowd wandered about," an eyewitness related. "People met each other with suspicion; one hardly dared to speak even in low tones. There was universal silence." Suddenly, from the quay, came a horseman carrying a tricolor flag. It was General Exelmans, coming from Fontainebleau and announcing that the Emperor would arrive that very evening.

A minute later the three colors floated from the balcony of the Salle des Maréchaux. Gradually there arrived at the Tuileries Napoleon's officers and former servants. Imperial uniforms and green liveries reappeared. There were congratulations and embraces. Stretched out on the floor, the ladies hastened to unpick the fleurs-de-lis from the carpet and the beloved bees reappeared. Similarly, on the boulevards, the shopkeepers unhooked their signboards, and violets and eagles succeeded the royal crowns. Some shops had been more cautious and in 1814 had merely displayed the backs of their boards on which they had painted the new emblems while keeping the imperial fauna on the reverse. Now they had only to turn the boards round.

In the courtyard of the Carrousel the Parisians shouted, "Long live the Emperor!" Dances were organized in the garden and as the couriers announced the approach of the Emperor the enthusiasm became wild. Everyone looked affectionately at the tree of the Swiss which, in the center of the still wintry garden, was all flowers. Paris seemed to have prepared an enormous bouquet for the town to offer its hero. The tree of the Swiss was forgotten. It had become "The chestnut tree of March 20," and on the next morning, when the Emperor opened his window, after a triumphal evening, it would be the first thing he saw.

One hundred days later came the last figure of the dance. Louis XVIII returned to the Tuileries and Napoleon left. For the third time the shopkeepers repainted their boards, or turned them round. The operation was carried out with an almost miraculous dexterity; admittedly it was becoming a habit. Paris, decked in white, "wept with joy" as it acclaimed the King. In the garden the enthusiasm was indescribable—as indescribable as on the evening of March 20. Quite without irony the *Moniteur* wrote the next morning: "The foreigners who witnessed this wonderful spectacle"—for the allies had returned with the Bourbons—"were able to see the French character in its true light."

The Bonapartists ground their teeth with rage. To console themselves they had only the Vendôme column and the chestnut tree of

156 • THE TURBULENT CITY: PARIS

March 20, now gone over to the opposition. But the royalists were laughing up their sleeves. The Cossacks encamped at the Tuileries in 1814 had installed their kitchen there and, according to them, the tree owed its early flowering merely to the grease with which it had been copiously watered. This explanation did not prevent the Bonapartists from going every spring to visit the chestnut tree of March 20. One morning its trunk was even found to be surrounded by a tricolor ribbon. For years and years the chestnut tree continued to be in advance of the other trees in the alley, and the veterans of the Grand Army, each year somewhat fewer, looked affectionately at the tree that had flowered for the return of their Emperor.

3

Thanks to a Pin

It was over. Waterloo had ended the Hundred Days. Napoleon had just abdicated for the second time. From the windows of the Elysée Palace he saw the several thousand Parisians filling the Rue du Faubourg-Saint-Honoré. Shouts reached him of: "Long live the Emperor! Do not abandon us!"

Napoleon had decided to go to Malmaison and await the passports which would enable him to reach America. Fearing that the crowd would prevent his departure, he had his carriage taken out through the main gate, while he crossed the garden on foot. At the gate leading to the Champs-Elysées Grand Marshal Bertrand's carriage was waiting. The sunshine was brilliant. For the last time Napoleon rode up the Champs-Elysées—down which his coffin would triumphantly pass a quarter of a century later, passed the unfinished Arc de Triomphe on which the workmen were still engaged, and then turned into the main road to Neuilly.

As soon as he arrived at Malmaison he received his banker, Laffitte.

"Here are 800,000 francs. Tonight I shall send you three million in gold in a wagon, and I shall have my collection of medals put in your carriage. You will keep all that for me."

"I went to his desk," Laffitte related. "I sat down in his chair, I took a piece of paper and was about to write when, catching my arm, he said: 'What are you going to do?'

" 'Give you a receipt, sire.'

" 'I don't need one.'

" 'I might die; I must keep the secret. If this sum is not entered in my books you need a title to it.'

" 'And suppose I were stopped on the way. I might compromise you.'

" 'When I do a service, sire, I do not calculate the danger.'

" 'Never mind, I must calculate it for you. I do not need a receipt.'

"Such a great sum," Laffitte went on, "handed over with no title! The remnants of his fortune, the bread of his exile! I have never received such a glorious proof of trust, nor one that touched me more."

When Napoleon had left for Saint Helena and Louis XVIII had returned to the Tuileries, Baron Louis, the Minister of Finance, asked Laffitte to declare on oath "if, yes or no, he had any funds of Napoleon's." The banker requested an audience of the King.

"Sire," he said, "on March 19, a few hours before Napoleon's entry into Paris, I received from Your Majesty a deposit of seven millions, of which Napoleon was informed through the indiscretion of his courtiers. He himself, however, took pains to reassure me, ordering me to have this money transferred to England, thus proving that I was worthy of the trust with which the King had honored me."

"I knew all that," replied Louis XVIII. "Baron Louis was wrong. Have no fear, and do with the money entrusted to you what you did with mine."

And so, thanks to Laffitte, Louis XVIII and Napoleon were able to exchange a few civilities.

But who was this banker of kings? Jacques Laffitte, aged twenty-two, the son of a poor carpenter of Bayonne overburdened with children, arrived in Paris on the eve of the Revolution. He had decided to present himself at Perregaux's bank and solicit the modest position of clerk at one hundred francs a month. The future financier put on his Sunday best as worn in Bayonne, a scarlet coat like a toreador's, green waistcoat, canary-colored breeches and an outsized hat. Thus attired, he did not go unnoticed as he went to Perregaux's bank, which was almost on the corner of the boulevard and the Rue du

Mont-Blanc, now the Rue Chaussée d'Antin. The pediment of the building was adorned with a sculptured group bearing little relation to finance: Terpsichore crowned on earth by Apollo. Laffitte was received by the banker himself, and shown the door. The sequel is well known and forms a typical illustration to a moral tale. As he passed beneath "Terpsichore crowned by Apollo," the young man from Bayonne perceived a pin on the ground, bent down, picked it up, stuck it into his lapel, was called back and immediately engaged by Perregaux, who from his window had witnessed this gesture that gave proof of undeniable qualities of method and economy.

It was not only M. Perregaux who took an interest in young Laffitte, but also his wife, who was young and pretty. She was in the habit of having her pens trimmed by one of her husband's clerks, a handsome man who was not a little proud of this favor and looked down on everyone else. A few days after Laffitte's entry into the "Temple of Terpsichore" Mme. Perregaux's sprightly maid put a whole bundle of goose quills on the "little Basque's" desk to be trimmed.

"But, mademoiselle," protested the reigning favorite angrily, "you know very well that your mistress always gives me . . ."

"No, sir," replied the girl, just like a maid in a play, "my orders are to give these pens to the 'handsome boy from Bayonne.' "

And so, thanks to a pin and to love, Jacques Laffitte started on a career that was to make him the king of bankers and bankers of kings. Soon Perregaux made him his right hand and it was at his master's side that he learned his profession during that extravagant epoch of the Directory when society resembled an immense gambling den. The bankers were the kings of the day and the entertainments given by Ouvrard might have come out of the *Thousand and One Nights*. Laffitte was intimate with the men called by the Goncourts "the Staircase Men," who stood at the top of the steps facing the Rue Vivienne. "It is the club of these arbiters of the exchange, these masters of the price of everything, who shake the market as they would a bottle, and raise, lower and overthrow, to suit their own calculations, currency, assignats, warrants and orders. They are in charge of the pulse of the dying public fortune and they cause it to leap from rise to fall and from fall to rise, altering it each minute, reviving it one hour and depressing it the next, forcing the louis to twenty-three thousand livres on June 6, 1796."

A whole crowd of employees milled round these "tyrants of credit." Everyone was yelling:

"Do you want any warrants?"

"Do you want any assignats?"

"Have you any quarters?"

When Bonaparte decided to create the Bank of France Perregaux was appointed governor and president of the administrative council. Laffitte did not leave him, and during the famous crisis of 1805 learned how a banker may become a political personage. This was a novelty. England had formed the scheme of breaking the Bank of France "by scaring the public and making them rush to the counters to have their notes reimbursed in gold. The national credit would be ruined and Napoleon would be halted in his march on Vienna." The politico-financial operation nearly succeeded. At dawn several hundred people were queuing in front of the bank. By evening, recounts an eyewitness, there were still a lot of people, "in spite of the cold autumn. The most determined brought mattresses so that they could spend the night in the Place des Victoires." Fouché took energetic measures. He declared that no one would be reimbursed unless they had first obtained a serial number from the town halls. Parisians in those days had less patience than they have today. The successive queues wore down even the most determined and the moneychanging came to an end.

On February 17, 1808, Perregaux died and his bank became Perregaux, Laffitte & Co. The business was so prosperous that when the Duchesse de Raguse, Perregaux's daughter, drew her dividends—one quarter of the bank's profits—she could not help saying to Laffitte: "Good heavens, have you robbed a mail coach that you can give us so much money?"

In 1814 the Prussians claimed 300,000 francs from the Parisians and camped their troops in the Rue Saint-Antoine until the money should be paid. The Prefect of the Seine hastily summoned two hundred financiers and bankers and asked for their help. There was a silence. "I do not dare ask you," said the prefect, turning to Laffitte. "Everyone knows that three days ago you lent two millions to the provisional government."

"Well, I shall subscribe again."

He had saved Paris twice in one week.

What became of Laffitte after that? "Not only," says Jules Bertaut, "did he appear as a formidable financial power in the somewhat naïve eyes of the contemporaries of the Restoration, but to his status as controller of money was added that of a politician of the first rank.... Brave, hard-working, honest, lacking general ideas, having had no time in his rapid rise to educate himself, he was so happy in his riches, so pleased to display them, so eager for popularity! With an open purse for all in misfortune, determined to play an important role in his class, which came to power under the Restoration, he possessed the plain dealing of M. Poirier, together with his self-sufficiency and high-flown speech which foreshadowed Joseph Prud-homme.* On every page of his memoirs he stands out as a good husband, a good father, a good citizen. He was a spectacle in himself, just like Emile Augier's hero. His life is a perpetual example, a moral history for grownups."

The great reign of Laffitte had begun. His "palace" was the pile of the Bourse, that neo-Greek edifice surrounded by its seventy Corinthian columns. The Emperor had agreed to the plans, but the Bourse was not inaugurated until the Restoration. From one o'clock onward the great hall was invaded by a crowd of *carottiers*—small investors who gambled for trifling stakes *(à la carotte)*—and newsmongers who, in low tones, spread true or false items of news. Jules Bertaut, who might have lived at that time, he describes it so vividly, gives the remarks one feels he must have heard himself.

"Martinez is leaving the ministry."
"It seems one of the bankers has fled."
"Who? Beauregard? I knew that yesterday."
"Does he leave a deficit?"
"Enormous."
"I believe he was the lover of little G—— of the Opéra."
"She put him through it."
"Ah! There's Rothschild!"
"He's the one who's selling in bulk."
"No!"
"Yes, he is!"

Laffitte's arrival would set them buzzing. While waiting for him

---

* These two characters, created by Emile Augier and Henri Monnier, typify the comic bourgeois of the nineteenth century. (Translator's note.)

to come in, an eyewitness recounts, they would watch a fat man "who blew like a grampus." This was Laffitte's confidential agent, "instructed to inform his master, hour by hour, of what went on on the Stock Exchange. The boss himself arrived regularly on the stroke of half past two. He made his way through the hordes of small investors, shaking hands to right and left, taking as much care of his popularity there as in the political clubs."

For Laffitte had gone in for politics, and on the opposition side. He was a power to be reckoned with. "The House of Bourbon is at war with the House of Laffitte," remarked the King ironically.

By then the banker had left La Guimard's old house and was living in the Rue d'Artois. All society flocked there and Laffitte was soon able to make his daughter Albine a princess. She married the eldest son of Ney, the Prince of Moskova, bringing him 100,000 livres a year and a capital of twenty-five millions. She also brought him her caprices, celebrated throughout Paris. Had she not one day insisted on the paths of the family garden being sanded with sugar?

4
A Jolie Laide

It is hot and stormy. Two lovers are walking arm in arm. He appears about forty, but has the manner of a young man. He is undoubtedly a soldier in civilian clothes. His companion is hardly more than twenty. She is small, fair, with a dazzling skin and an exceptionally slender figure. Her mouth is perhaps a little too "rosebud," her glance that of a coquette, and she walks with her feet turned in, but she is delicious. She seems to sparkle with life. She is surely a Parisienne. Without being beautiful, she is sweetly attractive. Her companion appears to be of the same opinion, for he is devouring her with his eyes.

In what year is this scene taking place? During one of the first summers of the Restoration.

Suddenly large drops of rain splash on the sanded path. The sky is black and the young woman sighs as she looks at her pretty muslin dress, which, according to descriptions of the fashion, must have been adorned with gathers, festoons and garlands. The lovers take refuge under a tree, but a few moments later the pouring rain comes through the leaves. The young woman could weep! A gentleman carrying a superb umbrella comes forward and offers it.

"But on one condition: to give the little lady my arm!"

There can be no hesitation and they set out boldly for the Rue du Faubourg-Saint-Honoré, where the little lady says she lives. Her original escort follows behind in the pouring rain.

When the trio arrives in front of the Elysée gateway the drums beat and the guard presents arms. Without doubt Monseigneur the Duc de Berry or Marie-Caroline of Naples, his wife, is about to come out. But no one comes, no equipage is waiting in the courtyard. The young woman bursts out laughing. Appalled, the man with the umbrella realizes that it is the Duchesse de Berry, Marie-Caroline, on his arm and that the dripping gentleman covered with mud who is following them is the King's nephew! The good man would like to flee, but still laughing the little duchess invites him to dinner the next day and the prince joins in his wife's invitation.

They had been married since June, 1816, and the duke was very much in love with his little scrap of a wife. But he had not given up his bachelor existence for her sake. He was of the opinion that he resembled Henri IV, from whom his family was directly descended, and his adventures were numerous. These adventures left visible traces. Marie-Caroline shut her eyes and appeared proud to be the wife of a Don Juan. It is related that in 1820 the Duchesse was visited by twenty women from Nantes all proclaiming themselves to be with child by the Duc de Berry. At first Marie-Caroline showed some incredulity.

"How long was monseigneur at Nantes?"

"A week, madame."

Marie-Caroline was thoughtful for a moment, then exclaimed: "Ah! in that case it's very possible!"

Louis XVIII took his nephew's love life more seriously. "If one marries at thirty-eight and does not settle down, it proves that one looks on one's wife merely as another mistress."

The King was right. This was exactly how her husband considered the charming Marie-Caroline. She pleased him, and he was able to write to his friend Roger de Damas, taking the Duc de Richelieu's saying to himself: "I would like to announce that the duchess is pregnant, but I cannot say, unless it be from last night or this morning." He was conquered by the urchin side of this Neapolitan, of whom it was said: "She is half Vesuvius, half schoolroom." She took her husband out into the streets of Paris and amused him with a hundred childish tricks. They went into shops. It was so funny not to be recognized, to haggle—and to be "called back." This was a curious custom then in vogue in Paris shops. The lady who had unsuccessfully made her offer went away, but was efficiently followed by a *grisette,* so called because in the eighteenth century she used to wear a gray cloak. The *grisette* would follow the reluctant shopper, but when she approached another shop the saleswoman would stop her and bring her back, willy-nilly, to the first shop, where the bargain was then made.

The Duchesse de Berry was particularly fond of the little side shows of the boulevard or the Palais Royal. Skipping along on her husband's arm, she would go into ecstasies before the dwarf of the Rue des Petits-Champs, who was twenty-seven inches tall, before the famous Mustapha, who hopped about on one foot while swallowing pebbles, before M. Conte, who, being of a nobler disposition, preferred swords to gravel and swallowed them up to the hilt. Swords paid, and soon Conte was able to have his own theatre, to which the Duc de Berry and his wife would go. But at that time only certain theatres were authorized to put on plays. In order to protect the "privileged establishments" all kinds of difficulties were put in the way and, in spite of the duchess's protection, Conte could get permission to present his "tableau plays" only on condition "that a gauze curtain would separate the actors from the public."

However, the Duc de Berry would not allow his wife to go wandering about alone, as she wanted to do. It was then dangerous to walk in the streets of Paris, which swarmed with "prickers." These had started in 1818, and according to a communiqué from the police prefecture got "a cruel pleasure from pricking from behind, either with an awl or with a needle fixed to a stick, young persons from fifteen to twenty years old." Many more mature women claimed to have been pricked, Henri d'Almeras relates. "To be pricked, even from behind, was for some women a homage, somewhat brutal perhaps, but having some value. Everyone could not obtain it!" This formed the subject of many conversations. Marie-Caroline must certainly have laughed when she learned that "in order to discover the perpetrators of this new crime, as a policeman of the time called the prickers, it was decided to take from various bawdy houses twenty prostitutes, who, having been well filled up with red wine, would brave the pricks and prickers and walk boldly through the streets. Police would follow them 'as scouts.' " But these piquant walks were without effect and a chemist of the Ile Saint-Louis began to sell an ointment for pricks, while an armorer invented a rear cuirasse in light steel. The affair was made topical. Songs were sung of the pretty little pricker—Cupid—"who gave women pricks that did not seem too disagreeable."

The Duchesse de Berry was later to be very excited by the new omnibuses, the great innovation of the age. One day she made a wager of ten thousand francs that she would travel alone in the "Madeleine-Bastille." She won her bet, and the coaches on that line were henceforth called "Carolines." There was an idea of putting into service, on the Vincennes-Neuilly line, a "colossus omnibus" thirteen feet wide and thirty-one feet long. It would have two decks surmounted by a bridge like a ship's. The engine, which never got beyond the drawings, was to be worked by four horses walking inside on a slope.

The companies had stuck enormous posters all over the capital in order to explain the workings of these public vehicles. "These coaches, whose number is shortly to be raised to one hundred in Paris, give warning of their passing by a newly-invented arrangement of trumpets. They are so organized that they will stop at the least sign made to the coachman or conductor. The door, situated at the rear, can afford no danger to persons entering or alighting."

Where did the Parisians take their walks under the Restoration? The Palais Royal had lost its former great popularity, but was far from attaining its present state of desertion. During the morning the light women who had "slept" in town would go that way before returning home, to drink a bottle of red-currant syrup, which they invariably paid for out of a five-franc piece, their night's earnings. During the afternoon the respectable women appeared. They would visit the lace sellers. A little later would arrive the "mustached young men," clerks or soldiers who had made appointments to meet their sweethearts. Finally, the sun set and the Palais Royal relived the days of its former glory. A crowd of "nymphs" invaded the garden. There were several hundred of them and they were divided into three classes: the "half-beavers," who walked up and down the little garden paths; the "beavers," who hardly ever left the galleries; and the "first-class beavers," whose stamping ground was the terrace over the cellars.

At the bottom of the garden shouts were heard from the Café Montansier. This was the meeting place of the "half-pays," former imperial officers retired by the Restoration. They received seventy-three francs a month for captains and forty-four francs for lieutenants. They listened with delight to the singer who demanded:

> Think you a Bourbon can be
> King of a great nation?

It was the custom to yell: "No, no, no, no, no, no, no!"
One evening an officer leaped onto the platform and sang:

> A fig for the King,
> For his brother the same.
> A fig for his nephews,
> Berry and Angoulême.
> A fig for the Duchess of Berry
> And for all who admire their name.

Only Madame Royale was left out!

It was impossible not to recognize the half-pays. Brandishing their canes as though they were sabers, they all wore long blue overcoats buttoned up to the chin and brought in at the waist, which resembled the coat of a uniform.

The aim of their life was to provoke the bodyguards into taking part in conspiracies that were mostly stillborn, to join secret societies—the "Black Pin" or "Bonaparte's Vultures"—to carry canes with Napoleon's picture on the knob, to wear tricolor braces, and to drink ostentatiously the "liqueur of the brave" or the "tears of General Foy."

The half-pays also walked in the Avenue des Champs-Elysées and the Tuileries, but were hardly ever seen at Longchamp, which had again become fashionable on Fridays. Idlers would come to watch the long line of coaches from the Marais, cabs, "cuckoos," landaus, *"demi-fortunes,"* barouches, not forgetting the dandies who rode on horseback carrying little canes, for, as a contemporary said, the fashion "forbade whips."

The Parisians also liked going to the new Tivoli, an entertainment Park which was to disappear in 1828. (The Casino de Paris, the Apollo and the Théâtre de Paris were erected on part of the site.) In that year it was showing an amazing "Incombustible Spaniard" whom all Paris flocked to see. Wrapped in a vast woolen cloak and wearing a kind of felt sombrero, he was shut up in an oven next to a chicken cooking there. When the chicken was cooked, he ate it, drank a bottle of wine, and hurried into a cold bath.

The Luxembourg gardens obtained a certain success as a result of the *draisiennes* that were presented to the Parisians on April 5, 1818, in the presence of Baron de Drais, an engineer from Karlsruhe and son of a councilor at the court of the Grand Duchy of Baden, who had had the idea of perfecting the French invention of the *célérifère,* straddled by the *Incroyables* of the Directory. M. de Drais's chief success was in having rendered mobile the front part of the wooden steed, which had formerly looked very like a horse on a merry-go-round. On the eve of its presentation the name of the *draisienne* was changed to velocipede. Let us hear a contemporary reporter's account of the first excursion. "With the help of this machine M. de Drais's footman should have covered 300 *toises* [about 650 yards] in three minutes, and yet the children always kept up with him without difficulty. This machine could never be of any real use. It could only be used in the well-kept paths of a park. The narrowest ditch, the smallest rut would force its rider to dismount and to lift his machine over the obstacles. At best the velocipede would serve as a plaything for children in the garden. But if the expectation of the numerous spectators was not fulfilled, the curious were recompensed by the presence of the prettiest women in Paris wearing their most brilliant clothes."

The day was marked by an accident, however. "An amateur, wishing to try one of the two 'toys' that had been in use until then, had a fall which greatly amused the spectators. One of the screws having fallen off, it was no longer possible to make the machine go. It was no more than a stick with a wheel."

But the French builder of "sticks with wheels," M. Garcin, persisted, and in the following month the *Petite Chronique de Paris* announced the new experiment as follows: "Decidedly the importer of velocipedes does not wish the whole affair to 'end in a song,' and a large poster on the walls of Paris informs us that a new kind of course will take place at Monceau, near the barrier. There one will be able to hire by the half hour one of these wooden steeds with two wheels. As a very necessary precaution riding lessons will be given before the experiments take place. We shall see whether this resumption of the conspiracy against horses and donkeys will have more success than the show in the Luxembourg."

The "conspiracy" succeeded. To the great astonishment of the *Petite Chronique de Paris* the "childishness" caught on, and its results are well known.

On the feast of St. Louis, 1818, the Parisians were given a free spectacle: the inauguration of the new statue of Henri IV erected on the Pont-Neuf, in the presence of King Louis XVIII, the Duc and Duchesse de Berry and all the members of the royal family.

Twenty pair of oxen had drawn the monument from the foundry in Roule to the Marigny crossroads. There they had halted, exhausted. Several hundred royalists had taken their place and managed to drag the great mass to the Pavillon de Flore. Two days later seventy horses of the marines were needed to bring the *Vert-Galant* to his final resting place. The statue had been cast in metal from the recently overthrown effigies of Napoleon, including that of the Vendôme column, which had itself been made with the bronze of an Austrian cannon taken at Austerlitz. Everyone knew this, and there were some smiles on the day of the inauguration, but it was not known that the sculptor Quesnel, who, after the casting, had to rectify any defects in the equestrian statue, was an ardent Bonapartist. In despair at seeing his Emperor transformed into a King, he had, as a reprisal, inserted a little statue of Napoleon into Henri IV's right arm and had stuffed the belly of the horse with songs and pamphlets against the Bourbons. Then he had placed an account of the whole operation in the head of the *Vert-Galant*.

All this arsenal, hostile to the new dynasty, which had raised the monument to its own glory, must still be there.

5

The Knife

On February 12, 1820, the Duchesse de Berry was completely engrossed in preparations for the masked ball to be given that evening by Comtesse Greffulhe. It was perhaps the last time she would go to a dance before her lying-in. Deneux, her *accoucheur,* would insist on her foregoing further parties, and he meant what he said. He was the author of a work on "the nipples and artificial teats," and his decisions were final. And so Marie-Caroline wanted to appear dazzling that evening. She had decided to go as a "queen of the Middle Ages," a fashionable period. She wore a dress of cherry-colored velvet trimmed with ermine and with wide, slashed sleeves. The dressmaker had pronounced it "suitable for dancing." A red velvet hat set off the sheen of her gold hair.

At ten o'clock the Duc and Duchesse de Berry arrived at Comtesse Greffulhe's. One of the guests, the Duc de Fitz-James, had chosen the costume being worn by the actor Potier at the Porte Saint-Martin in a parody of the opera *Les Danaïdes.* In the opera, the actor, having distributed to his daughters knives known as *eustaches,* added: "Run along, my lambs!"

And that evening Fitz-James was distributing daggers to all the ladies. "My lamb," he said to the duchess, giving her an *eustache,* "what place in the heart should one strike?" A little later on Marie-Caroline, returning to her coach with her husband, was still laughing. She was holding the knife Fitz-James had given her in her little red-gloved hand and looked at it, repeating: "What place in the heart should one strike?"

On the evening of February 13 there was a thick fog over Paris. It was damp and cold, about 40° Fahrenheit. Eight o'clock was about to strike. A man with light chestnut hair and blue eyes, small, a little over forty and respectably dressed, was watching at the corner of the Rue de Richelieu and the Rue Rameau, where, in 1820, the Opéra stood. At this spot today is the tiny green island of the Square Louvois.

Facing the house bearing the number 7, which still stands, an iron porch painted to imitate striped canvas jutted out over the street. It was the private entrance to the royal box. The man came closer.

A sentry was standing in his box. On the threshold the concierge of the theatre, a man called Bouchon, also paced up and down and waited. The Duc and Duchesse de Berry might arrive unannounced. Admittedly the performance, consisting of three pieces, the *Carnaval de Venise, Le Rossignol* and *Les Noces de Gamache,* had already begun, but the prince and princess could not easily get away from the Tuileries before eight. Charles and Caroline had already seen *Les Noces de Gamache* a few days before, but Virginie Oreille, one of Charles de Berry's mistresses, was to dance in the ballet and the duke might well come that evening.

Suddenly the rumble of several carriages was heard in the Rue de Richelieu. Soon an outrider in the Artois livery turned into the Rue Rameau. Bouchon cried, "Present arms!" and in the little vestibule the guard bustled about, took their rifles from the rack and hastily fell in. The Duc de Berry's equipage came from the Rue de Richelieu, turned left and halted between the gray-painted posts flanking the porch.

The waiting man came forward gripping a dagger that he concealed in his large coat pocket. The valet put down the steps and opened the carriage door. The prince got out and helped his wife.

The man was two paces away. No one paid any attention to him. He could have struck but "his courage failed him." Charles and Marie-Caroline had gone by. Mme. de Béthisy, Comte de Mesnard, Comte de Clermont-Lodève had got out of other carriages. Before entering the theatre, Mesnard turned round and ordered the equipages to come back at a quarter to eleven. The order was immediately transmitted from mouth to mouth until the last carriage at the corner of the Rue de Richelieu. "Quarter to eleven . . . quarter to eleven."

The man had heard. Reproaching himself for his lack of daring, "solitary as always," he plunged into the fog, in the direction of the Palais Royal. He intended to go to bed. A saddler, attached to the royal stables, he lived a short way off, in the Place du Carrousel. Beneath the arcades of the Palais Royal a whole "crowd of thoughts" pressed upon him. It was not the first time that at the last moment, his hand gripping the handle of his dagger, he had not dared to strike.

He had formed his scheme six years before. It was in 1814 and he was then at Metz. Napoleon was beaten and the royalists were cutting up sheets to make white cockades. The enemy was occupying Nancy and it was said in Metz that in the Place Stanislas the white flag had replaced the tricolor. Lost among the English, Russian, Austrian and Swedish uniforms, the Comte d'Artois strutted about surrounded by his band of scatterbrains. And meanwhile the banished Emperor had to leave France! All his former servants were rallying to the Bourbons. The man had wept for it. He could still hear the saddler Henry, with whom he worked, saying: "When one is on a man's side, even if he is a brigand, one should never abandon him."

The country was invaded. The Emperor reigned over his cabbage patch of Portoferraio. In the man's eyes the Bourbons were the greatest enemies of France, the Bourbons who were living in the Tuileries among Napoleon's furniture. He had sworn to exterminate them and dogged the Duc de Berry "because it was the only way to exterminate the race." The race . . . he spoke of it as of rats that had invaded a ship.

One day in April, 1814—he often thought of that day—he had gone on foot to Fontainebleau, where the Old Guard (what sacrilege!) were giving an entertainment for the Duc de Berry. The people's joy had made him think. "Could it be I who am wrong?"

The man had then left for the Island of Elba. "More to distract my mind from my schemes than to become settled in them." But his ideas "pursued him." Employed in the Emperor's modest stables, he did not stay long at Portoferraio. He returned to Paris, still haunted by the idea of his crime.

The Hundred Days brought him peace. But his schemes harassed him again when, after the Emperor's embarkation at Rochefort, he was at La Rochelle with the banished man's equipages. There he bought his dagger, a saddler's awl. On his return to Paris he obtained a small post in the royal stables.

Since then he had lived in a nightmare. For five years, while the Emperor was dying on his rock, he was accompanied by the haunting shadow of murder.

"I followed the Duc de Berry into the churches he went to, I went to the hunts. . . . I always accompanied him on foot. I went to

Fontainebleau in 1816 on the arrival of the Duchesse de Berry. . . . I tried to find opportunities."

He "tried to find opportunities." Nearly every evening during the last four years he had prowled in this way about the theatres to which he imagined the prince might go. The man lived alone, shunning everyone who came near him.

"With my plans I could not form any friendship."

Supposing he should compromise someone? He owed it to himself to conspire alone. When he went home in the evening he barely thanked the man who gave him his candle, fearing that he might be obliged to exchange a few words with the people of the house. He was soon nicknamed "the bear."

On arriving at the farther end of the Palais Royal, the man stopped. Should he go to bed? Should he return to the Opéra at a quarter to eleven? "I imagine that I should have fewer opportunities in future, for I had been notified that from the first of the following month I was to go to work at Versailles. There was a new 'revolution' within me. Am I wrong? Am I right? I said to myself. If I am right, why do I lack courage? If I am wrong, why do my ideas not leave me?"

Suddenly he made up his mind. It would be tonight! He made the journey between the Opéra and the Palais Royal several times. At twenty minutes to eleven, as he turned the corner of the Rue de Richelieu he caught a glimpse through the thick fog of the carriages that had just arrived. A cabriolet was there in the Rue Rameau, between the door of the theatre and the corner of the street. The man stood by the horse's head; he would be taken for a servant in charge of the carriage. The three-quarters struck. The outrider mounted his horse. The man's blue eyes did not leave the door at which the duke was to appear.

A few weeks before he had watched in this fashion for a whole day in the forest of Fontainebleau. But the prince passed at a distance. He had come back on foot, cursing his ill luck, dragging his leg. Suddenly a carriage stopped by him. He recognized Charles's equipage.

Through the door the duke had asked: "Are you tired? Get up behind."

Berry had then inquired who that man was. "He is employed in the King's stables," the outrider had explained. "His name is Jean-Pierre Louvel."

The first act of *Les Noces de Gamache* had just begun. The duchess, shielded from the heat of the footlights by three little blue taffeta screens, was yawning. She had danced so much the night before.

"You are tired, Caroline," said Charles. "Would you like me to take you down?"

"No, I want to see the ballet."

This, perhaps, was what the duke did not want. If he had been alone he could have made a sign to Virginie, who would have come afterward to join him in the little anteroom to the box.

The second act was over. Faced with another yawn, Berry turned to the Comte de Clermont-Lodève.

"What time is it?"

"Nearly eleven, monseigneur."

The prince rose.

"Come now, Caroline, be sensible! I shall accompany you to your carriage."

With a sigh the little duchess left her armchair of blue Utrecht velvet.

In the Rue Rameau, seeing the arrival of Comte de Choiseul, who preceded the Duc de Berry, the footmen hurried forward. The duchess, having her husband on her right and Comte de Mesnard on her left, appeared under the porch. The sentry, with his back to the Rue de Richelieu, presented arms. To the right of the royal guard stood Choiseul. Clermont-Lodève remained on the threshold. Marie-Caroline entered her carriage. The lady-in-waiting sat on the princess's left. The steps were put up. A footman spread a fur rug over the two women's legs.

"Good-bye, Caroline!" the duke called. "We shall see each other again shortly."

Charles, without coat or hat, could not remain forever in the open street on that damp, cold night. He turned back to enter the theatre. At the moment when Comte de Choiseul stepped forward to precede the prince Louvel darted like an arrow between the sentry and the carriage and literally fell on the duke.

"There's a clumsy lout!" exclaimed Charles.

"Mind what you're doing!" cried the Marquis de Choiseul, pulling at Louvel's coat. But the man ran away into the Rue de Richelieu.

At that moment the Duc de Berry uttered a cry: "I've been assassinated! That man has killed me!"

"What, monseigneur, are you wounded?" asked Mesnard, whose mind was far from being alert.

"I am dead. . . . I am dead. . . . I am holding the dagger!"

Clermont-Lodève, Choiseul, the footman and the sentry were already running after the assassin. Berry staggered, supported by Mesnard. Marie-Caroline wanted to jump out of the carriage, whose steps were not let down. Mme. de Béthisy tried to stop her.

"I order you to let me go!"

"Come, my Caroline," said the prince. "Let me die in your arms."

The princess pushed her lady-in-waiting aside, jumped and fell by the side of her husband, who was leaning against a post. He had just pulled out the dagger. It was a terribly sharp blade with a crude wooden handle.

The duchess and Mme. de Béthisy, whose dresses were already stained with blood, supported the wounded man, who walked painfully to the little vestibule where there was a red bench for the soldiers on guard. In order to find the wound Mesnard began to unbutton the green coat and yellow waistcoat of his master. The blood gushed out.

"I am dead," Charles panted. "A priest, quickly!"

At dawn Charles de Berry breathed his last. But Louvel's crime appeared to have been in vain. Seven and a half months later, on the morning of September 29, 1820, the cannon began to fire: twelve shots for a princess, one hundred for a prince. There was an interval of seven or eight seconds before the thirteenth shot. All Paris was holding its breath.

> As the bronze bell thunders
> France is roused—and wonders.

The thirteenth shot touched off an immense shout of joy. The Duc de Bordeaux was born.

> Born of a tardy oracle and a final sigh.

The joy was both great and sincere. Reading contemporary accounts one must believe that even those in opposition, disarmed by this miraculous birth, had been won over to the general rejoicing. The whole town danced, sang and embraced. That evening 200,000 bottles of Bordeaux were drunk in honor of the heir to the throne. Fashion even invented a new color: *caca Bordeaux*. Every elegant man had to wear a coat of this color if he did not want to be dishonored.

And it was sung:

> We feared that a girl
> Would make our hopes fall.
> But a good chap arrived
> Who was shown to us all!

The "good chap" was not to reign. He left for exile in 1830 under the name of Henri V and did not return to Paris until July 2, 1871, under the name of Comte de Chambord. A cab set him down at the palace where he was born. The last of the elder branch of Bourbons looked at the long façade blackened by the flames, and heavy tears filled his eyes.

Not wishing to abandon the flag with which France had been built, the flag his dying grandfather had given him and which had waved at Marignan and Fontenoy, he could only return to exile. Had he been brought up, not by Madame Royale, but by his parents, the Duc de Bordeaux might have stretched out his hand to tricolor France, might perhaps have understood that the three colors had ceased to be the symbol of the Revolution and had become the symbol of order.

The dagger that, one carnival evening, Louvel had plunged into the Duc de Berry's breast had indeed "destroyed the race." There was nothing left for "King" Henri V but to die and be buried in the folds of a white flag that had become the winding sheet of Royalty.

6
Dubourg and the Three Glorious Days

It was eleven o'clock on the morning of Thursday, July 29, 1830. The last day of the "Three Golden Days" had begun. The Parisians were preparing respectfully to turn out the old king, Charles X, for senility of thoughts, tastes and feelings.

In the Place de la Bourse, combatants uttered a yell of triumph as they saw coming out of the palace a man of about fifty, wearing a blue frock coat.

"Long live General Dubourg! To the Hôtel de Ville! To the Hôtel de Ville!"

Those present did not know who this general in a blue frock coat was. And yet he had fought heroically in the Vendéan, republican, imperial and royalist armies. But for the Parisians General Dubourg was making his entry into history on that Thursday, at eleven in the morning, in the Place de la Bourse. They asked no more of him. They possessed a general—without a uniform, it is true, but what did that matter? With him they could occupy the Hôtel de Ville and form "a government." And they set off.

Suddenly the man in the blue frock coat managed to escape from his admirers. When he returned he was wearing a general's uniform, unfortunately without epaulettes. But an actor called Perlet, who happened to be there, fetched him a pair from the wardrobe of the Opéra-Comique. General Dubourg being now presentable, the procession continued on its way to the Hôtel de Ville.

Nothing is known of how General Dubourg spent his time during the three days preceding his entry into history, but without doubt, like all Parisians then, when he opened the *Moniteur* on July 26 he must have been a prey to anxiety or fury—according to his opinions. The newspaper contained the text of royal decrees suppressing the liberty of the press, dismissing the Chamber, modifying the electoral law and summoning the electors to vote the following month. By these decrees Charles X wanted to "punish" the electors who, at the beginning of July, had sent 274 opposition deputies to the Chamber against only

143 representatives of the governmental party. The president of the Council, Prince de Polignac—the most insignificant minister France ever had—was quite sure that the decrees would save the monarchy. The Virgin had appeared to him, he declared, and encouraged him to proceed in this way.

"Given such high patronage," exclaimed the King, "it would be criminal to hesitate!"

Polignac declared, moreover, that Paris would not react and that it would be unnecessary to take any military precautions. The Secretary of State for War had not even been informed.

"He will be very surprised when he reads the *Moniteur*," the Duc d'Angoulême—the Dauphin—had remarked, rubbing his hands as though it were a good joke.

The reactions of the Secretary of State on reading the paper on the morning of July 26 are not known, but those of Thiers are. He immediately summoned forty-three journalists to the offices of the *National* and made them sign a text which smelled of powder: "The legal regime has been interrupted and that of force has begun. . . . Obedience ceases to be a duty!" Paris at once became stormy. People began to assemble everywhere. Stones were thrown at the lilies on the façades of public monuments.

Charles X, who was at the Château of Saint-Cloud, had sent for Marmont on the morning of July 27 and said to him: "It seems that there is some anxiety concerning the tranquillity of Paris. Go there and take command. If everything is in order this evening you can return to Saint-Cloud."

The Duc de Raguse had obeyed. During the afternoon three battalions of guards occupied the Carrousel and the Palais Royal, two more were installed in the Place Louis-XV, and a sixth encamped in the Boulevard des Capucines. But at every crossroad the insurrection was lurking. According to an eyewitness, Paris was like the bridge of a ship about to go into action. "Innumerable patrols of the 5th Regiment of the line were scouring the town, trying to disperse the gatherings that re-formed the moment they had passed. The Parisians grew bolder. From the top stories chunks of wood, flower pots and old saucepans began to rain on the heads of the troops. In the streets boys threw stones. Soon the soldiers opened fire in the Rue des Pyramides and the Rue Saint-Honoré opposite the Café de la Régence. Around five o'clock a baker's workman, bare-chested, was seen carrying on his shoulders the body of a woman who had just been killed. He advanced toward a company of the 5th regiment of the line and, swinging the bloodstained body, threw it at the heads of the soldiers, yelling: 'This is what your comrades do to our women! Will you do the same?' "

In the evening two companies of the 5th went over to the side of the revolt. The first tricolor cockades appeared.

Wednesday, July 28, dawned on a Paris that had decided to fight it out. Barricades were being erected everywhere. Crowns and fleurs-de-lis were torn off the shops. The trees in the boulevards were cut down and the ground strewn with bottles, to stop the cavalry passing.

The shopkeepers of the Palais Royal felt that the affair would be decisive when they saw the celebrity of the arcades, "the man with the long beard," take up his usual station, but dressed in an almost elegant way. This person usually wore shoes kept on by string and a frock coat "in which everything that was not a stain was a hole." His name was Chodruc-Duclos and he had ruined himself for the royalist cause during the Revolution and under the Consulate. In 1815 the Bourbons had shown him such ingratitude that Chodruc had decided to be a living reproach to them, which was why he displayed his sordid poverty two steps away from the Tuileries. On the morning of July 28 he watched the rioting turn into a revolution. Not far from him battle was joined with the Swiss Guards. "Seeing a group of young people armed with rifles, which they were using badly," a witness relates, "Chodruc went up to them and asked for a weapon so that he might show them how to shoot. He took aim and pulled the trigger. A Swiss Guard fell. He gave back the rifle. The man who had lent the weapon urged him to keep it, since he knew so well how to use it."

"Thank you," replied Chodruc, "but that is not my opinion."

And he continued to observe the combat as a spectator only.

Marmont had divided his troops into several columns and tried to keep a passage clear in the main highways. The Hôtel de Ville was the scene of violent fighting. The royal cannon swept the Pont de Grève. Massed in the Ile de la Cité, the Parisians hesitated. A lad of fourteen—apprentice to a locksmith—leaped forward carrying a flag.

"I shall show you how one should die. Remember that my name is Arcole!"

Before he had reached the middle of the bridge he fell, his hand still clutching the flag. That is why, since July 28, 1830, the former Pont de Grève has been called the Pont d'Arcole. Paris owed that much to the little locksmith's apprentice.

At the end of the day Marmont's situation was desperate. If the King would withdraw his decrees blood might perhaps cease to flow.

"I shall think about it," Charles X, still at Saint-Cloud, had replied. "But I consider it very bold to bring me such suggestions."

Having thought, he added with a "gracious" gesture: "Let the insurgents lay down their arms. They know my goodness well enough to be sure of a most generous pardon."

Charles X then began playing whist, not lifting his eyes from the cards and seeming not to hear the rumbling of the cannon. Through the windows of the Salon de la Vérité, as night fell, the smoke of the musket fire could even be seen rising in clouds above the houses. From the second floor, with the aid of a telescope, Mme. de Gontaut could see furniture, even pianos, being thrown out of windows in the Rue de Rivoli on top of the troops crowding the pavements. That evening Charles X was all the more sure of victory since he had just sent Marmont a note telling him to "assemble his troops and hold fast" and "await his orders tomorrow."

"Tomorrow" was to be July 29.

At the very time when General Dubourg arrived in the Place de l'Hôtel-de-Ville, the royal troops, having abandoned the Louvre and the Tuileries, were retreating in disorder and passing through the Rue de Rivoli under M. de Talleyrand's windows. The prince was engaged in dictating his memoirs. He broke off, looked at the scene and turned to his secretary.

"Put in a note that on July 29, 1830, at five minutes past noon, the elder branch of the Bourbons ceased to reign over France."

On entering the Hôtel de Ville, General Dubourg was greeted by the "government," which had been installed there for an hour: a journalist from the *Temps,* called Baude, and his "chief of staff," with no staff and no uniform, Colonel Zimmer.

"What do you want?" Baude asked the general.

"A chamber pot and a piece of bread," Dubourg replied.

Relieved and fed, he agreed to sign all the proclamations presented to him by Baude and Zimmer, who were delighted to possess a uniformed general. Dubourg's "reign" continued until the evening. When General Lafayette appeared he was obliged to give way to him and yield to seniority. His name can be seen in the "List of persons who distinguished themselves during the memorable days," between a "Dubourg, doctor" and a "Dubourg, shoemaker."

However, this official commendation cannot have been very lucrative, for in the following year he was found offering Charles X, for a consideration, his services and those of his "friends."

At Saint-Cloud, after the arrival of his routed army, the King asked the Duc de Mortemart to accept the post of First Minister and to try, by himself, to raise the barricades and get the Parisians back into their homes and the King into the Tuileries. The duke refused this herculean task and Charles X tried to press the nomination into his hand. "I recoiled several times, so much so that I backed into the tapestry," Mortemart told Alexandre Mazas. "The King kept on following me. Seeing me literally with my back to the wall and with my arms pressed against my sides, he stuck the paper into the belt of my officer's uniform. I took it out hastily to give it back."

"You refuse, sir, to save my crown and the lives of my ministers?"

Mortemart finally gave in. In the whole course of history no president of the Council can have been invested by the head of the state in such a way.

That evening the King's game of whist was dull. Everyone was obviously thinking of something else.

During the night the King's sleep was interrupted by several visits from M. de Mortemart, who, backed by Vitrolles, submitted to him the text of six new decrees. Wakened with a start each time, Charles X must certainly have regretted M. de Polignac, who never disturbed him, even when the Virgin came to chat with him in the middle of the night. Being in a bad temper, the King resisted all the more strongly his new minister's democratic schemes.

"The repeal of the decrees?" protested the former Comte d'Artois, furiously shaking his head in its cotton nightcap. "We haven't come to that! It's too much!"

Vitrolles, who was tireless, explained at length to the King that they had come to more than that. Mortemart was less resistant; he left these interviews absolutely exhausted and voiceless.

"I have no saliva left," he confided in hoarse tones to Mazas, who was waiting for him in his room.

Finally, at seven o'clock in the morning, the duke and Vitrolles gained their point. The King, still in bed, signed the new texts.

Yet Mortemart could not make up his mind to leave for Paris. "He dawdled," Vitrolles wrote, "like a man not eager to face difficulties he dreads. He came and went, stood before a cheese on a table. . . ." Finally, urged on by the baron, Mortemart entered a barouche with M. d'Argout, Langsdorff and Mazas, who had placed the texts of the new decrees in the pocket of his coat fastened with a pin. Such was the new team's ministerial portfolio.

The King was never to hear of it again.

In Paris, after a day spent in attempting the impossible, Mortemart summoned Mazas to the Luxembourg palace.

"You will inform His Majesty," he said, "that the royal decrees have been violently rejected at the Hôtel de Ville. The meeting, which is in permanent session there, has pronounced the King's deposition."

Yet Mortemart still had "some hopes" of treating with the Chamber of Peers and with a section of the Chamber which had not the slightest wish to accept Lafayette as President of the Republic.

"For my negotiations to be successful," Mortemart said, "the King must not budge from Saint-Cloud and must make all arrangements to defend himself there to the last, for he will be attacked tomorrow morning."

And Mazas left for Saint-Cloud, having placed in the knot of his cravat a scrap of newspaper on which the First Minister had written these words: "Every confidence in the bearer."

Held up in his journey by the heaps of paving stones and the barricades, Mazas had only reached Point-du-Jour at half past three in the morning. There he learned that the King, fearing an attack by the Parisians, had fled to Rambouillet.

On July 31 the curtain raiser to the future regime was played: Louis-Philippe, preceded by an urchin beating a broken drum, left the Palais Royal to embrace Lafayette at the Hôtel de Ville. Behind the man who in a few days would be the "bourgeois King," among a group of eighty deputies "in traveling dress," came two lame men:

Benjamin Constant, borne in an armchair, and Laffitte, sitting on a chair supported by two water carriers. There were cries of: "No more Bourbons!" So on all the walls posters were displayed, explaining that the Duc d'Orléans "was a Valois." This, in fact, was the title he had borne at birth. The scene is well known. At the beginning Orléans wanted to defend Charles X, and then gradually let himself be persuaded. Then came the final tableau: Lafayette and the future King embracing beneath the folds of a tricolor flag. Lafayette's "republican kiss," after the enthronement by Laffitte, had made a king.

But at Rambouillet Charles X refused to go into exile. He thought he could save the situation by himself nominating the Duc d'Orléans lieutenant-general of the kingdom. His councilors were dumbfounded.

"The rebels have nominated M. le Duc d'Orléans lieutenant-general of the kingdom," the King explained. "It may be that by nominating him myself I may make an appeal to his honor to which he may not be entirely insensible."

While the King lived out the day in hope, in Paris the lieutenant-general re-established the tricolor cockade, nominated provisional ministers and refused the royal appointment. He wished to receive his powers only from the Chamber. On the following morning, Monday, August 2, he summoned to the Palais Royal M. Tutpinier, appointed baron and Director of Ports by Charles X. Having promoted him to the rank of Director of the Department of the Marine, the lieutenant-general ordered him "to take steps to arm and direct to Cherbourg vessels suitably equipped to receive King Charles X, in order to transport him to England." It can be seen that the future King had not waited for Charles X's abdication to make arrangements for his predecessor's flight, even indicating the port of embarkation.

Lafayette, even more expeditious, sent out a call to arms, and thousands of Parisians—it is impossible to establish the exact number —piled into cabs, omnibuses and "cuckoos," and set off for Rambouillet. Five commissioners, sent by Louis-Philippe, preceded them and their task was to scare the King.

"We are followed by 100,000 men," one of them announced to Charles X.

Not without reason the King refused to believe him, and turned to Marshal Maison, who was one of the delegation.

"Marshal, in the name of honor and on your word as a soldier I summon you to tell the truth. Is it correct, as has been suggested, that the whole population of Paris is arriving spontaneously and in disorder?"

"At these words, and without hesitation—I saw it since I was looking straight at him," Mme. de Contaut relates—"Marshal Maison replied: 'I swear it, sire! They have told only half the truth!'

"The King bowed. 'I trust the honor and word of a soldier and I consent to leave.'

"The orders for departure and retreat were immediately given and carried out between half past nine and ten o'clock, with a speed that was almost miraculous."

The phantom of the great Revolution was in everyone's minds. Madame Royale, who had lived through October 6, seemed to see reappear the dreaded specter of Paris in revolt. She threw herself into her carriage with the air of one distraught. The Dauphin, who was sulking and declared "that the only thing he wanted to be bothered with was his dogs," mounted his horse. The King, leaning on the sub-prefect's arm, walked to his berlin. He had aged by ten years.

In the park, and at the advance posts toward Coigniéres, the boot-and-saddle was sounded. The royal army, still 12,832 strong, also fled. "It must be said," the bodyguard Théodore Anne admitted, "that our retreat bore somewhat the appearance of beaten and fleeing troops. Infantry, cavalry, artillery, all went by at the same time."

The enormous crowd of fugitives disappeared through the Guéville gate on the road to Maintenon. An hour later the vanguard of the Parisian army arrived: one general and two pupils from the Military Academy. The general, too, announced the arrival of eighty thousand Parisians and demanded thirty thousand bread rations, a figure he soon reduced to fifteen thousand. And in fact, during the course of the night, detachments arrived. When day came the "Paris column" was counted. It consisted of one thousand men. The remainder—if there were a remainder—had retreated. The "victors" piled into the court carriages still at Rambouillet—thirty and forty to a carriage—and went back to Paris, singing and waving tricolor flags, leaving the mayor with fifteen thousand bread rations that he had had baked for the "army of Parisians."

Now Paris thought of nothing but its dead, and the bodies of the "heroic combatants" were buried in the garden of the Louvre, at the foot of Perrault's colonnade, until a worthier tomb could be given them. When in 1840 the column in the Place de la Bastille was finished—a bronze shaft divided into three, as a symbol of the three glorious days—and when a prancing figure had been placed on its summit, representing "Freedom bursting its chains," a journey was made to the Louvre garden to disinter the heroes of July. It was discovered that their bones were unfortunately mingled with the remains of the mummies brought back from Egypt by Bonaparte which, under the Empire, had been hastily buried in the same spot, having been voraciously attacked by moths. No close examination was made and "the whole" was carried in great pomp to the column.

That is why there is today, buried in the Place de la Bastille, a whole series of Rameses and Egyptian queens who certainly never imagined that they would sleep their last sleep fraternally mingled with Parisian revolutionaries.

7
The Noble Faubourg

M. Jules Bertaut has very clearly shown to what extent the Faubourg Saint-Germain, that district "limited in extent but of capital importance," was for half a century "like an organic being, a sort of individual, having its own letters of nobility, education, customs, prejudices, loves and hates," in short, another world!

After the departure of the old King, of *their King,* after the accession of Louis-Philippe, this world shut up its houses and limited its expenses to what was strictly necessary.

"I grudge myself even the bread I eat in Paris," said the Comtesse de Gouvelle.

"I heard the Duc de Luxembourg-Montmorency," a contemporary reported, "end a conversation thus: 'For my part I congratulate myself on being a bachelor and leaving no posterity. There is no place left for us in these new times.' "

The legitimist faubourg had become a large village which one rarely left. Those who had ventured as far as the Tuileries—the "château," as they called it—had fled, appalled. Such a one was Comte Apponyi, the Austrian ambassador, obliged by his functions to attend a dinner presided over by the King. He had returned "frozen with horror," his neighbor having been bold-faced enough to fan herself at table with an enormous tricolor fan.

How could one possibly visit this murdering King? For the faubourg roundly accused Louis-Philippe of having committed a crime on August 27, a few weeks after the Three Glorious Days. In a word, the legitimist circles believed that the new King had had his cousin, the Duc de Bourbun-Condé, father of the Duc d'Enghien, assassinated for his private ends. The tale ran through Paris. On the morning of August 27 Lecomte, the old duke's valet, had knocked at his master's bedroom door. It was half past eight. Hearing no sound from the room, he thought that the prince was still asleep, and withdrew. A quarter of an hour later the same thing happened. Growing anxious, Lecomte went to fetch Chevalier Bonni, the duke's surgeon. They knocked again. No answer. The door was bolted from inside. There must have been an accident. The alarm was given, the door was broken down and the room entered.

The shutters were closed. By the light of a dying candle they saw the duke, motionless, standing by the window. He looked like a man listening to something. They drew near and then perceived that the Duc de Bourbon was hanging by a handkerchief from the *espagnolette* of the window. His face was discolored. First aid was tried, but all was useless. The last of the Condés was dead at the age of seventy-four.

There were no signs of struggle in the room. The dead man's knees were partly bent and the tips of his feet touched the carpet, so that, to escape death, the prince would only have had to straighten his legs. Was it, then, a suicide? But what a curious way to hang oneself! To kill himself in this way the Duc de Bourbon would have had to be helped by someone. Since his shoulder had been broken he had not been able to raise his left arm. Besides, in consequence of a wound received at Beristein in 1795, he no longer had the use of three fingers of his right hand. How then could he have tied a knot so complicated that the valet had difficulty in undoing it?

It seemed, therefore, to be a murder. The unfortunate man must have been strangled before being hanged. The legitimist circles were strengthened in this belief since the magistrates appointed by the

King to carry out the judicial inquiry seemed to favor the theory of suicide. Did not this denial of evidence denote a "controlled" attitude? Surreptitiously at first, then openly, the legitimists' attacks were made: Louis-Philippe was accused of being the instigator of the crime. The faubourg was all the more convinced because suddenly the King gave orders to suspend the inquiry. The Duc de Bourbon's death was particularly advantageous to the young Duc d'Aumale, Louis-Philippe's son, who would thus inherit the last of the Condés' vast fortune. The sum of eighty-four millions was mentioned—several thousand million present-day francs. The public was not unaware that Sophie Dawes—the Duc de Bourbon's mistress, who had become Baronne de Feuchères—had frankly offered her "services" to the Palais Royal, and that Louis-Philippe, when still the Duc d'Orléans, had accepted. The result of this association was highly successful: Mme. de Feuchères had forced the old man to sign a will in favor of his great-nephew Aumale. But after the revolution of 1830 the Duc de Bourbon, loyal to the elder branch, might revoke his testamentary dispositions. He might think of favoring the little Duc de Bordeaux, then in exile. The best thing to do was obviously to get rid of the old man before he changed his mind. A hidden staircase linked the duke's bedroom with Mme. de Feuchères's apartments. There was no doubt that the prince's mistress had helped the assassins. "Mme. de Feuchères," wrote *Figaro,* "is a little English baroness greatly resembling an *espagnolette*." * The nickname stuck to her, but, the faubourg asserted, Espagnolette had merely obeyed the King's orders. Even today many historians have thrown a veil over the origin of the Duc d'Aumale's fortune. The ground seemed to them rather slippery.

Today we know the truth from the documents of the inquiry which have been kept secret for over a century. The story is racy, and somewhat broad. I ask pardon in advance of my women readers.

Married at the age of fourteen, the Duc de Bourbon had started on an amorous career at an age usually spent in more innocent games. Sixty years later the duke had still not decided to surrender arms. But it is obvious that at that age it is often difficult to present them with the necessary alacrity. Mme. de Feuchères had heard that hanged men, before sinking into nothingness, often obtained a certain consolation.

* This is a pun, as *espagnolette* might also mean a little Spanish woman. [Translator's note.]

Might she not apply this bold method to the Duc de Bourbon and thus, in spite of his years, keep her power over him which was so important to her? This is why she would quite simply hang her elderly lover, for a few brief moments, from the *espagnolette* in the bedroom. One evening Mme. de Feuchères left the prince a second too long, and the poor man died. Horrified by her "negligence"—as well she might be—Espagnolette had had neither the courage nor the strength to unhang the duke and had fled to her apartments.

She had confessed the truth to Louis-Philippe, who had hastened to end the inquiry. One can imagine the shout of laughter that would have greeted the revelation of this ribald ballad of the hanged!

The legitimist newspapers, enjoyed by the inhabitants of the faubourg, constantly recalled this drama throughout "Philippe's" reign. For them—and some of them were sincere—the King was an assassin, and a thief. The *Charivari* discovered one day that a malefactor bearing Louis-Philippe's name had been arrested in the act of stealing an umbrella from in front of a shop in the Rue de Rivoli. The following day this headline appeared in large letters on the front page: ARREST OF THE GREAT THIEF LOUIS-PHILIPPE TAKEN IN THE ACT OF STEALING AN UMBRELLA IN THE RUE DE RIVOLI, NOT FAR FROM THE PALAIS ROYAL.

The article began: "For some time now watch has been kept on the actions of an egregious thief named Louis-Philippe, who for many years has not recoiled from any crime. This man, who even under the Restoration habitually prowled round the Tuileries, has at last been taken in the act of theft and all will rejoice at the thought that society will receive satisfaction. . . . This time it is an umbrella that the clever rogue made off with."

The faubourg's true newspaper was *La Mode,* which had fallen into the habit of referring to the King as "So-and-So" and announced imperturbably: "So-and-So has decided to procure some money by establishing at the entrance to the Tuileries gardens a stall for canes and umbrellas." *La Mode* was created by Emile de Girardin in 1829. During the last year of Charles X's reign the paper had confined itself to advising its male readers to wear "a bright chestnut coat shot with red," or telling its female readers that without Henri III or bishop sleeves they would be dishonored. On the accession of Louis-Philippe

La Mode's advice was interlarded with political counsels and formulas. In a few days the pacific newspaper became the most aggressive legitimist journal. It was directed by Vicomte Walsch, a man swollen with pride. One day a certain d'Arlincourt, whose fatuity equaled that of Walsch, declared to the director: "Do you know, my dear vicomte, that in this room where we are now are the two greatest prose writers of the century?"

"My dear sir," replied Walsch, "what you say may well be half true."

The "greatest prose writer of the century" sometimes wrote articles worthy of Père Duchesne. As witness one recommending a sovereign remedy against the cholera that was raging in Paris at the beginning of 1832. "Take 200 heads from the Chamber of Peers, 150 heads from the Chamber of Deputies, those of Casimir Périer, Sébastiani and d'Argoult, those of Louis-Philippe and his sons, send them rolling in the Place de la Révolution, and the atmosphere will be purified."

However, the dominant note of *La Mode* was gay. There was not an issue that did not sully—admittedly with a certain wit—the King and his "august family." The Duc d'Orléans, heir to the crown, was nicknamed *Le Grand Poulot,* and *La Mode* gave him as his motto: "Blessed are the poor in spirit, for theirs is the kingdom of heaven."

In the face of Walsch's attacks the King tried to play his role of citizen-King. "I know the French. . . . I know how to take them," he said to Apponyi.

And he began to distribute handshakes and embraces to such an extent that the workers soon called him *le père biseur.* It was wasted effort, for *La Mode* increased its attacks. It even had the idea, one Shrove Tuesday, of disguising a man as Louis-Philippe. Wig, large side whiskers, broad tricolor cockade, nothing was lacking, even the legendary umbrella. For the whole of the day the man walked from the Palais Royal to the boulevards, effusively shaking the hands of passers-by and exclaiming: "Gentlemen, it is with renewed pleasure that I salute you!"

For all that, the King continued to pose as the perfect bourgeois and to sing the "Marseillaise" to all and sundry. Even Guizot thought he was going too far.

"Don't worry," Louis-Philippe replied. "I only move my lips. I forgot the words long ago."

He was in fact playing a part, but he overplayed it. *La Mode* had plenty to go on. But it ended by lacking restraint. Walsch's subscribers—the whole of the Faubourg Saint-Germain—enjoyed reading news of this kind: "The Duc d'Orléans, son of the King, is about to lead an Austrian princess to the altar. It is true that Philippe-Egalité once led one to the scaffold."

And the faubourg rocked with laughter. The legitimists did not even behave becomingly at the time of the accident of July 13, 1842. On that day, setting out for Neuilly to visit his parents, the Duc d'Orléans left the Tuileries and entered a four-wheeled cabriolet drawn by two horses harnessed without a shaft, in the style made fashionable by the Duc d'Aumont. According to a contemporary, when the horses reached the Porte Maillot they were heated by the rapid journey from the Tuileries and began to get excited. "The postilion was already having difficulty in mastering them, although the near horse alone was galloping. On a very short rein, as is the custom when harnessing *à la daumont,* it felt constrained, reared several times and set off with a speed that carried away the other horse, which had hitherto remained calm." At that moment the cabriolet was at the top of the Chemin de la Révolte.

"Can you not master the horses?" the prince asked the postilion.

"No, monseigneur!"

So the heir to the throne opened the door and jumped, feet together, into the road. He fell heavily and remained motionless on the stones. He was carried into a small grocery nearby and died there four hours later. The grocery was demolished and in its place the King had a Byzantine chapel built that still exists and today puzzles passers-by in the Boulevarde Pershing.

The faubourg wore black, but did not disarm, in face of the terrible grief of the King and Queen.

This dying world contained a racy collection of originals, whom Jules Bertaut has shown us. Such was the strange Comte de Gerval, a slim, elegant, handsome cavalier with a youthful bearing, who was present at every party, except for two days a week. One morning, at La Muette, the comte was overtaken by a terrible storm. When he went home to the Rue de Lille he went to bed and summoned his friends. On seeing him they were thunderstruck: de Gerval, wrinkled, white-haired and bent, had aged fifty years. The comte told them the truth. He was eighty and had been page to Louis XV. During those mysterious forty-eight hours every week he entrusted his body to the specialists. They bathed him, dyed him, massaged him, wrapped him in flannel, made him up, gave him special meals and fortifying drinks, and then put him into circulation for the rest of the week. Had it not been for that unlucky storm this extraordinary arrangement might have gone on for a long time.

On the very evening of his confession M. de Gerval passed peacefully away. His death preceded by only a few months that of the whole faubourg, whose knell was sounded by 1848, that society full of good taste and elegance, no doubt, but so frivolous, so superficial, so blinded by prejudice, and which, according to the famous saying, "had learned nothing and forgotten nothing."

8

Two Women of Paris

They both lived in Paris. One was born during the winter of 1824, the other during that of 1825. Both were fashionable, both were adulated, both ate up their lovers' money like chocolate drops, and both died poor, abandoned and consumptive. One was called Elise, then Lise, Sergent; the other Alphonsine, then Marie, Duplessis. The first was "Queen Pomaré" of the Bal Mabille; the second the "Lady of the Camellias" of Alexandre Dumas *fils*.

Lise—she was then still Elise—was seventeen when her father was ruined and withdrew her from her school at Chaillot. Extremely well made, she was not "positively pretty," but was something better. Nowadays we should say that she had "sex appeal." One morning she informed her father that she had a toothache and was going to the dentist. Her father never saw her again.

The dentist was in fact a young sculptor called Marocchetti, who got rid of Lise after giving her a child, which was undoubtedly somewhat offhanded. The child died. Lise then rented a furnished room in the Rue de Ponthieu and began to live a life that was admittedly rather free, but that seems at first to have been very unsuccessful.

At this same period, Marie Duplessis, who was breathtakingly beautiful, had already been set up by a restaurant keeper of the Rue de Montpensier. He was far from being the first man to take an interest in her. Her father, a Norman peasant, had sold her at the age of fifteen to an "elderly amateur," who took it on himself to complete an education whose first rudiments the girl had learned from the farmhands. Abandoned after a few lessons, Alphonsine—she was not yet Marie—was living with some cousins, fruiterers of the Rue des Deux-Ecus, and had a job with a laundress. Roqueplan, the king of the boulevard, claimed to have met her at this time standing before a fried-fish stall. Alphonsine struck him as pretty, delicate and "as dirty as an unkempt slug." The future director of the Opéra-Comique bought her a big piece of pastry which the girl ate so greedily "that she seemed to grow fatter in three minutes." Roqueplan did not push his advantage, merely saying to her: "See you tomorrow." When he next saw her, two years later, she was no longer a laundress; she had already left her restaurant keeper and had begun to ruin Vicomte de Méril. She was to ruin a good many others.

At about the same time Lise Sergent was living with a young woman who was to become the famous dancer Rose Pompon, but who for the moment was merely a waitress in the Café du Divan, 3 Rue Le Peletier. The place was frequented by Balzac, Théophile Gautier, Gavarni, Gérard de Nerval and Henry Monnier, who, in order to get rid of the bourgeois who sometimes wandered into the establishment, used to pretend to be the Paris executioner. It was there that Rose had met Lise. Their friendship was not approved by the owner of the Divan.

"That woman's morals are more than just light. She changes her lovers as she changes her chemise."

The future Queen Pomaré certainly changed her lover more often than her chemise, for she had only one; she would wash it every Saturday evening and put it on, still damp, on Sunday morning. However, Rose did not care for the remark, and gave in her notice.

The two friends led a gay life, but they were too fond of love to get rich. "Soon," Rose was to relate in her *Souvenirs*, "we were so hard up that one evening Elise announced (with such solemnity that I at once believed her) that in eight days she would have a sumptuous apartment, horses, carriages and diamonds, or she would throw herself in the river.

" 'We shall go to Mabille this evening,' Lise decided. 'We shall dance, and I shall be very surprised if someone is not taken with me. I shall set my two legs flying and you'll see if I'm not as good as any of the celebrated women.'

"And in her short petticoat and white dimity corset she began to dance in such a strange, bold, graceful way that I was stupefied. Almost at once I tried to imitate her. Within me was the same spirit that possessed her. Quite naturally I discovered gestures, turns and movements whose grace I could feel. After this trial we threw ourselves into each other's arms. Our vocation was born."

And the two young women—Elise in a dress of green silk and a straw hat adorned with a bunch of daisies, Rose in a muslin dress and white cape ornamented with a branch of flowering may—made their entry into the Bal Mabille, which was in the Allée des Veuves, on the site of what is now 49-53 Avenue Montaigne. It was an open-air dance hall, brilliantly lighted, comprising paths, lawns and galleries surrounding a vast kiosk where played the best dance orchestra in Paris. The Mimi Pinsons,* *grisettes* with fingers roughened by sewing, came down from Montmartre with "their" painter or "their" poet. The Musettas or Louisettes, *lorettes* ** who would rather go without a meal than without rouge, came to Mabille every Saturday. While waiting for the rare, golden bird who would keep them, they applauded the dancing of Frisette, Carabine, Mousqueton, Brididi le Désossé and Prichard.

When Rose and Lise began their exhibition everyone stopped dancing. Lise was extraordinary. It appears that she possessed a "superb, impassioned" ardor. "When it was over," Rose related, "she was so closely surrounded that she could not get back to me, and so, excited by her triumph, she cried imperiously: 'Back, let me pass!'

"There was more laughter and applause: 'Bravo! Bravo! She is a queen! a queen!' And a voice in the crowd shouted: 'Queen Pomaré!' †

---

* Mimi Pinson, the heroine of a story by Alfred de Musset, is the type of the Parisian *grisette*. [Translator's note.]

** Elegant young women of easy virtue, who lived in the district of Notre Dame de Lorette. [Translator's note.]

† Queen Pomaré was the reigning queen of Tahiti. [Translator's note.]

"The name spread through the garden like an electric flame. Queen Pomaré! One heard nothing else!"

Eight days later "Queen Pomaré" did not throw herself in the river. She had her horses, carriages and diamonds. But every Tuesday, Sunday and Saturday she would return to the Bal Mabille, dressed in white or black. "With her wrists loaded with strange bracelets and her neck surrounded by fantastic jewels," Théophile Gautier related, "she brings to her dress a wild taste that justifies the name given to her. When she dances everyone forms a circle round her and the most inveterate *polkists* stop and admire in silence."

For Lise did no more than dance the polka or the quadrille. These words evoke memories of the quiet little dances of our childhood, but in 1843 they involved such swayings of the hips, such epileptic contortions that to be successful one had to be, as they said, "boneless." Among the figures of the quadrille, that of the "lone cavalier" turned into something quite extravagant. Incidentally, at the Bal Mabille the quadrille was soon called the *cancan* or the *chahut*. The famous Chicard, who was employed by an undertaker during the day and danced at Mabille in the evening, had perfected a certain number of "lone cavaliers" in the whirlwind style, such as the "stormy tulip" step or that of "the red herring returning to his family," which bordered on acrobatics. The *chahut* gave birth to the verb *chahuter* (to kick up a shindy).

All Paris wanted to see Queen Pomaré dance.

> O, Queen Pomaré, your throne is at Mabille!
> There your delightful kingdom ends and starts.
> There you amuse and charm, there your subjects kneel.
> You have no lover, though you rule all hearts.

This virtue was merely for the sake of the verse, for in fact Lise had a considerable number.

At eleven o'clock curfew sounded at the Bal Mabille. Lise, Rose, Céleste Mogador and Mignonnette, who had dethroned Carabine and Mousqueton, turned back into *lorettes*. But the spectacle was not over. It continued in the Allée des Veuves and along the Champs-Elysées, where there was an amazing number of a rather special kind of beggar. They were blind musicians, scraping out polkas. And, says an eyewitness, "carried away by the charm of the music, the frequenters of Mabille started dancing again even more enthusiastically and polkaed from blind man to blind man all the way to the Place de la Concorde."

As for Marie Duplessis, she reigned over the boulevard. At that time the whole of the elegant life of the capital was concentrated between the Chaussée d'Antin and the present Richelieu-Drouot crossroads. It was not done to show oneself beyond these limits. At a pinch one might dare to go as far as the Théâtre des Variétés, but beyond that were the Indies, as Alfred de Musset imperturbably remarked. A hundred times a day and a hundred times a night the boulevard was paced by the lions. "The 'lion,' " a chronicler tells us, "has pomaded hair, a gold-knobbed cane, turned-back cuffs, varnished boots and yellow gloves; he wears a medieval beard. He bites, he roars, he foams, he is insolent. He speaks thus: 'I declare that . . .' He is affected, tight-waisted, supercilious, full-blooded. He is not a man but a vignette. . . ."

All these "vignettes" watched enviously as Marie Duplessis went by on the arm of the lover she was in the process of fleecing. Like all the elegant people, she lunched often at Tortoni's and dined still more often at the Café de Paris, and at night, when she left the Opéra, she did not fail to stop her barouche in front of Tortoni's to eat the ices which, according to custom, were brought to her in her carriage. Marie had become the lady "with the camellias." She adored them and wore them in her corsage. They were white for twenty-seven days in the month; on the other three days, it is said, she wore red ones. In this way her lovers knew where they stood.

Marie now had such a great need of money that, if Villemessant's *Mémoires d'un journaliste* are to be believed, she had to agree to the formation of an association of seven sleeping partners. They were already joined by many ties of friendship; by having the same mistress they formed yet another. "I am assured," says Villemessant, "that to celebrate the signing of the articles they made a joint present. It was a very necessary piece of furniture: a dressing table with seven drawers. When the association broke up each one emptied his own drawer and took his possessions elsewhere . . . and Marie kept the table as a souvenir."

The little universe over which Marie reigned for two or three years included the most extraordinary set of eccentrics. The most astonishing of these was undoubtedly M. de Saint-Cricq, who amazed Roger de Beauvoir himself, and he was certainly an expert. "Nothing less than the pencil of a Goya is needed," he wrote, "to impress such a figure on the minds of our great-nephews." One day Saint-Cricq sat down at table opposite Roger de Beauvoir, whom he did not then know. After putting snuff in his beetroot salad, he called the waiter and asked for a pot of cold cream. Saint-Cricq literally smeared his face with the cream, then opened his snuff box and threw several pinches of snuff on his face, powdering himself as abundantly as he had his salad. De Beauvoir was stupefied.

"It is for my headaches," the strange diner explained. "Pay no attention! Sometimes I add Condrieux or Canary wine as an astringent. My doctor sees no harm in it."

In winter Saint-Cricq had his own way of warming cabs: he sent his valet to pick out four fat, strong porters from the market. He had them shut up in a cab with all the windows closed and sent it to drive round the boulevards for two hours.

"In this way," he said, "when I go out in my turn I shall be able to enter a well-warmed cab."

On the other hand, when it was very hot, Saint-Cricq had a no less sure way of cooling himself: he entered Tortoni's and asked for three ices. He swallowed the first, dropped the second into his left boot and the third into his right boot.

Sometimes at night he would borrow a louis from each diner in the Café de Paris. He would put the money in his hat, go down the boulevard and toss it out in handfuls like sweets. He called this "giving largesse to the people."

There was also M. de Courchamps. At that time memoirs were very fashionable and Courchamps began inventing the alleged recollections of a certain Marquise de Créquy, who was supposed to have known all the best society in the old regime.

He had identified himself so closely with his pseudo-marquise that he finished up by dressing as a woman, with an old checked shawl. One day, when dressed in this fashion, he opened the door to Beauvoir, who had come to interview him for *La Mode*.

"Don't be surprised to see me dressed like this," he said, "I should not be able to work otherwise."

If Marie Duplessis was for a time one of the queens of the boulevard, the king was undoubtedly Nestor Roqueplan. The arbiter of taste, he declared he was unable to sleep a wink the night before he had to try on a new suit. The dandies accepted his tastes as gospel. Roqueplan was not rich and sometimes, at the Café de Paris, he would for the sake of economy refuse the services of the wine waiter, declaring: "Give me some water. Wine is common, plebeian!"

And during these hard times he would order a pot-au-feu or a mutton stew. Immediately the "lions" would call loudly for boiled beef or mutton and a jug of water.

The great event that set all the boulevard talking was the creation of the first Paris–Saint-Germain railway and, in particular, the building of the famous Batignolles tunnel under the Monceau hill.

"What? Underground? But we shall be unable to breathe," it was said. A scientist, indeed, affirmed that the temperature in the tunnel would be unbearable and that, by thus passing from cold to heat, the unfortunate travelers would run the risk of death. Mme. de Girardin was the first person brave enough to undertake the adventure. She came back still alive, bringing with her the little guide given to the intrepid travelers at the Saint-Lazare station. "The Mont Valérien," it said, "bends down to watch the whirlwind as it passes." A whirlwind—the Saint-Germain railway in the time of Louis-Philippe!

Paris amused itself, Paris mocked, Paris dressed. Paris seemed to have recovered its futile grace of the eighteenth century, with, in addition, a careless fancy, an unembittered irony, an absurd oddity and a skepticism. And it forgot the growing scandals, the murmuring revolts, the big words bandied about, which all lead to riots and sweep away thrones.

What became of Lise Sergent?

In *Nana* Zola has related that evening when his heroine, together with Satin, watches, through the open window of her house in the Avenue de Villiers, a rag picker searching the gutters.

" 'Look!' Satin exclaimed. 'Queen Pomaré with her basketwork shawl!'

"And while a gust of wind whipped their faces with fine rain, she told her darling the queen's story. Oh! she was a superb girl once, all Paris was taken with her beauty. And such effrontery, my dear: men treated like dogs, great men weeping on her staircase. Now she had become a drunkard; to amuse themselves the women of the district would give her absinthe to drink. Then the urchins would follow her along the pavements, throwing stones. . . . Nana listened, chilled.

" 'You'll see,' Satin added.

"She whistled like a man. The rag picker, who was under the window, raised her head and was revealed in the yellow light of her lantern. In the bundle of rags and beneath the tattered scarf was a bluish face, seamed, a toothless hole for the mouth and inflamed bruises for eyes."

Shortly before the end of the century, when *Nana* was staged, a whistle sounded from the stalls during the rag picker's scene. It was Céleste Mogador, now the Comtesse Lionel de Chabrillan, who was protesting.

"Yes, it is I!" she cried. "I could not allow myself to see the truth so basely outraged in the person of a dead woman who was my friend!"

Through the former dancer it became known that Queen Pomaré never became a rag picker but had died of consumption.

"I went to see her at her home," Céleste Mogador recounted. "It was in the Rue Saint-Georges, where, between two windows, a gilded wooden pedestal supported a plaster Virgin. Lise's cheeks were hollow, her lips too red, her breathing harsh. Her sister was there and, full of hate, cried: 'You thought yourself loved by everyone. Where are your friends now?'

"Lise pressed my hand. 'She is right. I am abandoned by everyone.'

"She looked at her thin arms and said to me: 'You did well to leave this kind of life. People will forget your past; perhaps you will forget it yourself.'

"She twined her rosary round her arm. . . . 'What a beautiful bracelet!' Her childhood's prayers returned to her lips. She asked me to leave her alone."

The next time Céleste Mogador returned to the room Queen Pomaré was dead. It was December 8, 1846. She was twenty-two years old.

Marie Duplessis soon followed her. She died less than two months later, February 3, 1847, at 8 Boulevard de la Madeleine. She, too, was undermined by tuberculosis and died alone. At her bedside there was only a former lover, Comte de Saint-Yves, who followed the funeral with a friend. Alexandre Dumas *fils* dedicated some verses to them. They might also apply to Lise's few friends who accompanied Queen Pomaré to her tomb in the Montmartre cemetery, a little grassy enclosure paid for by Céleste Mogador by selling a lace dress.

> A blessing on you
> Who loved her and went with her to the grave.
> You are not like the marquis, duke or peer
> Who when she lived were proud of what they gave,
> But saw no pride in following her bier.

9
Two Princes

The Duc d'Orléans sons: Aumale! Joinville! When one evokes the life of Louis-Philippe's sons at the Tuileries, at Neuilly or in the Palais Royal the past emerges from the mists of time and suddenly becomes present. Many of our contemporaries knew them and they themselves remembered having met relics from the court of Louis XV. They had taken tea with their grandmother—"Widow Egalité"—and with their great-aunt, the mother of the Duc d'Enghien, who had seen survivors from the age of Louis XIV.

The great event of their childhood was the arrival of two tutors chosen by Louis-Philippe and called Fleury and Trognon, names which stimulated Victor Hugo's wit in *Ruy Blas*.

> ... *affreuse compagnonne*
> *Dont la barbe fleurit et dont le nom trognonne.*

"*Fleurit,*" Joinville wrote later in his memoirs, "was an allusion to Cuvillier-Fleury, my brother Aumale's tutor. Victor Hugo thought he had grounds for complaint against these two gentlemen." Trognon, the Prince de Joinville's tutor, had formerly been professor at the college of Langres. One morning, before giving his lessons, he found his chair occupied by a donkey his pupils had tied to it.

"I leave you, gentlemen, with a professor worthy of you," he had remarked as he retired.

Now he had only one pupil, but one who by himself gave as much trouble as the whole of his old class. Every day Trognon gave the Duc d'Orléans a note of "the situation": "Writing and arithmetic: good. Employment of time: bad. Conduct: he was not docile on his walk; he has again picked flowers in the park, although monseigneur reprimanded him yesterday about this." And monseigneur added a note in his own hand: "If Joinville continues to amuse himself by devastation he will force me to take severe measures to correct him. He must not pick anything without having first asked and obtained permission."

How could he resist picking the flowers at dear Neuilly! "Neuilly!" Joinville sighed, sixty-five years later. "I never write that word without emotion, since for me it is linked with the sweetest memories of my childhood; I salute it with the respect with which one salutes the dead. Let those who never knew the Neuilly I speak of imagine a vast château, without pretensions and without architecture, composed almost entirely of ground floors one after the other, on a level with enchanting gardens."

"Enchanting gardens," where the band of brothers and sisters ran till they lost their breath, while their tutors panted after them.

Cuvillier-Fleury was "aggressive, contradictious, as uncomformist as possible, playing at revolutionaries under the nose of Charles X." He did not merely make young Aumale work; he also took him to the theatre.

Incidentally, Cuvillier-Fleury and Trognon were really only in charge of homework, for Joinville and his brothers attended the Lycée Henri IV. Out of courtesy the Duc d'Orléans had asked the permission of Louis XVIII, who had replied:

"This is vulgarity, sir! If you ask me for my approval, I tell you distinctly: no! . . . All the same, you are free to do as you wish!"

The future Louis-Philippe had taken this as permission and had bowed respectfully in thanks.

One morning, one of Joinville's young friends at the Lycée Henri IV jostled him, crying: "Take that, little majesty!" That morning Louis-Philippe had become King of the French. "I am absolutely certain," the prince was to say later, "that my father never wanted it. When Charles X's throne crumbled, without his being able in any way to defend it, without doubt he wished passionately to escape into the common exile. When France rose from one end to the other, he understood that he would escape exile only by joining the movement."

When he became a King's son Joinville worked no better than before. "My time at school will always remain, as they say in mathematics, marked with a minus sign." He preferred listening open-mouthed to the stories of Comte de Houdetot, now a colonel in the cavalry, who had begun under the Empire as a naval officer. When he was not yet one year old Houdetot had sailed in the arms of his nurse, who was bringing him back from Mauritius. The ship was attacked by the English and the nurse cut in two by a cannonball. Which caused Houdetot to say: "I have more claims to advancement than most. Everyone has had horses killed under them, but I am the only man in the French army who has had a woman killed under him!"

The colonel had fought at Trafalgar, and little Joinville was never tired of hearing the former sailor evoke the battle during which he had been seriously wounded. Left out in the sun on the quayside at Cadiz, he had been saved by a ravishing woman who, touched by his youth, spread a fan over the "poor boy's" head. Half dead, Houdetot kissed the providential hand and the young woman immediately had the officer taken to her house, thus avoiding for him a period in a hospital ravaged by typhus and preparing for him a delightful convalescence which had left him with many happy memories. Hearing this, Joinville's heart beat faster; he wanted to be a sailor. Louis-Philippe yielded, took his son from school, entrusted him to the inevitable Trognon, and himself put them in a carriage that took them to Toulon, where they embarked in the *Artémise* for a cruise in the Mediterranean.

Aumale, who was four years younger than Joinville, was still at school, but was a very bad pupil.

"Pupil Aumale," declared his professor at the Lycée Henri IV, "let So-and-So's example be a lesson to you. Like him you will end your existence as second violin at the Théâtre Français."

His neighbor, little Emile Augier, to whom the master made a similar prediction, turned to Aumale and murmured: "You have such good connections, perhaps you'll be first violin."

Since Joinville, although a dunce, was an excellent sailor, why should not Henri d'Aumale, an equally bad pupil, be a good soldier? And at the age of fifteen the young prince received a second lieutenant's commission.

When Joinville returned to Paris he was captain of a corvette. The women of Paris found him irresistible, and the young prince did not wish to disappoint them.

"As the King has sent me to roam the seas, he must allow me to roam after the girls," he declared. And he did not stint himself.

But this kind of "roaming" is expensive, and the King was extremely tight-fisted. And so, on one particularly difficult day, Joinville decided to pawn a present from his mother: a gold watch ornamented with jewels.

Like everyone else the prince imagined that he would be able to redeem the watch before anyone noticed it, but, as with everyone else, time went by. Joinville was still without money and the inevitable happened.

"What have you done with your watch?" the Queen asked him one day. "It's a long time since I saw you wearing it."

Taken unprepared, Prince de Joinville replied: "I must have left it at my aunt's."

"My aunt" was Madame Adélaïde, the King's sister. Queen Marie-Amélie immediately gave orders for her son's watch to be fetched from her sister-in-law's. Obviously it could not be found, and Joinville, not without embarrassment, was forced to admit the truth.

The word made a hit. The expression "aunt" ousted the expression "the nail" (formerly applied to hock shops), and that is how, without wishing it, the pious and charitable Madame Adélaïde gave her name to the pawn office.

In 1841 Colonel d'Aumale made a joyous entrance into Paris, followed by his regiment, the 17th Light. "Erect on his white horse, his shako on his brow, the chin strap at his mouth, his gorget at his throat, the Duc d'Aumale appeared like an archangel." This, at least, is what Robert Burnand assures us. And the young Parisiennes of the day must undoubtedly have been of the same opinion, for they cast flowers, smiles and glances at the nineteen-year-old colonel. Suddenly, at the Rue de Charonne, a shot rang out. The duke had been fired on. Only a horse was wounded. Aumale was not in the least moved and, with his sword, gave the signal to proceed. But his order could not be carried out, for the girls rushed at the handsome colonel, trying to lift him from his Arab saddle and carry him in triumph. The prince laughed heartily as he tried to defend himself.

"Those devils would have killed me," he said later, "just to show how glad they were I was alive. I have never seen such a dangerous hand-to-hand fight. The Arabs were much gentler!"

Soon, at the Tuileries as at Neuilly, when the young colonel entered the drawing room his brothers and sisters—and even stern Queen Marie-Amélie—would hum Raimbaud's big aria from *Robert le Diable*. This was a transparent allusion to the Duc d'Aumale's love for the enchanting Alice Ozy. When she was born in the Rue Saint-Denis, in 1820, her father, M. Piloy, a jeweler by trade, had given her the names of Marie-Justine. After being a shopgirl and then a seamstress at Belleville, she had fallen into the arms of the actor Brindeau, who got her a part at the Variétés and gave her her stage name of Alice Ozy. In private she was called Alicette. She was so pretty that when she walked in the street passers-by stopped to look at her. One day she sang in *Robert le Diable* at the Tuileries theatre. Aumale was dazzled, and Alicette was easily persuaded to be dazzled in her turn. The colonel would go to fetch her at her home in the Rue Laffitte, would dress her as a man and then they would both walk arm in arm along the boulevard. Or else he would ask her to go to Courbevoie in the morning to watch the maneuvers of the 17th Light. The regiment would file past her barouche, where the charming girl sat smiling in an organdy dress—a smile that seemed addressed to each of the soldiers. The whole regiment was in love with "its *colonelle*." The idyll lasted until the day a banker sent an overwhelmingly elegant coupé to the stage door of the Variétés. The footman opened the door and Alicette, forgetting Raimbaud and the 17th Light, drove away to fresh loves.

Joinville was the first of the brothers to marry. He had sworn that he would not let himself be married, but would seek his happiness for himself. On one of his voyages to Mexico he fell in love with Princesse Françoise, second daughter of Pedro I, and informed his father by letter that he wished to marry her. Louis-Philippe and Guizot were discussing the matter, solemnly weighing the pros and cons, when a message came by telegraph that Joinville's frigate, the *Belle-Poule*, had just arrived at Toulon. The prince had disembarked with his wife on his arm.

She was called Chica, babbled in Franco-Portuguese, and soon made the conquest of the whole family. Nevertheless she caused some surprise when, having caught a cold, she asked for some parrot broth.

Aumale found his happiness under the sky of Naples at his uncle's, the Prince of Salerno, whose daughter, Princesse Marie-Caroline, had also fallen in love with her irresistible cousin. On learning of her former lover's marriage, Alicette sent back the love letters the prince had written her. Aumale thought he ought to send a few bank notes. Alicette returned them with the words: "I should have preferred a souvenir." Much later, after the long exile, after 1870, Alice Ozy, then a lady with prematurely gray hair, would often receive a note saying: "The ex-Raimbaud will come and shake the ex-Alicette's hand on Monday, between four and six." It was not a lovers' rendezvous. The two of them would just talk quietly about the good old days. But Aumale—who was forty-eight in 1870—had not settled down and at that period both society women and women of the *demimonde* would fight over the duke with as much ardor as had the girls of Charonne. In the six o'clock train one evening coming back from Chantilly a female passenger said: "My dear, he received me with his usual graciousness. He is to come and dine with me next week. I have his promise."

"I expect him to tea on Saturday, after the hunt," said another.

"You can envy me, my dears; I had monseigneur to myself for a whole hour," replied a third.

One lady in the compartment, however, said nothing. When the train was entering the Gare du Nord she rose and remarked mockingly: "Ladies, you have had monseigneur to lunch, to dinner, to tea, to talk. As for me, last night I had him to sleep, and if things go as I hope I shall have him tonight for the same reason. Good evening, ladies."

It was Léonide Leblanc, who with the prince was ending an amorous existence full of racy adventures. Robert Burnand tells us that Léonide Leblanc, who was much sought after, "had found a way of discouraging, while not discouraging. It is said that she had had an effigy made of the Duc d'Aumale, the head of wax and the body of goldbeater's skin. When her suitors became too pressing she had a way of half opening the door and showing them from a distance a noble form in an armchair: 'Hush! Monseigneur is there!' which calmed impatience."

I once knew an old lady who, when a young bride, had been shut up for an hour with the Duc d'Aumale in a lift that had broken down between floors. This adventure—she always called it "our accident"—which took place in a palace in Ems, had really set its mark on her life. Forty years later, when she spoke of the "prince" her eyes became strangely brilliant. She grew instantly younger. And yet, as the heroine herself admitted, the two had done no more than exchange banalities on the various methods of ascension practiced at the time.

Old age came at last even to Aumale. And, before his flower beds at Chantilly, he consoled himself as best he could.

"I love roses. All old soldiers love roses," he said. "There is no better way of forgetting the sadness of retirement than pruning one's rose trees."

He would then pin a scarlet Maréchal Niel to his lapel. He was not displeased that a soldier's name should have been given to a flower. Then he would stroll away, twirling his cane and humming in his somewhat cracked voice the regimental march of his dear old 17th Light.

Joinville, too, had returned to Paris. Passers-by in the Rue de Rivoli had seen him on the day of his return kiss the threshold of the Palais Royal, the house where he was born, the house of his childhood. Two departments elected him to the Chamber, but two years later he retired definitely from public life. Henceforth, in the twenty-seven years left to him, he killed time by writing his *Souvenirs,* painting charming water colors and, above all, by hunting.

It was Aumale who died first, in 1897. Joinville survived him for three years. He hunted almost up to the last day of his life. One winter's day, in the forest of Chantilly, a boar pursued by the prince's hunt dashed into the frozen lake of Reine-Blanche. The ice gave way, taking the beast and part of the pack with it. To save the hounds, which could be heard howling, faggots and logs were thrown among the floating ice. Prince de Joinville was on the bank. He had become very deaf and asked a charming girl of sixteen, who was standing near him: "Can you still hear them, my dear? Will they save them?"

"Yes, monseigneur, I can still hear them."

The young girl—she is now Comtesse d'Ydeville—has described the scene to me. The prince questioned her incessantly, in anxious tones.

"Can you still hear them, my dear?"

"I replied, pointing to a corner of the lake: 'Yes, I can still hear a howl.' Finally I had to answer: 'No, monseigneur, I can hear nothing more.'

"The prince's hand had dropped from my shoulder and I saw the old man raise his handkerchief to his eyes. . . . Seventeen hounds had drowned beneath the ice."

This is the final image of Prince de Joinville that one would like to retain: this rather bent old man, enclosed in his deafness, this admiral of France, weeping in the cold for the death of his hounds.

PARIS BLEEDS

1

The Infernal Machine

"He was an old night bird. Wearing a black skull cap, his head sunk between his shoulders, thick-set, bent, seeming to ruminate sinister schemes, he spent all day in his dark shop in the Rue Saint-Victor, working with his awl and punching leather." Such is the portrait J. Lucas-Dubreton has drawn of Pierre Morey. At the time of the Terror the saddler was twenty, and he still pined for his twenties. He read only Cabet's *Populaire, Chains of Slavery* or *Exposition of Republican Principles.* Resembling in this thousands of other Parisians at the time, he had only one thought: to assassinate Louis-Philippe, who in 1830 had filched "his Republic" for his own profit. In those days the King was as much shot at as a rabbit, which did not prevent the sovereign's conscientiously performing his job. He even consulted a professor of deportment in order to learn the best way of bowing to the crowd after being shot at by a regicide.

Between attempts at murder the belated Robespierrists spent their time making the citizen-King's life a misery. They were as good at it as the legitimists. To the irony of the Faubourg Saint-Germain, and in default of the anarchists' pistol shot, the Republicans preferred insurrection. Certain days in 1832, 1834 and 1837 gave grounds for a belief that some Parisians were past masters in the art of rioting. One day one of these specialists was arrested by the police.

"What is your profession?"

"Rioter!"

Rioter-conspirators and candidates for regicide lived in those "dishonored streets" Balzac speaks of—a network of stinking alleys, muddy lanes and airless culs-de-sac which at that time covered the whole center of Paris, from the Montagne Sainte-Geneviève to the boulevards. Escaping from the rarefied air of their lodgings, the conspirators would meet at the wine merchants', of which there was an almost incredible number. There, to swigs of coarse red wine, they would join in hate of the "tyrant" by preparing the next insurrection, or would expound their schemes. Morey himself wished to buy a house near the Palais Bourbon and dig a tunnel under the Chamber. Barrels of gunpowder would be stacked there and, on the occasion of a royal session, everything would be blown up: deputies, ministers, government, peers of France, "Philippe" and his family. What a magnificent fireworks display! Unfortunately 100,000 francs would be needed, and old Morey did not have them. In his shop in the Rue Saint-Victor, a street dating from the time of Philippe Auguste, he pondered.

One day toward the end of 1834 a man entered Morey's shop. With his pointed nose, scanty hair, boot-button eyes and thin mouth, the man looked like a rat.

"Can you put me up?" he asked.

Morey said he could. The man—a Corsican called Joseph Fieschi —was in Morey's eyes a true blue, an ardent Republican, a victim of tyranny. He was mistaken.

Fieschi was a man sold in advance—to whoever wanted to buy him. He had admittedly distinguished himself during the Russian campaign, but after that his existence had been infinitely less honorable. He had been given ten years for forging, a penalty involving loss of civil rights which, with the help of forged certificates, he managed to pass off in 1830 as a political sentence. Having become a "victim of the Restoration," he became a spy at police headquarters, which did not prevent his secretly distributing Bonapartist newspapers. Shortly afterward he became guardian of the Croulebarbe mill, which the city of Paris had bought with a view to cleaning the River Bièvre. In these surroundings, dating from the twelfth century, Fieschi was happy, and he loved, and was loved by, a girl young enough to be his daughter—*La Borgnotte,* who, it seems, was pretty in spite of having only one eye. Incidentally, the Corsican liked to keep to the same family, for the charming one-eyed girl's mother had been his mistress for many years.

Then misfortune had struck. He lost his jobs as guardian and spy, the police having noticed that the "martyr's" certificates were forged. In those days police inspectors were not to be trifled with.

"If I were accused of having stolen the towers of Notre Dame," someone said at the time, "I should begin by running away."

Fieschi took pains to hide himself, and before he knocked at Morey's door he had been living from hand to mouth. Now, wounded in his pride and embittered, he never ceased his vituperations against the royal government that forced him to lie low in old Morey's shop. He, Fieschi, a man who could render incomparable services! Had he not invented an extraordinary weapon?

"Suppose," he told Morey, "there is a besieged garrison that still has arms, but whose defenders are gradually reduced. How can they resist? I, Joseph Fieschi, have invented the means: twenty-five rifles mounted on a frame. One man, one alone, would be needed to set them off. Then what an explosion!"

And from his pocket he pulled out a sketch of the machine.

"Eh! old Morey, that's what you want for your barricades!"

Morey looked for a minute then remarked in his gentle little voice: "It would be even better for Philippe!"

Fieschi gasped. "You're right! It would be better than your scheme . . . and it would cost less."

"But I've not enough money to pay for such a fine machine."

"Neither have I."

"Give me your sketch. I know a rich man who is a good patriot; if he thinks it can succeed he will pay the expenses."

The next day Morey crossed the Seine and paid a visit to the grocer merchant of opinions, Théodore Pépin, who lived at 1 Rue de Faubourg-Saint-Antoine. He was an emphatic, vain and imbecile bourgeois. With his long face framed in mutton-chop whiskers, he looked like a merino sheep. He took pride in being a revolutionary, and by loudly proclaiming his opinions he had become "someone" in that Republican district. When he was with his colleagues of the Society for the Rights of Man he had not enough words to condemn "Philippe," but this did not prevent his bending double with respect if any of the nobility entered his shop.

When Morey showed him Fieschi's sketch the grocer did not understand it very well.

"Bring me the man," he ordered importantly.

The following day Fieschi's formidable Italian accent did not make matters clearer, so the Corsican agreed to make a scale model of the *machina*.

When he brought Pépin the model the grocer understood. Undoubtedly Fieschi was very clever! Nothing could be simpler—it only needed thinking of—than those twenty-five rifle barrels neatly arranged on a wooden frame whose upper part could be raised or lowered in such a way as to permit accurate aiming. The fire would be simultaneous, thanks to a trail of powder lit between the twelfth and thirteenth breeches. All that was needed was to place the machine in a window and set fire to it the moment Philippe passed the house. (Fieschi's *machina* is now in the National Archives.)

"How much would it cost?" the grocer asked anxiously.

"For everything, including making the machine and renting the house: five hundred francs."

At five hundred francs it seemed a pity to go without it! Pépin agreed to finance the operation. In addition the grocer opened an account for Fieschi at his shop which would allow him to satisfy his hunger without paying.

The trio decided to operate on the following July 28. On that day, the anniversary of the Three Glorious Days, the King would hold a general review of the National Guard, who would be drawn up from the Bastille to the Madeleine. It would be enough to find, along the route, a house that was "ordinary, inconspicuous, sheltered from the curious and the indiscreet." They found it at 50 Boulevard du Temple. It was a narrow, three-storied building, huddled between two cafés, the Mille Colonnes and the Bayadères. Opposite, on the other side of the boulevard at No. 29, was the famous dance hall, the Jardin Turc.

For 330 francs a year—a quarter's rent in advance—Fieschi rented a suite of three rooms on the third floor. One window opened onto the boulevard and the others onto a little courtyard giving access to 41 Rue des Fossés-du-Temple. (The conspirators were unaware that this house already had a revolutionary past. In 1793 it had been used as a meeting place for the Gravilliers section, of which the celebrated Simon, "little Capet's tutor," was one of the most active members.)

Prudently, Pépin did not show himself there, but faithful to his word paid the bills presented by Fieschi: *chese,* 5 francs; *chandelli,* 1 franc; *glasse,* 5 francs; *por de boa à charbon,* 6 francs, etc. The grocer also paid with a good grace for the wood for the machine and for the 25 rifle barrels, on which the Corsican took a commission of 37.50 francs, incidentally the only cash the affair was to bring him.

Soon everything was ready. On the evening of July 27 Morey arrived in the Boulevard du Temple and carefully charged the barrels to the top: ten or twelve balls in each barrel, not to mention the buckshot.

Although Fieschi had promised his accomplices to kill himself once the affair was over, the saddler was suspicious and, being an expert shot, he took care to load one or two barrels leaving a gap between the powder and the shot. They would explode and unfailingly kill the regicide. The two men got a confederate to ride on horseback along the boulevard and aimed the machine "at the level of the rider's breast." The train of powder was placed and Morey advised Fieschi to light a fire in the fireplace the next morning. He would then merely have to take a brand and put it to the powder.

At half past ten on July 28, the King, followed by his sons Orléans, Joinville and Nemours, by Marshals Mortier and Maison, by Thiers, the Duc de Broglie and a crowd of generals, arrived opposite No. 50. Suddenly Louis-Philippe saw a wisp of smoke issue from the window of the third floor. He had time to say to Prince de Joinville:

"This is my affair!"

At the same moment the fusillade cracked out "like a firing squad."

"Here I am!" cried the King, waving his hat.

One ball merely grazed his forehead, but around him it was a hecatomb. Fieschi's infernal machine had mowed down the crowd: eighteen dead and twenty-two wounded lay on the pavement. Marshal Mortier was killed instantly by a ball in his left ear.

What irony! That morning the readers of *Charivari* had read this announcement: "Yesterday the citizen-King came from Neuilly to Paris with his splendid family without being in the least assassinated on his way."

Fieschi, horribly wounded by the explosion foreseen by Morey, his skull fractured, the skin of the forehead falling over his eyes, was arrested as he tried to escape by the Rue des Fossés-du-Temple. Morey and Pépin took so many precautions that they ended by being taken prisoner too.

Fieschi—he proudly signed his letters "the *rézisside* Fieschi"—a real "showman of assassination," directed the inquiry and trial. No accused was ever seen to be prouder of passing into posterity. All three conspirators were guillotined on February 19, 1836. Pépin, who had been pitiable during the pleadings, died with courage. Morey was heroic. He could have spoken and saved his own life, but he preferred silence for, as we know today, he had warned the leaders of the Republican party. Cavaignac, Bastide, Recurt and others were waiting on the morning of July 28 in a workshop on the corner of the Boulevard Beaumarchais and the Boulevard du Temple. Barbès and Blanqui, warned by the saddler, were standing by to act. If the attempt had succeeded the second Republic would have been born thirteen years earlier. Blanqui—a detail that does not embellish his memory—in order not to be suspected prepared a "moral alibi" by sending his son and nurse to watch the review in front of the Jardin Turc. They were knocked down but escaped unwounded.

(Assuredly it was in memory of Morey that General-Engineer Kostikov should have had a religious service held in 1942. The inventor of Stalin's famous "organ," at the head of his staff, was present at a mass said in honor of Fieschi, "republican, revolutionary martyr," to whom, he admitted, he owed "the sole idea of his battery." But the general-engineer of the Soviet Army did not know his history. Fieschi was by no means a victim of tyranny; he had killed, not from republican ideals, but for 37.50 francs and a few pounds of lentils and prunes.)

2
A Banquet Smelling of Burning

At the beginning of February, 1848, the XII *arrondissement* of Paris was getting ready to give a political banquet in favor of the reform of the Constitution. In order to gain its ends—since Guizot no more than the King would hear of changes—the opposition had the idea of making use of the euphoria of banquets. A thousand, two thousand, three thousand persons were gathered around a few deputies. One ate one's fill, drank copiously, felt one's importance grow with each dish, and by the time the champagne was reached the sated guests, made cheerful by the wines, heartily applauded the orators who showed them the urgency of that "Reform" to which those present, mostly bourgeois, had until then lent an unattentive ear. Surprisingly enough, the government, which had overlooked up until then several hundred banquets at which people were stuffed with both food and words, found it necessary to take offense at this banquet of the XIIth *arrondissement,* and the meal immediately took on a revolutionary flavor. A police note informs us that on February 14 there was "some unrest in people's minds." On the 15th, 16th and 17th similar notes occur: "Rather lively unrest . . . Paris is still in a state of unrest. . . . The population is still very restless."

M. de Rambuteau, Prefect of the Seine, went to see the King. Louis-Philippe displayed a disarming optimism. In his opinion it was merely bluster, nothing more.

"My dear prefect, eight days hence you will be ashamed of the foolish fears with which you have been inspired and which I am quite unable to share."

Incidentally the opposition seemed to prove that the King was right. Not for a moment did radicals, socialists and republicans imagine that the projected agapes were the "liberating spark." Indeed, in order to prevent the people from taking part, the price of the banquet was raised from three to six francs. (In those days a worker earned between two and three francs a day. A woman's wages were rarely more than one franc.) It was also decided that the banquet "of the

XIIth *arrondissement*" should take place at the Etoile barrier on a piece of wasteland in the Rue du Chemin-de-Versailles, now Rue Galilée.

Battle was joined. Instead of letting well enough alone, the government sent delegates to the organizers. Guizot's representatives proposed the following scheme: just as the guests were unfolding their napkins a police commissioner would appear and tell the assembly to break up. Odilon Barrot would make a speech, the commissioner would draw up his report and all present, with empty stomachs, would return to their distant homes. The program did not specify whether the commissioner, as the only man remaining, would be condemned to eat the meal prepared for fifteen hundred people.

When the delegates had left the organizers argued hotly. What were they to do? This procedure, which consisted, in short, of making a great many people from a distance lunch off a speech and the smell of a banquet, seemed dangerous. And yet no decision was reached. In Paris unrest increased.

"I wish this banquet were over," one man said.

"Yes," replied a wit. "We can see it cooking, but I would rather digest it."

On the morning of February 21, the banquet began to burn and smell scorched. The *National* and the *Réforme,* wishing to force the hand of the overcautious Deputies, declared "that nothing in the program would be changed and that everyone would go to the banquet in procession with the National Guard." At once Guizot, relying on old laws signed by Louis XVI and Bonaparte, decreed:

"1. The meeting and the banquet are forbidden;

"2. The present decree shall be notified to all whom it may concern;

"3. All measures are being taken to ensure the carrying out of the present decree."

The measures announced were grave. Nearly thirty thousand troops were to occupy Paris. Faced with this development of forces, the opposition, terrified, canceled the banquet by eighty votes to seventeen. The painter Ary Scheffer, a frequenter of the Tuileries, hastened to the château to acquaint the King with the good news.

"You see," exclaimed Louis-Philippe. "I was sure they would withdraw."

The final touch to this feeling of well-being was brought by General Jacqueminot, commander of the National Guard, who was sent by Duchâtel, Minister of the Interior, to suggest that the sovereign should suppress some of the military measures. The old King agreed, and went to bed.

At the same time, the leaders of the extreme left were meeting. Should they march? Admittedly the republicans had troops. Indeed there were many out of work in Paris; the railway lines were finished and the new fortifications built. The paid-off workers had chosen to remain in Paris, where they hoped to earn three or four francs a day, rather than return to the provinces, where wages were sometimes as low as 1.50 francs. These jobless men, some of whom belonged to "secret societies," would if necessary be excellent fighters. Unfortunately, nothing was prepared.

"Have you arms and organized men?" Ledru-Rollin asked. "My opinion is that, if undertaken under present conditions, the affair is madness."

Louis Blanc spoke even more strongly.

"You can decide on insurrection if you like, but if that is your decision I shall go home, put on sackcloth and weep over the ruins of democracy."

Nothing, therefore, would be done. The next day the *Réforme* wrote: "Man of the people, beware of any rash undertaking. Do not give power the opportunity for an easy success."

It seemed, then, that everything would go off quietly.

Tuesday, February 22. A gray day. Fine, cold rain was falling. Still in bed, the King smiled as he saw the great rain clouds scudding before the wind above the bare trees in the Tuileries.

"I knew quite well no one would make a revolution in winter."

Guizot and Jayr, the Minister of Public Works, entered the room.

"Well, you have come to congratulate me," the King said to them. "The affair is going splendidly. You know that they have canceled the banquet. They saw, somewhat late it is true, that the stakes were too high. And when I think that many of your friends wanted to give way!"

Jayr did not share this opinion. On leaving his house he had seen the crowd: workingmen from the suburbs making for the Place de la

Concorde. Of course, the banquet and march past were canceled; of course the *Réforme* had warned its readers; of course the republican leaders had ordered "total abstention." But many Parisians, who had risen before dawn, were unaware that the organizers had retired and were going to the appointed meeting place. The King's optimism was not in the least shaken.

"Paris is disturbed? How should it not be! But this disturbance will calm down of itself."

Meanwhile, some professional rioters were mingling with the onlookers, perhaps members of the "Dissident Society," with five hundred adherents, twelve of whom were policemen. Was it these twelve inspectors, acting as *agents provocateurs,* who, as Alexandre Zévaès imagined, succeeded in bringing the whole society into the movement? What a wonderful haul for the police! This hypothesis is not untenable, and would to a certain extent explain the King's optimism.

Early in the morning Louis-Philippe received the artist Horace Vernet, who spoke to him of the columns of workers coming from the Bastille whom he had passed on the boulevard. The King answered absent-mindedly, and preferred to talk to the painter of the voyage the latter was about to make to Pau, to paint Abd el-Kader's portrait. Before taking his leave, Horace Vernet again expressed his fears.

"Have no anxiety, my dear Horace," the King replied. "It will die down of itself without having to be blown out."

At about ten o'clock in the morning several hundred students arrived at the Madeleine, skirted the gates of the monument and went down the Rue Royale singing. On the pavements the crowd applauded. Encouraged, the students crossed the Seine, jostled several Municipal Guards and entered the Chamber of Deputies, which at that hour was empty. After gazing defiantly at the scandalized ushers and wandering about the rooms, they left the Palais Bourbon, whose gates were hastily closed behind them.

Still in front of the Chamber, the students shouted: "Long live reform!" and "Down with Guizot!" but it was still more a students' procession than a revolution. They were playing at rioting. Since 1830 disturbances had been so frequent that a student rag was not alarming. And yet, round about noon, in anticipation of the sitting to be held in the Chamber, General Sébastiani arrived with a battalion of the 60th of the line and a squadron of the 6th Dragoons. The cavalry charged at a slow trot. The students crossed the bridge and dispersed in the direction of the Rue Royale and the Rue Saint-Honoré. One demonstrator, wounded by a blow with the flat of a saber, was tended at the Café des Ambassadeurs. Would the drama now begin? Not at all. For, at the same moment, some wags set the fountains of the Place de la Concorde playing. An old lady, who had rashly sat down near one of the sirens, was soaked. Everybody laughed. The band of the 60th of the line played waltzes and polkas. It seemed more like a fair than the beginning of a revolution!

The square was black with people. The crowd did not know quite what it was waiting for. To warm themselves they lit fires with the Punch and Judy stalls and the wooden horses in the Champs-Elysées.

It was some boys who first took on a more bellicose attitude. They began by throwing stones at the dragoons' backs and then, at the beginning of the afternoon, built barricades with chairs, an omnibus and three cabs. One squadron, having taken the Cours-la-Reine, returned toward the square and came up to the obstacle. The apprentice rioters at once politely made a gap and then closed it after the last horseman.

Thiers was present at the incident. He was therefore somewhat reassured as he went to the sitting of the Chamber where the deputies were discussing . . . the privileges of the Bank of Bordeaux. People were yawning. Odilon Barrot rose to speak, and the Chamber became more attentive. Would the tedium disappear? The opposition deputy surpassed all hopes. Wishing to be pardoned for his escape from the banquet affair, he coldly demanded that the ministry should be indicted for having, abroad, betrayed "the honor and interests of France" and, at home, "thrown the country into profound disturbance."

The Chamber was stupefied. The ministers had violated no law, nor governed otherwise than through a majority. Constitutionally the government was irreproachable. Guizot, solemn, icy, disdainful, mounted the tribune and asked that the debate should be adjourned to Thursday, February 24. The Chamber agreed, with a majority of 110, and went back, with a sigh of resignation, to the Bank of Bordeaux. Nevertheless, some deputies were uneasy. They questioned Guizot. Was not all Paris in the streets? Were the troops calm?

"Gentlemen, I shall answer for the day!"

However, by dint of crying: "Long live Reform!" and "Down with Guizot!" by dint of being jostled by the horses' rumps and waiting in the rain for something to happen, the crowd was beginning to be more nervous. At about four o'clock in the afternoon the fever rose. With the exception of a few suburbanites provided with poles snatched from the vineyards, the demonstrators were not armed. As in 1789 they wrenched open the gates of Saint-Roch church. There were pikes for defending themselves and levers for tearing up the paving stones. Then—the Parisian is ingenious—with the help of an omnibus shaft they broke open the gunsmiths' shops. The shops of Lepage, in the Place du Théâtre-Français, Trébut, in the Rue Saint-Honoré, and Lefaucheux, in the Rue de la Bourse, were ransacked. Even the fencing foils were taken.

"A foil?" said one of the rioters. "That doesn't matter. I shall get my hand in again. I have tyranny as my target."

Finally, in order to "stake out the revolution ground," a few barricades were erected here and there. Very politely the occupants of cabriolets were made to get out. A carriage full of paving stones became a heavy obstacle that the soldiers of the 17th of the line had difficulty in moving. Behind the line the cavalry trotted by.

But immediately they had passed the barricade was restored to its position. Since the Revolution of July, 1830, and the riots of June, 1832, April, 1834 and 1837, the Parisians possessed an extraordinary feeling for street warfare. In a few seconds a pavement was torn up and the stones heaped together. Nevertheless, on that evening there was nothing that could be compared to the preceding days.

"The barricades are ill built," Prefect of Police Duchâtel was to say to Chancelor Pasquier. "And they give the impression of being erected merely for form's sake."

It was still raining, and during the first part of the night many of the brawlers went back to the suburbs. Ledru-Rollin thought that everything was over. On the other hand, the true blues, such as Grandmesnil and "the worker Albert," saw things more clearly and thought they should profit by the occasion to seduce the National Guard and arm the populace. Ringleaders of the Dissident Society, sitting in the wine shops in the Halles district, swore "to resume the struggle until the aristocrats were exterminated." Having drunk well, a certain Sobrier, who was later to be nicknamed the "madman of the Revolution," swept several comrades off to his home and distributed an odd selection of weapons among them. They went drunkenly down the Boulevard Saint-Martin and clashed with a detachment of cavalry. There was immediately a general flight, and all of them, staggering slightly, went home to sleep off their wine and their enthusiasm.

The prefect reported to the King on the day. There had been one dead, near the Louvre. About a hundred barricades had been erected. More serious troubles could be expected the following day. The monarchy was in danger.

"Come now," said the King. "You will regret having spoken to me like that. The Parisians know what they are doing. They will not exchange the throne for a banquet!"

The upper classes shared this feeling. There was a ball at the Duchesse d'Estissac's and one at the Princesse de Ligne's. The political world was more disturbed. That same evening the English ambassador, Lord Normanby, was dining in the Rue de Rivoli at the Finance Ministry. In order to let his carriage pass a breach had to be made in a barricade in the Rue de Rohan. "We sat down eighteen at a table set for thirty-six," he was to recount later. "Many of the guests, in fact, had preferred to stay at home rather than having the paving stones moved. . . . We carefully avoided talking about politics. The talk was only of the opera and of Fanny Elssler." As they left the dinner the guests felt the night to be heavy with threats. Fresh troops had arrived. They were bivouacked in the rain around fires whose flames were kept down by the icy wind. On the outer boulevards the rioters took possession of the barriers. The little customs houses at the Etoile, Monceau and Batignolles were occupied. The National Guards' post at the Courcelles barrier was burned down.

The King did not hear the muffled tumult rising from the city. He went to bed, peaceful and calm. Guizot was less sure of himself. The shouts of "Down with Guizot!" uttered even under his windows, had perhaps slightly shaken his assurance. Perhaps he thought of Lamennais's prophecy, already five years old: "It is Guizot who must lead Louis-Philippe's monarchy to its last resting place. He is a born gravedigger."

As for old Thiers, he had understood nothing.

"It is all over," he said as he went to bed. On the contrary, it was just beginning.

"It is raining; nothing will happen today," Pétion used to say at the time of the great revolutionary days. On that Wednesday, February 23, it was raining torrents. The air was damp and the south wind incessantly drove fresh clouds to pour down on the capital. It was a day on which to stay at home by the fire. Yet on that morning the beating of drums, the sound of omnibuses being overturned and paving stones being torn up brought all Paris into the streets.

Guizot had redoubled his precautions. The troops were occupying the Bourse, the Carrousel, the Hôtel de Ville and the Saint-Denis and Saint-Martin gates. During the night, particularly round the Hôtel de Ville, the barricades had sprung up like mushrooms. Omnibuses and cabs were not enough; in the Rue Quincampoix two traveling coaches, filled with great paving stones, barred the way. At break of day the troops, coming from the Place de Grève, launched an assault on this redoubt. They were met with heavy fire. Sixteen soldiers fell. It was no longer a matter of vine poles. In the backs of shops the Parisians were melting shot. On the doors of many houses could be read, written in chalk: ARMS GIVEN, or SALE OF ARMS. Urchins broke bottles and strewed the fragments under the horses' hoofs. The soldiers began to get angry and in the Rue Vieille-du-Temple started to demolish a barricade with cannon fire.

The situation was undoubtedly serious, but very few people were yet thinking of the fall of the regime. They had seen so much since 1830!

"General," a young officer asked his commander, "shall we be here for long?"

"Why?"

"Well, I'm having dinner in town."

Meanwhile—which was very significant—the first red flag appeared in the Rue Montmartre. It was planted on the summit of a barricade as strong as a bastion. Admittedly it was, more prosaically, a purple blind torn from inside a cab and nailed to the shaft of a wine cart, but the symbol was there, and one must do as best one can.

The government was stupefied. How, in one night, could matters have got so much worse? At about eight o'clock the prefect decided that they might perhaps try to arrest the leaders of the extreme left. Too late: they were no longer at home, but in the streets.

Why not summon the National Guard? It might play a pacifying role. And they hastened to have the drum beaten. The result of this step was catastrophic: an hour later the bourgeois, disguised as warriors, arrived at the town halls. No orders were awaiting them. They wandered about woefully and to everyone's astonishment shouted, not "Long live the King!" but "Long live Reform!"

However, the officers managed finally to assemble part of their men. The Xth Legion was reviewed by Colonel Lemercier. One man stepped out of the ranks and cried: "Down with the ministers and long live Reform!"

Lemercier had not recovered from his surprise when his whole troop replied in echo: "Down with Guizot!"

The colonel, completely shattered, decided to go back to bed.

It was then that the leaders of the Society of the Seasons had a brilliant idea. From old-clothes shops they procured uniforms of the National Guards in which they dressed some hirelings. Their work and mission can be guessed. The result did not have to be long awaited. An hour later National Guards were shouting, "Down with Guizot!" under the minister's windows and "Long live Reform!" under the King's. Better still, the VIIth Legion took the liberty of sending a deputation to the Hôtel de Ville, and the IVth signed a petition roundly demanding the "indictment of the corrupt Ministry."

The final blow came from the IIIrd Legion. In the Place des Victoires rioters were attacking the guard post with paving stones. A battalion of National Guards watched the scene with indifference. A detachment of dragoons appeared; the horsemen, amid a rain of projectiles, trotted slowly toward the crowd. As one man the National Guard stepped forward and crossed bayonets under the horses' noses. The crowd applauded them with shouts of "The National Guard is with us!" And the dragoons could only retire, pursued by jeers.

At almost the same moment identical scenes were taking place in the Rue Le Peletier and the Rue Saint-Antoine. The news ran through Paris like wildfire: "The National Guard has mutinied!"

The King, informed at once, was overwhelmed. He was flabbergasted! The National Guard was his hope and pride. He wore its uniform; he reviewed the men; he took an interest in them. He who, for eighteen years, had carefully disguised himself as a bourgeois! His umbrella, his toupee, his thick whiskers, his muddy boots, all the panoply in the Joseph Prudhomme fashion which he had chosen, certainly not because he liked it, but in order more closely to resemble those bourgeois from the Marais, those shopkeepers who had emerged powerful from the great Revolution and on whom he considered he should depend in order to reign . . . And those people, his "comrades," as he called them when he asked them to dinner at the Tuileries, were now betraying him. What appalling ingratitude! He could scarcely believe it, even so. In a broken and suddenly aged voice he asked each person who entered his office: "Is it true that the National Guard is making common cause with the rioters?"

He paced up and down, stammered, looked vaguely about him, and finally took the only measure possible: the dismissal of Guizot.

Once his decision was made, the King calmed down. The evening was peaceful and the Tuileries as boring as on its finest days, while mounted National Guards rode through Paris announcing the good news of Guizot's departure and Molé's arrival. There was general embracing. Apart from a few recalcitrants, a few professional rioters, the joy was complete. Admittedly the barricades were not destroyed, but they were illuminated, and as night fell lamps were hung on the trees.

Everything was over!

And yet, on the following day, at the beginning of the afternoon, with the King in flight, the Parisians, completely astonished by the unexpected success of their upheaval, were to impose a Republic on France.

3

The Man in the Yellow Coat

Paris was illuminated on that evening of Wednesday, February 24, but Sobrier could not be consoled for "having let the Revolution escape." He decided to go into action. Followed by a few hotheads, members of secret societies, he ran from barricade to barricade. In the Rue Montmartre he climbed on the side of an overturned omnibus and yelled:

"Citizens, the satisfaction given to the people is derisory. Molé, or even Thiers, instead of Guizot, is nothing to us! The rights of the people have been ignored for fourteen centuries and they must be solemnly recognized! Forward!"

Fresh recruits joined him. From barricade to barricade the group grew. Sobrier was indefatigable. That evening he was seen in the Rue Montorgueil, the Rue Saint-Denis, the Rue Saint-Martin, at the Hôtel de Ville, the Tuileries and even in the Marais. It was near the Louvre, in a little café in the Rue du Coq, that he collapsed, drunk with exhaustion and wine. But the impetus had been given. The little band, with candles stuck in rifle barrels, went to shout its anger in front of the offices of the *National*. Its editor, the Republican Armand Marrast, somewhat scared, spoke prudently. In the front rank of his listeners could be seen a bearded fellow, dressed in an astonishing yellow coat, his long, curly hair falling down to his shoulders. He generally posed for the "heads of Christ" in Montmartre studios. Suddenly he interrupted Marrast and shouted in a hoarse, vinous voice: "Forward, my friends!"

This man in the yellow coat, a man whose name no one knows, was to dethrone Louis-Philippe. His vitality was extraordinary. He was tall, thin and with bright eyes; "the total effect was of a man about to face gunfire." Carrying a torch, and without ceasing to shout, the model led the crowd along in marching step. It was ten o'clock in the evening. In the Boulevard des Capucines, by what is now Rue Cambon, where the Foreign Ministry was then, the way was barred by the 14th of the line, commanded by Lieutenant Colonel Courant.

"What do you want?" the officer asked, stepping forward.

"We want the Ministry to be illuminated," the man in the yellow coat replied.

"That has nothing to do with me."

"All right, let us pass."

"I am a soldier. I must obey. I have been ordered to let no one pass, and you shall not pass."

The man thrust forward his torch and threatened the lieutenant-colonel with it, shouting: "You are all nothing but scum, and I tell you we shall pass. It's our right!"

He came nearer. The torch was nearly touching Courant's mustache. It was then that the Grenadier Sergeant Giacomini threw up his rifle, aimed and fired. The man in the yellow coat fell, killed at almost point-blank range.

It was irreparable. The soldiers, irritated by the insults, harassed, hungry—they had eaten nothing since morning—were no longer in command of their reflexes. They thought it was a signal, and fired. Fifty-two people lay on the ground. In a second there was no one left in the boulevard. The rioters had disappeared and the terrified soldiers fled down the Rue des Capucines. Gradually, however, the fugitives listened to their colonel's voice and returned to their post. The battalion re-formed, and the demonstrators came back in their turn, shouting: "Assassins! Vengeance!" At that moment a wagon belonging to the Messageries Royales Laffitte et Caillard crossed the boulevard, taking three travelers and their luggage to the Havre station. In a few minutes occupants and baggage were turned onto the pavement and about fifteen corpses were piled into the cart's yellow box. The body of the man in the yellow coat and of a half-naked woman were placed well in sight. Four men bearing torches climbed onto the shafts, and the vehicle, drawn by the Messageries' white horse, set out for the center of the city. As this funeral procession passed the illuminations were extinguished and the tocsin sounded. They stopped first in front of the *National*. Garnier-Pagès, seeing the tragic carriage, spoke of a misunderstanding and begged the demonstrators to go no farther. The bloodstained exhibition had a better welcome at the *Réforme*. Flocon, a man possessed of the faith acquired in dungeons, advised them to show "every family the appalling outrage" that had been perpetrated. He added: "Public execration must abolish tyranny!"

The phantom coach, signal of the death of the regime, pursued its way. It went toward the Bastille. The cart dripping with blood halted in front of the July column where slept the combatants of the Three Glorious Days. It was getting late. What should they do? It was cold and beginning to rain. The torchbearers were terribly thirsty. They had shouted so much. It seemed difficult, however, to leave the macabre load at the door of a bistro. They therefore went down the Rue Saint-Antoine, without quite knowing where to go next. Fortunately, the door of the town hall of the IVth *arrondissement* happened to be open. The Messageries driver drove his cart into the courtyard and, before going to have a drink, the demonstrators laid out the corpses in a ground-floor room. It was then that they perceived that among the victims of the "terrible outrage," next to the body of the man with the yellow coat, were the corpses of a soldier of the 14th of the line and of an officer of the National Guard. The rioters, too, had fired.

In his bedroom at the Tuileries King Louis-Philippe listened to the sinister murmurs from the city. The news of the firing at the Capucines had left him crushed. In all the streets fresh barricades were being erected. There would soon be not one paving stone in place. The trees in the boulevards were cut down. The street lamps were broken and the gas ran along the ground in long, bluish whirls. From time to time a rifle shot startled the King, sunk in his armchair. They were shooting at random, here and there, "to prevent sleep soothing the city's anxiety and anger."

"Everything may yet be saved," the mayor of the VIIIth *arrondissement* said to Victor Hugo on that Thursday morning.
"Yes," the poet replied. "If Bugeaud will forego being the savior."
Louis-Philippe had just dismissed Molé, called on Thiers and charged Bugeaud, the conqueror of Isly, with saving the monarchy. The marshal was sure to succeed. On arriving at his headquarters at three in the morning, he had placed his watch in front of him and given his orders—and what orders!
"If necessary I shall make the Parisians swallow the saber of Isly up to the hilt!"
Four columns were to go through the capital and get by at all costs. The first, commanded by General Sébastiani, would go from the Tuileries to the Hôtel de Ville; the second, with General Bedeau, was instructed to reach the Bastille by the boulevards; the third would follow the two first, so as to prevent the barricades from re-forming; the fourth would push on to the Panthéon. And the National Guard? They could do without it, since the marshal had at his disposal nearly twenty-seven thousand men.
At five o'clock in the morning this plan went into action. The Panthéon was quickly reached. On his side, Sébastiani arrived without

hindrance at the Hôtel de Ville. Seeing him, the defenders in the square scattered. General Bedeau's column, eighteen hundred strong, did not have the same good fortune. At the Montmartre barrier the rebels defended themselves hotly. Volley firing finally enabled the troops to advance as far as the Gymnase Theatre. At that point officers of the National Guard and unarmed bourgeois came to parley with the general, assuring him that the population of the suburbs was still unaware of the government changes and that calm would certainly be re-established once Thiers's arrival in power was known. Bedeau halted his advance and sent a messenger to the marshal. "I approve what you have done," Bugeaud replied, "and I send you proclamations announcing the new Ministry. Distribute them by every means at your disposal. . . . But it is understood that if rioting begins you must read the riot act and be energetic in the use of force."

But a quarter of an hour later there was a counter-order from the marshal. "My plans have been modified. Announce everywhere that there is a cease-fire and that the National Guard will act as a police force. Speak conciliatory words. P.S. Withdraw to the Carrousel."

What had happened was this:

Not without difficulty, from barricade to barricade, Thiers and his Cabinet had reached the Tuileries. At eight o'clock in the morning, Thiers and Odilon Barrot had seen the King and extracted the cease-fire order from him. This was communicated to Bugeaud. Furthermore, the following announcement was ordered to be posted throughout Paris:

> Citizens: Order has been given to cease fire everywhere. We have just been entrusted by the King with forming a new Ministry. The Chamber will be dissolved. An appeal is made to the country. MM. Thiers, Barrot and Duvergier de Hauranne are Ministers.
> *Liberty, Order and Reform!*
> General Lamoricière is appointed commander of the National Guard.

This appointment was an idea of the new ministers. Lamoricière, who was very popular, was the leading spirit in the conquest of Algeria. It was he who, in the preceding year, had captured Abd el-Kader. Perhaps by his very presence he would be able to rally the National Guard and calm public feeling. Lamoricière, who did not know what was wanted of him, arrived at the Tuileries. Unfortunately he was in civilian dress. Without delay an officer put a tunic on him on which a general's epaulettes were pinned, and he was given the first kepi that came to hand. The cap was too large and the tunic too small. It was impossible to find a pair of trousers that the general could wear. He therefore kept his civilian trousers, checked ones. And in this get-up African Lamoricière mounted his horse and rode down the street.

He was acclaimed. Too well! The rioters asked him to put himself at their head. This was by no means Lamoricière's ambition and he hastily turned back. Annoyed, the combatants fired on him and wounded his horse.

The situation was becoming worse each minute. General Bedeau's retreat—from the Gymnase to the Concorde—ended in a rout. The crowd had gradually infiltrated the soldiers' ranks. Girls took their arms, men snatched their rifles and cartridges and it was an anonymous rabble that entered the Place de la Concorde by the Rue Royale. The troops were so mixed up with the rioters that the Municipal Guards occupying the Peyronnet pavilion at the top of the Avenue Gabriel fired on the disorderly mass. The rioters rushed forward and butchery resulted. The Guards were cut down with sabers. General Bedeau was not even able to intervene. It was not until half past ten that, with the help of the men remaining to him, he was able to take up his position in the square before the "swing bridge" of the Tuileries.

At the same time the 45th of the line was fraternizing with the people and returning to barracks; military students led the insurgents; prisoners for debt were freed and swelled the ranks of the combatants; bullets were whistling and cracking all over the town, particularly in Rue de Chartres, Rue Saint-Nicaise, Rue des Froimanteaux, all winding alleys at that time separating the Palais Royal from the Place du Carrousel.

At a short distance from the château, right on top of a barricade, a man blackened with powder was fighting like a demon. Tirelessly he repeated: "My friends, we must shoot General Aupick!"

It was Charles Baudelaire, who had not forgotten his hatred of his stepfather.

As was to be expected, it had not been possible to post the announcements and the town had turned into a battlefield. Odilon Barrot decided to go on horseback to speak to the rioters. He was received somewhat coolly. There were shouts of: "Down with the humbugs! No more Barrot! The people are the sole masters!" There even began to be yells of: "Down with Louis-Philippe!" At the corner of the Rue de la Paix Arago shouted: "Abdication before noon . . . or else revolution!"

In consternation Barrot returned to the Tuileries. He found the King in the Galerie de Diane, beginning his lunch. General Bedeau's lamentable retreat, which Captain de Laubépin had just announced, did not prevent his sitting down to table with the Queen, his sons, Thiers and Duvergier de Hauranne. Suddenly Rémusat, one of the new ministers, arrived. He was stupefied on seeing the King begin eating a chicken.

"Sire, the King must know the truth. To hide it at such a moment would show complicity in the event. Your very serenity proves that you have been led into error. Three hundred paces away from your palace the dragoons are exchanging their sabers and the soldiers their rifles with the insurgents."

"But it is impossible! . . . impossible!" the poor man stammered, rising hastily from the table.

"I must add, sire, that the King is no longer in safety in the Tuileries."

"What is to be done? What is to be done?"

Thiers advised a retreat to Saint-Cloud, where sixty thousand men could be assembled.

"We shall then march on Paris. We shall perhaps be obliged to destroy the Hôtel de Ville and I should have to use cannon, but I would destroy six similar palaces in order to crush the revolution."

The little man had become a fire eater. There was now no question of "the old man's abdication." There is nothing like giving power to a man in opposition to see him become more governmental than his predecessor. The Queen thought a retreat to Saint-Cloud was premature. Why not first try to review the troops defending the château, as Louis XVI had done on August 10?

Louis-Philippe was a cork tossed on the waters. He was incapable of commanding and could barely obey. With a sigh, he agreed and went to put on his uniform of general of the National Guard. Followed by

Montpensier, Nemours, Marshal Bugeaud and Lamoricière—still as oddly dressed—the King mounted his horse. From the windows in the Galerie de Diane the Queen, the princesses and the ministers watched the scene, as once had Marie Antoinette and Louis XVI's last defenders. Not far away the battle could be heard. The water tower, three hundred yards from the Tuileries, was being violently attacked.

At first the review did not go too badly. There were present nearly four thousand troops, among whom were three battalions of the National Guard. The King first passed an infantry company. The men cried "Long live the King!" But a little farther on, the National Guards of the Ist Legion yelled "Long live Reform!"

"Reform?" answered the King sadly. "But you have it, my friends. There is no longer any pretext for unrest."

And he spurred on his horse. As the procession passed the IIIrd Legion the bourgeois uttered loud shouts: "Down with the ministers! Down with the regime!" The King faltered. He was seventy-five. Instead of pressing on and being acclaimed by the soldiers waiting for him, he turned round and went back to the château, where he sank into a chair near the window.

He had aged by ten years. Around him his family, his ministers and his officers were thinking of the inevitable abdication, but no one had yet dared utter the terrible word which would overwhelm the old man. It was Emile de Girardin, press director, who was to dare. Coming from the street, he burst into the room.

"Sire, the ministerial fumblings are no longer of any use. In an hour there will be neither king nor royalty in France. There is only one word that meets the situation: abdication."

There was a heavy silence. The shots could be heard striking the front of the château. The King looked at those about him and said: "You wish it? All right, then, I abdicate."

A few minutes later Louis-Philippe was hastening to the passage leading to the garden. The wind blew. It was not even a flight, but a panic. No royal dignity, but an old man hunted by rioters. He had even forgotten to take 700,000 francs from the drawer of his desk. He left with 15 francs in his pocket. On arriving in the Place de la Concorde the King pushed his way through the crowd and with the Queen entered a court brougham. An unknown man shut the door.

"Thank you," said the King mechanically.

"Not at all," the man replied. "I have been waiting eighteen years for this day!"

Louis-Philippe stamped with impatience. "Go on, go on at once!"

The coachman cracked his whip and the modest equipage, surrounded by a cavalry escort, moved off toward Saint-Cloud, the first stage on the way to exile.

That same evening Frédérick Lemaître was playing in his great triumph, Félix Pyat's *The Ragpicker,* at the Porte Saint-Martin theatre. One line of dialogue was particularly famous. Returning from his rounds the hero says: "Let us empty the dustbin and draw up an inventory of my night's work. To think that I have all Paris in this basket!"

And on that evening, to the applause of the public, who began singing the "Marseillaise," Frédérick Lemaître added to the diverse objects in his basket a royal crown. For the Parisians the bourgeois monarchy—eight hours after its fall—was only fit for the scrap heap. It was well and truly dead.

The man in the yellow coat had killed it!

4

The Orbit of a Comet

The King had not passed the Passy barrier when the Tuileries were invaded. The victors immediately sat down to the royal family's interrupted dinner. In the cellars the barrels were pierced and there was soon two feet of wine in the basements. The next day drunkards were found drowned. In the drawing rooms some people dressed up in the garments of the King and Queen. Mirrors were fired at, statues broken. Into the courtyard were thrown portraits by Mignard, papers found in the King's desk, the little Comte de Paris's exercise books, the bust of Voltaire, pictures by Delacroix . . . and everything burned together with the coaches. Only the Saverne, the King's armored carriage—a real fortress—refused to burn. Shortly afterward it was tipped into the Seine from the Pont des Saints-Pères. The throne was burned in the Place de la Bastille, in front of the July column, but the great crucifix from the chapel, saved by military students, found a refuge in the church of Saint Roch.

In the Chamber M. de Lamartine's hour was about to strike. "Lamartine's political principles were those of the eternal truth represented by the Gospels." It is no use trying to find the name of this panegyrist of the author of *Les Méditations*. The phrase was written by Lamartine himself.

But in spite of this "eternal truth," the Chamber did not take the poet-deputy very seriously. When he wanted to speak on the conversion of government stock, he was interrupted by shouts that "the conversion of stock was not as good as the conversion of Jocelyn" (reference to a poem by Lamartine). However, on February 24, 1848, a few moments after King Louis-Philippe's abdication, all his colleagues had their eyes fixed on him. The Chamber was in a state of disorder and it was felt that the writer would now emerge from his silence. Some remembered M. de Humboldt's amusing remark: "M. de Lamartine is a comet whose orbit has not yet been calculated." This February 24 was to be the great day of his life.

Suddenly the ushers carried in an armchair and two chairs and put them down at the foot of the tribune. At the same moment the Duchesse d'Orléans entered the hemicycle. On her right was the litttle Comte de Paris, aged ten, in whose favor the King had just abdicated; on her left was her second son, the young Duc de Chartres. Hélène de Mecklembourg-Schwerin had been a widow since the accident that brought about her husband's death in the Chemin de la Révolte. On seeing the young woman, whose frail figure appeared weighed down by her mourning veils, all the deputies rose and applauded. The princess looked so tiny, so fragile, so touching. "A pretty face under a bonnet," Mme. de Girardin said of her. "A pretty figure under a coat, a pretty foot in a slipper and a pretty hand for a well-made glove." In short, a Parisienne, in spite of her German birth.

"I am a republican, but I am moved by that woman and her two orphan children," Armand Marrast confided to his neighbor.

The monarchists wished to exploit this success. Dupin, one of Louis-Philippe's counselors, mounted the tribune, followed by Odilon Barrot, whose long-drawn-out speech sounded hollow. No one listened. Everyone was looking at Lamartine, whose hour had struck.

Later he was to assert that everything would have been different if at that moment he had exclaimed: "This revolution is just, it is generous, it is French. It does not fight against women and children. Go on and reign! The people adopts you! It will be your grandfather. You had only a prince as tutor; now you will have a mother and a nation." But Lamartine said nothing of the kind. He mounted the tribune and demanded the creation of a provisional government " that will prejudice neither our rights nor our resentments, neither our sympathies nor the right of the blood that flows, the right of this people made hungry by the glorious work it has accomplished in the last three days."

At this moment the orator was melodramatically interrupted. The doors of the sessions hall were broken in and the "hungry people," pursuing their "glorious work," invaded the Chamber. The drunken rioters were shouting: "Down with the bourgeois! Down with the traitors!" One of them waved a weapon in the direction of President Sauzet—a complete nonentity—who sank down behind his desk and escaped, taking the hat of one of the secretaries by mistake. The enormous room had now no resemblance to a parliamentary assembly. Taking advantage of the crush, one of the rioters approached the Comte de Paris and threatened him with a knife. A group of deputies stepped in, saved the child and managed to get the "regent" away.

The session continued under the presidency of Dupont de l'Eure, an elderly remnant of the Council of the Five Hundred. He was born in the reign of Louis XV, had been a deputy since the Year VII, and his antecedents and well-known incapacity had summoned him to the presidential armchair. His quavering voice was quite unable to enforce quiet. The crowd yelled: "Provisional government! Names! Give us names!" Scraps of paper were handed to Dupont de l'Eure, who droned into the tumult. Finally Lamartine returned to the tribune and shouted: "Dupont de l'Eure, Ledru-Rollin, Arago, Marie and Lamartine."

One is always best served by oneself. There was applause.

"To the Hôtel de Ville!" It was Lamartine who gave the order. If this self-appointed "government" stayed in the Palais Bourbon it would be lost. At the Hôtel de Ville, the headquarters of the revolt, the new masters could hope to retain their power. And they set out by the Left Bank. Two drummers and four workmen in blouses preceded Lamartine, who gave his left arm to an armed workman and his right to a National Guard. Dupont de l'Eure had been hustled into a cab. Without ceasing, now from one window, now from another, he begged in broken tones: "My friends, no civil war."

Indeed, the affair was far from being over. Cavalry squadrons could be seen riding in good order along the quays on the Right Bank. A party of them would only have had to cross the bridge to carry off this "government by acclamation." Lamartine was afraid of this. He was a prisoner of the riot. A drunken woman, brandishing a saber and displaying, in spite of the cold, strong, bare breasts, wanted to kiss the poet, who drew back, scared by this sight so different from the pale, romantic heroine dear to his heart. The woman consoled herself by kissing the National Guard, who was delighted by this windfall.

As they passed the d'Orsay barracks the poet stopped and spoke to one of the cuirassiers through the railings: "Soldier, give me a glass of wine."

He was not thirsty, but he wanted to turn a phrase.

"My friend, here is the banquet!"

And he drank, to the applause of the crowd.

Near the Hôtel de Ville the barricades were more numerous. Dupont de l'Eure's cab could no longer follow. The "old flag" was taken out of his vehicle, two stalwarts took him under the arms and, lifting him from the ground, got him over the tree trunks and pools of blood. In front of the Hôtel de Ville the "government" was separated by the crowd. Dupont de l'Eure escaped suffocation thanks to a fat old woman who took the old man in her arms. Surrounded by pikes and sabers, the deputies reached the main porch. Inside it was a different matter. It was impossible to find a single room for their discussions. The rioters were everywhere. The "ministers" wandered about helplessly until a municipal employee called Flottard led the new masters of France into a dark corridor. In order not to be separated, the deputies held hands. Dupont de l'Eure followed, still carried by the sturdy old woman. At the end of the corridor Flottard opened a door. It was a narrow little room, furnished with a table and some rush-bottomed chairs. Rifles were piled in a corner. On the chimney piece were some empty bottles.

They began to get organized. While the crowd yelled and rioters were constantly entering the room, the cake was divided up. Dupont de l'Eure was nominated president, Lamartine took Foreign Affairs,

Ledru-Rollin the Interior, Arago the Marine and Marie Public Works. They needed a Minister for War. As in 1830 there was, it seemed, a general who had just appeared in the Hôtel de Ville and who could be found. He turned out to be an actor called Chateaurenaud. Dressed as General Kléber—a play he was rehearsing—and mounted on a cab horse, he had been declaiming speeches from his part at the neighboring crossroads to frenzied applause. Lamartine preferred to choose a real general, the only one who, in view of his age, had not fought against the people: General Subervie. While waiting for the old soldier to arrive they hastened to dispatch a proclamation to the army, assuring the troops that "all would be forgotten except their courage and their discipline." This brilliant formula was suddenly interrupted by a group of men entering the room. Surprise! It was another government! The radicals of the National and the socialists of the Réforme had also formed a Ministry. There were Louis Blanc, Marrast, Paguerre, Flocon and "the worker Albert." Fortunately these gentlemen were well disposed and accepted the title of Secretaries of State.

Now to work! But no! The door opened once more. A worker appeared and cried: "If in half an hour you have not recognized the sovereignty of the people, the people will be here."

The memory of the Terror hung over the Ministry. Lamartine rose. "I shall speak to them!"

He had barely reached the corridor when a whole crowd rushed at him. They shouted: "For far too long ambitious men have been making use of us to make revolutions and then getting rid of us on the day of victory!"

The whole question was there. The Parisians feared another juggling trick like that of 1830. Lamartine stood on a chair and tried to speak. There was a general outcry. "Humbug! Go and mend your lyre!" In order to gain time Marrast gave him the list of members of the provisional government to read out.

"I cannot," replied Lamartine, more modest than he had been just now on the tribune. "My name is on it."

Marrast held the list out to Crémieux.

"Are you being funny? My name is not on it." (It was on it the next day.)

Finally Lamartine agreed to shout the names over the tumult.

"By what right," someone yelled, "do you set yourselves up as a government?"

By what right? This time the poet was able to answer: "By the right of the blood that has flowed, by the right of the people without leader, without guide, without orders and tomorrow without bread."

Applause broke out. Lamartine had won . . . for a few minutes. Returning to the office, he asked his colleagues to proclaim a Republic as a matter of urgency. If they wavered there was a risk of being thrown out the window, or of the arrival of the terrible Caussidière, a cynical giant who, with a saber attached to his belt by string, had just taken police headquarters single-handed and was calling to arms "the people so often deceived by treachery."

It was nine o'clock in the evening. They were beginning to feel hungry. While a concierge brought some bread, cheese and a bucket of water, someone discovered a half sheet of paper on which a temporary secretary, after smearing it somewhat with Gruyère, wrote at Lamartine's dictation:

"The provisional government declares that the provisional government of France is the republican government and that the nation will be immediately called on to ratify the resolution of the provisional government and of the people of Paris."

"Three times provisional," Ledru-Rollin exclaimed, with reason, "is twice too often!"

This grammatical observation, which was quite simply a political revolution, as Victor Hugo was to remark, seemed justified to those present. One of the "provisionals" was replaced by the word "present" and the seal of the City of Paris was fixed to the bottom of the sheet, but upside down, they were in such a hurry. This scrap of undated paper—no one had thought of putting the date—contained a people's whole future.

Now they had crossed this Rubicon, perhaps these gentlemen would go on to organize the republic imposed by the people of Paris and of whose existence twenty-nine million Frenchmen were still unaware? Perhaps these improvised ministers would give orders for the return home of the hungry populace still yelling in the square who on the morrow would nearly massacre these bourgeois dictators and impose the red flag of France? Would the provisional government proclaim the country in danger since, it was said, Marshal Bugeaud was preparing to march on Paris with the royal army? No. Before going to bed, the members of the new government—and this, as far as I know, has never been noticed before—decreed "in the name of the people" that "the jury charged with receiving pictures for the annual exhibitions of painting shall be appointed by election. The artists will be summoned for this purpose by a future decree. The Salon of 1848," the text continues, "will open on March 15." This time the date was not forgotten: "This 24th day of February, 1848."

Surely no government, in such a dramatic and precarious situation, has ever issued such an unexpected decree!

5

Freedom Goes to the Head

Parisians are lightheaded—or so those people assert who do not live between the Vincennes and Saint-Cloud gates—and the wind of independence brought by the 1848 Revolution turned the Parisians' heads until they nearly lost them. Paris had abandoned all sense of restraint: freedom had gone to its brain. A simple lamplighter, who had taken part in the attack on the château, died a few days later at the Tuileries itself, which had been transformed into a civilian hospital. It was decided to give him a sumptuous funeral. He was magnificently dressed from head to foot, an oculist gave him glass eyes and the body was seated in Louis-Philippe's armchair. All Paris filed past "this child of work people whom death had given a throne." To be truthful, it was not entirely for the sacred cause of freedom that the "child of work people" had died. When the château was being sacked he had stolen a few diamonds, but on learning that National Guards posted at the gates were searching everyone who left and shooting thieves, he took fright and swallowed the stones in their settings. He trusted to his strong digestion and hoped soon to recover his treasure, but nothing happened. Fearing to be shot if he confessed the cause of his illness, the lamplighter preferred to be silent, and died of it. As a result of this "indigestion of diamonds," in Lenotre's words, he was borne to Père Lachaise cemetery in a hearse drawn by six caparisoned horses, to the sound of muffled drums and between two rows of troops. Behind the coffin walked delegations from the "Holders of July decorations," the "Victims of April," or the "Wounded of February," members of those innumerable societies that sprang up after the Revolution, the reds and blues Flaubert writes of, the rioters, the mystics and the drunkards who had formed "clubs," "cleubs" or "clioubs"—the pronunciation varied according to one's opinions—gatherings at which the death of kings was decreed and the fraudulence of grocers denounced. Over one of these societies the men and women of Paris nearly came to blows.

This was the "Vésuviennes." Their spiritual father, a certain Borme, Junior—no one knows, incidentally, who Borme, Senior, was —claimed to have invented "a Greek fire enabling a woman to destroy a whole arsenal with ten francs' worth of material." An ardent feminist, he had also conceived a method by which "two thousand citizens could fight fifty thousand men at once." It must be mentioned that after a brain fever in 1841 Borme, Junior, had had to be shut up. Under the Second Republic he can only have been relatively cured, but he thought otherwise and considered that his inventions gave him the right to put himself at the head of his "sisters of the Republic." And so one morning the citizenesses of Paris read the following notice posted on the walls of the capital:

"I have asked the provisional government to engage you under the title of Vésuviennes. The engagement will be for a minimum of one year and a maximum of thirty years. Signed: Borme, Junior."

I do not know how many aspirants signed on for thirty years, but there was a rush of candidate Vésuviennes for twelve months who cheerfully enrolled under the banner borne by Citizen Borme, Junior. Their male contemporaries were interested by the name Vésuviennes and one of them asked for an explanation.

"Deep down in our hearts," replied one of the new recruits, "we have a whole volcano of revolutionary fire and ardor."

The "fire and ardor" were first revealed by a splendid formula of which Borme, Junior, was very proud: "Woman must not emancipate herself by becoming a man; she must emancipate man by making him woman." One suspects that the Vésuviennes were not going to stop at that point on their road. A draft constitution was soon drawn up and submitted to the provisional government. The first article dealt, naturally, with fashion: feminine dress should be as like as possible to that of men. Love came next: marriage was made obligatory for the Parisian at twenty-six and for the Parisienne at twenty-one. "Remarriage" was also an obligation for widowers of less than forty-five. Above this age the ladies left you in peace. However, sometimes they confided you to a foreign woman who, by adopting an old man, became French. Before marriage a recruiting board, presided over by Vésuvienne officers, could exempt dunces, cretins and deformed people from marriage. Ladies with a particularly volcanic temperament who did not want a disappointment would be allowed to live for a year with a postulant before appearing at the town hall. This novitiate had to be certified by witnesses.

Up to this point the men had not taken things badly. The Vésuviennes were women of Paris—that is, naturally charming—and it was not difficult to shut one's eyes to their eccentricities. But things went wrong when the last article of the constitution appeared: "The males will henceforward have their share [what share was not specified] in household duties." Justifiably anxious, a certain Muré announced that one could perfectly well do without women thanks to compressed air, which, according to him, could be distributed in the home so as to "wax boots, grind coffee, make the beds and snuff the candles." The Vésuviennes, annoyed at being compared to wind under pressure, replied by singing "their" "Marseillaise":

> Work, you trousered tyrants!
> Women, our day is come!

The "trousered tyrants" thought the joke had lasted long enough and that it was time to put a stop to it, particularly as the evil was spreading. Other utopian societies were formed in imitation of the Vésuviennes. One Parisienne, Mme. Nicoyet, dared to announce on the platform of the Feminist Club that she was going to found a newspaper dealing with the art of having children without the help of the stronger sex. Mme. Nicoyet was pretty, and in order to set her back on the right road some gentlemen waited for her as she left the club and smacked her bottom out on the boulevard.

War had been declared.

The men, considering ridicule to be a sure weapon in Paris, composed the "Farewell Song of the Vésuviennes":

Onward, Vésuviennes, we must be bolder
And throw off the yoke that weighs down on our shoulder.
Let us do what they dared not in '93
And abolish our husbands by decree.
    May unheard-of vengeance light
    On mankind and teach it sorrow.
    May the cocks of yesternight
    Be the capons of tomorrow!

    It must be admitted, looked at objectively, that freedom went to other heads besides those of the Parisiennes. The newspapers of the day, whose names made the bourgeois tremble—*Lave Sociale, Journal de la Canaille, Aimable Faubourien, Christ républicain*—were filled with masculine proposals giving rise to anxiety about the minds of their authors. Citizen Muré—the compressed air man—affirmed: "It is not a question of organizing work; we must organize leisure. The workers must be replaced by trained dogs charged with running the factories." Finally, an "advanced mind" of the Society of the Rights of Man and of the Citizen—who must be awarded the palm—declared in all seriousness: "For putting our doctrines into practice and frankly accepting their consequences men who have reached the age of thirty are too corrupted by the old ways. These men must disappear from society so that it can be regenerated." The "advanced mind" explained his thoughts as follows: "In a word, it is indispensable to suppress men of thirty and over. Those who are devoted to our principles, and who sincerely wish for their triumph, must therefore generously take the initiative by voluntarily quitting life and immolating themselves in order to assure the regeneration of the world and the happiness of humanity." This proposal, it appears, was much applauded . . . by those under thirty, of course.

    A few days after the storm the Revolution of 1848 was already appearing inexplicable. "How this sad phenomenon came about," wrote Albert de Broglie, "is something I still only imperfectly understand, in spite of the many eyewitness accounts I have heard, for the event came upon me like a thunderbolt, and whatever one does to explain the unexpected after it has happened, it always remains incomprehensible."

    What had been gained by the operation?

Royalty, according to Lamartine, may have succeeded in making of a nation of citizens "a vile rabble of traffickers," but the small bourgeoisie thought it better to put up with "the official vices" than to have bloodshed. Admittedly, during the night of February 25, Lamartine, climbing once more onto his chair, had managed to impose the tricolor flag, "which had gone round the world with the name, glory and freedom of the fatherland," and the specter of the red flag, "which had only gone round the Champ-de-Mars," had vanished. But for all that the great shadow of '93 covered the sky. They thought of Sanson, and an inventor was already proposing to create an improved guillotine, with linked holes, that would enable several heads to be chopped off at once.

People sang:

> On your knees before the worker,
> Hats off to the cap!

But the bourgeoisie of Paris was to have its revenge.

On the morning of June 23, 1848, several hundred Parisians, out of work as a result of the closing of the famous national workshops, went on their knees in the Place de la Bastille to listen to a fanatic called Pujol, who, standing on the base of the July column, like a goat on a rock, addressed the shades of the unfortunates who fell in the attack on the fortress in 1789:

"Heroes of the Bastille, the heroes of the barricades come to prostrate themselves at the foot of the monument erected to your immortality! Like you they made a Revolution at the price of their blood, but until now their blood has been sterile. The Revolution must be begun again!"

And they began it again.

Four hundred barricades rose up out of the earth as by magic. The Minister for War, General Cavaignac, undertook to bring Paris to its senses. He avoided involving his twenty-three thousand troops in the "chamber-pot war" that had defeated Marmont in 1830. In certain districts he let the revolt form, ripen and burst. Then he brought the lancet to bear on the abscess. Setting out from healthy districts, he advanced, cleaning up each block of houses, machine-gunning, shooting, laying waste. On June 25, forty thousand insurgents were surrounded in the area of Saint-Lazare, the Rochechouart barrier and the faubourgs Poissonnière, du Temple and Saint-Jacques. There was a desperate resistance. In vain Monseigneur Affre, the Archbishop of Paris, carrying a crucifix, tried to force them to lay down their arms. He died, hit by a stray ball, and the combat ended only when there were no more combatants. Nearly five thousand dead lay on the bloody pavements.

"The Republic is lucky," Louis-Philippe remarked in his exile. "It can fire on the people."

There were fifteen thousand arrests and four thousand deportations. The bourgeoisie had conquered.

Henceforward freedom was only a word; the societies were persecuted, working hours were increased and the law on the press partly re-established. Illusions were dead. Admittedly there were some people with enough acquired momentum to continue attacking the Jesuits or wanting to free the oppressed Poles. But it was no good stuffing oneself with the "immortal principles of republican idealism," it was no good applauding high-sounding speeches by young men who would soon become the old fogeys of "forty-eighters," it was no good rejoicing on hearing of the Italian risings, the Austrian insurrections, the Bavarian upheavals, the Prussian riots—a revolution a day, the *Charivari* gloated! The pure enthusiasm was over. Blood had flowed. The ditch between classes was more deeply dug. The Parisians had not even the courage to smack Borme, Junior's Vésuviennes. They had no heart for it.

At the beginning of December, 1848, in an end-of-year revue called *The Watch Night Lanterns,* the comedian playing "the sovereign people" sang this significant song:

> The supreme rank, oh! what a bore!
> I don't want to govern any more!
> I'll send myself to the right about
> For there's no one left to turn me out!

No one left? The "sovereign people" were very blind! For at that very moment there was a new deputy in the Assembly. Impassive, with a heavy mustache and a little, pointed beard, he did not say much . . . but he observed. Lamartine called him "a hat without a head." He bore a magic name: Louis-Napoleon Bonaparte.

6

The Rubicon

A few days after the vote of December 10, 1848, which, by a large majority, gave the presidency of the Republic to Louis-Napoleon Bonaparte, there was a solemn session of the Constituent Assembly. "It was about four o'clock in the afternoon," Victor Hugo wrote. "Night was falling, the vast hall of the Assembly was half plunged into shadow, the chandeliers hung from the ceiling and the ushers had just brought the lamps for the tribune. The President made a sign and the door on the right opened. Then there was seen to enter the hall and walk rapidly to the tribune a man still young, wearing black and having on his coat the Star and Grand Cordon of the Legion of Honor. Every head was turned toward that man. A pallid face in which the shaded lamps brought out the thin, bony angles, a heavy, long nose, mustaches, a curled lock on a narrow forehead, small eyes with no sparkle, a timid, anxious bearing, no resemblance to the Emperor: it was Citizen Charles-Louis-Napoleon Bonaparte."

On mounting the tribune, the first President of the Second Republic declared calmly and in a deep voice: "In the presence of God and before the French people represented by the National Assembly, I swear to remain faithful to the democratic Republic, one and indivisible, and to fulfill all the duties imposed on me by the constitution."

How could this man dare to violate his oath? Did not Article 64 of the Constitution say that "any means whereby the president of the Republic dissolves the Assembly is a crime of high treason. The President is *ipso facto* deprived of his functions. The citizens are obliged to refuse obedience to him"? There was nothing to fear.

"He is a fool who can be easily led," Thiers declared.

But in three years this "fool" had revealed himself to be particularly intelligent and now, in the autumn of 1851, Paris talked of nothing else but a *coup d'état*. Without doubt, it was said, Louis-Napoleon was going to re-establish the Empire and send the deputies packing.*

---

* This chapter, and the one following, owe much to *Louis-Napoléon et le coup d'Etat du deux décembre* by Pierre Dominique (Amiot-Dumont).

"What are they saying in Paris and in the Assembly?" he asked Deputy Flandrin one day.

"Well, prince..."

"What?"

"Everyone is talking..."

"Of what?"

"Of the *coup d'état.*"

"And does the Assembly believe in it?"

"A little, prince."

"Do you?"

"Not in the least."

"I thank you, Monsieur Flandrin," Louis-Napoleon exclaimed, seizing both the deputy's hands. "You at least do not think I am a scoundrel."

The future Napoleon III was neither a fool nor a scoundrel; he was simply a born conspirator, and as he mused in front of his fire, watching the smoke rise from his cigarette, he was not a mere visionary, as those declared who did not know him well. He was in process of building up the finest plot in history. In that autumn of 1851 things could evidently not go on much longer. The war between the representatives and the presidency had entered on an active phase. The deputies refused the President of the Republic a supplementary credit and, being a spendthrift like his grandmother Josephine, he was forced to get into debt and sell some of his equipages. There was the same lack of success—but here the Assembly, blinded by hate, committed a grave error—when the President asked the deputies to repeal the stupid law of May 31 regarding universal suffrage, which was practically done away with by a thousand difficulties. (Had it not been for a certificate of residence provided by his mother-in-law Thiers might not have been able to be an elector.)

What would happen in May, 1852, when, according to the Constitution, Louis-Bonaparte was supposed to leave the Elysée Palace to his successor? In London the "red" exiles were counting the days. They reveled in this declaration: "On May 8, 1852, at midnight, M. Bonaparte's presidential fortunes will expire."

"M. Bonaparte" had not the least intention of "expiring" on May 8 at midnight. Who had he about him to help in keeping power? First of all his three faithfuls: Mocquart, Persigny and Fleury. Persigny was also a born conspirator and had been at Strasbourg and at Boulogne.* A shaggy watchdog, with bristling mustache, eyebrows and whiskers, he was the typical hired bravo. Fleury would do anything to make the affair succeed. A horseman, a man of the world, a man of pleasure—which, incidentally, ruined him—he had become the jack of all trades of the Elysée. But these three were only hangers-on. Louis-Napoleon had near him only one leader: Morny, the future Emperor's half-brother, son of Queen Hortense and Comte de Flahaut, himself son of the Prince de Talleyrand and Comtesse de Souza, who, in the time of Louis XVI, had granted her favors to a certain abbé of Périgord. It is difficult to admit that one is the son of a Queen of Holland, grandson of an Empress of the French, grandson of a prince who was a bishop and one of the most famous of ministers, and registered under the name of "Demorny." He therefore decided to call himself Comte de Morny. Under Louis-Philippe he was an officer, dandy, arbiter of fashion, fanatical Parisian, lover of the Belgian ambassadress, who helped him live in a princely style—or so she was to declare. But 1848 had destroyed this gilded existence. Fortunately, the brother he had seen only from a distance became installed in the Elysée Palace. Everything would turn out all right. At first Louis-Napoleon was rather embarrassed by this "living sin" of his mother's, but then he was almost charmed, although retaining a little mistrust. In any case, Morny had a decisive influence over his brother. He seemed to have been right when he wrote in his, as yet unpublished, papers: "I think I may assert that without myself the *coup d'état* would never have taken place.... When I saw the prince for the first time after his elevation to the presidency I found him full of prejudices, false systems and suspicion. He had those ideas one naturally acquires during a prolonged exile, a kind of sentimental liberalism natural to banished men, but which do not enable one to govern for long. His entourage was composed of a collection of fools who had passed their lives in opposition or in prison and were incapable of advising the prince to a right course of action."

Morny took charge of this "right course of action." But a brain is not enough; two arms are also needed, one for the police and the other for the army. For the first post Louis-Napoleon thought at once

* The scenes of two previous attempts by Louis-Bonaparte to seize power. (Translator's note.)

of Maupas, the Prefect of Haute-Garonne and the youngest prefect in France. In his post he had displayed a firmness that impressed the prince. He recalled him to Paris, unfolded his projects and offered him the Ministry of the Interior.

"Monseigneur," Maupas replied, "the Minister of the Interior's influence is only in the provinces; his work begins principally after the event; it is in Paris, in the prefecture of police, in the office of the direct head of the commissioners and agents that you need a man of action and zeal."

Maupas was therefore appointed to the police prefecture.

The main point remained to be settled: who to place at the head of the army. It was Fleury who discovered the man at Constantine, in the person of General de Saint-Arnaud, a man with an eagle's nose and a steely eye. He was unfortunately only a brigadier general; to be Minister of War he would have to be a divisional general. A little campaign led by Saint-Arnaud against the Kabyles was puffed up and he was appointed divisional general over the heads of fifty-two more senior generals. As a result of a Cabinet change adroitly brought about by the President he became Minister for War, chief minister, indeed, of this temporary team, convoked on October 27. Naturally, Saint-Arnaud agreed to get rid of the chatterboxes and to help in arresting ringleaders, but the Assembly was on holiday. They would have to wait until the deputies returned to Paris.

"What the devil!" Saint-Arnaud exclaimed. "When one tells someone to jump off the roof one may well allow him to choose his own moment."

General Magnan, commander of the Paris garrison, agreed to come into the affair, but prudently asked to be informed only "at the moment of mounting horse." This did not prevent his summoning the twenty generals present in Paris on November 17 and speaking to them as follows:

"Gentlemen, it may happen that within a very short time your commanding general may think fit to associate himself with an extremely important decision. You will obey his orders passively.... Whatever happens you will be shielded by my responsibility.... The only responsible person, gentlemen, will be myself, who if necessary will bear my head to the scaffold or my body to the Grenelle plain."

Then Magnan, who seemed to think he was on the stage, added: "Let us all now swear that none of us will speak to anyone whatever of what has just passed between us."

Not one general appears to have spoken, and yet the plot was in the air. It was the subject of every conversation. At the end of the month a few deputies met at Molé's house and questioned their colleague, General Changarnier, whom the Assembly would place at the head of the troops in the event of any disturbance.

"I undertake to make the *coup d'état* fail," he kept on repeating.

Now he was pressed for details. What did he intend to do? Had he taken any precautions? Changarnier assumed a self-satisfied air.

"My apartment is a little fortress. The inhabitants of the house are absolutely devoted to me, particularly the pastry cook who lodges on the ground floor and all his boys."

The deputies were dumbstruck and separated "in silence and consternation," repeating to themselves—as they later admitted—"Tomorrow the country will fall to the most daring or the most cunning."

As against General Changarnier's pastry cook's boys, Prince Louis-Napoleon had sixty thousand soldiers. The barracks were packed with men, and regiments had had to be lodged even in the casemates of the outer fortifications. The officers lectured the troops, but now they were really political talks. Officers spoke of nothing but hate and contempt of the Republic. "The deputies were chatterboxes who were wasting France's fortune," Pierre Dominique relates. "Faced with these speech makers, whose external appearance, conversation, cares and interests were so different from the appearance, conversation, cares and interests of the soldier, the military men spoke of showmen and of the lesson to be taught to babblers. What were the republicans? Antipatriots, drinkers of blood, looters, enemies of the uniform, the scum of the nation." And soldiers could be heard calling the bourgeois of Paris "Bedouins." One knew what that meant from an African fighter.

The army was ready to obey the Little Corporal's nephew.

On the evening of December 1 Morny was at the Opéra-Comique for the first night of *Bluebeard's Seven Castles*. Two lines were applauded:

> Without caring a single jot
> Let us now arrest the lot.

People smiled as they looked at the President's brother in his box. Morny appeared to nod in approval and the theatre broke into applause. In the interval he went to speak to Mme. Liadères in her box and, naturally, they talked of the famous clean sweep.

"What side will you be on, my dear count?"

"On the side of the handle, of course, madame," Morny answered, smiling.

Morny did not see the last act. He went to the Elysée, where the President was receiving, as he did every Monday. There were not many people and at ten o'clock the guests were already leaving. Louis-Napoleon took his brother's arm and quite naturally led him to his office, the silver boudoir in which the Emperor had signed his second abdication. Saint-Arnaud, Maupas, Persigny and Mocquart were already there. The prince took a key, opened one of the drawers in his desk and took out a folder on whose cover the conspirators could see these seven letters written in blue pencil:

RUBICON

It was for that night.

Since it would soon be time to mount horse, General Magnan had been informed during the course of the evening, as had Saint-Georges, director of the national printing works, and Colonel Vieyra, the new chief of staff of the National Guard, who had gone to break the drums, so that the citizen soldiers could not be summoned the next day.

Louis-Napoleon opened the folder and took out the text of the posters—a summons to the people, the army and the Parisians—which had to be printed during the night and posted before dawn. The Parisians would learn that the Assembly was dissolved, universal suffrage re-established, a state of siege proclaimed and that elections were to be held to approve or condemn the *coup d'état*, which provisionally gave all power to the President of the Republic.

Everyone knew his part. Maupas would have the biggest role to play during the night, as he was entrusted with arresting the hotheads of the Assembly. The following morning Morny would take possession of the Ministry of the Interior. For the moment Saint-Arnaud would merely have to provide the prefect with a few detachments. He would intervene later if things went badly. In any event he would show only a third of his forces the next day so that in no case would the men remain more than twelve hours under arms. The riot—if there was a riot—would not be able to make use of the troops, as in 1830 and 1848. Everything was also arranged for provisions and stores. There would be as little bivouacking as possible.

Louis-Napoleon opened another drawer, put forty thousand francs on the table and turned to the Minister for War.

"This is all my riches. You will need it tomorrow in order to distribute a few gratuities."

The prince rose. Morny thought the meeting needed a final word: "It is understood, gentlemen, that each of us is risking his skin."

"Mine is already worn out," Mocquart replied. "I have not much to lose."

So, as Véron has pointed out, nothing was arranged in case of failure: no money, no passport, not even a position to fall back on. "The gamblers threw everything on the table, in one stake. . . . If they failed there would be only the firing squad."

Louis-Napoleon went to bed. Morny left for the Jockey Club, while Maupas went to his prefecture and Colonel Biéville, the President's aide-de-camp, who was also in the plot, left in a cab for the national printing works. In front of the building there was already drawn up a company of mobile gendarmes, brought by Fleury. The cab was unharnessed, and the coachman locked in a ground-floor room with twenty francs and several bottles.

"These bourgeois pay too well for there not to be something going on," the man remarked philosophically.

Inside the printing works Saint-Georges was awaiting the colonel. He had summoned a night shift for some urgent work—which often happened. However, the workers were republicans and some of them, guessing what was in question, appeared unwilling. A few gendarmes were brought up and calm was restored. Saint-Georges and Biéville cut up the copy in such a way that the text could not be understood by the compositors.

Finally, having set the type themselves, the two men printed, and then, to judge the effect, read the presidential text to the gendarmes. These learned that the overtalkative civilians would be thrown out of their jobs and that Napoleon's nephew would be the sole master. They applauded and approved so noisily that they had to be quieted down in case the whole neighborhood came to the windows. Biéville freed his coachman, the cab was harnessed and the officer, with the posters under his arm, left with Saint-Georges for the police prefecture, where the usual teams, protected by policemen, would start off at six o'clock to post the decrees all over Paris.

It was a little after four in the morning. Since eleven, eight hundred policemen had been assembled in the courtyard and the various police stations on the pretext of a new raid against refugees from London, said to have returned to Paris. Maupas had taken the precaution of assembling his forces on several occasions during the past few weeks against alleged revolutionaries, so that the men would not be surprised when they went into action. One by one Maupas received forty police commissioners. This time the prefect was obliged to tell them that it was not a question of action against the exiles. He told them of a conspiracy that had been discovered against the presidency of the Republic.

"We know all the accomplices. Justice is informed."

It was precisely the "accomplices" who had to be arrested. Each officer had only one or two persons to apprehend during the night and was therefore unaware of the scope of the arrests. There were to be arrested eighteen deputies, including two of the Assembly's questors, and about sixty ringleaders capable of leading a possible uprising. The plan was carefully conceived. Each police commissioner found in the street a group of policemen and gendarmes who knew nothing. The precaution had even been taken of adding a locksmith to each expedition. The riding schools and horse hirers were closely watched. Orders had been given to cafés with meeting rooms not to open their doors.

The most delicate matter would seem to be the arrest of the questors, who lived in the Palais Bourbon. As the gendarmerie was not enough, a backing of troops was necessary and Colonel Espinasse, commanding the 42nd of the line, was summoned. By an irony this was the same regiment which, eleven years before, had had the task of arresting Louis-Napoleon on his Boulogne adventure.

Two-thirds of the regiment arrived in the Rue de l'Université at twenty past five. As though by coincidence, the rest of the unit was on guard in the Palais Bourbon itself. Seeing his colonel arrive with police commissioners, the commander of the guard understood at once. He broke his sword and tore off his epaulettes so that he might not be considered a traitor—he seems, by the way, to have been sincere—and everything went off perfectly well. One of the questors, Baze, appeared in his night shirt; he tried to harangue the troops, but his unusual attire and his strong accent—he was from Languedoc— made the soldiers laugh. He was dragged half-naked to the station in the Place de Bourgogne, where he was allowed to dress. Then he was hustled into a cab, which trotted rapidly off to the Mazas prison.

The same scenes took place everywhere: Deputies and generals tried to resist, to invoke the famous Article 68, to speak of assassination, to promise to shoot Louis-Napoleon at Vincennes, or to banish him to Nouka-hiva, but these fine words were incompatible with nightcap, tousled beard and hair, bare feet and hairy legs under a nightshirt. Everyone laughed and thought of the last farce they had seen in the Boulevard du Temple.

Changarnier, who had not been warned by his baker boys, appeared, like the rest, in night attire, yet brandishing two pistols.

"General," a commissioner hastily cried, "do not resist. Your life is not threatened."

"I was expecting a *coup d'état*. Here it is," Changarnier declared.

Then philosophically, throwing away his pistols, he offered his services.

"When the foreigner makes war on us, the President will be glad to find me ready to put myself at the head of an army."

General Cavaignac was even calmer. Lamoricière let himself be arrested quietly, but when the cab taking him to Mazas passed the palace of the Legion of Honor, he stuck his head through the window and wanted to harangue the troops on duty. The commissioner took a gag out of his pocket and African Lamoricière instantly calmed down.

Out of all the soldiers only General Bedeau shouted on his staircase: "Treachery! Outlaws! Help!"

He was hustled into a cab and as he continued to yell the police drew their swords and galloped after the carriage.

Thiers was sleeping so soundly that the commissioner had to shake him. A nightcapped head appeared.

"What is it? What's going on?"

"We are arresting you."

Maupas, after the report of his men, alleged that Thiers was then stricken with terror. "His speech was incoherent, he did not wish to die . . . he was not a criminal." However, he agreed to get dressed. After stripping to the buff he tied round his chest a broad flannel belt "held round the neck by a ribbon." The police watched this spectacle with mocking eyes. In his overcoat Thiers regained courage.

"And supposing I blew out your brains, sir?" he asked the commissioner. "Do you know the law?"

"I do not have to answer you, sir. I am carrying out the orders of the Prefect of Police just as I carried out yours when you were Minister of the Interior."

The final word of this dawn of December 2 was uttered by the Deputy Roger, who, awakened with a start, exclaimed as he rubbed his eyes: "Ah, so I am arrested? Very well! Joseph, give these gentlemen some sherry and come and help me dress."

7
First Steps of the Second Empire

That morning a fine rain was falling. The Parisians, with their loaves under their arms and their milk cans in their hands, gathered in front of the posters, whose paste was still damp. The first reaction was favorable to the conspirators.

"It's a bold stroke!" the workers exclaimed, delighted by the trick played on the Assembly that had muzzled them in June, 1848, that Assembly "the lair of conservatives, monarchists and clericals," that Asssembly composed of provincials of another epoch. Now Paris, as Pierre Dominique has written, "the Paris of the artisans' and workers' suburbs, bold, noisy, revolutionary, wearing its bonnet, even a red bonnet, cocked over one ear, looked down on the provinces." Besides, was not universal suffrage re-established? Were not the people summoned "in electoral meeting" to say whether or not they approved the clean sweep? One could always say no! One would see! As for the bourgeois, they were delighted to see order return and the specter of revolt disappear. Moreover, the Stock Exchange would begin to look up.

Meanwhile, with the printing presses occupied, the shops shut, the large cafés turned into traps, these police measures made the hearts of many Parisians beat a little faster. There was a kind of invisible threat hanging over the city. The fever mounted when troops were seen to occupy the Invalides, the Champs-Elysées, the Tuileries, the Palais Royal, the Hôtel de Ville, the Cité and certain points on the boulevards. The whole town, whose streets were covered with large paving stones (replaced since they had been last used as barricades), rang to the tread of the hoofs of cavalry detachments going to their posts or of dispatch riders galloping with their orders.

At half past eleven, the Parisians who happened to be in the Champs-Elysées saw a veritable cavalcade leave the Elysées Palace through the gardens. The President was in front, preceded by a squad of horsemen carrying pistols and followed by King Jerome, Napoleon's last surviving brother, Marshal Exelmans, Prince Murat, Generals Magnan and Saint-Arnaud. Behind them rode about forty generals without commands and other high-ranking officers.

The conspirators were going to take the pulse of Paris.

Along the avenue a few cries of greeting broke out, but there were no enthusiastic acclamations. There were even occasional cries of "Long live the Republic!" which, in the circumstances, was very like a call to order. But when the procession came out into the Place de la Concorde General de Cotte's brigade came forward shouting, "Long live the Emperor!" There were some mobile guards who broke ranks and, more prompt, cried: "To the Tuileries!" Louis-Napoleon seemed to want to follow their advice. He had the grilles of the swing bridge opened and galloped quickly across the gardens. Jerome caught up to him and shouted:

"Louis, you're going too fast. Believe me, don't enter the château."

It was good advice, although it came from Jerome. The ex-King of Westphalia, that comic-opera sovereign, was somewhat under the influence of his son, Prince Napoleon, who, that morning, his monocle worn as a battle signal, yelled that "that wretched Louis is dishonoring the family." The President pulled up and at a walking pace passed through the grille of the Pavillon de Flore and rode along the quays. After going along by the waterside gallery he entered the Cour du Carrousel by the Pont-Royal gate. There were two regiments of the line. The first presented arms, but the second did not budge. The drummers left their drums lying on the ground in front of them;

there was not one shout. The crowd came out of the populous little streets leading into the square. At scattered intervals there were shouts of: "Down with Bonaparte! Down with the lancers!" Louis-Napoleon turned round, passed through the gate and crossed the bridge. On the left bank, in the Quai d'Orsay and the Rue de Bourgogne and in front of the Chamber the troops shouted: "Long live the Emperor!" but nearly everywhere the crowd replied: "Long live the Republic!"

The cavalcade returned to the Elysée Palace. As a whole, apart from certain line regiments, one could depend on the army. As for the Parisians, perhaps they were not shouting what one might have wished, but they did not seem aggressive. Besides, life was quietly resuming its course. The omnibuses rolled by, the shops gradually opened their shutters, the tribunals were working. Alone, on that morning of December 2, the deputies were up to their old tricks.

About forty representatives, in spite of the barriers, had managed to slip into the Palais Bourbon, but the president, the elderly lawyer Dupin—it had been thought useless to arrest him—had no idea of giving any resistance.

"What would you have me do?" he asked his colleagues, who tried to drag him to the sessions chamber. *"Uni nihil, nihil.* We have right on our side, that is obvious, but those gentlemen have might. *Dura lex, sed lex.* We can but go away. I have the honor to take my leave of you."

A few handfuls of deputies had been arrested, but 220 representatives had managed to assemble in the Rue de Grenelle-Saint-Germain, near the Croix-Rouge crossroads, in the town hall of the Xth *arrondissement,* today the VIIth. The deputies immediately resumed their old habits: they shouted, yelled and insulted one another, in spite of the ushers who repeated endlessly: "Silence, gentlemen, silence!" All were of course agreed in voting a decree of deposition and enjoining "all functionaries and holders of force and authority to obey any request made in the name of the National Assembly, under pain of breach of trust and high treason." The freeing of their arrested colleagues was also decreed, then vociferations, clamors and proposals rose from all sides and in the middle of the uproar this dreaded cry was heard: "Hurry up, the forces are arriving!"

They were arriving, indeed, but were not very large: a captain, two sergeants and a handful of cavalry. General Oudinot stepped forward.

"I order you to leave and to clear the town hall. Will you obey?"
"No," the captain replied.

And that was all. A few moments later the 220 were in the street and demanded to be sent to Mazas. These gentlemen had suddenly developed a taste for martyrdom. They were quickly given satisfaction. They were surrounded by soldiers, and the long procession took its way to the d'Orsay barracks, for the Mazas prison was full.

"That is well done," a few "white blouses" grouped in a wine merchant's window cried.

The "220" were placed at Mont-Valérien, at Vincennes, in the d'Orsay barracks, and all Paris guffawed on learning that the deputies were encamped in the barracks. There was nothing better for removing political barriers than communal life. One lends a blanket, one exchanges a pillow for a dressing gown brought to the guardroom by a resourceful wife and opinions become merely shades.

"I spent the night on a Bonapartist mattress," one of the deputies said the next day, "wrapped in an extremist shawl, my feet in a social-democratic sheepskin and my head in a legitimist nightcap."

During the evening a whole section of the population of Paris became excited. The heavy cavalry from Versailles rode down the Champs-Elysées and up the boulevards. At a cry of "Long live Napoleon," uttered by Fleury, who was accompanying the regiment, the crowd replied in a louder voice, with a touch of anger: "Long live the Republic!" Suddenly a shot—the first—rang out, and it was Fleury who received it. He was only slightly wounded in the head, but the wound bled copiously and he made a heroic return to the Elysées Palace. The fever grew, but the people of Paris were far from losing their calm and passively watched a handful of hotheads going from the Bastille to the Saint-Denis gate singing the "Marseillaise." Maupas, however, was pessimistic. "The chief districts are in favor of barricades," he wrote to Morny. "Saint-Marceau, Saint-Antoine and Trône barrier. The sections are summoned for a quarter to eleven; everyone will be at his post. The munitions are bombs that can be carried in the hand. The 44th of the line will be with them; three hundred men follow them crying: 'Long live the socialist republic, and no pretender!' They intend to ring the tocsin; in several churches the ropes have been cut. The night will be serious and decisive. There is a scheme to attack the police prefecture. Hold some cannon at my disposal; I shall ask for it when necessary." In spite of this alarmist dispatch, Morny and Magnan remained faithful to their principle: the troops were to regain their barracks; only a few posts would be manned. However, there were increased arrests and all night the capital was scoured by police vans and cabs surrounded by policemen.

On the next morning the barricades had not risen and the troops, rested and refreshed, took up their positions of the day before. In the Rue du Faubourg-Saint-Antoine about ten left-wing deputies, some republican journalists and two or three workmen went up the street shouting: "To arms! Long live the Republic! Long live the Constitution!" But the faubourg did not stir. From their doorsteps the workers watched the little band go by. The deputies addressed them: "Will you let Napoleon do as he likes? Will you defend the Republic?"

The replies were mixed: "Haven't we got universal suffrage?" "But we have no arms!"

As for arms, they were on their way to look for them. There were some at the post near the Rue de Montreuil. They went there, and the soldiers on guard let themselves be disarmed. The handful of demonstrators now had twenty-two rifles. A few workers had joined the deputies and they began to build a barricade at the corner of the Rue Sainte-Marguerite and the Rue de Cotte.

The barricade was livid in the dawn. . . .

But a company of the 19th of the line hurried up from the Bastille. Some of the workers faded away.

"Do you think we are going to get killed so that you can keep your twenty-five francs a day?" (The daily sum the deputies had voted themselves.)

"Stay here for a moment," Baudin replied, leaping onto the barricade. "And you will see how one dies for twenty-five francs a day!"

The soldiers were a few yards away. A sergeant discharged his weapon in the air. One or two men on the barricade thought the troops had started to shoot, and opened fire. The regiment replied. Baudin fell and the insurgents fled in terror. Gradually the news of Baudin's death spread through the town and, for certain minds, provided the necessary leaven, but at the moment Paris was relatively calm. The Bastille, the bridges, the Hôtel de Ville were solidly occupied. Morny and Magnan were in command of their nerves, while

Maupas sent terrified dispatches. However, he was in the right when he said: "I must say that I do not believe that popular sympathy is with us. We find no enthusiasm anywhere. Those who approve us are lukewarm; those who fight against us are inexpressibly vehement." That was true, but he should have added that those who fought against them were only a few hundreds. Admittedly each of them fought like ten men, and soon the winding streets between the Hôtel de Ville and the boulevards were bristling with barricades. On the boulevard it was difficult to get along; the crowds were dense and the lancers, out on reconnaissance, were booed and insulted. Near the water tower there were cries of "Long live the Assembly! Down with the traitors!" In the Rue Greneta, the Rue Transnonain and the Rue Beaubourg things were more serious. There were about one hundred rioters there holding a barricade, and they were not content with shouting. They fired on a cavalry squad. The soldiers took them from the rear and shot a handful of them on the spot, in accordance with the Minister for War's orders: "Any individual taken while building or defending a barricade or while bearing arms shall be shot." The last word had been with Morny. Saint-Arnaud merely wanted offenders to be brought to military justice.

Night falls early in December and it was by the light of torches, as in 1848 on the occasion of the Capucines shooting, that a few groups of demonstrators carried two corpses from the Chaussée d'Antin to the Faubourg du Temple, shouting, "Vengeance! To arms!" This did not prevent Morny, Magnan and Saint-Arnaud, faithful to their technique and in spite of Maupas's heavy sighs, from sending the troops back to barracks. As in 1848 a whole district was abandoned to the rioters. The insurrection ripened there and the following day it was to be attacked in force. Magnan explained to Maupas: "All my troops are going back to their quarters to rest. I am leaving Paris to the insurgents. I am letting them build barricades. If they are behind them tomorrow, I shall teach them a lesson."

At dawn on December 4 Paris was peaceful, with the exception of the district around the Rue Montmartre and the Rue du Temple, where seventy-seven barricades had sprung up. Some reached the second stories of the houses. From the Rue Mazagran to the Rue de la Lune there rose a gigantic barrier. It was occupied by a hundred men with rifles. The onlookers—for, of course, there were onlookers—saw a woman standing on the summit reading a proclamation written by Victor Hugo and signed by twenty-two deputies: "Louis-Napoleon is a traitor!" The crowd, who seemed to think it was at the Olympic Circus watching an up-to-date "great historical tableau," applauded the names of the "twenty-two." Paris was present as a spectator and there were hardly more than twelve hundred rioters. Opposed to them were sixty thousand men, who went into action around ten in the morning and were resolved to end things quickly and, if necessary, to use cannon. Before the great barricade of the Boulevard Bonne-Nouvelle the artillery fired balls and shells. The republicans returned their fire and the colonel of the 72nd and thirty men were killed, but, taken in the rear, the defenders were obliged to abandon their shelter of paving stones, carriages and furniture. The other barricades were quickly removed. The whole district was traversed by infernal columns that took no prisoners. Every man taken bearing a rifle, or with his hands blackened by powder, was shot at once.

The revolt was mastered, but during the afternoon a bloody drama was played out that the future Second Empire would have difficulty in effacing.

It was three o'clock. The struggle was nearly over and the last fires were being extinguished. The boulevard, between the Gymnase Theatre and the Madeleine, was full of idlers watching the troops who occupied the road in close battalions. Every window was packed. The crowd was well dressed and that December 4 was to be called "the day of greatcoats." It was a Thursday and many families were taking their children for a walk. People were amusing themselves and, partly to tease the soldiers, "just to see," some cried, "Long live the Republic!" Suddenly a shot rang out. Where from? No one knows. Historians do not agree. According to the Bonapartists someone fired from the window of a house in the Rue du Sentier; according to republican writers the detonation came from the middle of a squad. However that may be, the men turned to face the pavement and there was a terrible salvo. While the crowd stampeded the soldiers continued firing. In vain did their officers shout: "Cease fire!" The machine was in motion. From the Boulevard Bonne-Nouvelle to the Boulevard des Italiens firing broke out. Worse still, squads were seen to attack the crowd and enter the houses. And it lasted for ten interminable minutes. When the wind of madness had ceased to blow dozens of corpses lay on the pavements. There an old man was stretched out, still holding his umbrella tightly against his chest; here a child, whose body was pierced by eighteen balls; thirty-seven corpses were laid out at the Cité Bergère, about fifty in front of the Hôtel Sallandrouze. According to the republicans—Odilon Barrot—"this massacre was not simply the result of a deplorable misunderstanding but a coldly decided and atrociously calculated execution." I think, rather, that the massacre is to be explained by fear, a fear incapable of hearing reason. The troops, according to Pierre Dominique, "were seized with panic, and being able to escape the danger through flight or through that kind of attack which is often a flight forward, saved themselves by firing on what was in front of them, on the crowd, that shapeless and multicolored monster, that ocean of heads and arms from which sprang, like foam from a storm at sea, a mass of boos and gibes."

Life resumed its course. People ended by believing the government's theory: "The president has crushed a band of evil doers." The bourgeois were confident; the Stock Exchange rose five francs in two days. "Dictatorship is fighting demagogy," Morny wrote. "There is no doubt; dictatorship must triumph," and arrests were rapid: 26,642 people were apprehended; 9,530 were deported to Algeria, 239 to Cayenne, 2,804 interned and 1,545 expelled.

The plebiscite was an overwhelming victory for Louis-Napoleon: 7,439,216 "yes," against 646,737 "no." The Empire was made. On January 1 a solemn *Te Deum* was sung at Notre Dame. They waited a few months, until the anniversary of December 2, in order finally to bury the Second Republic. A second plebiscite gave 7,800,000 votes for the re-establishment of the Empire against 280,000. The stain of blood was effaced and forgotten. In spite of a severe cold spell the crowd frenziedly acclaimed Napoleon III, who saluted them from the balcony of the Tuileries.

"The Empire is peace!" the new regime had promised. The Parisians who were to fall in Mexico, in Italy, in the Crimea, or in the shell hole of Sedan would perhaps think that in political matters it is wise not to make too many promises.

PARIS PLAYS AND SUFFERS

1
In Offenbach's Day

Immediately after the establishment of the Second Empire one had no choice if one wanted to go from Montrouge to Saint-Ouen: one had to follow the through roads that were already frequented in Gallo-Roman times: Rues Saint-Jacques, Saint-Denis and Saint-Martin. From west to east there were only the boulevards that, from the Madeleine to the Bastille, allowed free circulation. Of course one could also use the inner boulevard that ran along the Farmers-General wall, dating from 1785, or the circular road on the other side of the same wall, but at each barrier the press of traffic made one lose a great deal of time. One will remember Gervaise, whom Zola shows us at the Poissonière barrier, waiting for her man, who had spent the night away from home, "giddy at the sight of the uninterrupted flow of men, beasts and carts between the two squat customs houses, coming down from the heights of Montmartre and La Chapelle. There was stamping of herds, a crowd that sudden halts caused to spread out like a lake over the roads, an endless file of workers going to work, carrying their tools and their loaves of bread. And the mob was swallowed up and continuously lost in Paris."

On May 26, 1859, the Farmers-General wall around Paris was

demolished and in its place the boulevards and circular roads were joined to make up our present boulevards. In one bound Paris extended as far as its fortified outworks, those walls bastioned in the manner of Vauban, twenty-four miles long, whose construction had begun in 1841. Henceforth Paris had twenty *arrondissements,* an area of 440 square miles, and in 1867 would have 1,825,274 inhabitants.

The man who performed the operation was Baron Haussmann, but everything was decided and conceived by the Emperor, haunted by the memory of foreign capitals. An army of demolishers swooped down on the network of sordid alleys, stinking culs-de-sac, streets older than the oldest dowager, of which Balzac speaks, those streets of assassins and of bad company. The operation cost only 2,115 million francs, but the town received four times more in taxes (52 millions in 1852, 232 millions in 1869), which did not prevent grumblers from talking ironically of "The Fantastic Tallies *(Comptes)* of Haussmann." Admittedly, by straightening the avenues many memories dear to lovers of the past had been abolished: the tower of the Hospitalers of Saint John Lateran, the Innocents Market, Saint-Benoît's church, what remained of Cluny College, the Hôtel Coligny and several dozen churches, chapels and oratories.

But now Paris could breathe. Another motive had urged on Napoleon III and Haussmann: the fear of revolt. These rectilinear avenues that cannon could rake with fire would put an end to the eternal street-corner fighting in which the Parisian had excelled since the famous "Day of the Barricades" in Henri III's time. This argument did not prevent the Goncourts' sighing at these "boulevards with no turning, with no adventures of perspective, implacable in their straight lines." Proudhon no longer recognized Paris in "this new, monotonous, exhausting town."

"Regret the old Paris who will," said George Sand, who although from Berry loved Paris, "my intellectual faculties never allowed me to know its turns, although like many others I was brought up there. Now that the great cuttings, too straight for the artist's eye, but eminently safe, enable us to walk for a long time, hands in pockets, without losing our way or being forced every moment to consult the policeman on the street corner or the affable grocer, it is a blessing to be able to wander along the wide pavement. . . . For my part, I like to realize that no vehicle, from the sumptuous equipage to the modest four-wheeler, is so good for gentle, smiling reverie as the pleasure of using two good legs, obedient, on asphalt or stone, to their proprietor's wishes. . . . But go down the street, follow the quays and boulevards, cross the public gardens . . ."

In the Place de l'Observatoire one might meet a bearded character, wearing a blouse and exhibiting a hare that played the drum. From time to time a shot was fired past the hare's ear, but it remained impassive. On the parvis of Notre Dame was another hare, of a less warlike turn: it played cards with a spaniel. It was alleged that when they were not watched the two animals cheated. In the Place de la Madeleine Pradier the cudgel player, who prided himself on his elegance, threw tiny rings into the air which he caught on a horn fixed in the middle of his forehead. In the Place du Château-d'Eau Sabra told fortunes; in the Carré Marigny Cantru swallowed swords; in front of the Bourse a medieval knight, Mengin, installed in a carriage under a vast umbrella, sold pencils; in the Place de la Bastille Bouvard played waltzes on a pig's bladder over which he had stretched a violin string; in front of the Military Academy Voelina showed white mice, and not far away an old soldier of Napoleonic days, "Tripoli, son of Glory," sold conscripts a powder for polishing the belts and buttons of their uniform. On the boulevard was a clarinetist, the "musician by intimidation," whom one could never hear, for the moment he put his instrument to his lips people hastened to give him a few coins to go and play farther off. Until the day a passer-by felt obliged to intervene.

"Let the poor man play us a little piece. Can't you see you humiliate him by refusing to hear him?"

The musician grew pale. "He took a handkerchief from his pocket," Henri d'Almeras relates, "wiped a few drops of sweat from his forehead, blew his nose, looked at the public, looked at his clarinet, wiped it thoroughly as who should say: 'Well, old girl, we're for it!' Then, taking his courage in both hands and trying to smile, he declared: 'Ladies and gentlemen, I must confess to you that I have never known how to use this instrument.'"

After this adventure he changed his district.

Restaurants abounded. From 1852 menus were posted in the windows. It was a restaurateur of the Rue Saint-Sauveur who had had the idea. In a modest establishment a meat dish cost thirty centimes, and twenty centimes for a half portion. For fifteen centimes a good vegetable was served and the whole washed down with ten centimes of wine. Set meals began at eighty or ninety centimes.

Of course, if one had large means and a still greater appetite, one could try for admission to the Club of Large Stomachs, whose members, every Saturday at the Restaurant Philippe, remained at table from six in the evening to noon on Sunday and swallowed three meals: the first from six to midnight, the second from midnight to six in the morning and the third from six until noon. Without giving the endless list of dishes let us merely mention that at the first meal six bottles of burgundy per head were allowed, at the second three of bordeaux and three of burgundy and on Sunday morning, instead of coffee, four bottles of champagne were served.

One day Viel-Castel made a wager—and won it—that by himself he would eat the following dinner for twenty-five louis:

> Potage Essence de Gibier
> Vin de Tokay
> Laitance de Carpe au Xérès
> Cailles désossées en caisse
> Truites du Lac de Genève, essence d'écrevisse
> Vin de Johannisberg glacé
> Faison rôti bardé d'ortolans
> Pyramides de truffes entières
> Clos-Vougeot de 1819
> Compote de fruits martinique à la liqueur de Mme. Amphous
> Sorbet au marasquin Stilton
> Marsala glacé
> Raisin de Malaga frais en grappes
> Vin de Chypre de la Commanderie
> Vin de Constance.

This light dinner was prepared by the famous Casimir—Casimir Moisson—and served at the Café Anglais in the well-known room No. 16, doubtless in the presence of," Ludovic, Duc de Gramont-Caderousse, king of the "Great Sixteen," who for ten years, from 1855 to 1865, was sovereign of the boulevard and the dandies.

Very inbred, red-haired, thin, stooping, a pale complexion with red spots on the cheekbones, and with a deep voice, he was undermined by consumption. He did not reign only over his companions in pleasure; he also reigned over waiters, shopkeepers, commissionaires and even the doormen of the boulevard. He also reigned over the Jockey Club, on the corner of the Rue Grange-Batelière. Bets were laid; one man defied another to be able to play a game of billiards while two terrified ponies ran round the room. . . . He reigned over the Café de Paris, over Tortoni's, and above all over the Café Anglais and its Great Sixteen, whose windows looked out over the boulevard and over the Rue Marivaux. There would forgather the Prince of Orange, Prince Paul Demidoff, Princesse Mathilde's nephew, Prince d'Arenberg, the young Duc de Rivoli, the witty Marquis de Modène, Prince Galitzine, the financier Raphaël Bishoffsheim, the two Turks Khali Bey and Mustapha Pasha, who did not know what to do with their money. Gramont-Caderousse was most intimate with Aurélien Scholl, who had founded a newspaper printed on rubber—the *Naiad* —that one could read in the bath. On May 16, 1863, he became editor-in-chief of the famous *Nain Jaune (Yellow Dwarf)*, a new type of paper that in its first issue alleged that the Vaudeville Theatre, at that time directed by an actor known for his avarice, had printed in the cast list of some play:

Double rank of women of the people..........Mme. Alexis
Crowd of spectators ....M. Ricquier.

Another frequenter of the Great Sixteen was the Duc de Brunswick, who possessed an imposing collection of busts of himself. Each copy had a different hairstyle and was carefully numbered. So in the morning, when his valet asked him respectfully: "On what model should His Highness's hair be dressed today?" Brunswick replied by giving a number.

Gramont-Caderousse's most faithful friend was Comte Germain, who wore 300,000 francs' worth of rubies on his person. His great pleasure was to ask friends to go to the theatre with him. When he was seated in his coupé lined with salmon-pink satin, Louis Sonolet tells us, he would take a bundle of theatre tickets and ask, sure of the effect he would produce: "What show would you like to go to? Variétés? Vaudeville? Opéra? Palais-Royal? Gymnase? Bouffes-Parisiens?"

When his guests had reached agreement he would calmly roll up the useless tickets and use them to light his cigar.

It would be unfair not to mention Comte d'Osmond, who had lost a hand in a hunting accident. This did not prevent his being most amusing, and, whenever he saw a piano, playing a waltz he had entitled "Farewell to My Left Hand."

When King Gramont-Caderousse and his "court" left their Great Sixteen and crossed the rooms papered in red with gold hieroglyphics, the clients of the Café Anglais watched them with respect and envy. The *lorettes* would be there with their "apprentices," the *biches* being taken out by rich lovers. There were also the fops *(petits crevés)*, degenerate dandies, their faces anointed with cream and their beardless chins nestling in their wide collars. There were also the *cocodès*—a more distinguished variety of *petit crevé*—and their companions, the *cocodettes*, "who were to the cocotte what the amateur is to the professional."

The professionals appeared on the boulevard at about nine o'clock. It was like an invasion. "One could see on the pavements of the Rue Notre-Dame-de-Lorette," wrote Zola in *Nana*, "two rows of women brushing by the shops, their skirts tucked up, noses to the ground, hastening to the boulevard with a busy air, without one glance at the shop windows. It was the famished raid by the Bréda district in the first light of the gas lamps. . . . A hundred yards from the Café Riche, as they were arriving on the field of maneuvers, they let down their dresses, hitherto carefully held up, and from then on, risking the dust, sweeping the pavements and rolling their hips, they proceeded in little steps. They slowed down still further as they passed the bright lights of a great café. Strutting along, laughing loudly, with a backward glance for the men who turned to look at them, they were at home. . . . But as the night wore on, if they had not made one or two journeys to the Rue de La Rochefoucauld, they turned into trollops and their hunt became fiercer. At the foot of the trees, all along the dark and emptying boulevards, there was ferocious bargaining, oaths and blows."

Sometimes one of the ladies would leave the mud and perhaps become one of those celebrated gold diggers of the Second Empire, one of those women who, like Nana, cleaned out the richest man in Paris "with one bite," those women "like an invasion, like one of those clouds of locusts whose passing seared a province. They scorched the ground on which their little feet passed. . . . Every day they drove round the lake, making acquaintances that were strengthened elsewhere. It was the great street walking, the beat in broad daylight, the accosting of famous whores, taking place in the tolerant smile and dazzling luxury of Paris."

Their style and air were all the more remarkable in that these ladies generally came from some porter's lodge. La Païva was an exception. Her father was a grand duke, it was said. She came from Moscow and her salon, if Sainte-Beuve is to be believed, was as well frequented as that of Princesse Mathilde. She was not lacking in wit.

"Was it love that taught you French?" Arsène Houssaye asked her one day.

"No," she replied. "It was the French who taught me love."

The most famous after La Païva were Anna Deslions—Nana—and Juliette Beau. The former had black hair, a matt complexion and sparkling eyes. She died of an enlarged heart, which is a good mark for a courtesan. Her rival was nicknamed "Juliette la Marseillaise" and, in private, her gold hair could clothe her entirely. It was more difficult to be received by Juliette or Nana than in a drawing room in good society. If one wanted "to be in the swim" one had to try to receive the two competitors at the same table. It would appear to have been easier to have the Empress to dinner. There was also Cora Pearl, whose real name was Emma Crouch (one can understand her taking a pseudonym). She was "as fresh as a moss rose," a contemporary assures us, but she must have looked rather artificial with her yellow hair, mascaraed eyelashes, eyelids too black and lips too red.

There was also Mme. Musard, a former cabaret waitress, who had the finest equipages in Paris. She used to organize sumptuous dinners in her stables and this hippic dandyism was great appreciated by Gramont-Caderousse.

One day the latter had to leave his kingdom for Egypt, to take care of his lungs. He came back to Paris in 1865 to die. He was only thirty-two. "He was," said Rochefort, "one of those predestined men who have intelligence and almost genius, senses and a tender soul, vices and never any absurdities."

He expired in the arms of Hortense Schneider, with whom he had had a long liaison—long for the boulevard, of course. He disappeared just as Hortense was beginning to become the queen of Paris.

Hortense Schneider had mounted the throne—a stage throne—at the very end of the preceding year.

A few months previously—Gramont-Caderousse was still in Egypt —the pretty young woman was packing her trunks. Anger had brightened the pink of her dimpled cheeks and her uncombed fair hair seemed to shoot out sparks. Mlle. Hortense Schneider was in a rage because the Palais-Royal Theatre had just refused her a raise and, on that summer's day in 1864, she had decided to leave Paris and quit the theatre "forever." What! they dared do *that* to her! The only actress in Paris who could link the sensual and the comic, roguishness and distinction! She who could utter peals of laughter capable of bringing all the men to her feet! Had she not been "delicious" in Offenbach's *Tromb al Kasar?* She preferred "to go back to her mother" at Bordeaux. They'd see!

Mlle. Hortense Schneider was acting stupidly. It must be said that she was not very intelligent.

The trunks were numerous. They were needed to take the fashionable crinolines that were so ample in 1864 that a young woman returning from shooting had been able to get forty partridges by the customs under her dress. Hortense stuffed the dresses in. She did not need to buy "rubber shapes and corsages that can be blown up at will." She would have been Rubens's delight.

Suddenly the doorbell rang. Hortense did not bother to answer. It rang again.

"Who is there?"

"I, Offenbach! I'm with Halévy. I've brought you a wonderful role."

"Too late, my dear," Hortense replied, still not opening her door. "I am renouncing the theatre."

Jacques Offenbach, who knew actresses, was not put off by so little. "A superb creation. For the Palais-Royal!"

It was the open sesame. The Palais-Royal! A piercing cry rent the air and the door opened. A theatre that had refused to recognize her talent—never! She said other things as well. One of her friends alleged that Hortense had learned French "from Cambronne." Offenbach, climbing over the trunks and pushing the blonde fury before him, explained: "A marvelous play! A Greek play! The abduction of Helen by Paris! You will be the beautiful Helen. All Paris . . ."

"Never!"

Offenbach, his eyeglasses cocked, had already sat down at the piano and as he played hummed the verses of "Divine Loves," "A Wise Husband" and "Invocation to Venus."

> Tell me, Venus, where's your pleasure
> In thus making virtue tumble,
> Tumble down beyond all measure?

Seated on a trunk, Hortense listened with delight. But all was in vain. Neither Offenbach nor Venus and her virtue could persuade her to tread the boards of the Palais-Royal again. That same day she left for Bordeaux. There she received a telegram: "Affair failed at Palais-Royal, but possible at Variétés. Reply. Offenbach." She replied: "I demand 2,000 francs a month." This astronomic salary was agreed to, and on December 17, 1864, was a triumph, a triumph that would not be surpassed until April 12, 1867, the year of the Exhibition, by the famous *Grand Duchess of Gerolstein*. All Paris, all Europe was humming:

> Here behold my father's sword.
> At your side it must be worn.
> Your soul is proud, your shoulders broad.
> This sword will be nobly borne.

Before the curtain rose Hortense looked at *her* audience with pride. Not only was all Paris there, but the Kings of Portugal, Sweden, Norway and Bavaria, the Prince of Wales, the Czar of Russia, the Prince of Orange and the Count of Flanders were there. Kings telegraphed asking for a box for the evening of their arrival and the theatre staff could be seen rushing through Paris trying to buy back a box.

In Hortense's dressing room after the performance there really should have been a master of ceremonies. Crowned heads were jostled. She also received them in her own home and Hortense was nicknamed "Princes' Way."

Hortense Schneider's dressing room was an image of Paris at the end of the Second Empire, with not only the kings and emperors of Europe but also the whole of international society gathering there. Paris had become the crossroads of Europe and the Tuileries themselves had a motley, cosmopolitan side. It derived, too, from the forty years of exile and adventurous life of the master of the house, from the Empress's foreign origin, from her Spanish family and her English or Austrian friends. The court gave the impression of playing an operetta, a very brilliant and well-produced operetta, admittedly, but one rather put together for the sake of the cause.

"It was, in fact, very boring," said Mme. des Garets. But what court is not boring? And yet the Tuileries were not in the least stiff, as in the uncle's time. There reigned good temper, kindliness and even, during the holidays, moments of gaiety that Napoleon I's court had never known. Cordiality and amiability were, of course, not absent from the Tuileries in Louis-Philippe's reign, but the citizen-King's court was singularly lacking in style. In 1867 the time was far away when the sovereign of France could be seen returning on foot from the Tuileries to Neuilly, his trousers mud-splashed, his umbrella under his arm, or the ministers coming to Neuilly for the weekend with a razor and a spare collar wrapped in a piece of paper as all their baggage.

Napoleon III pushed his care for the right setting so far as to forbid cabs to enter the Tuileries courtyard. But on reception evenings there were not enough vehicles to bring all the guests, so the cab drivers were allowed to extinguish their lamps as they passed the gate. A hired cab whose number could not be read became a livery or private carriage. On those evenings the Tuileries sparkled with a thousand lights. At one's first steps on the grand staircase one was stupefied by the amazing immobility of the household cavalry standing stiffly on each stair. Their impassivity was such that one day the Empress amused herself by slapping the face of one of these living waxworks. The jest was in doubtful taste, but not one hair of the horsehair plume stirred.

In the drawing rooms one had to blink so as not to be dazzled by the jewels, the gold of the uniforms, the diamonds of the orders, the women's bare shoulders emerging from gigantic dresses as brilliant as flowers.

But at that time there was another Paris, a Paris often forgotten: the Paris of the retired shopkeeper, the Paris of the small bourgeois, the Paris of Labiche.

As in Labiche's plays, all the girls were alike. They had hardly any personality, and when a suitor was suggested to them they replied to their papa: "I shall do whatever you wish."

If, by chance, they were offered two young men to choose from, what a terrible alternative!

"Goodness!" they would then reply. "You put me in a difficult position, and I am ready to accept the one you prefer."

Were they ever bold? Undoubtedly, but so timid!

"Mama thinks you a man of heart and an honest man," Mlle. Perrichon confessed to M. Armand.

And M. Armand sighed: "And you, mademoiselle, will you allow me to hope that you may feel the same benevolence toward me?"

To which the young girl replied: "Sir, when a young lady is well brought up she always thinks like her mama."

And she slipped away, blushing, ashamed of her temerity, leaving the "good young man," a boy like all Labiche's young men, "affectionate, steady, never any liquor except coffee." This young Paris bourgeois would grow old before his time, wear a smoking cap, sign contracts before the notary, drink his camomile infusion every evening, walk for twelve hours at a time carrying a pot of myrtle or a kettle, and climb a ladder to calm his toothache. Even when deceived he would be the happiest of the three. As for the erstwhile well-brought-up girl, now a laughable mother-in-law, cooking her stew, knitting woolen stockings for her husband, she would principally despise any Italian straw hats that might offend her eyes!

These puppet couples sometimes tried to escape from their incurably bourgeois life, but without success. Potard, in *La Baron de Fourchevif,* even announced with pride: "We are bourgeois, let us stay bourgeois!" And he sent his wife back to the washtub.

A stupid, simple Paris, waving its indelible stupidity like a flag, but a touching Paris, too, a Paris that seemed to come out of an old family album with a big steel clasp, found one day by chance and opened with amusement. And then one is overcome by a slight feeling of emotion on seeing once more the photograph of the aunt eternally playing bezique, wearing her flowered slippers and her indefinable bonnet with strings.

And this forgotten Paris lived at a stone's throw from the Tuileries, rustling in purple and gold, from the boulevards where no one thought of anything but love and wit, from the theatres where one rubbed shoulders with kings, from the Paris of Gervaise and Nana.

2
An Acrimonious Parisian

"I came into the world during a sad century, with a soul inclined to sadness, but I have never given anyone the right to suspect this. On the contrary I pass for being a gay man. But sometimes people are surprised at hearing what sounds like a sob in the concert of my airy indifference."

This "unhappy man" was Comte Horace de Viel-Castel and was the type of the embittered misanthrope. His father had held the posts of chamberlain and lover to the Empress Josephine. Viel-Castel's brother had for his part been the lover of Mme. de Montijo, mother of the Empress Eugénie. In spite of his "connections" the writer, author of twenty-seven books, was in no way considered by Napoleon as being "an illustration of his reign." He had merely been granted—partly out of weariness, for he had pestered his cousin Nieuwerkerke with requests—the post of secretary general of the national museums.

"I register debates in which I take no part," he joked, with a sour smile.

His twenty-seven books are forgotten today—they were already in his lifetime—but his *Memoirs*, published twenty years after his death, earn a kind of immortality for Viel-Castel. Each night, like a good viper not wishing his venom to be lost, he would note down what he had said and heard. For the most part it is gossip and tittle-tattle, but leaving aside some flagrant backbiting history can glean some profit.

Bald, his slack face framed in bushy whiskers like those of Franz-Joseph, with a steely eye and a mouth that under his *schnauzer* mustache was seen to be ironical, he would go each Wednesday and Saturday to the house of Princess Mathilde, daughter of King Jerome. At the beginning of the Empire Viel-Castel liked "the character and person" of Napoleon III's first cousin. "With her," he wrote, "frankness is a virtue pushed to extreme limits." Later on Horace de Viel-Castel was to be infinitely less appreciative of this "frankness," for it would be exercised at his expense, but for the moment he was delighted and received with joy the princess's confidences concerning the Emperor.

For example, on Thursday, September 28, 1858, he carefully noted down the conversation of the evening before. They had been talking about Walewski, the natural son of the great Napoleon and Maria Walewska. His wife, little Marianne, was for the moment Napoleon III's mistress. According to Mathilde, Walewski was unaware of his misfortune.

"Marianne is a little libertine who has managed, while sleeping with the Emperor, to become a friend of the Empress. But she is terrified of her husband and I would swear that Walewski knows nothing."

Chaumont-Quitry, the Emperor's chamberlain, did not share this opinion. According to him Walewski was a complaisant husband. He *leased* his wife to the Emperor for a high price, as witness the land worth 100,000 francs that he had just received from Napoleon.

"Walewski's ignorance is put on. I have seen him, with my own eyes, in Villeneuve park, turn round and go back when he caught a glimpse of the Emperor and his wife on a path. But I saw more than that this year at Cherbourg. One morning Walewski and I were in a room adjoining the Emperor's bedroom. Mocquart arrived to speak to his sovereign, opened the door without knocking, then recoiled in surprise and nearly fell into my arms. Through the open door I was able to see Mme. Walewska in the Emperor's arms and Walewski, who was standing next to me, must have seen everything I saw."

"I know," Mathilde admitted, "that the Emperor is very imprudent, that he does not restrain himself and that last year, at Compiègne, when we were all in the imperial railway carriage divided into two compartments, Mme. Hamelin and I were witnesses of His Majesty's amorous impulses toward Marianne Walewska. Mme. Hamelin and I were seated near the swing door separating the two compartments. The Emperor was alone on one side with Marianne; the Empress, Walewski and, in fact, everyone else, were in the other compartment. The door swung open with a movement of the train and enabled us to see my very dear cousin astride on Marianne's knees, kissing her mouth and with a hand in her bosom. In any case the Emperor does not dissemble much. He is not entirely indiscreet. For example, he is never the first to speak of his success, but if he is questioned he answers frankly. Last year, during a ball at the Tuileries, I saw him looking anxious and I asked him the reason. 'I have a very bad headache,' he said. 'Moreover, I am pursued by three women.' 'What!' I replied. 'Why do you give yourself all this trouble? Three women, it's madness!' 'Well, you see,' the Emperor continued, 'I have the blonde on the ground floor'—Mme. de Labédoyère—'whom I am trying to get rid of. Then I have the lady on the first floor'—Comtesse de Castiglione—'who is admittedly very beautiful, but she is insignificant and insipid and she bores me. And then I have the blonde on the second floor'—Mme. Walewska—'who is in quest of me and pursues me.' 'But what about the Empress?' 'As for the Empress,' said the Emperor, 'I was faithful to her during the first six months of our union, but I have need of little distractions and I always return to her with pleasure.' "

If Horace de Viel-Castel is to be believed, Eugénie took pleasure in "fulfilling the role that Mme. Du Barry fulfilled with Louis XV." It was Mme. de Pompadour above all who filled this role with Louis XV. She became friends with the women who attracted the Emperor; more, "she forwarded their relations with her husband; she pushed them into his arms so as to obtain a little more influence through them." It is certain that Comtesse Walewska, Comtesse de Labédoyère and little Pommayrac were members of Eugénie's circle. La Castiglione, who was only a courtesan and who became Napoleon's mistress by order of the King of Italy, was an exception to the rule.

If Princesse Mathilde felt some regret when faced with these love affairs on every floor, she must also have found some consolation. Twenty-two years earlier, at Arenenberg, the future Emperor had been greatly excited by his cousin's pretty, low-cut dresses. He indulged "in all the silliness of a man in love," an intimate of the household tells us, while young Mathilde, between meals, "stuffed herself with cakes so that at table she would look sentimental and have to be tenderly pressed to food." Soon there were kisses as they walked along the alleys in the park and the engagement became official. Louis-Napoleon gave his fiancée a lock of his hair, and Mathilde handed him a cane, whose gold knob was in the shape of a little dog.

"Take great care," she murmured to him. "It is the symbol of fidelity."

She would have done better to give him a sword for, while indulging in his "silliness" Louis-Napoleon was preparing a plot to overthrow Louis-Philippe's throne. As he wandered along the paths of

Arenenberg he had been careful not to inform his cousin of his projects. It was through the newspapers that she learned of the arrest of her fiancé, who had attempted in a cavalier fashion to rouse the garrison at Strasbourg. The details of the escapade sent King Jerome into a fury: Napoleon's enterprises had succeeded because he had genius, but that a young dandy, a writer of verse and a reader of philosophy, should make the attempt was too much.

But it was better to be a conspirator—and Napoleon was to remain one all his life, even on the throne—than to be, like Jerome, a ridiculous puppet who, trembling with fear, protested his loyalty to Louis-Philippe, disavowed his nephew, broke his daughter's engagement and forbade her to write to the outlaw, whom the French government embarked in the *Andromeda* for New York.

Jerome preferred to sell his daughter—there is no other word—to Demidoff, grandson of an enriched moujik, who in private beat her and in public slapped her face.

The intervention of Czar Nicholas, Mathilde's cousin, was needed to break this unfortunate union with a man of whom Viel-Castel said: "Nothing viler and baser can be imagined! False, cowardly, every vice, in fact, and not one good quality!"

The fiancés of Arenenberg were to meet again after the 1848 revolution. The interview took place in the Hôtel du Rhin, Place Vendôme, and Louis-Napoleon pretended to have forgotten Mathilde's long silence. He needed her, her connections and her purse as well. Would the idyll of Arenenberg begin again? Rumor had it that the princess was doing all she could to seduce her cousin and become his mistress.

When the new President was installed in the Elysée Palace there was no more talk of a liaison but of a marriage. Louis-Napoleon undeceived his friends, putting on an air of weariness and describing a large circle in the air, "indicating that Mathilde's dimensions awed him, who liked slender, supple women." The low-cut dresses of Arenenberg had spread somewhat. For her part—and she seemed sincere—Mathilde was not much more attracted to her cousin.

"He is neither frank nor impressionable," she confessed. "Nothing moves him. If I had married him I think I should have cracked open his head to find out what was inside." This is not the language of Arenenberg.

Napoleon III's marriage with Eugénie de Montijo effaced old memories still more. Yet it was Princesse Mathilde who presented the young Comtesse de Teba to her cousin in the hope that he would make her his mistress and break his liaison with Miss Howard. Only the second part of the program succeeded. It was probably not without a slight feeling of jealousy that Mathilde left the first place to the woman who had been her protégée, but Eugénie did nothing to smooth things over, treating Mathilde merely as the Emperor's cousin, pretending to ignore the bonds of affection uniting the former fiancés and the material aid Mathilde had given Napoleon on his return to France. Mathilde consoled herself for giving the throne to the "Spanish woman" by saying all the ill she could about her.

The many unpublished documents recently discovered by Mme. Castillon du Perron revealed what King Jerome's daughter thought about the Empress. "God knows," the princess wrote toward the end of her life, "one had reason to dread that woman's influence! With however much indulgence one tries to judge her, one is still astonished at the amount of cunning and pride united in one person. If I did not fear to sound pretentious, I should compare her to Sixtus V deceiving the Conclave until the moment he threw down his crutches. She let fall the mask after the birth of the Prince Imperial; her vanity knew no limits." Princesse Mathilde even said once: "She is an unnatural wife and mother!" It is true that in another unpublished letter Mathilde admitted frankly that Eugénie had the gift of making her unjust. It is true too, as Mathilde told Horace de Viel-Castel one day at lunch, that the Empress sometimes adopted a questionable attitude and made unfortunate remarks. For example, in March, 1858, she made "scenes of sobs and tears" to the Emperor, asking him to pardon the Italian Orsini, who had thrown three bombs at the imperial carriage. The attempted assassination resulted in six deaths and ninety-five wounded. Eugénie claimed that the assassin was "an excellent patriot."

"Orsini," she affirmed, "did not wish to assassinate the Emperor of the French, but the friend of the Emperor of Austria. What led him to assassination was the heightening of a generous sentiment. He loves freedom passionately and no less forcibly detests the oppressors of his country."

And she apparently added this explanation, all the clumsier, in the mouth of the Empress of the French, in that she admired Napoleon I: "I remember very well the hatred we had in Spain for the French after the wars of the First Empire."

Can we believe Viel-Castel when he relates a saying of Napoleon III told to him by Mathilde? It was during lunch at the Tuileries. The only guests were the princess and Doctor Conneau. The Empress, wrote Viel-Castel, spoke with such harshness and with such a decidedly hostile bias against French policy that the Emperor got up impatiently and exclaimed: "Really, Eugénie, you forgot two things: that you are a Frenchwoman and that you have married a Bonaparte!"

King Jerome's son was Viel-Castel's *bête-noire*. He had not words enough to condemn him. In his opinion Prince Napoleon was a man without bravery, without gratitude, without honesty and without generosity. "The first impression produced by Prince Napoleon is not a favorable one," Viel-Castel wrote. "And when one knows him better one despises him profoundly. If he were brave one would pray that he might be taken from us by a bullet, but one has not even that resource." It was he who had one day dared to say to his imperial cousin:

"You have nothing of the Emperor!"

"You are mistaken; I have his family."

As he sighed Napoleon III was certainly not thinking particularly of Mathilde, but there were all the other members of the clan. The only thing with which he reproached his former fiancée was her irregular attendance at the official receptions in the Tuileries. "It is indispensable," he wrote to her, "that I should have the members of my family around me."

Mathilde, and one can understand her, preferred staying at home where—in the Rue de Courcelles in the winter and at Saint-Gratien in the summer—she received artists and men of letters, which has given us several outbursts from the pen of Viel-Castel, who had nothing but contempt for painters and writers, those who had no title, of course! He disapproved of Mathilde. "The princess has been badly advised," he wrote. "In my opinion she makes a great mistake in admitting artists to the intimacy of her home. She does not know their moral nature. Artists, far from being flattered at finding themselves in the drawing rooms of the nobility, are very unhappy there. Their touchy character makes them morose, they are jealous of any superiority, they form a hatred of social distinctions that do not set them in the first rank and in their presence conversation becomes very difficult since every word from a person in society seems to them to indicate an intention to wound. Artists do not admit that a 'man of the world' can be a true artist, but they do not know why they, the artists, will never be true men of the world."

On June 5, 1853, Alexandre Dumas was invited to the princess's. Viel-Castel considered the presence in the Rue de Courcelles of the author of *The Three Musketeers* "an error," for Mathilde allowed him to take on "a lofty tone." He was a vain clown, a liar and a coward! The Emperor had just signed a decree appropriating the possessions of the princes of Orléans, and Dumas improvised this verse, which from Mathilde's drawing room made the rounds of Paris:

> Uncle and nephew are alike
> In their pomp imperial.
> The uncle took our capitals,
> The nephew takes our capital.

Viel-Castel did not treat Hugo any better. In his opinion: "No one in the world is at once more despicable and more denuded of moral sense. He speaks constantly of the family, of the sanctity of the home, of the respect due to the mother, but all his fine preaching is nothing but the utterance of printed gossip. . . . He has never deprived himself of mistresses, whom he has enshrined in his poetry, and his family is composed of an equal proportion of legitimate children and bastards."

He dealt even more briefly with George Sand and disposed of her in a few words: "A week ago I was dining with the painter Eugène Delacroix and I asked him: 'Have you been Mme. Sand's lover?' 'Of course,' he replied. 'Just like everyone else.'"

On the other hand, the Tartuffe-like Horace de Viel-Castel was full of indulgence for Alfred de Musset. Was this because he was a "man of the world"? "In spite of his rather disordered life," he wrote, "Musset has remained young in heart and mind. He was quite delighted to meet me again. 'Young people today,' he said, 'are no longer young, they are no longer gay, they have not even that worldly politeness that formerly indicated well-educated men. They no longer laugh, they no longer amuse themselves, they are gamblers without passion, lovers without passion, debauched without enthusiasm. And then they are profoundly ignorant, so ignorant as to envy the knowledge of a donkey.' "

When Musset died, on Monday, May 2, 1857, Viel-Castel wrote the next day: "Musset did not drink in order to be gay, he drank to live another life, strange, inner, fantastic, of which he revealed nothing. . . . He was a true poet, a great poet, but poetry had already died in him and today it is only the human body that we give back to the earth. Poor Alfred! I can still see him, fair, pink and shy with his seventeen years, coming to read me the manuscript of his *Tales of Spain and Italy*. Poor poet, no one will ever know what cup of bitterness you emptied before seeking oblivion by emptying the dirty glasses of cabarets."

In spite of his nobility Vigny was very roughly handled. Viel-Castel saw him "as chubby as an old angel, his face shining and pomaded like that of an old actress who has just removed her make-up."

It is through Viel-Castel's *Memoirs* that we know the racy story of La Païva, mirror of the life of Paris of the time. It was in 1857. The "marquise" was not yet living in her sumptuous neo-Greek house in the Avenue des Champs-Elysées; she was still studying the plans. It was not until a little later that Henry Murger was able to say: "La Païva's house will soon be finished. They have just laid the pavement."

The woman who, it was said, had taken as her motto *Qui paye y va*, declared one day to an importunate suitor: "You absolutely must sleep with me, you're set on it, it's a fixed idea, so one must finish with the business in order to live in peace with you. What can you offer me? You are poor, you have thirty thousand livres a year, I love money, I never have enough, and yet I have more than you. I want you to buy the favor you ask for. Have you ten thousand francs?"

"No."

"You answered well, for if you had admitted possessing ten thousand francs I should have asked you for twenty thousand. Since you haven't ten thousand francs bring them to me. We shall burn them and I shall be yours for as long as the bonfire of ten thousand francs lasts."

The lover bowed and said: "Until tomorrow, marquise."

"The following day," writes Viel-Castel, "the marquise, seated on the divan in her boudoir, was at her most attractive. A marble table, like an antique altar, seemed to await a victim; the air was perfumed and the daylight filtered through the thick curtains to the windows. The lover came to the goddess not wearing a fillet but adorned with twelve banknotes for one thousand francs; he had wanted to make his sacrifice more complete. La Païva, without changing her attitude and with the smile and look of an amorous viper, felt the twelve thousand francs, found them adorable, and set them out on the marble table so that they would burn one after the other, and lit the first. At once the young man flew into La Païva's arms and leaving aside all preliminaries went straight to his goal and enjoyed his good fortune as one who knows the price of time. When the notes were burned the satisfied lover and the smiling, rumpled and mocking La Païva faced each other, and while the lover was adjusting his clothes he said, in reply to the courtesan's amused glances: 'My poor girl, I've made a fool of you. The notes were so well photographed by my friend Aguado that they deceived you.'

"At these words La Païva leaped like a panther toward the impudent man. . . . She heaped abuse on the satisfied man, who was no longer in love, and who left, dusting off his knees."

There is also the story of Alexandre Dumas, his wife Ida and Roger de Beauvoir. The scene took place in the Rue de Rivoli, in the home of M. and Mme. Dumas. A fire crackled in the grate. Outside it was raining torrents. Ida was in bed. Alexandre, in full evening dress, left for a reception at the Tuileries and returned three-quarters of an hour later.

"My goodness, I wanted to walk to the Tuileries, I got soaked to the skin and I'm no longer presentable. I shall stay here. You have a fire and I shall work."

All Ida could say was no use. Dumas wanted to work by the fire, and when Dumas wanted something . . . An hour went by. Ida cursed, Dumas's pen scratched, the fire crackled and the rain continued to fall. Suddenly the bathroom door opened and Roger de Beauvoir, wearing nothing but a shirt, made his entry. He had formerly been Ida's lover, and indeed it was at his house that Dumas had met his future wife, but although Dumas was not attacked by retrospective jealousy he did not relish this evening at his expense. He made a dramatic scene, to which Roger de Beauvoir replied:

"Good heavens, you arrive like a bomb, you settle down at your ease by the fire, you announce your intention of spending the night in the chimney corner, while I freeze in a bathroom like an ice house! It's quite unbearable, I couldn't stand it, and here I am!"

Dumas continued dramatically: "Very well, sir, we shall have an explanation tomorrow morning. Meanwhile do me the pleasure of leaving my dwelling."

Outside it was raining like a deluge.

"I can't send you away in this rain," Dumas declared, having looked through the curtains. "One wouldn't send a dog out. Sit down, Monsieur de Beauvoir, spend the night in my armchair. We shall have our explanation tomorrow morning."

With great satisfaction Roger de Beauvoir stretched his bare legs out to the fire. Dumas went to bed with Ida, who did not utter a word. At the end of an hour the fire went out. Beauvoir's teeth began to chatter.

"The wretch will catch a cold, I'm sure," Dumas murmured. "Monsieur de Beauvoir, I do not want you to catch a cold. Come to bed. We shall have our explanation tomorrow morning."

M. de Beauvoir promptly slipped into bed and the melodrama became a farce.

At nine in the morning Dumas woke up, looked at the guilty pair— who did not seem overcome with remorse—and woke them up.

"Roger, old friends do not quarrel over a woman, even a legal wife. It would be stupid."

He took Beauvoir's hand and placed it on Ida's body.

"Roger, let us be reconciled like the ancient Romans, on the public thoroughfare."

And so it was done.

Viel-Castel's diary also gives us details dear to lovers of sidelights on history. Thanks to Nieuwerkerke, who was present at the execution of Verger, Horace was able to relate the death of that interdicted priest, that unbalanced man who, on January 3, 1857, had assassinated Monseigneur Sibour, the Archbishop of Paris, in the church of Saint-Etienne-du-mont, "on account," he said, "of the Immaculate Conception."

The murderer's awakening was atrocious.

"He flew into a fury, rolled on his bed, crying that he wanted to live, that he would fight to the death and, as the almoner tried to calm him, he pushed him away.

" 'You are going to talk to me again of the Virgin, of scapulars and rosaries. You know my convictions; leave me in peace! I do not want to die thus, with only strangers near me. They cannot, in my last moments, deprive me of the presence of my friends, of my relatives. I want to live.'

"The hour drew near, and the condemned man, deaf to the almoner's exhortations, shouted, fought, bit his sheets. The governor of the prison had summoned the executioner, a large, athletic person, nearly six feet tall, with a broad, hard, common face, wearing a greasy hat with a narrow brim and a dirty, worn black suit. This person unceremoniously and with some brutality took hold of the condemned man, who was rolled up in his sheets and blankets. He dressed him forcibly and carried him to the room in which he would wash for the last time. On his arrival Verger was calmer. He asked that they should not take so many precautions against him and promised to make no resistance. In a quarter of an hour Verger had aged ten years, his eyes were haggard and the contraction of his features was hideous, yet he retained his presence of mind. The almoner profited by these moments of calm to make a last appeal to his Christian sentiments and to try to awaken sincere repentance in his heart. This time Verger listened. For a few seconds his head was bent on his breast, then he raised it and made a complete apology. He repudiated his crime and the principles he had professed and was finally reconciled with the idea of religion and embraced the almoner.

"Eight o'clock was about to strike; the funeral procession set out. Verger grew paler and paler, his eyes became scared, his head sank on his shoulder, but he went forward, supported by the almoner and the executioner. On the platform of the scaffold, at the moment of being fastened to the swing plank, Verger cried in a fairly strong voice: 'Long live Jesus Christ! Long live the Emperor!' "

On March 11, 1863, Horace published an article in the newspaper *La France* criticizing the measures taken by Nieuwerkerke regarding the exhibition of paintings and the rules drawn up by the director of the national museums. On the following day Viel-Castel received this letter from his "boss," a letter he described as "stupid in its swollen vanity and crudeness."

Sir,
    I have read in *La France* of 11 March an article entitled "The Exhibition of 1863." You will understand that I cannot tolerate that a person who is a member of my administration should permit himself to criticize its actions. You have attacked the most important points in the regulations I proposed, which have been approved. You know quite well that mine was the initiative in all these measures and that I had just given H.E. the Minister of State a report entirely in favor of annual exhibitions. It would, I think, have been good taste to choose between the independence of your pen and the respect you owe to your chief.
    I might perhaps have the right to invoke other motives for being surprised by such a procedure.

And Comte de Nieuwerkerke ended his letter by informing the culprit that he "was no longer a member of the personnel of the general directorate of the imperial museums."

Princesse Mathilde associated herself with the steps taken by her lover, and Comte de Viel-Castel was received no more in the Rue de Courcelles. His rage was enormous. In his *Memoirs* he heaps abuse on "the pasha Nieuwerkerke," whom he accuses of sponging on Mathilde. As for the princess, whose "character and person" he formerly admired so much, she becomes, under the "outlaw's" pen, a vulgar and stupid fat woman. The drawing room he liked so much to visit was now merely "a bazaar" full of "false grandeur" that needed "to take only one step to become an anteroom."

Viel-Castel's bitterness knew no limits . . . and perhaps that was what he died of in the following year.

The punishment seems disproportionate to the crime and historians sought to find a meaning in the last, somewhat obscure, sentence of Nieuwerkerke's letter: "I might perhaps have the right to invoke other motives for being surprised by such a procedure." What were these "other motives"? They were looked for in the *Souvenirs* of Philippe de Chennevières, who spoke of "extremely shady acquisitions" made by Horace for the Louvre.

It is Mme. Castillon du Perron who has given us the final explanation by recently publishing the following letter from Nieuwerkerke dated December 1, 1882, which the author of *La Princesse Mathilde* had the good fortune to find in the Primoli archives:

Dear Reiset,
 I shall give you a categorical reply to your question concerning Viel-Castel. He was not relieved of his post; he was dismissed as a thief. Out of respect for the name he bears and for his brother Louis, who is a very honorable man, I took as a pretext an article in *La France*, of which he was one of the editors, and which contained attacks against the office of which I was director. But there was proof of several thefts not only from me but from other people, among whom was the Marquise de Gabriac, from whom he stole five hundred francs while her back was turned and during a visit he was paying her. He had taken some of the objects under his care to sell to dealers, but had had to bring them back on their refusal to take them. I had a collection of five-franc pieces bearing the effigy of Louis XVIII and I saw their number diminish. I informed Moissenet, who, with his skill as a detective, gave me proofs that it was Viel-Castel who was stealing them while I dressed.

 Everyone who was smeared by Comte Horace, everyone he spoke ill of is today fully avenged.

3
Virginia

In Louis-Philippe's day the Bois de Boulogne was so dreary that Parisians never ventured into that "pitiless desert." At the beginning of the Second Empire Napoleon III, who remembered Hyde Park, laid out winding roads, planted trees, dug lakes and a serpentine river, built restaurants, kiosks and chalets. Soon, Comtesse d'Agoult relates, "in the broad, well-sanded, well-watered *allées* would pass, at the fashionable hours, four or five rows of equipages, phaetons, victorias, calashes, pony-carts and *huit-ressorts*." Henceforth the guests of Napoleon III and Eugénie went to the Château of Saint-Cloud through the new wood.

 At the end of a hot day in June, 1856, there were many carriages entering the Bois through the Porte Maillot—a mall game had given it its former name of Porte Mahiau—and proceeding along the Allée des Acacias. That evening the Emperor and Empress were giving an evening party at their little château of Villeneuve-l'Etang, near Marnes-la-Coquette, in honor of their cousin the Dowager Grand-Duchess of Baden.

Inside a calash, filling the whole of the carriage with her crinoline of transparent muslin, was the prettiest woman imaginable. On her hair, which fell in silky black curls onto her shoulders, was placed a hat adorned with a halo of white marabou feathers that gave pearly tints to that perfect face.

The young Comtesse Virginia de Castiglione—she was just nineteen—was also going to Villeneuve-l'Etang. At the request of the Emperor the Empress had invited her herself. Virginia smiled happily, lulled by the regular trot of the horses, letting her thoughts wander, remembering the stages of her career as imperial mistress—or rather, future mistress, for as far as one can be accurate in such matters, when Napoleon III had received the beautiful comtesse at the Tuileries he had confined himself to stroking his mustache nervously and uttering banalities. However, what a long way had been covered since that evening of January 9 when young Mme. de Castiglione had been presented to the Emperor! The setting had been Princesse Mathilde's house in the Boulevard Haussmann. Virginia, with her hair drawn back, pink feathers mingling with her black hair with its tawny lights, had that evening resembled "a marquise of former days wearing a royal bird," as Vicomte de Reiset wrote. As he twisted his mustache —a sign of emotion—Napoleon addressed a few pleasant words to the young Italian, but Virginia had lost all her self-assurance. She had remained silent and when he left her the Emperor had said: "She is beautiful, but she appears to be without intelligence."

Three weeks later Comtesse de Castiglione had somewhat redeemed herself at a ball given by old King Jerome. It was midnight when, wearing a white-and-gold dress, she entered the Palais Royal, where the "comic-opera king" lived. Napoleon III was already leaving and passed her on the staircase.

"You are arriving very late, madame."

"It is you, sire, who are leaving very early," she had replied, with an almost bold look at the sovereign.

This time the Emperor presumably found she was a little more "intelligent." Virginia redeemed herself completely in the Tuileries on January 29. Her sumptuous dress of silver blue had been a sensation, and that night, when she returned home to 10 Rue de Castiglione, she was able to write in her private diary: "The Emperor came to speak to me. Then everyone looked and came to see me. I laughed." As one looks through this diary, recently revealed by Alain Decaux in his book *(La Castiglione, Dame de coeur de l'Europe)*, one observes that Napoleon III found Mme. de Castiglione increasingly "intelligent": "Saturday, February 2. Talked with the Emperor, who gave me some oranges. Tuesday, February 5. I went to M. Le Hon's costume ball, where I spoke to the Emperor who was masked. Thursday, February 21. Combed with powder, pearls, feathers. Went to concert at the Tuileries. Dined, talked with the Emperor."

Cavour, who was then in Paris for the Peace Congress, at which he was representing Piedmont, wrote to a friend on the day after the concert at the Tuileries: "I warn you that I have set the very beautiful Comtesse de XXX on her career and I have invited her to flirt with and seduce, if the opportunity arises, the Emperor. She began her 'mission' discreetly yesterday at the concert in the Tuileries."

It was, in fact, a mission with which the comtesse was entrusted, and it was King Victor Emmanuel himself who had asked her to serve the cause of Italy with Napoleon III in this extra-diplomatic fashion. He had had his own way of handing the young woman her letters of credit: "December 17, 1855," one reads in the diary. "While my hair was still undressed Persano came to tell me that the King was waiting outside! I dressed in black velvet, combed my hair, sent everyone away, left everything and went into the drawing room. Persano had taken the key of the garden, through which he had entered the drawing room. At eleven he left. I accompanied him into the garden, where he . . . . . . I came to my dressing room to tidy things." She had become the mistress of the King, who had been able to judge for himself the arms Virginia would wield in the cause of Italian unification. In case Victor Emmanuel, somewhat distracted by the Castiglione garden, had not made his intentions clear, Cavour had summed up the royal wish in one sentence:

"Succeed, my cousin, by what means you please, but succeed!"

The means that pleased her were undoubtedly love. That was why the comtesse had come to Paris, accompanied by her husband, who, in love and completely dazzled, apparently suspected nothing.

One may imagine Virginia's joy at receiving, on June 25, this letter from Eugénie's lady of honor:

"Dear Madame, I am instructed by the Empress to tell you that you will receive an invitation for Friday evening at Villeneuve-l'Etang, and that you are asked to come in day dress and in hat, as there will be excursions on the lake and in the park."

As she drove toward Saint-Cloud had Virginia any idea that this time, on June 27, her "mission" would take a great step forward?

The calash crossed the Seine, climbed the slope toward the château and entered the park. The little château of Villeneuve-l'Etang, which during the Restoration had belonged to Madame Royale, was hidden in the midst of fields and water. The lake, fed by a spring, had the limpidity of a Swiss lake and the Emperor, in memory of Arenenberg, had had a Swiss farm built on its bank that looked rather out of place under the sky of the Ile de France. The warm, perfumed night— the hay had been cut that very morning—was falling. Mme. de Castiglione descended from her carriage and in "her ghostlike dress," in the words of a guest, walked toward Napoleon, who was receiving on the lawn by the lake. When he noticed Virginia he came toward her. It was obvious that the comtesse dazzled him. "What virtue would have been needed," an eyewitness wrote, "to resist her, and in that kind of gathering it was not virtue on which men prided themselves!" The party began. Already the Emperor was leading her smilingly toward one of the boats adorned with lamps that awaited the guests. He helped the young woman to get in, seized the oars and, while the music of the guides and of the choirs of the Conservatoire could be heard, steered the boat toward a little island in the center of the lake. Those present displayed some respectful astonishment. "The Emperor," wrote Mme. de La Pagerie, "seemed to me to forget rather too completely that the whole of Europe had been surprised by his love match and had not yet got over its surprise. As for Mme. de Castiglione she gave me the impression of a perfectly calm, cool person, preparing and managing her effects and proceeding without swerving to the goal she had set herself."

If Viel-Castel is to be believed, the Emperor and the comtesse wandered "for a long time" on the island. When Virginia returned to land, to watch the fireworks and take supper in the château, everyone was able to notice that her dress had been "somewhat crumpled" and that the Empress, pale in her white dress lined with pink, "revealed some vexation."

The famous liaison had begun.

Very frequently during the following winter the Emperor's little coupé could be seen standing in front of 28 Avenue Montaigne, where the Castigliones were living. One evening, just as Napoleon was leaving the house to return to the Tuileries, three men emerged from the shadows and rushed at the sovereign. They were three Italian anarchists, who had received fifty napoleons to kill the man whom Comtesse Castiglione had rallied, perhaps too well, to the cause of Victor Emmanuel. The coachman whipped up his horses, they leaped forward, knocking down one of the men, and the carriage drove on. On the following day all Paris was talking of the event.

They also repeated the Empress's saying at the costume ball at the Ministry of Foreign Affairs. Virginia had gone as Queen of Hearts in a vaguely Louis XV costume, all sprinkled with hearts. Eugénie looked at her rival, fixed her eyes on one of the hearts and said aloud: "Her heart is a little low."

Virginia was admiring herself so much that she may not have heard the insulting remark. That evening, says Viel-Castel, who seems to have regarded her with a great deal of attention, "she carried the weight of her beauty with insolence; she displayed the proofs of it with ostentation. We cannot say that her dress was décolleté; but we can affirm the nudity of her bosom, barely covered with transparent gauze. The eye followed the contours and the slightest details. . . . Her bosom is really admirable; it rises proudly like the bosoms of young Moorish women. In a word the two breasts seem to lay down a challenge to all women."

It was at Compiègne, during one of the series of receptions, that Virginia was able to observe how much she was detested. Her boundless pretentiousness had turned all the guests away from her. "She seemed so imbued with her triumphant beauty," Princesse de Metternich wrote. "She was so entirely preoccupied by it that after a few moments, when one had looked well at her, she got on your nerves! There was not a movement, not a gesture, nothing that was not studied!" So when, during an excursion to Pierrefonds, she was seen to slip in the ruins and fall, displaying the prettiest legs in the world, everyone was convinced that her fall was voluntary and formed part of the program. The Emperor had remained at Compiègne, and no one took pity on her. And yet Virginia had broken several bones in her wrist. She was bandaged and merely reconducted to the charàbanc that had brought the guests. She had to wait until the visit was over before she could return to the château. "When everyone came back to take their seats in the carriages," General Fleury related, "no one came to sit with the unfortunate injured woman, no one bothered to play the part of escort. It was sad to see all those courtiers, as in *La Favorita,* turn from the king's mistress."

It was at Compiègne, at the end of the season of 1857, that the imperial liaison came to an end. Through pride, perhaps in reply to a woman who looked down on her, the comtesse paraded Napoleon III's feelings for her. Later on, the Emperor confided to Poniatowski: "Her need to be talked about was the cause of the rupture. I never said anything to anyone. If people talked, it was because her friends would find her lying in her bed surrounded by costly sheets and laces."

Sheets and laces whose source she had certainly mentioned. Her "mission" was over.

"I have barely passed through life and my role is already ended," she sighed.

The end of her adventure did not serve her as a lesson. She continued to believe herself superior to all other women, and she expressed this primacy in these modest words: "I equal them by my birth. I surpass them by my beauty. I judge them by my intelligence."

With men she behaved as "an uncontested queen." Feeling sure of herself, seeing them at her feet, she made unreasonable demands or played with her lovers' hearts. Perhaps she wished to avenge herself for having been abandoned by the Emperor. One evening, "as a distraction," she confessed in her diary, she invented a long story that made one of the unhappy men caught in her toils weep. "He could not bear it," she wrote, delighted. Each page of her private diary reflects her love affairs. What stormy liaisons! What betrayals! What dreadful blackmail! What lies! What cruelty! Everything she confided to her little notebook now bears pitiless witness against her.

The end of her life was terrible. She who had been the most beautiful and most desired woman of her time became a half-mad woman driven by a mania for walking. She was living at 26 *bis,* Place Vendôme, and every evening, dressed in black, her face hidden by veils, dragging along two miserable, fat, asthmatic dogs, she would leave her house, taking care not to be recognized, go to the arcades of the street whose name she was once so proud to bear, in the direction of the Rue de Rivoli. For hours and hours she would walk, coming back to her house only when the dawn was beginning to disperse the darkness she now cherished. She did not want to be seen, shunned herself, and in her bedroom all the mirrors were shrouded.

"I have become horribly ugly!"

While waiting for the following night she would slip between her black satin sheets—which had the main merit of not showing the dirt —and write innumerable letters in which her mind wandered. She constantly relived her past. Now that she was only a poor woman whom passers-by turned to look at, she liked to stroke with her thin hands "the nightdress of Compiègne," a souvenir of glory—unless it was the nightdress of the rupture, the dress of the final night—in which she wished to be buried.

She also liked to reread the letter that Thiers had written her on December 21, 1872. "I recall what you did at Florence in the interests of our poor France, then most unhappy." She remembered the little man, his white hair standing up in a tuft, who had entered her house on October 12, 1870, a few weeks after Sedan. He had come to ask Mme. de Castiglione to intervene at the court of Prussia and with Bismarck in order to obtain an interview from the latter and sound out the enemy's intentions regarding a possible armistice. She had been glad to have once more a part to play. She knew Bismarck and kept up a correspondence with Queen Augusta, the future Empress of Germany. "The French have lost," she wrote to the Chancellor. "They are lost, and it is for you to yield. You must have enough proud generosity for this. . . . Make a step toward the Parisians, allow them to live, since they agree to the occupation of Paris."

One knows the reply that Bismarck wrote in history; the comtesse was deeply affected by it. She claimed that she had failed completely, forgetting that, thanks to her, Thiers had been able to make contact with Bismarck. Admittedly the two men had not been able to agree, but what could she do about it? She should have been satisfied with the success she had obtained, but in politics as in love and beauty her mind craved the absolute.

Since Compiègne she had tried to live over again the wonderful hours when she was twenty. She had tried many times, but in vain. This frustration had finally led to a lack of balance in her brain that increased with the years. "In her gloomy bedroom," her last biographer has written, "every day and every night she celebrated the funeral of her beauty." Soon Virginia no longer left her bed. She thought she was ruined, although her jewels and Italian estates were worth a fortune. Moreover she received a pension from King Umberto, in memory of what she had done for Italian unification.

One of her few friends, in order to get her out of her slough, begged her to adopt another mode of life.

"It is too late," she replied, her eyes shining with tears. "It is too late to begin again to live when one has already begun to die."

She died at the age of sixty-two, completely forgotten. She had demanded that her death should be surrounded by silence and she was obeyed. At her interment there were only two friends, who had been informed by chance. She was not dressed in "the nightdress of Compiègne." Her body was refused transport to Italy, to Spezia, where she had wanted to rest. Today, in the cemetery of Père Lachaise, the stone covering her tomb is bare. Even the inscription has been effaced.

4

At "My Aunt's"

In *Le Siècle* of March 4, 1856, one could have read this poignant anecdote that must have made all Paris weep. "A poor young girl came one day to one of the offices of the Mont de Piété to pawn a bundle of clothes, on which she was given three francs. For fifteen consecutive years she regularly paid the interest on this small sum, amounting to a few centimes, without ever having enough to redeem the bundle." Being moved, the management finally made inquiries. Of course the working girl was pretty, meritorious, pure and hard-working. "In the conduct of this hard-working, beautiful and good woman," the paper went on, "there was a great courage that had its source in noble sentiments." The young girl was called to the pawnshop, which undertook to return her "few clothes" without repayment. "It was then that the beautiful soul of the unhappy woman could be seen. The little bundle was composed of a woman's skirt and kerchief. Hardly was it opened when the young girl" (she was still "the young girl" after fifteen years) "took these objects in both hands and, bursting into tears, covered them with kisses. They were all she had inherited from her mother, who had been dead for fifteen years, and in order to preserve these precious relics she had religiously brought her pious tribute, just as one goes to the cemetery to lay flowers on a beloved tomb on the anniversary of a death!"

Note that this pathetic story may be true, as in 1901, in the Rue des Francs-Bourgeois, there was pointed out the presence of an umbrella belonging to the granddaughter of one of Louis-Philippe's ministers who, for twenty-five years, had been paying interest on it. (Talking of umbrellas, Maxime du Camp relates that around 1865 he saw an umbrella in one of the pawnshops that had been repawned for forty-seven consecutive years. It was quite famous and was talked about in the head office. An employee was mentioned who had come into the office "before" or "just after" the arrival of the umbrella. The object had become a "standard." Hanging from a rack, it was completely covered with tickets that gave it an armor of paper scales. One day a member of the supervisory council took pity on it, freed it and sent it back to the legal owner, who became extremely angry and declared that he did not intend that anyone should take in on themselves to give him charity—and the umbrella returned to the Rue des Francs-Bourgeois.)

But if the Mont de Piété has made generations weep, it has also made them laugh. It was a blessing for cartoonists, who loved to show the taxpayer leaving the pawnshop with his legs bare under his coat, having pawned his trousers for the benefit of the tax collector.

An official sculptor, who was paid by the state only when his commission was finished, discovered an ingenious method of carrying on his work. Once a piece of his statue was finished—head, arm or foot—he would take it to the Mont de Piété. With the money advanced on it he bought bronze and could pay the caster for the next piece. In this way there exist effigies of heroes, so Maxime du Camp assures us, that have passed "limb by limb" through the pawnshop before being erected on a pedestal in one of our public squares.

On the death of Comtesse de Castiglione, at the end of November, 1899, it was noticed that some of her jewels and furs had been in pawn for several years. There was surprise. Had she not often been seen wearing the ermine for which a receipt was found among her papers? Had not her pretty neck been adorned by that famous necklace of 279 pearls, "those tears changed into pearls," as she herself had sighed? Later the truth became known. She who had been the mistress of Napoleon III—and of so many others—was very intimate with the director of the Mont de Piété. (Some people said indeed that she was on the best possible terms with him.) Before going to a dinner she would pass by the Rue des Francs-Bourgeois and the director would "lend" her her pearls and furs. Before she went home, or the next morning before the shop opened, the objects resumed their place in the iron safe which, according to rules, could be opened only by two keys, one belonging to the shop keeper and the other to the supervisor.

But what is the origin of this institution, that seems so typically Parisian and that, particularly during the Second Empire and at the beginning of the Third Republic, enabled so many of the inhabitants of Paris to make both ends meet?

The first royal act authorizing usury was signed by Charles V on June 2, 1380. From his château of Vincennes the sovereign authorized, for fifteen years, five inhabitants of Troyes to "trade and lend money." Pledges—hitherto considered fraudulent—were allowed, with the exception of "holy relics, sacred church ornaments, plowshares, coulters and the ironwork of plows." The rate of interest was fixed at two Paris deniers a week. Charles V, in spite of his name of "The Wise," thus opened the door to the Lombards and Jews, the scourge of the Middle Ages. These latter were even authorized by his son to charge borrowers a rate of 43 percent a year. It may be said, as an excuse, that Charles VI was mad.

In Italy usury, which in the fourteenth century had been tolerated by certain Popes, had spread considerably. In the middle of the fifteenth century the Recollet friar Barnabas of Terni was particularly moved by this evil and began to fulminate daily against the usurers from the pulpit. He attacked the Jewish moneylenders with such force that when the Jews saw the friar arriving toward their town they would send a deputation asking him to preach elsewhere. But Barnabas turned a deaf ear.

One day in 1462, in Perugia, he decided after his sermon to take a collection to set up a charitable bank, a mass, a *mountain* of piety, *Monte di pietà*. The phrase was launched, the organization created. "The Perugians breathed again," a contemporary tells us. "The indigent of hard-pressed citizen was no longer reduced to humbling himself before the usurers and begging his ruin from them. The beneficent dew fell alike on creditors and debtors who each had satisfaction, the one of extinguishing his debt, the other of receiving his due."

From Perugia the "beneficent dew" spread over the majority of Italian towns.

But in France usury continued freely on its way. In vain, at the States General of 1614, the nobility proposed the creation of a Monte di Pietà "in which there would be deniers to lend." The Third Estate refused "this invention" that it considered "a means of introducing fresh usurers into France, where there were already too many." To counter the evil it was necessary to wait for an edict by Louis XIII authorizing the creation of "offices for lending on pledges" in which the *"denier seize,"* that is, 6.25 percent would be levied. The rate was so modest that no one was tempted except, a few years later, Théophraste Renaudot, to whom we also owe the first French newspaper and the first office of public assistance. In 1627 the "French father of the Mont de Piété" decided to open "at the information office in the Grand Coq, Rue de la Calandre, at the exit of the new market, near the palace in Paris a sales office for the exchange and redeeming of furniture and various property." The editorial office of the *Gazette* and an office for charitable advice were already functioning at the same address.

At first it was greeted with success and enthusiasm, then the inevitable jealousy crept in. Théophraste Renaudot, as formerly Brother Barnabas, was insulted and called a usurer. His children, who were studying medicine, had to leave the faculty "for reasons of immorality." "The Renaudots," Guy Patin explained, "are linked with a traffic and business that aims at selling gazettes, registering servants, lands and houses, at dealing in second-hand goods, lending money on pledges and other things that are unworthy of the dignity and calling of a physician."

The quarrel became so violent that the Parliament took a hand and declared the "second-hand dealer" Renaudot to be in the wrong. He was "expressly inhibited and forbidden to sell or lend on pledges in the future."

Under the Regency matters merely became worse. You pledged heavy silver plate and got it back much lighter. The usurer who lent at 120 percent was considered to be a philanthropist, and the one who took 300 percent a "good fellow."

On his arrival in power Necker waged war against usury.

"It is an abuse of strength against weakness; it is the empire of avarice and cupidity over a certain class of men. . . . But the laws against usury, the punishments inflicted on those guilty of it have not halted its progress in the capital and one cannot conceal the insurmountable difficulties in the way of reform, for as the administration's supervision becomes more alert the usurers redouble their precautions for hiding their criminal trade under apparently legal forms. It has therefore become necessary to oppose a new kind of obstacle to this depravity."

On December 9, 1777, Louis XVI, at Necker's request, signed letters patent beginning in these terms: "Louis, by the grace of God, King of France and of Navarre, to all who will see these presents, greeting! The good effects that have been and are still produced by the monts de piété in different nations in Europe, and notably those formed in Italy, do not allow you to doubt of the advantages that would result for our peoples from such establishments. These means have seemed to us the most apt to put an end to the disorders introduced by usury which have only too frequently entailed loss to many families."

Our present Mont de Piété was then created, at the very place where the central office is today, that is between the Rue des Francs-Bourgeois and the Rue des Blancs-Manteaux. The building, rented by order of Louis XVI, belonged to the Procureur-Général Joly de Fleury, who was later to succeed Necker. On January 5, 1778, the agreement was signed for 6,400 livres a year.

A year after its founding the Mont had received 128,505 objects, nearly half of which had been redeemed. "Nothing better proves the need that the capital had of this 'Lombard,' " a contemporary chronicler writes, "than the inexhaustible flow of borrowers. There is talk of forty barrels filled with gold watches!"

But everything crumbled with the Revolution and the abundance of assignats. The money offered by the Mont de Piété did not represent a hundredth part of the real value of the pledge. The establishment ceased to function without having been officially closed and the reign of the usurers started again. Not only was the interest asked more than 300 percent, but the "lenders, when they had need of money, would themselves pledge articles they had taken as security."

It took Napoleon's arrival to reopen the Mont de Piété, whose doors were henceforth never closed, and, above all, to lay down this absolute rule: "The establishment must never make a profit."

The great rule of the pawn office is discretion, and once an operation is ended—either by the withdrawal of the article or by its sale—the relevant papers are destroyed. All that remains are the account books and figures dealing with the movement of operations, which are worth a study. Graphs indicating the number of pledges and amounts advanced enable one to follow the after-effects of historical events. In this way the appearance of the machine can clearly be seen. The surplus of manufactured articles automatically created a surplus of pledged articles. One can also observe a curious phenomenon: following upheavals the Mont de Piété did very bad business. After the Revolution, after Waterloo, after the Revolutions of 1830 and 1848, after the Commune, the curve delineating the number of pledged objects falls rapidly. The most brutal descent was in 1919-1920. There was a slump equally in 1945-1947. In a normal period work is no longer the standard of the value of things—money can be procured by so many means!—and, moreover, the Mont needs some time to adapt its prices. From 1949 the curve begins to rise again, and in 1951 three or four times as many Parisians as in 1945 went to the Municipal Credit office.

Sidelights are thrown on history too. In 1870, the approach of the German armies brought a rush to the Mont de Piété of a whole crowd of Parisians who, without being either poor or needy, wanted to place their precious possessions in safety for a fee of 9.5 percent on the value of the money lent. That showed a great confidence in the establishment, but in a few days the pawnshops were so full that the mayor of Paris had to take a revolutionary step: "As long as the abnormal position of the city continues it will not be possible to agree to advances above the sum of fifty francs."

In 1860 the standard pledge was the mattress. Today there are not two hundred mattresses in the keeping of "my aunt"; under the Second Empire there were more than fifteen thousand. The story was told of the poor woman who, each morning, would pledge her mattress. With what she received she would buy potatoes from the market gardeners and sell them retail. In the evening, out of her profits, she ate and reclaimed her mattress—and began all over again the next day.

How many objects were in this way taken out every Saturday and brought back every Monday! During all this period, and until the end of the century, the Mont de Piété was the dramatic inspiration of realistic ballads, beginning:

> A workman's wife, and mother of six,

and ending each verse with these dramatic words:

> At the Mont de Piété, é, é, é.

5

The Last Inhabitant of the Tuileries

In that tragic summer of 1870 a frail woman, almost pitiful in her little black cashmere dress adorned with linen, would wander through the château of the Tuileries, in which the armchairs and sofas, as they were every summer when the court was at Compiègne or Saint-Cloud, were covered with dust sheets printed with large bouquets of mauve iris. At mealtimes the frail woman was brought a few dishes on a tray, which she barely touched.

That woman was the Empress Eugénie, the Regent of the Empire while her husband was following his retreating soldiers across the plains of Champagne. He had become a miserable wreck relegated to the baggage wagons, undermined by sickness, no longer able even to sit a horse. The unhappy, vanquished man was now proceeding in a berlin, whose jolting gave him terrible stabbing pains in his kidneys and bladder, toward the stage where his surgeon was waiting to sound him, toward the stage that took him nearer every day to Sedan.

Sedan. The Empress heard of it for the first time in the evening of September 2. "Our communications with Sedan are cut. Our army may be blockaded at that place."

That was all she knew at the end of the afternoon of September 3. She was unaware of the magnitude of the disaster. That evening the Empress was alone. Henri Chauveau, Minister of the Interior, was announced. He was ghastly pale. In silence he handed his sovereign a telegram, the telegram from Sedan:

"The army is defeated. Having been unable to be killed among my soldiers, I have had to constitute myself prisoner to save the army. Napoleon."

A minute later Eugénie's two secretaries, Conti and Filon, saw their mistress appear at the head of a little spiral staircase linking the Emperor's apartments with those of the Empress on the first floor overlooking the gardens. The unhappy woman was "pale, her hard eyes blazing with anger." She cried out to them, panting:

"Do you know what they say? That the Emperor has given himself up, that he has capitulated! Do you not believe this infamy?"

Horrified by this apparition, Conti and Filon did not dare utter a word. In a hoarse voice she resumed, almost menacingly: "You do not believe it?"

Conti gathered up his courage.

"Madame, there are circumstances in which the bravest . . ."

Eugénie, her features convulsed, interrupted him, shouting: "No, the Emperor has not capitulated! A Napoleon does not capitulate. He is dead. . . . You hear me, he is dead and they want to keep it from me."

Then, when she was forced to admit the facts, raising her arms, "her eyes haggard like those of a Fury," she almost yelled: "Why did he *not* let himself be killed? Did he not feel he was dishonoring himself? What kind of name will he leave his son!"

The terrible news had run through Paris. Already the faces of 1830 or 1848 were appearing in the suburbs. Insurrection was in the air. Would the Tuileries be defended?

"Whatever happens," the Empress decided, "the soldiers must not fire on the people."

The Empress could still have tried to save the regime by giving executive power to the Chamber. She did not decide to do so.

Night fell on the city. In her bedroom Eugénie could hear dull rumblings. Soon she saw filing down the Rue de Rivoli men bearing torches and crepe-hung flags. Through the confused noise she heard cries of "Long live the Republic!"

The governor of Paris, General Trochu—that "past participle of the verb *trop choir* [to sink excessively]"—did not interfere.

At one o'clock in the morning Jules Favre mounted the tribune in the Chamber demanding the deposition of the imperial family. But the deputies took no decision and separated, adjourning the session until noon the following day. At dawn on the next day, September 4, at dawn on that fine, warm summer Sunday, the uprising began. It was the third revolution in forty years, without counting upheavals and insurrections. But this time a few hours would suffice for the street to be master of the Tuileries. It is true that Paris was fighting a woman.

Very early the city was awakened by cries of paper sellers: "The Emperor a prisoner!"

At eight in the morning a great murmuring came to the windows of the Tuileries. "On all sides," wrote the Goncourts, "a movement was growing that bore toward the center of Paris the inhabitants of the outer districts. The Rue de Rivoli and the Place du Carrousel were black with people. The weather was wonderful and everyone knows that the Parisians are always in a flutter on Sundays. Some walked peacefully round the arcades and along the pavements; others hurried feverishly to the Palais-Bourbon, where they foresaw work to be done. Others again massed at the crossroads, on the top of the pavements, waited, watched, drinking in the warm air of a real summer's day."

Soon demonstrators invaded the Chamber of Deputies and tore down the imperial eagles.

"This time," the workers cried, "we must have the Republic! No republic that allows a king to return when the bed is well warmed, and no republic of deputies either!"

The Place de la Concorde appeared like a stormy sea beating against the gates of the swing bridge. Troops raised the butts of their rifles. What was to be done? Shouts came from the street, shouts insulting the woman whom the Parisians considered responsible for the war and the defeat: "Down with the Spaniard!"

"You do not want to abdicate, madame," faithful Conti said to her. "Very well, in an hour you will be in the hands of people who will make you abdicate by force. If you escape, wherever you go you will take your rights with you."

"Remember the Princesse de Lamballe," Henri Chevreau murmured quietly.

To bring the Empress to the decision to flee required the immense clamor of the crowd which, forcing the gates in the Place de la Concorde, rushed into the garden, an immense clamor that was like a blow to the Regent. For the fifth time in eighty years the Tuileries was to experience the dreaded invasion.

"Madame," implored Nigra, the Italian ambassador, who had hurried to the château with Metternich, his Austrian colleague. "Madame, do not delay any longer."

Distracted, the Empress threw a glance of distress on everything about her. Would she have to leave all that? Was it really the end of the fairy tale that had made of Eugénie de Montijo the Empress of the French?

It was a quarter past one.

Eugénie put on a hat and a thin coat and left the room, followed by the two ambassadors, her reader, Mme. Lebreton, and a few faithfuls. The little group went down to the ground floor by the Empress's staircase and reached the stairs which were a private exit from the Prince Imperial's apartments, on the very site of the former entrance to M. de Villequier's apartments by which, formerly, Louis XVI and his family left the château for Varennes. The Empress's coupé was waiting for her as usual. On the door were painted the arms of the French Empire and the coachman was wearing imperial livery. How could they cross Paris in such a carriage when, behind the Carrousel gates, the crowd was already calling for death? There was only one solution: to attempt to leave by the Louvre museum. Eugénie took the narrow corridor that ran the whole length of the château; it was lit by gas both day and night. Through the great gallery, the Carré room, the gallery of Apollo, the little group reached the Hall of the Seven Chimneys. There, in front of Géricault's painting of *The Raft of the Méduse,* the Empress stopped. She gave her hand to her faithful companions to kiss. After the last bow, in company with Mme. Lebreton and the two diplomats she hastened toward the staircase. Before going down she looked for the last time, through the window of the small Salle Henri II, at the long façade of the château. At that moment the flag floating on top of the central pavilion of the Tuileries came slowly down its pole. This happened every time the sovereigns left the château for another residence. But today, when the victorious revolution surrounded the Tuileries and the Louvre, where was Eugénie to go? Mme. Lebreton had five hundred francs on her. The Regent's only luggage was two handkerchiefs, and she had a very bad cold.

Through the Egyptian section the fugitives reached the vault that opens onto the Place Saint-Germain-l'Auxerrois, under Perrault's colonnade. The crowd was too busy shouting, "Long live the Republic!" to pay attention to those two women in black and those two bourgeois in their tall hats. Nigra hailed a cab that was jolting by. How is one to explain the fact that the two ambassadors, who had been the Empress's friends for years, left her, on the pavement, after entrusting her to a passing cab? The fact is there, completely incomprehensible. Eugénie gave the two ambassadors her hand to kiss and entered the carriage. Mme. Lebreton followed her, giving the coachman the first address that came into her head, that of State Councilor Besson, in the Boulevard Haussmann. Not without difficulty the cab went up the Rue de Rivoli through the yelling mob. Eugénie could see the rioters, who were already breaking the stone eagles adorning the façades.

"Long live the nation!" cried a workman, sticking his head through the window.

At Mme. Lebreton's request, the coachman left the Rue de Rivoli and soon arrived in the Boulevard Haussmann. Calm succeeded the storm. The district was deserted. M. Besson was not at home and no one opened the door. There was the same failure at the house of M. de Piennes, the Empress's chamberlain, who lived in the Avenue de Wagram. Eugénie then thought of her American dentist, Dr. Evans. She gave the coachman the address: "Avenue Malakoff, at the corner of . . . Avenue de l'Impératrice."

The dentist was out as well.

The visitors, who refused to give their names, asked the valet if they could wait for the dentist and the servant showed the two women into the library.

Dr. Thomas W. Evans, who had been living in France since the end of Louis-Philippe's reign, was a man of forty-six, with an open, attractive countenance. He had spent the day watching Paris live through its first republican hours. Jules Favre had managed to get the crowd out of the Palais Bourbon by crying: "No day of blood! It is not here that you must proclaim the Republic, it is at the Hôtel de Ville!"

And the crowd, suddenly docile, had followed Jules Favre and Jules Ferry along the right bank, while another column of Parisians marched behind Gambetta and Pelletan along the left bank. At the Hôtel de Ville they found the leaders of the extremist parties—Blanqui, Delescluze, Flourens, Pyat—who were preparing to form a government. The competition was serious. How was it to be neutralized? Ferry proposed:

"The Paris deputies, to the government!"

The proposal was accepted. Trochu became president of the government, Jules Favre vice-president. Rochefort, just freed, entered the Government of National Defense with Arago, Gambetta, Jules Ferry, Garnier-Pagès, Pelletan, Crémieux and Simon.

The Third Republic had taken power without one drop of blood being shed.

Dr. Evans has left a picturesque account of his walk through Paris, in which one sees the children in the Champs-Elysées "disporting themselves in the care of their nurses, riding on the roundabouts or gathering round the puppet shows," while a short distance away, in the Place de la Concorde and around the Palais Bourbon, was "a black, stormy, tumultuous mass," shouting for the downfall of the imperial regime.

The doctor returned home at the end of the afternoon. He was accompanied by his compatriot and friend Dr. Crane. One can imagine

Evans's stupefaction when he pushed open the door of his library. The Empress was there, tragically pale, sunk in a large armchair near the window. She was dressed in a black cashmere dress and wore a "Derby" hat to which was attached a dark veil. She blew her nose continuously; tears filled her eyes.

"You see, I am no longer happy. The bad days have come."

Without hesitation the two doctors agreed to help the Empress. Mrs. Evans was at the moment in the Hôtel du Casino at Deauville. Would not the best plan be to try to join her by road, first taking the doctor's carriage, then trying to find post horses? From Trouville the fugitives would perhaps be fortunate enough to find a boat to take them across the Channel.

It was ten o'clock in the evening and the Empress wished to leave at once. Evans calmed her. She had had hardly any rest for three days. It was settled that they would leave the following morning at half past five. While Eugénie and Mme. Lebreton tried in vain to sleep the two doctors went to take the pulse of the town. Everything was calm at the Porte Maillot, through which in a few hours the fugitives would try to leave Paris. Around the Tuileries there was great animation, but the château was not occupied by the people—they would make up for it later. The sentries were on duty as usual. The words "National Property" had simply been written on the walls in chalk. The N's had disappeared from the pediments of all the public monuments. The Rue du Dix-Décembre had become the Rue du Quatre-Septembre. The crowd moved happily about. It sang, laughed and acclaimed the National Guards, whose rifles were now carrying bouquets. The café terraces were full of customers. The regime had crumbled with an almost miraculous rapidity. The "Third" was indeed mistress of Paris.

On their return from their expedition Crane and Evans did not go to bed. They feared at each instant to learn that the order had been given to close the city gates.

The sun had not yet risen when the dentist's landau left his house and drove down the Avenue Malakoff. The road sweepers were already at work and the shopkeepers were taking down their shutters. In those days Paris rose early. At the gate of the Porte Maillot the soldier in charge signed to the carriage to stop. Evans, who was sitting on the bench on front, opened the window and leaned out so as to mask the opening almost completely. So that the N.C.O. could not see anything inside the landau the dentist held an open newspaper in his left hand, on the side of the Empress.

"I am an American. I am known to everyone in the neighborhood. I am going to the country with some friends."

The soldier took a step backward.

"Go on!"

A second later the carriage was rumbling over the bridge across the moat of the fortifications.

The last French sovereign had left Paris.

6

Paris Besieged

The Germans were approaching.

Paris was about to fight, without hope perhaps, but not without glory.

On September 14, 1870, Trochu, governor of Paris and president of the Government of Defense, reviewed the army that was to defend the capital. From the Bastille to the Arc de Triomphe, along the boulevards and the Champs-Elysées were massed 115,000 mobile guards—the *moblots*, young men who had drawn a "lucky number"— summoned from the departments to contribute to the defense of Paris, and 200,000 citizen-soldiers from the capital—the National Guard— half of whom had not known, a fortnight earlier, how to present arms. There would soon be 384,000 Parisians of every kind defending the city. The real soldiers were not there. They were on the watch. Trochu could, in fact, also count on 50,000 men of the line to whom there would soon be joined 18,000 men escaped from the Sedan basin. At that moment they were trying to halt the march of the pointed helmets. The seventeen forts surrounding Paris were occupied by 15,000 sailors and naval gunners. The city possessed a good store of artillery: seven hundred pieces. There was also an "armed navy": five floating batteries, eight gunboats and seven vedette boats. To sum up, as Trochu admitted, "plenty of men, but few soldiers."

The roads and pavements were hidden by the helmets, police caps, kepis and hats of all kinds. Here and there bayonets gleamed. The defense of Paris had been divided into nine sectors commanded by two generals and seven admirals. One of the latter—with long white hair and snowy whiskers—rode a very restive horse. At the Boulevard Poissonnière he had great difficulty in maneuvering his mount in front of the governor so as to present his division. At that moment drums and trumpets joined in and the horse decided to gallop quickly away. "The old admiral," wrote Hérisson, Trochu's aide-de-camp, "had lost his hat, and his trousers were rucked up to his calves. Being encumbered by his bare saber and his reins he was quite simply clinging onto the mane. We saw him disappear along the road, followed by a large dog that had got through the lines of troops and was barking loudly after him."

In spite of this comic incident the day had been a heartening one. Trochu had few illusions about the worth of these improvised soldiers who had left workshop, factory or drawing room to form the great mass of defenders. Nevertheless, on that evening of September 14, the governor addressed a vibrant proclamation to the mobile and National Guards: "Never has any army general had before his eyes the spectacle you have just given me: three hundred battalions of citizens, organized, armed, surrounded by the whole population acclaiming in an immense concert the defense of Paris and freedom! . . . Therefore, have complete confidence and know that the area of Paris, defended by the persevering efforts of public opinion and by 300,000 rifles, is impregnable."

The next day the Prussians were in front of the forts. On September 16 one could still reach Saint-Denis and Athis, but on the 18th the encirclement was complete. The woods surrounding the city were fired and the villages in the suburbs evacuated. While the professional soldiers entered into contact with the enemy, beyond the belt of forts, the "300,000 rifles" were on watch on the ramparts. Many were those, however, who preferred to stay at home or to play interminable games of cork-penny rather than freeze on the fortifications. "Pay and the cork," wrote Catulle Mendès. "Under this title one could sum up the history of the National Guard. The wife is hungry, the little children are hungry, but the father of the family is thirsty. He draws thirty sous, the daily pay of the National Guards. What does he do? He goes to have a drink. When he has drunk, what remains? A few sous, the empty bottle and the cork. Very well, he stakes the few sous on the cork and in the evening, when he goes home, what does he bring back to the house? The empty bottle." It was only after more than two months of siege, on November 23, that the National Guard—the Passy battalion—exchanged a few shots with the Prussians, near Bondy. Four men were wounded in the arm or leg. These improvised soldiers were not thought much of by the military. On December 16 the commander in chief of the National Guard received this dispatch from the general commanding Vincennes: "Battalion head of the 200th, drunk.—At least half the men, drunk.—Impossibility of assuring the service.—Necessity of relieving them from their posts."— That same day, December 16, the battalion on duty at Maison-Blanche was at the advance posts, at Issy, in a complete state of intoxication.

The officers, too, took things easily. Later a curious-looking colonel was seen to review the troops on the Champ-de-Mars. He had a wasp waist, rounded hips and a chest to match.

"But it's a woman!" exclaimed a National Guardsman.

It was, indeed, a woman, for the colonel appointed to take the review had not finished his game of manilla and had sent his mistress in his place.

Discipline was a relative matter. "Besides," an orator at the Favié Club exclaimed, "what use is discipline? It has helped us to get beaten by the Prussians. It was the disciplined troops that were beaten at Reichshoffen, Forbach and Sedan. Can one demand from a 'reasoning' republican that he should submit to discipline like an automaton?"

Why discipline, since one could conquer by means of Greek fire? At that time the Parisians believed implicitly in the virtues of this means, which was already in vigor in the Middle Ages, and had founded a newspaper called, naturally, *Greek Fire*. There had been some hesitation between *Picrate of Potassium, The Gas Bomb, Nitroglycerine* and other peaceful titles. *Greek Fire* had won the day. An orator from the Folies-Bergère Club declared that these "rockets of Satan" should be able to kill one thousand Prussians a minute. In five hours of bombardment the siege would be lifted, for want of besiegers. Unfortunately, as Delescluze pointed out, this Greek fire did not easily catch "dry matter." So an orator from the Batignolles Club proposed "as a preliminary" that each Prussian should be watered with the help of a fire hose. This seemed hardly convenient, and a member of the Reine-Blanche Club was in favor of a "hot-water rifle." The Cour des Miracles Club had discovered another method for breaking the grip of William's army: let the lions and tigers from the zoo into the battle. But how to teach the beasts to respect the Parisian and eat the Prussian? The plan came to nothing and a more daring scheme took its place: to furnish the women of Paris with a thimble containing prussic acid and ending in a needle.

"Though many may approach," affirmed the inventor, the prophet Jules Allix, "what matter for those who possess the 'prussic thimble'? They stab the enterprising Prussians and remain peaceful and pure, having around them a crown of dead."

On January 6 the cannon disturbed these wonderful plans and the Prussian shells, that fell on Paris at the rate of eighteen an hour, made the club orators realize that the time for hot-water rifles had gone by. The first shells fell at Auteuil, in the Rue Boileau and the Rue La Fontaine.

"It's going along nicely," a member of the National Guard declared that morning, while quietly continuing his sentry duty.

Indeed, people were much more preoccupied with food difficulties than with the bombardment. What would one eat at midday? Rat, cat or elephant's trunk? Such was the serious problem. Rat was not bad, "a mixture of pork and partridge," one gourmet declared. Rats were sold in the Place de l'Hôtel de Ville, at the rat market. The animals were sold live for ten or fifteen sous each. The animal you had chosen was pushed with a stick toward another cage in which was a bulldog that neatly strangled the rat. Well nourished, the bulldog was the only member of the canine race in Paris that was able to eat its fill and one of the few that did not finish its life in a stew, for dogs were also eaten. "Properly killed," the *Chronique du Siège* said, "well-cleaned, suitably seasoned, well-flavored by a sauce made in the usual way, the dog is an excellent food. The meat is delicate, pink and not at all tough." The brains were particularly appreciated. They were sold in the Halles for 1 fr. 50 or 2 francs.

A butcher in the Boulevard de Rochechouart, besides selling rats at 50 centimes and dogs at 4 francs a pound, also sold cats at 20 francs, crows at 100 sous and sparrows at 1 fr. 25. During the siege it appears that 25,523 cats were eaten. One wonders how this figure was arrived at, for alley cats, caught and eaten, can certainly not have been declared.

There was a special market for horses in the Rue d'Enfer. The price was 40 or 50 centimes a kilogram, whether the horse came from the imperial stables or those of a cabby. The two famous trotters given by the Czar to Napoleon III were sold for 800 francs and were turned into "equine sausage," although Alexander II's gift had been valued at 56,000 francs. Every three days the Parisian had a right to 33 grammes of horse and to get them he had to queue in the terrible cold. There was the same wait before the baker, who sold bread that in theory was made of wheat, rice and oats but which, as Henri d'Almeras remarked, "seemed to have been made from old panama hats picked up in the gutter."

"Do you know what the bread we eat is composed of?" asked an orator from the Revolution Club in the Elysée-Montmartre. "I shall tell you. Firstly of hay; secondly of oaten chaff; thirdly of sweepings from the mills; fourthly of clay. At the moment you are being made to eat the Buttes Montmartre."

Note that the first inhabitants of Paris—long before the arrival of the Parisii—nourished themselves with clay and that, apparently, the clay of Montmartre was what they particularly enjoyed!

The art of cooking had not abdicated and on December 4 *Les Nouvelles* gave their readers a menu that had been served on the previous evening to a few gastronomes:

> Consommé de cheval au millet
> Brochettes de foie de chien à la maître d'hotel
> Emincés de rable de chat sauce mayonnaise
> Epaule de filet de chien sauce tomate
> Civet de chat aux champignons
> Cotelettes de chien aux petits pois
> Salmis de rats à la Robert
> Gigot de chien flanqué de ratons
> Salade d'escarole
> Bégonia au jus
> Plum-pudding au jus et à la moelle de cheval
> Dessert et vins

At Brébant's one day a dish was served called "saddle of mutton" which did not inspire confidence. It was, in fact, saddle of dog.

"Oh!" exclaimed Hébrard. "At our next dinner they will serve us the shepherd."

Things did not come to that, but thanks to the zoo the most unexpected dishes appeared on Parisian dinner tables. At the English butcher's at 173 Boulevard Haussmann were found dwarf zebu, buffalo, "Aristotle's deer," nilgai, peacock, camel, yak, Gambian or Danube geese, kangaroo, cassowary, bear and zebra. On December 30 Castor and Pollux, the two elephants dear to Parisian children, were shot. A kilogram of trunk attained the fabulous price of 80 francs. It is true that the butcher had bought the two pachyderms for 27,000 francs. "I was curious enough to enter Roos, the English butcher of the Boulevard Haussmann," wrote Edmond de Goncourt in his diary on December 31. "Amid the anonymous meat and extraordinary horns a boy was offering camel's kidneys. . . . Tonight I see that Voisin has the famous elephant sausage and I am dining off it." On the menus there appeared "fillet of elephant with madeira sauce," "haunch of bear" and "galantine of peacock."

It grew colder and colder and the benches on the boulevards and all the trees in the capital were sacrificed. "In the Champs-Elysées," wrote Edmond de Goncourt, "there is a felling of trees on which, before they are hoisted into the carts, a whole crowd of children throw themselves, armed with axes, knives, anything that cuts, to hack off pieces with which they fill their hands, their pockets, their aprons, while in the hole left by the felled tree can be seen the heads of old women occupied in grubbing up what remains of the roots with picks."

Meanwhile the life of Paris did not die and those theatres that had not been turned into hospitals gave readings. François Coppée did not lose the opportunity of giving us the *Letter from a Breton Guard,* who wrote to his countrywoman to announce that

> Le neveu du sonneur
> Est mort au champ d'honneur.

At the Opéra there were readings from the *Châtiments* and a collection was made in Prussian helmets, but as there were not enough enemy helmets a Russian helmet captured at Sebastopol was added. No one dared present a play to the Parisians; it would have been thought too frivolous. The Comédie-Française ventured on fragments:

last act of *Hernani,* last act of *Lucrèce Borgia.* Which enabled a contemporary to remark that the public had been given "eight deaths accompanied by candles, biers and the *De Profundis."* This was quite a lot. Pasdeloup, as reported by Georges Duveau, dared to give a concert in aid of the soup kitchens, but was violently criticized by Blanqui in these terms: "M. Pasdeloup is doing wrong. At the moment when our wives are dying of hunger and our brothers expiring in the Paris moats, it is not decent to scrape fiddles in the besieged city."

Fortunately for those who wish to think of something else, there was no lack of patriotic distractions. One could go to hear the tribunes occupy themselves in withdrawing from the battle the fathers of acknowledged natural children and putting them on the same footing as fathers of families who did not go to fight.

"If illegal households are formed more easily in Paris than elsewhere," one orator explained, "it is because in Paris, among the people at least, inclinations are followed, whereas for the peasant marriage is an association of parcels of land and for the bourgeois an association of capital."

One could also indulge in spy hunting, for "spy fever" was rife. In the Ternes district one was sure to see red and green signals go up from a window on the fifth floor of a house. One evening the police went to the spot. The door was opened and placed between the window and the lamp of a working woman was a red-and-green parrot that greeted the policemen by asking: "Have you had a good lunch?"

An ironic question, to say the least, in those days of famine.

But the greatest distraction was the departure of the balloons that were the sole link between Paris and the provinces. On September 24 the *Neptune,* the first postal balloon, left from Montmartre. "The day promised to be fine," wrote a contemporary journalist. "While the artillery thundered on the Prussians, at Villejuif and Arcueil, the military observation balloon from the right bank had been requisitioned to transport dispatches and was preparing to take flight. At a quarter past seven the loading was finished. For the first flight Nadar had chosen M. Duruof, already famous for his flights over the sea from Cap Gris-Nez and Monaco. M. Duruof uttered the sacramental 'Let go!' and the balloon had barely left the ground when to the airman's cry of 'Long live the Republic!' the crowd massed in the Place Saint-Pierre replied with unanimous applause. The *Nep-*

tune soon reached the height of five thousand feet, the level that had been indicated for its journey, and set off in a direct line for Calvados."

On Friday, October 7, a more important departure took place. Four thousand people wished to see Gambetta, the Minister of the Interior, fly off on his way to organize resistance in the provinces and, with the help of the army of the Loire, try to relieve Paris.

"It was at Montmartre," Alphonse Daudet related, "at the foot of that escarpment of plaster and ochre which the work on the Sacré-Coeur church has since covered with debris, but where at that time, in spite of the numerous footsteps of Sunday idlers and of boys' sliding, a few fragments of worn turf still showed their green, though rubbed and cut about. Below us, in the mist, was the city with its thousand roofs and its great murmuring that from time to time died down so that in the distance the dull voice of the cannon in the forts could be heard. There on the square was a little tent and within an enclosure marked out by a rope was a large yellow balloon tugging at its cable and swaying.... In the middle of a group Spuller and Gambetta, both wrapped up in furs. Spuller was very calm, courageous with simplicity, but unable to remove his eyes from that enormous machine in which he was to take his place in his position as departmental head, and murmuring in the voice of one who dreams: 'It is a truly extraordinary thing.'

"Gambetta, as always, talking and hunching his shoulders, almost delighted with the adventure. He saw me and shook my hand, a handshake full of meaning. Then he and Spuller entered the nacelle. 'Let go!' cried Nadar's voice. A few greetings, a cry of 'Long live the Republic!' the balloon rushing away, and nothing more."

Three balloons went off in this way from the Place Saint-Pierre, twenty-six from the Gare d'Orléans, sixteen from the Gare du Nord, three from the Gare de l'Est, two from the Tuileries gardens, two from the Boulevard d'Italie, one from Vaugirard and one from La Villette. The *Jules-Favre* fell into the Channel and the Prussians shot down the *Vautour*, the *Liberté* and the *Ville-de-Paris*.

So that the balloons could take the maximum of letters, the administration put special, extremely light cards on sale and Dagron invented the photo-microscopic telegram; these were the first steps in microphotography. A whole newspaper was reproduced on a square seven centimeters by nine. From October 21 *La Gazette des Absents* was printed on thin yellow paper for air transport, in order to give news of the besieged to the rest of France. After that were published the *Dépêche-ballon,* the *Ballon-poste,* the *Journal-poste,* the *Montgolfier* and the *Journal-ballon.* The Parisians were doubtless delighted to show the rest of the country that they "could take it," but they also wished to receive news from outside. So the balloons took carrier pigeons with them. Better still, M. Dagron left Paris, installed himself at Tours and managed to reproduce twelve to sixteen printed pages on one roll. So the pigeons returned to Paris bearing, in the hollow of a feather, twenty-five grams of film on which were fifty thousand dispatches.

For idlers there were also less peaceful distractions than watching for the return of the pigeons. The terrible capitulation of Metz, which gave the enemy 173,000 soldiers and a large quantity of material, was known in Paris on the rainy morning of October 31. The city was struck down with stupefaction. The "reds" considered that the moment had come to sweep away the government of September 4, which, after Thiers's journey, thought it might perhaps conclude an armistice. The National Guard of the working-class districts marched on the Hôtel de Ville, the seat of the government, with cries of: "Down with the traitors! Down with Trochu! No armistice! Fight to the end!" The demonstrators uttered another cry, a distant memory from '93, a cry that in a few months was to become a tragic reality: "Long live the Commune!" The members of the government were made prisoner, but one of them, Ernest Picard, managed to escape, called on the help of the National Guards of the bourgeois districts and freed the Hôtel de Ville. Paris was soon delivered from this revolutionary nightmare and the ministers, in order to establish their authority, organized a plebiscite. Paris gave its approval, by 557,976 votes to 68,638. The Government of Defense, now without fearing to be stabbed in the back, would be able not to make peace, but to try to loose the vise that was tightening each day.

Trochu had a plan, a plan that was much talked about, but the governor refused to reveal it, even to the Council.

"I have my plan. I will not be harassed with questioning as indiscreet as it is useless. I have my plan which posterity will know. This plan has been deposited with my notary." (Or so it was affirmed at the time. According to M. Jean Brunet-Moret, who is preparing an important work on Trochu, this is a legend.)

Paris roared with laughter and began to sing:

> I am Trochu's plan.
> Plan, plan, rataplan!
> What a plan indeed!
> I am Trochu's plan,
> All may yet succeed!

On November 14 a pigeon from Tours arrived in Paris. It did not bear an olive branch like the dove of the Ark, but a wonderful and important piece of news: the army of the Loire had succeeded in recapturing Orléans. Trochu immediately drew up a new plan, whose chief merit was that of not being deposited with his notary: the army of the Loire and the Paris army could push on toward each other and meet at Fontainebleau. In order to make a breakthrough the Parisians launched an attack on Champigny, which they managed to take. Magnificent pages of heroism were written on the plain of Villiers and the slopes of Champigny. But losses on both sides were so great that a truce was proclaimed so that the wounded could be taken away and the dead buried. The omnibus company sent its vehicles onto the battlefield, where the Christian brothers appeared as admirable nurses. In the evening Monseigneur Bauer was seen to arrive "on horseback, in violet breeches and boots, escorted by bodyguards wearing curious costumes and carrying torches." The prelate loved the theatre—and proved it a little later by unfrocking himself in order to marry a young and pretty actress.

On December 2, after furious fighting, the Germans failed to recapture Champigny. But on the next day it proved necessary to recross the Marne and bow to force. Moreover, Orléans was recaptured and the meeting at Fontainebleau did not take place. "One may say," Georges Duveau writes with justice, "that after Champigny the military history of the siege is finished." Soon the Prussians tightened their grip. The Parisians managed, with the energy of despair, to maintain themselves at Garches, Saint-Cloud and Montretout, but then came the tragic Sunday of January 22. On that day there was an affray at the Hôtel de Ville, and the "reds" had to be fired on. That same evening, when calm was re-established, Jules Favre, Minister of Foreign Affairs, asked Bismarck to receive him at Versailles.

Paris agreed to surrender.

On January 23 Bismarck replied through the intermediary of Comte d'Hérisson. "This very day the Chancelor agrees to receive Your Excellency and, at the Sèvres bridge, firing is suspended until six o'clock." While Saint-Cloud burned, throwing a tragic light on the scene, the minister, in a small, rotting boat, crossed the river floating with ice.

On January 28, at eight in the evening, the armistice convention was signed and at once there was a rush of Parisians to the country. "A curious procession," Edmond de Goncourt wrote in his diary, "of all those people, men and women, coming from the Neuilly bridge. Everyone was loaded with sacks, necessaries, their pockets swollen with something to eat. Bourgeois carried five or six chickens on their shoulder, balanced by two or three rabbits. I noticed an elegant little woman bringing back potatoes in a lace handkerchief. And nothing is more eloquent than the happiness, the tenderness I might almost say, with which people hold in their arms four-pound loaves, those beautiful white loaves of which Paris has been deprived for so long."

This consolation, after the defeat, of finding once more all that had been lost was overshadowed by two horribly humiliating days. The negotiations for peace began and the Prussians proposed a bargain to Thiers: either France gave Belfort to Germany, or thirty thousand men of the victorious army would occupy a part of Paris until the National Assembly ratified the peace preliminaries.

In accordance with the special convention of February 26, 1871, Paris sacrificed itself for Belfort.

The entry of the German army was to take place on March 1. On the previous day, Jules Favre related, as night was falling, the city, "instead of offering the spectacle of movement and life that gave an air of festivity to its most ordinary evenings, wrapped itself in voluntary darkness. None of its inhabitants dreamed of crossing the threshold of a café."

The following morning, while William was reviewing his troops on the Longchamp hippodrome, Paris seemed dead. "The city no longer has its great, humming life," wrote Edmond de Goncourt. "The horizon is empty, uninhabited. Only a few Uhlans have been seen so far, searching the Bois de Boulogne with every precaution." They made their entry into Paris by the Avenue de l'Impératrice, the present Avenue Foch, and by the Avenue de la Grande-Armée. Four Prussian regiments, headed by their bands, passed under the Arc de Triomphe; the others went round the monument. The whole army went down the Champs-Elysées, to the sound of fifes and drums. In the Place de la Concorde, in front of the statue of Strasbourg, soldiers left the ranks and began to dance. A few detachments went on to the Carrousel, but the major part of the forces went no farther than the Place de la Concorde. Palisades separated free Paris from occupied Paris. On March 3—the Assembly having voted ratification in record time—the occupation was over. Two large cafés at the Rond-Point which had served Prussian officers were sacked by the crowd, and in the same district several prostitutes guilty of having "consorted" with the occupiers were whipped.

The Parisian—in this case Comte d'Hérisson—tried all the same to swagger and joke. As the Prussian officers continually asked him how Paris had managed to hold out for so long, the captain replied: "We got by. I think people must have nourished themselves with policemen. At the beginning of the siege they went round in threes. Today they go around in pairs. What have they done with the third? They have doubtless eaten him."

7

A Mild Spring

A paradise, a mild weather made for love, one of those extraordinary Parisian springs that envelop everything in a pink or blue mist. Such was the spring of 1871. From March 18 to May 28, during those seventy-two days that were perhaps the most dreadful in its history, Paris was one bright ray of sunshine, a sun to make one stand at the window and sing with the barrel organ in the street endlessly repeating its refrain: "But cherry time is short," that air composed by the son of a miller of Meudon, the worker Jean-Baptiste Clément, one of the leaders of the Commune.

It all started with the affair of the guns.

The National Guard possessed 227 guns, 200 of which had been cast during the siege thanks to private subscriptions. The inhabitants considered them with the tenderness of parents caring for their children. When the Germans came to occupy Paris for forty-eight hours the Parisians hastened to place the guns in a safe place, outside the occupation zone, right at the top of the Montmartre hill, "under the guardianship of the people," that is of the Federates. For the siege was over, the war finished, but the greater part of the citizen-fighters had remained under arms. Moreover, the government, still at Bordeaux, having wished to disband them, delegates from 200 battalions had met and decided to create a "federation" at whose head a "central committee" was set.

When the Prussians had left there began to be a rumor that the government intended to take the Paris artillery. "The pieces of cannon are our property; we paid for them," wrote one of the Federates. "We do not want civil war, but if anyone tries to take our cannon away from us we will burn Paris rather than let ourselves be conquered by those bandits."

On March 8 the "bandits"—in fact, the regular troops—had tried to take the guns. The operation had failed, but in alarm the central committee had issued this revolutionary manifesto to the army: "Soldiers, children of the people! The men who organized the defeat, dismembered France, delivered up our gold, wish to escape the responsibility they have assumed by giving rise to civil war. . . . The people of Paris wish to preserve their arms, choose their own leaders and dismiss them when they have no more faith in them. No more permanent army, but the nation itself all armed!"

Thiers, who had not finished negotiating with Germany, could not tolerate such an appeal for desertion. Besides, he needed money, and the businessmen—as he related later—never ceased repeating: "You will never carry out a successful financial operation unless you get rid of all those scoundrels and unless you first take away their guns."

While the National Assembly installed itself at Versailles Thiers arrived in Paris with his ministers. It was March 15. The conflict between two powers—that of Paris and that of France—seemed inevitable.

On the morning of March 18 the snow that had fallen during the night melted, and a warm sun appeared. Spring was three days in advance of the calendar. The Parisians rose all the earlier since a government notice had been posted during the night. People hurried down the stairs and gathered in front of the yellow poster.

"Inhabitants of Paris, for some time now ill-intentioned men, under pretext of resisting the Prussians, who are no longer under your walls, have constituted themselves masters of part of the city. The guns taken from the state will be sent back to the arsenals and, in order to carry out this pressing act of justice and reason, the government counts on your help. Let the good citizens separate themselves from the bad, let them help the public forces instead of resisting them. Parisians, you will approve our having recourse to force, for at all costs order, the condition of your well-being, must be reborn, entire, immediate, unalterable."

In order to recover the guns Thiers had indeed decided to "have recourse to force," and the inhabitants of Montmartre had been awakened by the measured tread of soldiers of the line going to take up their positions. The whole hill was held by the troops. General Susbielle, in command of the operation, was in the Place Pigalle, General Paturel in the Rue Lepic, General Vinoy in the Place Clichy and, at the center of the contingent, General Lecomte, who, with the 18th battalion of cavalry and the 88th of foot, had succeeded in entering the artillery park at the top of the hill after a scuffle with the Federates on guard. There he awaited the harness necessary for taking away the cannon. It was late. It was so late, nearly four o'clock, that gradually the housewives of Montmartre and the prostitutes from the furnished rooms appeared in the street and, infiltrating the ranks, proposed that the soldiers should "drink a glass" with them. Soon the tocsin was heard, then the general call for the National Guard. Finally there appeared in the Place Saint-Pierre a group of Federates among whom could be seen a few soldiers of the 88th of the line come from their posts in the Boulevard Ornano, who had already deserted. General Lecomte ordered crossed bayonets and cried to the mutineers:

"Scum! It is all up with you."

"You are not going to fire on us," cried a few voices in the crowd.

The National Guards advanced, threatening, brandishing their rifles. Lecomte gave the order to fire. The troops hesitated, then made up their minds and reversed their rifles. The crowd rushed forward, embraced the soldiers and dragged them to the wine counters, which were all open. General Lecomte was unhorsed and dragged to the Château Rouge, a former dance hall in the Rue de Clignancourt that had become the headquarters of the Federates of the district. Fraternization spread all over the hill and Lecomte was forced to sign the evacuation of Montmartre. Yet he was kept prisoner. He was soon joined by a general with a long white beard, the septuagenarian Clément Thomas, who in June, 1848, had ordered a "charge on the scum." He was taking a walk in civilian dress in the Place Clichy and, being recognized, was immediately taken to the Château Rouge. In the middle of the afternoon the Federates took the condemned men— as they already were—by Rue Custine, Rue du Mont-Cenis and Rue de la Bonne to a house standing in its own grounds at 6 Rue des Rosiers. A yelling crowd surrounded the house, "smelling out the blood like wolves," shouting, "Death to them! Shoot them!" While in a ground-floor room, hung with flowered wallpaper, the two prisoners had a more than summary trial. Clément Thomas was the first to appear in the garden—"a real suburban garden," Alphonse Daudet related, "in which every tenant has his corner for gooseberries and clematis, separated by green trellises with banging doors." Pushed by rifle butts toward a little wall, Thomas was shot several times before reaching the place of execution. Although seriously wounded, the old man remained upright, his hat in his hand, while he was shot at from every side of the garden. General Lecomte underwent the same fate. A man shot him in the back, he fell, was picked up and carried to the wall, where he was finished off by several point-blank shots. There were present, at least among the killers who were later arrested, a clockmaker, a decorator, a plumber, a plasterer, a tinsmith, a grocer, a locksmith, a saddler, a mercer, a launderer, a lithographer, a day laborer, a supervisor of roads and bridges, a man of letters (Simon Mayer), three cobblers, two lemonade sellers, a clerk, a sergeant of the 88th, employed on the railways, and a sergeant-major of the 26th of the line, employed in trade.

Street by street the insurrection had spread over Paris, but outside Montmartre it was a "good-tempered" riot. "If all the men were not wearing the uniform," an eyewitness said, "one could believe it was the evening of a public holiday. The conquerors enjoy themselves." While enjoying themselves they built a few barricades—in the Faubourg Saint-Antoine and at Ménilmontant—occupied the Luxembourg, where the men of the line fraternized with them, and marched on the Hôtel de Ville.

At the Ministry of Foreign Affairs Thiers was in a panic. Only six thousand National Guards were ready to side with the army, or rather with what remained of it. Could they try to resist at the Hôtel de Ville?

"No, gentlemen," Thiers replied to the ministers. "It is obvious that the troops will no more hold on at the Hôtel de Ville than elsewhere. There is but one radical resolve that can save the country: Paris must be evacuated, and evacuated completely and immediately. That was the plan that gave success to Field-Marshal Windischgraetz at the time of the events in Vienna. I am not abandoning the game; I am saving it!"

Certain ministers wanted at least to halt the withdrawal at the line Chaillot-Etoile. But no. It was at Versailles that they must install themselves. Suddenly three battalions of National Guards, headed by a drum band, passed the Ministry. Thiers threw himself into a carriage escorted by cuirassiers and gave the order to set off at full speed. At each instant he thrust his head through the door, crying: "Go on, go on! As long as we have not crossed the Sèvres bridge there will be danger!"

Once the Sèvres bridge was passed the head of the government grew no calmer. He repeated endlessly: "Go on, go on!"

He regained his calm only at Versailles.

"What a day!" Jules Vallès wrote the next morning in *Le Cri du Peuple*. "That warm, bright sun gilding the mouth of the cannon, that odor of woods, the shivering of the flags, the murmur of that revolution going quietly and beautifully by like a blue river, those shudders, those gleams, those fanfares of copper, those lights of bronze, those blazes of hope, that perfume of honor—all was enough to intoxicate with pride and joy the victorious army of republicans!"

At Belleville and Montmartre the republicans were intoxicated by those lights of bronze, but the rest of Paris retained its usual appearance. "In Rue La Fayette," wrote an eyewitness, "all the shops were open, the cafés full of customers, the omnibuses, the cabs, the public went around without bothering about the new riot."

And yet it was not a riot, but a revolution.

How beautiful the Revolution seemed on that warm, sunny afternoon of Tuesday, March 28, that was to see the proclamation of the Commune. All the people of Paris, the craftsman, worker, shopkeeper, "advanced" intellectual part of Paris, were there in front of the Hôtel de Ville, shouting their joy, singing, embracing. All the Place de Grève, all the Rue de Rivoli sparkled with uniforms, flags, bright dresses. Bands tried, with all their brass, to dominate the joyful tumult, and suddenly an immense silence reigned. On the flag-bedecked dais that had been erected in front of the porch of the Hôtel de Ville a hundred men made their appearance, wearing red scarves crosswise. They were the members of the central committee, which was to disappear, and the newly elected men, the new members of the Paris Commune. The mayor of Belleville, Gabriel Ranvier, stepped forward and cried in a clear voice:

"In the name of the people the Commune is proclaimed!"

An immense ovation rose from the square; frantic applause broke out. People pointed out the militants with pale complexions—the prison complexion—those journalists, those tribunes they would go almost religiously to hear in the dark, smoky rooms of little cafés that were sometimes raided by the police. They were all there.

In the crowd, near Maxime Vuillaume, was a man in the uniform of a National Guard. His wife was holding the hand of a boy of three or four. The man was explaining: "You see that big bearded man, with large eyes and thick, graying hair? That's Félix Pyat, whose portrait we have at home. The other one, with the white beard, drawn features and severe face is Delescluze. The big chap standing up, wearing a major's kepi, is Protot, the right sort, from the XIth *arrondissement*, who defended Mégy in the Blois trial. That one, with the long mustaches is Clément, you know, the one who wrote 'Cherry Time.' Ah! everything will go all right with those fellows!"

The woman listened, "her eye lit with a fine flame."

"Lift the boy up; he must see too, the little fellow! Days like this make a mark in one's existence."

Suddenly his eyes were fixed on a corner of the dais.

"There's the best. Do you see him, sitting down, with his mouth like a blade, his thin lips and his deep eyes. How he has suffered! All his life in prison. I'll read you all about it. His wife died while he was in Mont-Saint-Michel. A real martyr, Citizen Blanqui."

Vuillaume intervened. "You are mistaken, citizen. That is not Blanqui you see. He was arrested at his nephew's in the Lot. At this moment he is in prison at Figeac."

"They've arrested him! Him! He will not be one of the Commune!"

"I saw a veil of sadness," wrote Vuillaume, "suddenly spread over the face that had been so joyful."

As Albert Ollivier has written, "more than a joy, an immense, overwhelming hope seized the spectators standing in the square, leaning from the windows, who communicated as they had not been able to do for a long time. The city, whose districts had lived isolated for some months, regained its unity in a kind of ideal transfiguration. The Hôtel de Ville, that had seen many riots, many betrayals, gave witness again of how much the autonomous action of Paris counted for in the communal "French gesture." The victory was a splendid one, a new fraternity enveloped the Parisians and who could not think that from this victory and this fraternity everything became possible?"

In the evening, while the troops of the Commune were filing past in an order that had not been seen for a long time, the central committee posted its farewell message: "Today it was given to us to be present at the most grandiose popular spectacle that has ever greeted our eyes and moved our hearts: Paris saluted, acclaimed its revolution; Paris opened a blank page in the book of history and there inscribed its powerful name."

There was no question of a red dictatorship wishing to impose itself on the country.

"As for France," one of the new masters of the Commune was to say, "we do not claim to dictate laws to her—we have groaned too much under hers!"

Paris was a "free city," wishing to liberate itself from the guardianship of provincial deputies.

"Paris aspires only to enclose itself in its autonomy, full of respect for the equal rights of other communes."

And the Parisians rejoiced on learning of the creation of the communes of Lyons, Marseilles, Narbonne, Toulon and Limoges.

But, by rising against the central power, Paris the decentralizer would, whether it wished it or not, appear as a usurper. On the following day the council of the Commune took governmental decisions infinitely more political, legislative and dictatorial than social or communal: suppression of the religious budget, of religious teaching, of ministerial offices, of certain newspapers, confirmation of the 437 political arrests ordered since March 18.

And the inevitable happened: armchair theorists and café ideologists clashed. Jacobins, Federalists, Hébertists, Socialists and the newcomers—Proudhonians and Bakuninians—succeeded, often with disarming good will, in creating intense confusion. Changes of governors and forms of government, brutal disgraces, sudden returns to favor, arbitrary arrests, incoherence and, above all, incapacity and indiscipline on all levels. That was what the Commune was soon to become. The agitators, those thirsting for blood, the haters blinded by their hate would be able to indulge in their usual games.

8

Paris Torn Asunder

Among the fanatics of the Commune the one who was most noticeable and, as a result of his functions, was most to be dreaded, seemed to be the Prefect of Police, soon Procureur of the Commune—for they were aping 1793. His name was Raoul Rigault. A former medical student, a master of sciences and arts, he was dirty, hairy, sputtering, lyrical, peevish, anticlerical. He had three gods: Hébert, Chaumette and Saint-Just. Someone who knew him well said that "it was the most complete extravagance of ideas that can be imagined." When he was sent to take possession of the prefecture he was met in the antechamber by a functionary of the building.

"Who are you?" Rigault asked him.

"Coré, director of the depot."

"Well, Citizen Coré, I have to announce to you that you are dismissed."

And as the "citizen" tried to explain that such a dismissal was illegal he was quickly interrupted.

"I am not making legality; I am making a revolution."

This revolution consisted first of all in surrounding oneself with friends who, when they were not armed to the teeth, were mostly dull and incapable of doing anything but drink heavily, as for example the new police commissioner of the Champs-Elysées district, who stuck this notice on his door: "In case of absence apply to the wine shop next door."

Rigault's right arm was the bloodthirsty Ferré, deputy Procureur of the Commune. The Hébert of the new regime was a lively little man—he was called "Quicksilver"—with a sharp, piercing voice, a wobbling eyeglass and a black beard. With him Rigault could give free rein to his anticlericalism. On April 2 he received congratulations from the Père Duchesne (still 1793!) for having forbidden prison almoners "to take drinks every Sunday morning under pretext of saying mass to people who don't give a damn."

When Rigault was able to question an arrested priest himself he was delighted. His eyes sparkled as he asked: "What is your profession?"

"Servant of God."

"Where does your master live?"

"Everywhere."

Then he turned to his clerk: "Write: 'Calls himself the servant of a certain God, who on the accused's own admission lives in a state of vagrancy.'"

Anticlericalism went so far as to force the nuns of the Hôtel-Dieu to wear red sashes over their black robes. Rigault was helped by other fanatics, such as Viard, a member of the Commune, who yelled in the church of Saint Elisabeth, transformed into a club: "We must get rid of the ignoble race of priests. Let each of us kill one and tomorrow there will be none left!"

It was much worse when there were discovered in the vaults of the church of Saint Laurent, in the Faubourg Saint-Denis, eighteen skeletons of women who, in the opinion of a professor from the medical faculty, had been buried there "in the days when it was customary to be buried in churches." This did not prevent the *Journal officiel de la Commune* from asserting that it was a question of recent crimes, of alleging that the skeletons had all "the legs apart and the knees close together" (sic) and making the victims utter these words: "The priests, our pitiless torturers, have dragged us here by force or by cunning, having assuaged on us their brutal lubricity, stripped us of our clothes and bound us so firmly that one can still see the contraction of one bone against another." Then they were buried alive: "Touch our bruised, horribly open jaws. So many bodies, so many martyrs. . . . The unpunished crime is there! Visible! Palpable! Make yourselves judges! Be our avengers!"

The call to murder was all the more dramatic in that the prisons at that time contained more than one hundred priests arrested as hostages. The affair began the day after the fighting of April 2. On that day, for the first time, the Versailles troops had attacked rebellious Paris. There had been fighting at Courbevoie. At Neuilly and Ternes the shops had hastily closed. In the evening the Federates had had to withdraw to the right bank. The next day it was the Commune's turn to attack. One of the columns had been commanded by fair-haired Flourens, who during the siege had nearly captured the Hôtel de Ville with the battalions from Belleville and Ménilmontant. He was one of the most popular men in the city.

"Go on, crowd," cried one of his partisans, pointing him out to the Parisians. "Make him a king of Paris, nominate a dictator."

Yet in spite of his popularity Flourens did not manage to keep his troops, who fled under the withering fire of the Mont-Valérien guns. At Rueil he had only a handful of men left. Seeming to seek death, he refused to withdraw with his little troop and went on alone, through Chatou. Near the bridge he took a room in an inn. There he was found by Versailles men and massacred with saber blows. That same day another leader was taken on the Châtillon plain and shot.

Following these executions the Commune decided to turn the imprisoned suspects into hostages and to add to them priests and the Archbishop of Paris. The execution by Thiers's troops of a Communard would be followed by the death of three hostages. However, although the Versaillais continued to shoot the rebels the Commune did not put its decree into practice until its last moments. In acting thus the master of the Hôtel de Ville showed a certain moderation, since at Versailles the convoys of prisoners were struck by the maddened crowd. "I saw some of them," wrote Barrère, the future ambassador, "bleeding, their ears torn off, their faces and necks gashed as though by the claws of wild animals."

Thiers was waging total war. The little man was eaten up with hatred of Paris. Gradually the vise was closing on Paris. Villacoublay, Nanterre and the bridgehead at Neuilly were in the hands of government troops. But it was not a "second siege," as some have said. The Versaillais were only to the west and southwest. To the east the Germans were encamped a few yards from the outer walls, but part of the north was free. Until March 31 one could even go directly by train to Versailles. Afterward one had to go by Saint-Denis and Conflans, or by Villeneuve-Saint-Georges, whose railway station was occupied by the Bavarians. Many bourgeois thus managed to leave the town, although without taking any luggage.

Soon the gates were more strictly guarded and to leave Paris became an exploit. "The most romantic people," wrote Alphonse Daudet, "climbed the ramparts at night with rope ladders. The boldest joined in parties of thirty to take a gate by assault. Others, more practical, managed quite simply with a five-franc piece. Many followed hearses and went out into the suburbs, wandering through the fields with umbrellas and silk hats, black from head to foot like country bailiffs. Once outside all these Parisians looked at each other laughing, drew deep breaths, danced about, thumbed their noses at Paris, but they were soon overcome by nostalgia for the asphalt."

For the life of Paris went on. People fell in love that spring and even got married. The amusing part was that Thiers later abolished all the certificates of births, marriages and deaths registered during the Commune from March 18 to May 28. Marriages had to be renewed, but experience had disillusioned many of the spouses. So, in the Xth *arrondissement,* out of sixty-two marriages only forty-eight were renewed and, in the XVIIIth, thirty-three out of fifty-five.

There was no lack of "spectacles" for the idlers. One could go and question those returning from the firing line.

"The park at Neuilly is wonderful," a major told Vuillaume. "Everything is in flower. We spend the night in the shrubberies where honeysuckle and periwinkle climb, breathing out perfume."

Maxime Vuillaume stood at the window of the Ministry of Justice, where he was lunching with the delegate. "The spectacle in the square is always amusing. At this warm hour there is no sound. Everything seems to sleep. Leaning against the barricades closing the Rue de la Pais and the Rue de Castiglione, the Federate sentinels are snoring. Only a small squeaking noise breaks the monotony. It comes from a saw slowly worked by two men squatting on the pedestal of the column. A tiny dust cloud rises from the bronze shaft." For the Commune had decreed the demolition of the Vendôme column. Vuillaume was there again on May 16 when, under the orders of the painter Courbet, "the monument of tyranny" was pulled down. (Courbet, whose guilt was incidentally not proved, was condemned to pay 350,000 francs for rebuilding the column. Faced with such a large sum—70 million present-day francs—Courbet preferred to go to Switzerland and pay nothing. In the place of the cylindrical blocks of stone was put a spiral staircase of 180 treads covered by new bronze plaques molded after the original forms, that had been greatly damaged. So the Vendôme column is today no longer in "Austerlitz bronze.") What a sight! The crowd was thick right to the beginning of the Boulevard des Capucines. Suddenly "before my eyes there quickly passed something like the wing beat of a gigantic bird. . . . A monstrous zigzag . . . A cloud of dust. All was over. The column was on the ground, open, its stone entrails bare to the wind. Caesar was lying on his back, decapitated. The head crowned with laurels rolled, like a pumpkin, to the edge of the pavement."

In spite of everything a few theatres continued to play. Eight establishments out of twenty-seven remained open, not to mention the puppet show in the Champs-Elysées until the flying bullets moved the shows to the Palais-Royal. There was even a first night at the *Gaîté*, on the night of May 18, three days before the "beginning of the end": *Two Unfaithful Races,* a vaudeville by Vazeille. An Englishman visiting Paris went on May 17 to the Opéra-Comique. "The theatre was full from the pit to the gallery," he related. "The noise was terrifying. . . . One saw nothing but uniforms in the boxes and stalls, but the higher regions were invaded by blouses, with a few overcoats. The women particularly made an infernal noise." But after the interval, when a singer, Mme. Ulgade, was about to begin her big aria "a trumpeter of the snipers appeared at the front of an empty box and sounded the charge. The effect was striking. The audience rose as one man and rushed for the doors. In less than five minutes the theatre was empty." It was only a joke, but no one came back to his seat to hear Mme. Ulgade begin her trills.

There were great crowds at the Tuileries, where, during May, three big entertainments were given for the benefit of the wounded and orphans of the Commune.

"Vermersch and I went for a walk," Vuillaume related. "Enormous crowd. The shrubs were illuminated by red lanterns hanging on the trees. Red lamps bordering the baskets and lawns. Through the windows of the palace, streaming with light, came waves of noise and singing. We crossed the portico of the central pavilion, the Clock Pavilion. To the left two Federates, leaning their elbows on their rifles, guarded the entrance to a vast room which everyone entered without the least difficulty. We entered. Along its whole length was a long, long table. Hundreds of glasses, bottles, cans of light beer, mountains of brioches, packets of biscuits. . . . We went upstairs. The door of the Salle des Maréchaux. A mist of burning heat. The enormous chandeliers hanging from the cupola shone brightly. . . . A strongly-built woman appeared on the stage. Her name ran through the benches. It was La Bordas. She spoke, she roared the song that had already made her famous. At the chorus there was wild enthusiasm. The whole audience sang together.

"La Bordas made a sign. From backstage came a Federate guard carrying a flag rolled round its pole. He gave it to the artist, who took it, unfolded it slowly, spread it right out and wrapped herself in it. It was a gripping spectacle. I shall never forget that apparition: on the white peplum, like a large patch of blood, the red of the gold-fringed flag."

On Sunday, May 21, a warm, sunny day, the Parisians returned to the Tuileries for a charity fête. The orchestras drowned the noise of gunfire. On the quays were crowds of people watching the fishermen. It was the opening of the season. Suddenly the news ran from mouth to mouth: at four o'clock the Versailles troops had entered Paris.

Around three o'clock, near the Saint-Cloud gate, a man had appeared on the rampart. He was a certain Ducatel. He had waved a handkerchief. A Versailles officer had approached and Ducatel had announced the incredible news: no one was guarding Bastion 64, the Point-du-Jour; they had only to enter. It was Delescluze who was now in command of the Commune troops and his authority was relative.

He was a cold, incisive, distinguished man, with yellow eyes "like those of a bird of prey." A retarded Jacobin, he ignored Socialism and dreamed of a universal republic. His health had been ruined by long deportation and at the end of May he was seized by illness. He had known of the abnormal situation at Bastion 64 for two days but had done nothing to remedy it. The Versailles officer commanding the sector did not dare make the attempt without reference to the government. He telegraphed to Versailles and Thiers gave the authorization for the troops to enter the city. The gates of Passy, Saint-Cloud and Auteuil had only a handful of defenders and seventy thousand government troops slipped into Paris. When night fell on the town Thiers, who was following operations from Mont-Valérien, noticed his troops occupying the top of the Chaillot hill; Passy and Auteuil were in the hands of the Versaillais; Delescluze was about to retire, but before doing so he posted a proclamation: "Enough of soldiers, no more braided staff officers! Make way for the people, the bare-armed fighters. . . . March on the enemy and let your revolutionary energy show him that one can sell Paris, but one cannot yield or conquer it!"

On Monday, May 22, the working-class districts once more—and for the last time—came down into the town to help the Federate soldiers, who were fighting with the energy of despair, while the "braided" soldiers put up a weaker struggle. The Versaillais continued their advance and were soon occupying a line from the Ternes to the Montparnasse station by way of the town hall of the VIIIth *arrondissement*, the Saint-Lazare station, the Palais Bourbon and the Invalides. National Guards began to abandon the fight. "I cannot stay at home," Goncourt wrote. "I need to see. On going out I find everyone gathered in the doorways—an agitated, grumbling, hopeful crowd, already becoming bold enough to hiss the dispatch riders. Demoralization and discouragement are visible in the National Guards, who are coming back in little groups, sad, exhausted. . . . We go up the boulevard. Half-finished barricades in front of the old Opéra House, and the Saint-Martin gate, where a woman with a red sash is pulling up paving stones." Paris, in fact, was having recourse to its old method of defense—the barricades. In one day five hundred were built, while the battle raged in the Rue Royale, Faubourg Saint-Honoré, Rue de Rivoli. The Place de la Concorde still held out, but it was the extreme limit of the defenses. Night fell. "We go home. . . . At this hour there is something frightening and mysterious in this battle that surrounds us, in this occupation silently approaching and seemingly without a struggle."

The fighting seemed to die down somewhat. Paris held its breath before setting off the last defense of the Communards: fire. And suddenly, between the two armies, a blaze arose. It was a sight worthy of the Apocalypse. The Hôtel de Ville, the Quai d'Orsay, the Legion of Honor, the Audit Office, the Palais de Justice, the Louvre library, the Tuileries, soaked in kerosene, stuffed with powder, were nothing but torches. At five past nine the château clock—that clock which had rung so many tragic hours—was stopped by fire.

"Look!" one of the incendiaries exclaimed. "Isn't it fine to see the king's palace burning? The bird will never want to return to its nest!"

From the balcony of a friend's apartment Raoul Rigault watched the terrifying spectacle. Like Nero he smiled at the sight of those enormous plumes of flame, those "whirlwinds of smoke sprinkled with holes of gold."

"Well," he exclaimed calmly. "There go the Tuileries to hell."

"What Rigault had just seen," reported Vuillaume, "was the cupola of the Salle des Maréchaux falling into the flames. It was exactly an hour and a quarter past midnight."

Amid the blaze, reflecting the purple and gold sky, flowed the Seine, like a river of blood. On Wednesday, May 24, in the reddening sky, the dawn broke revealing new fighters pursuing each other between the flames, from barricade to barricade. Blinded by the smoke, terrified by the cannon balls on all sides, the Versailles troops, composed almost exclusively of countrymen, fought with fury, rage and hate. "I shall be pitiless," Thiers had said, and his men were too. Shooting went on everywhere. In the Rue Saint-Jacques forty Communards were massacred without trial. Rigault was a short distance away. If he heard of the execution he must have rejoiced at having given the order, the day before, to kill all the hostages. Three victims had already been shot. The Procureur of the Commune wanted to direct the defense of "his" district in person. Standing at the window of 29 Rue Gay-Lussac, he watched the fight with the help of glasses. From there he could see the barricade of the Rue Gay-Lussac and that of the Rue Suofflot, and from his observation point shouted orders that his lieutenants took to the defenders. When the barricades were taken the house was surrounded. Wearing the uniform of a major of the Federates—blue tunic with red collar and revers—Rigault appeared.

"Here I am. It is I."

The Versaillais did not know whom they were arresting and took him in the direction of the Luxembourg, but at the corner of the Rue Royer-Collard a colonel intervened.

"Who is this man?"

The prisoner stepped forward.

"I am Raoul Rigault, Procureur of the Commune of Paris."

The officer calmly drew his revolver.

"Ah! So you are Raoul Rigault. Very well, shout: 'Down with the Commune!'"

"Long live the Commune! Down with the assassins!" replied Rigault.

The colonel took careful aim and fired at point-blank range. Rigault fell. Until the next the day the body remained there, on the pavement, the skull smashed, the brains leaking out. People stopped, hit at the body with a cane or a foot, then went on. A prostitute bent down, looked at the face covered with blood and declared calmly: "It's Rigault all right. I've often had a drink with him."

Although Raoul Rigault was dead his orders regarding the hostages were carried out just the same. At La Roquette, at six in the evening, Monseigneur Darboy, President Bonjean and five priests were shot. Here and there other prisoners were put to death. On Thursday, May 25, toward the end of the afternoon, the whole of the left bank was in the hands of the Versaillais. While the battle drew nearer to the last districts held by the insurgents, the five Dominicans brought from Arcueil, with six employees of their college, were shot in the Avenue d'Italie. At the same hour Delescluze left his bed, dressed carefully in black, put on his red scarf, silk hat and polished boots and went in search of death. He walked down the Boulevard Voltaire, toward the barricade of the water tower, opposite No. 5 on the boulevard. It was half past seven in the evening. The sky was still red; the Gobelins, the Arsenal, the warehouses of La Villette, the public granaries, were burning. Delescluze came near the barricade and from paving stone to paving stone climbed to the summit. "For the last time," wrote an eyewitness, "that austere countenance, framed in its short white beard, appeared before us turned toward death. Suddenly Delescluze disappeared. He had been shot dead."

On the following day, May 26, when the Commune was holding out only at Belleville, Charonne and La Villette, Rigault's orders brought death to forty-seven hostages: ten priests, a seminarist, a National Guard, a police officer, a clerk and thirty-three gendarmes. They were taken from the La Roquette prison and brought, on foot, to the execution place, at the top of Belleville. The long procession stretched out along the Rue de la Roquette, the Boulevard and Rue de Ménilmontant, the present Rue des Pyrénées and, after a halt at the town hall of the XXth *arrondissement,* climbed the interminable Rue de Belleville. Preceded by a pretty *vivandière* on horseback, the condemned men walked in pairs, surrounded by a double rank of guards. All along the route the crowd yelled, shouted, hurled abuse: "Down with the clergy! Down with the gendarmes! Death to them!"

Women showed their weapons to the condemned men. "This is what we shall strike you down with presently."

The forty-seven hostages finally arrived in the peaceful Rue Haxo, where, at Number 85, was a piece of wasteland covered with mossy turf. This was the setting for the horrible butchery carried out as much by the crowd as by the men charged with the execution. There was first of all a silence; the rifles seemed to hesitate. Then the *vivandière* intervened: she yelled, rose up, holding a pistol, and fired the first shot. The massacre began. Everyone fired at will, with no orders. For twenty-five minutes, as long as there was a moving body, the killers discharged their weapons. Then the crowd left the garden. As she passed the railings surrounding it the *vivandière* said:

"An old wretch of a priest would not die. I broke his jaw with my revolver. Then, with the heel of my boot, I smashed his face. I shoved my hand into his jaw to tear out his tongue, but I couldn't."

Near at hand the battle could be heard approaching. Farther off, to the east, scraps of music rose from the plain. The Germans were giving a concert.

All during Saturday, May 27, the battle continued. The Buttes-Chaumont were taken, then Père Lachaise cemetery, where they fought among the tombs until the middle of the night. Finally on Sunday, at one o'clock in the afternoon, the last barricade was taken in Rue Ramponneau. One man was still defending it.

The tragic week was over.

The Commune massacred 480 people. Thiers massacred 20,000, not 35,000, as Rochefort and certain other historians have asserted. Twenty thousand. Five times more victims than the Terror had claimed in Paris. The repression was atrocious, inhuman, monstrous. Everyone was shot who wore a jacket, a pair of trousers or even a pair of shoes belonging to the National Guard. Women were shot accused of being *pétroleuses* because matches or a taper had been found on them. All who appeared to be Italians, Poles, Dutch or Germans were shot. The wounded in the hospitals were shot—"they began at one end of the room." Mothers suckling their newborn were shot. Women chatting on their doorsteps, or the woman carrying bread who happened to be passing, were shot. They were shot for shooting's sake. Even the conservative newspapers ended by protesting. "These are no longer soldiers fulfilling their duty. They are creatures returned to the state of wild beasts," *La France* observed, while *Le Siècle* exclaimed: "It is raging madness. The innocent is no longer distinguished from the guilty." In a single night they managed to kill nineteen hundred people in the courtyard at La Roquette.

Some may find an excuse for the murdering madness of the Belleville mob when, a stone's throw away, the Versaillais were shooting the fighters of the barricades.

"What would you; it was as though we were mad!" one of the murderers of the Rue Haxo was to say later.

But how can one explain the attitude of General de Galliffet, watching a column of prisoners pass and taking out of the ranks, to have them immediately shot, those with gray hair "because they saw June, 1848," or those wearing a watch "because they must have been officials of the Commune"?

"I go out to discover burnt-out Paris," wrote Edmond de Goncourt. "One walks in smoke, one breathes an air that smells both of scorching and of varnish. . . . Through little paths between barricades that have not yet been demolished, I arrive at the Hôtel de Ville. The ruin is magnificent, splendid, unimaginable: a ruin color of sapphire, ruby, emerald, a dazzling ruin on account of the burnishing of the stone heated in the kerosene."

The Tuileries presented the same extravagant appearance, but darker, being more smoky. Everywhere else the ruins were rebuilt; at the château, perhaps, no one dared. The stones were sold. *Figaro* bought the chimney pieces of marble, which it made into paper weights for its subscribers. The English dressmaker Worth acquired the windows, doors and columns, that became sham ruins in his garden at Suresnes. The city of Paris put other remains in the Parc Monceau, along the supporting wall of the Jeu de Paume and in the garden of the historical museum of the city of Paris.

Jerome and Charles Pozzo di Borgo bought the central pavilion and, at the cost of millions, transported it to Ajaccio. It is now the castle of La Punta, dominating the bay. Divided up and transported—like the castle in *The Ghost Goes West*—have the Tuileries lost their evil genius? That evil genius which, since October, 1789, seemed to pursue with its curse the successive inhabitants of the old palace. All perished on the scaffold, died a violent death or had to leave for harsh exile, often in pitiful conditions. Six times in a century the Parisians had attacked the old dwelling place of kings. The sixth time the Tuileries died of it, for they had brought with them kerosene, powder and torches. The old château had become the very symbol of the power they were always trying to overthrow in order to impose their Republic. Perhaps, as long as it still stood, the dream some people had pursued since 1789 could not come true.

While the Tuileries were being demolished—Lenotre has reported—the contractor hung this notice on the gate:

NO ADMITTANCE TO THE PUBLIC

Underneath a wag wrote these two words that sum up a century of history:

YES! SOMETIMES!

The provinces, so often disdained, despised, looked down on, the provinces on whom, for eighty years, the capital had imposed by telegraph governments risen for the most part from its pavements, the provinces and Thiers had conquered Paris. The capital would never raise itself completely; it had been wounded more deeply than one imagines. Its pride had been humiliated, its faith in its destinies cast down; Paris would know again hours of exaltation, but, deep down inside, a flame had been extinguished.

About the Author

André Castelot, French historian and biographer, was born on January 23, 1911, at Anvers, Belgium, but received his education in France. He now lives in Paris, except for part of the year which he spends in the province of Charente, of which his wife is a native. It is there that he does all his writing.

In 1933 he began his career of journalism, historical research and dramatic criticism. At present he is associated with various publications, among them *Figaro-Litteraire, Carrefour, Miroir de l'Histoire* and *Historia*. He is also editor of two series of history books.

His books, all of which are on historical subjects and based on research in original, unedited documents, include *Queen of France,* a biography of Marie Antoinette, which was awarded a prize by the Academie Française, and *King of Rome,* a biography of L'Aiglon.

Format by Sidney Feinberg
Set in Intertype Garamond
Composed, printed and bound by American Book–Stratford Press, Inc.
HARPER & ROW, PUBLISHERS, INCORPORATED